Canon®
Speedlite System
Digital Field Guide

3rd Edition

Michael Corsentino

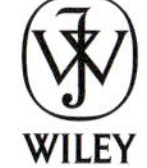

WILEY

John Wiley & Sons, Inc.

Canon® Speedlite System Digital Field Guide, 3rd Edition

Published by
John Wiley & Sons, Inc.
10475 Crosspoint Boulevard
Indianapolis, IN 46256
www.wiley.com

Copyright © 2012 by John Wiley & Sons, Inc., Indianapolis, Indiana

Published simultaneously in Canada

ISBN: 978-1-118-11289-2

Manufactured in the United States of America

10 9 8 7 6 5 4 3 2 1

WILEY

About the Author

Michael Corsentino is an award-winning contemporary wedding and portrait photographer, Adobe Photoshop and Adobe Lightroom expert, author, national speaker, and workshop leader based in Northern California. Shooting digitally since 1999, he made his first exposure when he was 12 years old and hasn't put his camera down since.

His 35-year love affair with the magic and science of photography is more passionate today than ever. Stylish, dramatic, edgy, and modern images set Michael's photography apart. His award-winning blend of photojournalism, fashion, and editorial styles have made him an in-demand portrait and destination wedding photographer.

Equally passionate about educating, Michael loves to share his lighting and posing secrets, post-processing techniques, time-saving workflow strategies, and shooting philosophy with other photographers during his inspiring workshops and speaking engagements.

Credits

Senior Acquisitions Editor
Stephanie McComb

Project Editor
Kristin Vorce

Technical Editor
Michael Guncheon

Copy Editor
Beth Taylor

Editorial Director
Robyn Siesky

Business Manager
Amy Knies

Senior Marketing Manager
Sandy Smith

Vice President and Executive Group Publisher
Richard Swadley

Vice President and Executive Publisher
Barry Pruett

Project Coordinator
Katie Crocker

Graphics and Production Specialists
Carrie A. Cesavice
Andrea Hornberger
Christin Swinford

Quality Control Technician
Dwight Ramsey

Proofreading and Indexing
Susan Hobbs
BIM Indexing & Proofreading Services

Vertical Websites Project Manager
Laura Moss

Vertical Websites Assistant Project Manager
Jenny Swisher

Vertical Websites Associate Producer
Josh Frank
Shawn Patrick
Doug Kuhn
Marilyn Hummel

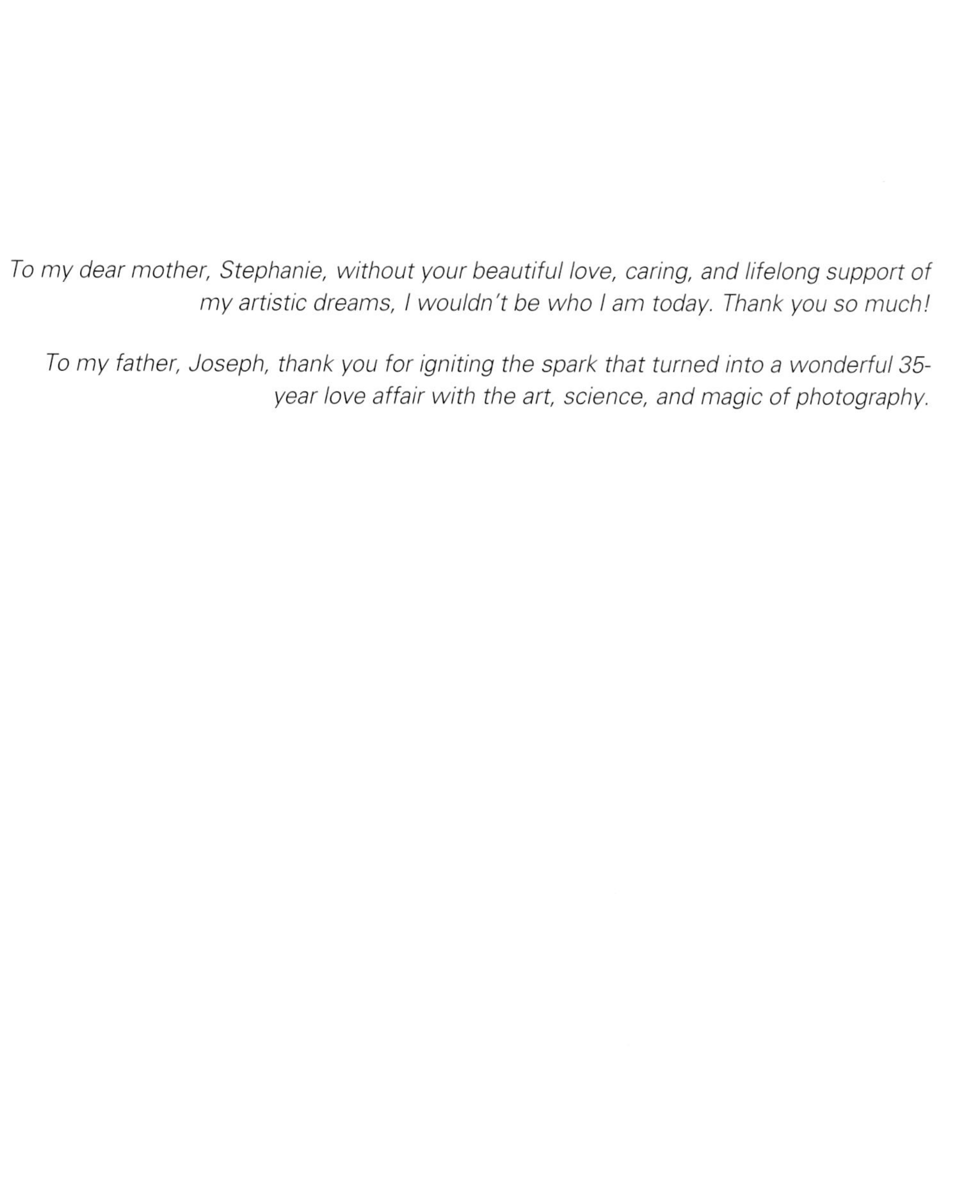

To my dear mother, Stephanie, without your beautiful love, caring, and lifelong support of my artistic dreams, I wouldn't be who I am today. Thank you so much!

To my father, Joseph, thank you for igniting the spark that turned into a wonderful 35-year love affair with the art, science, and magic of photography.

Acknowledgments

I owe a great debt of gratitude to the many wonderful people and innovative companies who have helped make this book a reality. Were it not for their generosity, time, and endless patience with all my crazy and repeated questions, this book would not have been possible.

A big thank you to the following companies and individuals who have generously provided equipment, educational materials, images, software, supplies, and technical assistance for this book: F.J. Westcott, Manfrotto Distribution, Lastolite, Honl Photo, MAC Group, ExpoImaging, iDC Photo, Drop it Modern, Syl Arena Photography, Kubota Image Tools, Nik Software, OnOne Software, Sylights.com, Amherst Media, TriCoast Photography, Backgrounds by Maheu, Canon U.S.A., The Eyelighter, MOLA Softlights, Fotodiox, Vello, Barbour Backdrops and Props, Shannon Michelle Photography, Gary Fong, PhotoshopCAFE, Steele Training, Photogenic, Fstoppers.com, Karl Taylor Photography, LEE Filters, ProPhoto Connect, HoneyGrids, Tether Tools, Think Tank Photo, California Sunbounce, Mike Larson Photography, RadioPopper, Photek, Lovegrove Consulting, Lightware Direct, Michael Bass Designs, Hildozine, Enlight Photo, Lensbaby, Don Gianatti Photography, Joe McNally Photography, Graphic Authority, and RPG Keys.

Special thanks to the talented photographers who've graciously contributed their images: Dennis Urbiztondo, Adam Duckworth, and Stacie Frazier.

Throughout my career, I've been lucky enough to connect with some truly amazing people in this industry and, in the process, have made many treasured friendships. There are so many individuals and companies who deserve special thanks for their support, help, and mentoring along the way. These are the folks who've believed in me from day one and shown incredible generosity and kindness for which I'll always be grateful. For them I would do just about anything. They are Dennis Urbiztondo, Sal and Taylor Cincotta, Kevin Kubota and the Kubota Image Tools team, Andrew Funderburg, Skip Cohen, Scott Bourne, Christopher Becker, Stephanie Devaux, Elena Hernandez, Colin Smith, Kevin La Rue and the team at Nik Software, Mike Wong and the team at OnOne Software, Jules and Joy Bianchi, Joey Lawrence, Amber McCoy and my friends at F.J. Westcott, Doug Gordon, Charlie Moshure, Candice Cunningham, RC Concepcion, Mark Astmann, Frederick Van Johnson and, of course, Tim "I gotta run!" Riley.

Thanks to following photographers who have mentored, educated, and inspired me from afar through their websites, and blogs: David Hobby, Scott Kelby, Joe McNally, Syl Arena, and Chris Orwig. I am indebted to each of you for sharing your knowledge and passion as well as helping me and countless others become better photographers.

To Stephanie McComb, my awesome Acquisitions Editor, for her always-calming demeanor, handholding, and gentle yet firm adherence to the deadlines. She kept me on track, told me everything would be okay when I was stressed, organized all the details involved in producing this book, and was always quick to reply to my many, many questions.

To Kristin Vorce, my Project Editor, for her cheerful attention to all the bits and pieces of the book, for helping to organize my scattered brain, and for her patience while explaining the various processes to me again and again. She was a true pleasure to work with and her contributions definitely made this book better and made me look better!

To my fine editing team at Wiley for their marketing insight, skillful editing, and continuous support and encouragement.

A special shout out goes to my buddy, Dennis Urbiztondo. Thank you so much for your amazing friendship, endless patience, and support. You are one of a kind, and I'm honored to call you my friend. Everyone should be lucky enough to have a friend like you.

Finally, eternal thanks to my mother, Stephanie, for her boundless love, support, and infusing me with her love of the arts at an early age. Throughout my life, your encouragement, endless laughter, belief in my dreams, work ethic, and class have been my guiding light!

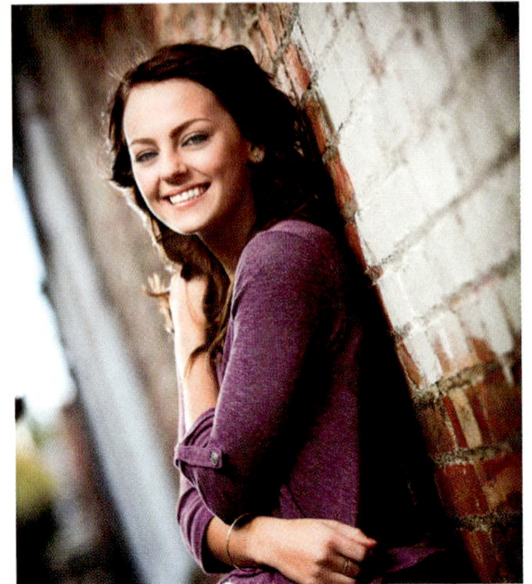

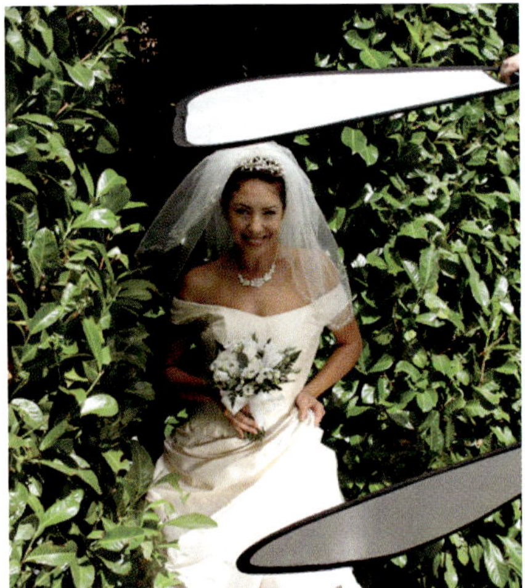

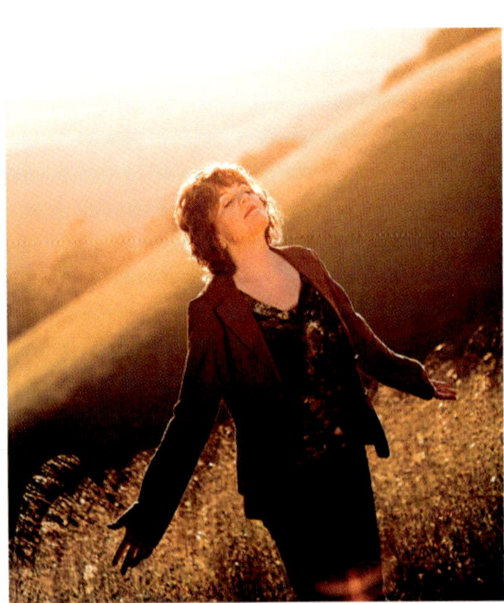

Contents

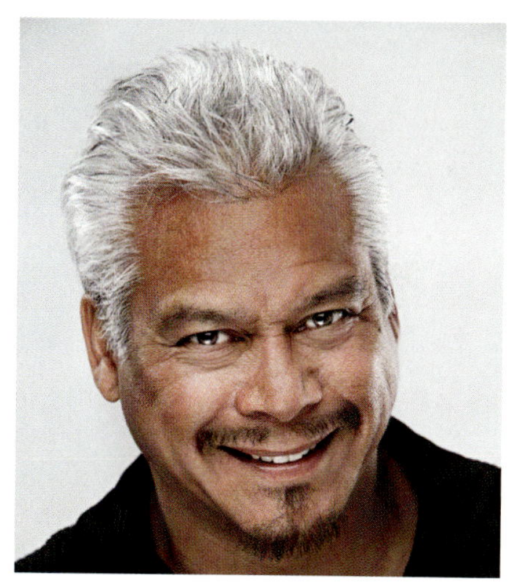

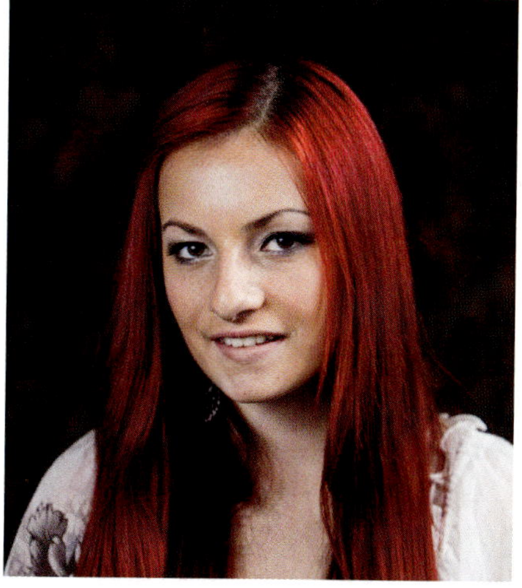

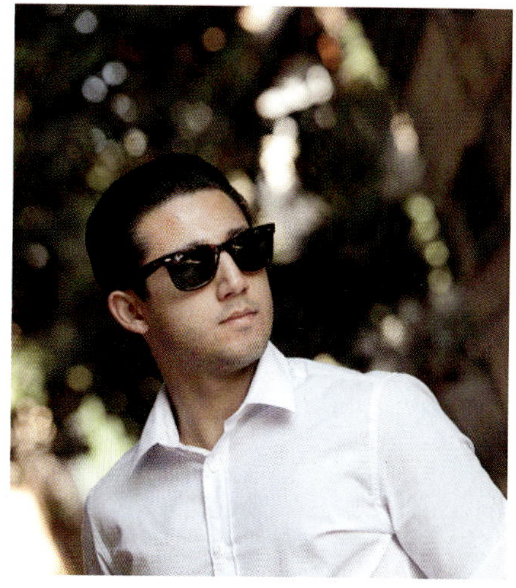

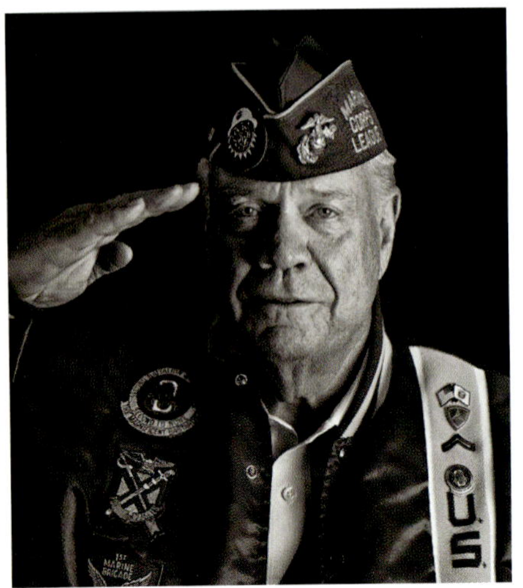

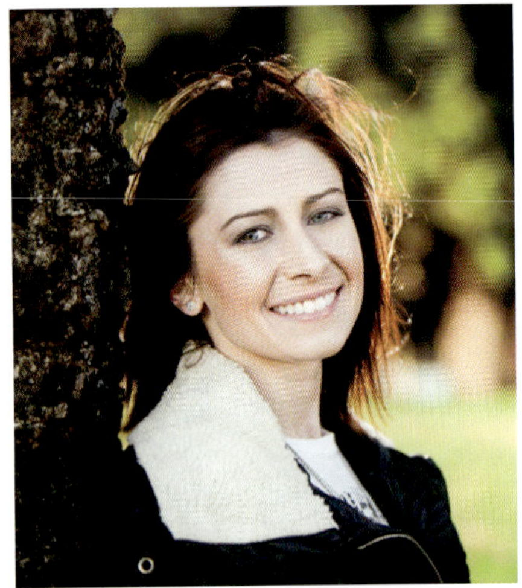

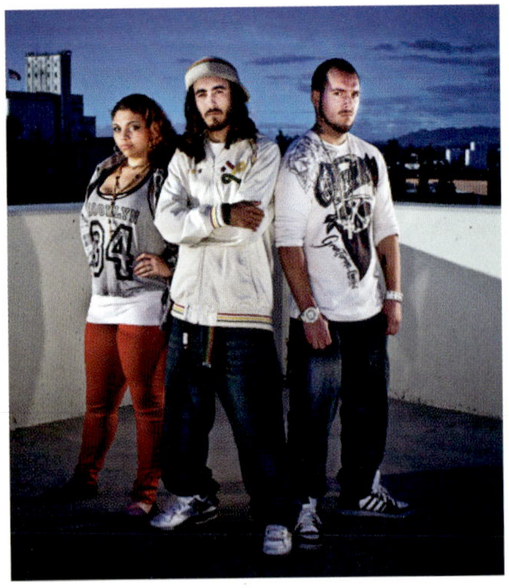

CHAPTER 4
Using Your Flash Off Your Camera   99

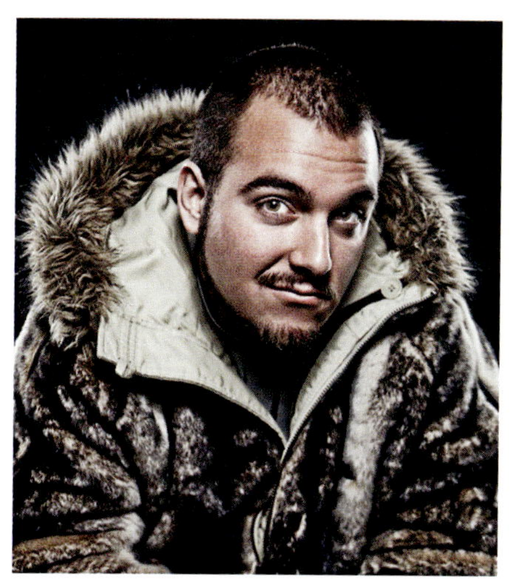

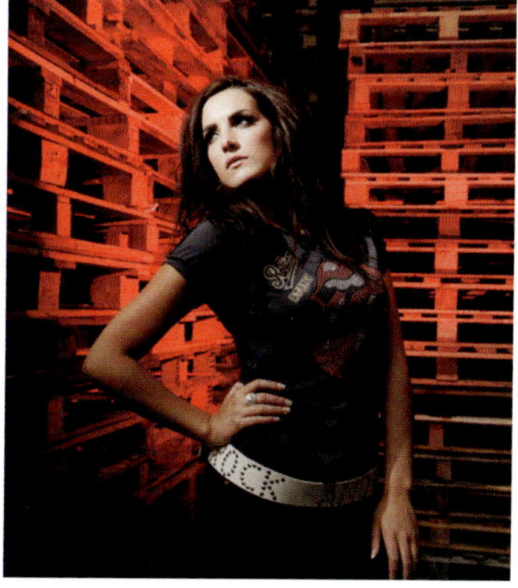

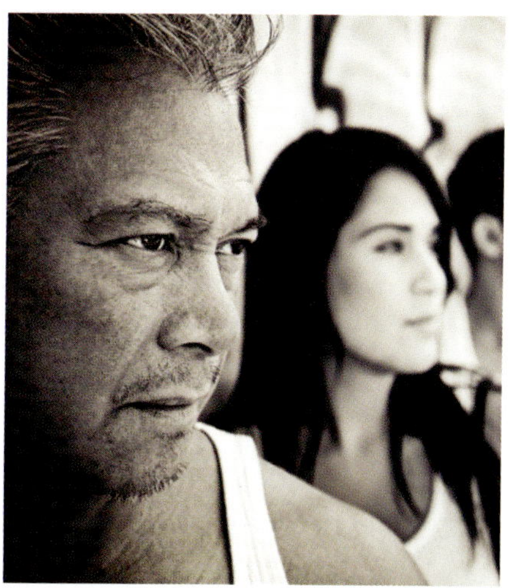

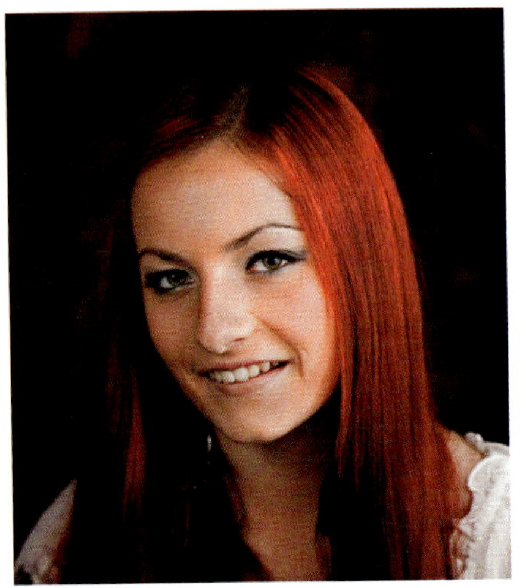

APPENDIX A
Posing Basics 231

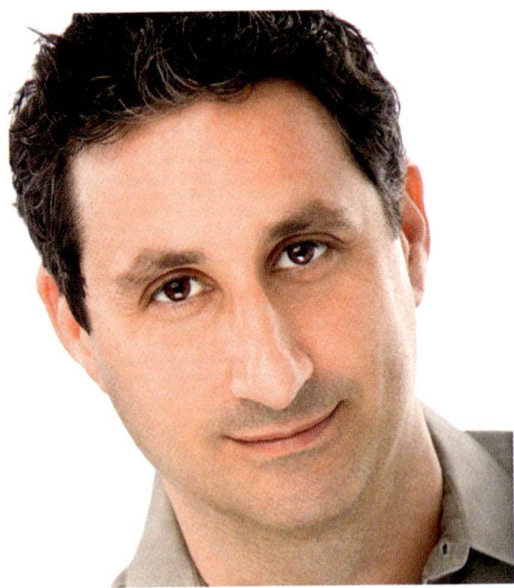

APPENDIX B
Rules of Composition 247

APPENDIX C
Resources 259

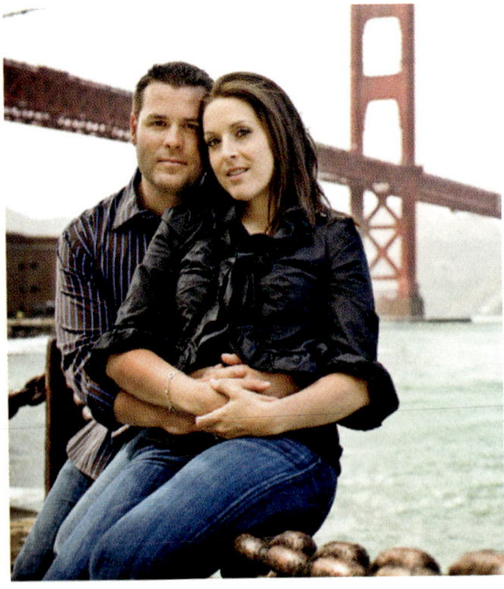

APPENDIX D
How to Use the Gray Card and
Color Checker   268

Glossary   270

Index   279

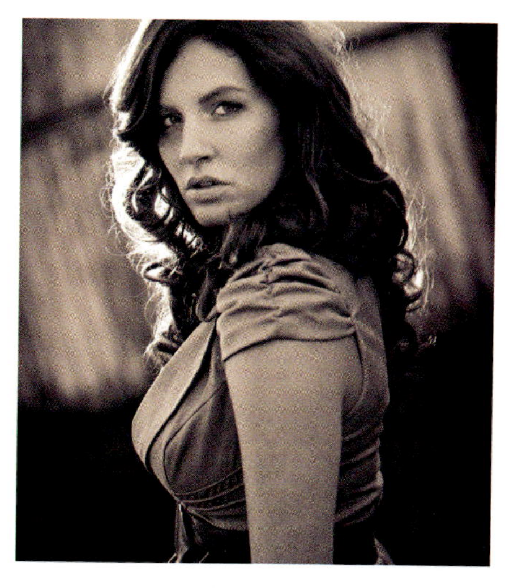

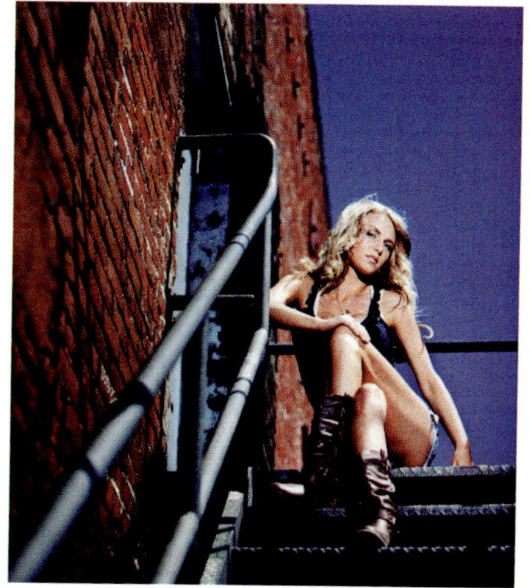

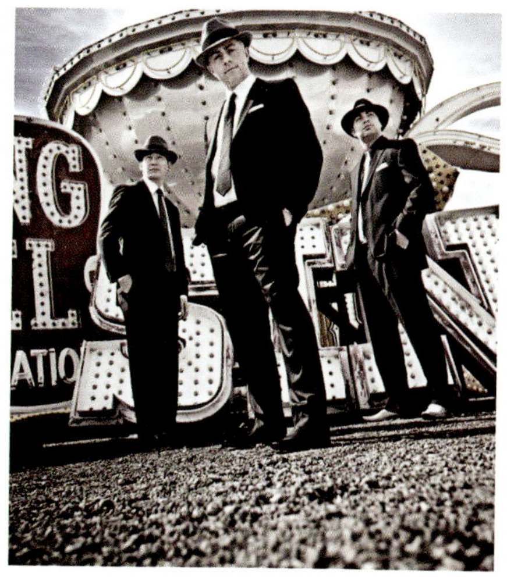

Introduction

Welcome to the *Canon Speedlite System Digital Field Guide, 3rd Edition.* Your Canon Speedlite and this book are a powerful combo! Together, they can help you create the photographs you've always wanted. With a little of your time and effort, this book will guide and inspire you to create images that you will be proud to present to clients and share with your family and friends. Flash technology evolves rapidly, bringing with it new features and capabilities. These are exciting opportunities for creative and business growth. The goal of this book is to get you excited about light by helping you understand the possibilities of your Speedlite System, the nuances of lighting, and camera flash terminology.

These powerful, handheld lights are simply amazing. Sophisticated in their features but simple enough to learn to operate, these technological marvels open a whole world of creative possibilities. With the Canon Speedlite System, you can literally just point and shoot! But why would you want to? That's only half the fun. A Canon Speedlite is able to do the complex exposure calculations for you, balancing the flash exposure with the ambient lighting and allowing for a more natural look to your images. I'll dig deeper and show you how to take control of your Speedlites by making creative and technical choices that will take your flash photography to the next level!

Learning how to understand and control your Speedlites is just the beginning. You will also learn about the different qualities of light and light modifiers, and when, how, and why you should use them. I will also cover light placement and styles of lighting for different and creative effects, and I'll address posing and composition. This book takes you beyond "point and shoot" and starts you on the road to creating truly cool images.

Short History of Canon's Speedlite System

The first Canon Speedlite that offered any type of automatic flash was the 300TL, introduced in 1986, which employed the TTL (Through-the-Lens) metering system and was designed to be used with the Canon T90 film camera.

Essentially, how the process of standard TTL auto flash worked was that a sensor in the camera measured the light reflected off the film plane. When the sensor determined that there was enough light to sufficiently expose a neutral subject, the flash automatically cut off. Although TTL was better than manually setting the flash, it did not always produce great results. Canon set out to improve this when it introduced A-TTL (Advanced Through-the-Lens).

The A-TTL auto flash system, first seen on the Canon T90 camera, was a great improvement, considering that before this, all calculations had to be done by hand. You had to measure the distance from the flash to the subject, figure out the guide number of the flash power, and decide how much power to use for the selected aperture that was required for the image.

A-TTL was Canon's advancement on standard TTL auto flash. Available with the EZ-model Speedlites, A-TTL fired a preflash before the actual exposure while the camera was metering, thus determining the proper flash exposure while retaining readings for the ambient light. The camera then used both of these readings to provide a natural-looking picture by using the ambient light for the main exposure and light from the Speedlite as a fill flash. This was known in Canon's nomenclature as "auto-fill reduction." When the camera meter determined that there was not enough ambient light for proper exposure, the flash was then used as the main light for the subject's exposure.

Although A-TTL seemed like a good thing, it did have a few shortcomings. Some of these included using a sensor on the flash to determine the light output instead of using a sensor in the camera, and having the preflash fire when the shutter button was half-pressed. It also wasn't very useful when attempting to employ bounced flash techniques.

In 1995, Canon introduced E-TTL or Evaluative Through-the-Lens flash metering. The advancement on A-TTL was that E-TTL fired a low-power preflash immediately before the shutter opened, rather than when the shutter button was half-pressed.

Canon's E-TTL metering system also improved on A-TTL by providing a more subtle and natural-looking fill flash when used in daylight situations. It did this by partly basing the exposure on the autofocus point that was locked onto the subject rather than by using an average of the light from multiple zones, as it had done in the past.

In 2004, with the advent of the EOS 1D Mark II, Canon introduced the E-TTL II metering system. This is very similar to the original E-TTL but with a couple improvements. Canon improved the way E-TTL II meters the scene. With E-TTL II, the camera takes a reading of the scene both before and after the preflash fires to help reduce false readings that can be caused by small, reflective substances in the scene. A second improvement was adding the capacity to use distance information supplied by the camera's lens to help obtain the correct flash exposure.

What You'll Learn from This Book

Although this book strives to be a great resource for learning about the Canon Speedlite System, please keep in mind that it is not meant to be the definitive guide for all things Speedlite. For that, you have your manual, which, as painful as it sounds, I suggest you read. Rather, this book is a digital field guide, small enough to be portable for easy reference in the field. It's here to help you to understand your Speedlite's capabilities, and to demystify its technical aspects, buttons, and menus. Along the way, you learn to take control and create flash photographs that really pop.

This book shows you what's possible with your Speedlites, and how they can be used in different situations. I provide an overview of lighting patterns, throw in some helpful tips and tricks, and give you advice about what's worked best for me. At the end of this book, in Appendix C, you'll find a comprehensive list of continuing education options. I am excited to share my love of flash photography with you. The journey can be a little intimidating from time to time, but hang in there, have fun, and experiment. The rewards are well worth the trip!

Quick Tour

For many photographers, the small pop-up flashes on many prosumer cameras are the first electronic flashes they use. These built-in flashes do a fair job of introducing you to the concept of fill flash. They can also be somewhat effective for creating catch-lights in a subject's eyes or for brightening small, shadowy areas. That's where the benefits start to trail off.

Due to their small size and close proximity to the lens axis, pop-up flashes are prone to overexpose subjects that are too close to the camera. When pop-up flashes are used as the main light source, they create harsh shadows. After dealing with these limitations, most photographers are ready to make the leap into the world of external flash units like those in the Canon Speedlite System.

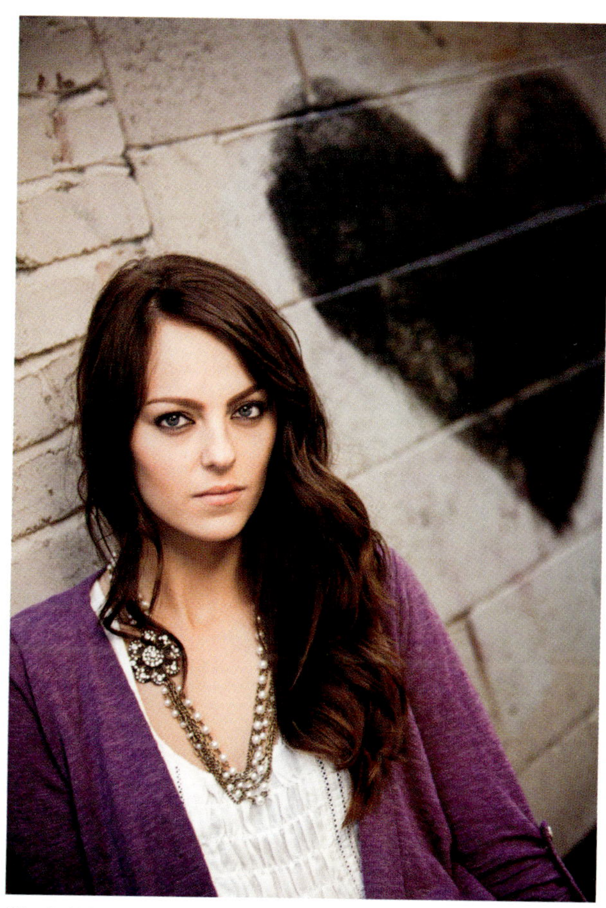

Model Taylor Anderson photographed using one 580EX II Speedlite fired through a Lastolite TriGrip diffusion panel above and camera left. A gold Lastolite TriGrip reflector was used below and camera right. Exposure: ISO 200, f/2.8, 1/160 second with an EF 70-200mm f/2.8L USM lens.

In this Quick Tour, I get you up to speed quickly, introduce you to some key Speedlite features, and encourage you to start exploring what's possible with your new flash!

Getting Up and Running Quickly

As with any new piece of photography gear, you'll want to start using your new Canon Speedlites right away. All you really need to do is pop in some batteries, attach the Speedlite to your camera's hot shoe, and then turn both the Speedlite and the camera on. Almost as soon as soon as you start using it, you'll be pleasantly surprised at the high-quality flash pictures you can make with your new Speedlite.

> **NOTE** The Speedlites accept alkaline, lithium, or NiMH rechargeable AA-sized batteries.

To attach the Speedlite to your camera, follow these steps:

1. **Turn the camera and Speedlite off before connecting.** This is a good habit to get into before connecting any type of electronic equipment.

> **CAUTION** Sliding the flash into the camera's hot shoe while it's powered on can cause it to fire unexpectedly, sometimes right into your eyes, and that's no fun!

2. **On the Speedlite, press the Bounce Lock Release button, and turn the mounting foot's lock lever to the left to the unlock position.**

3. **Slide the Speedlite's hot shoe into the camera's hot shoe, and turn the Speedlite mounting foot's lock lever to the right until it clicks to lock the Speedlite into place.**

4. **Place the flash head in the normal horizontal position.** You'll be repositioning the flash head differently later, but for now, leave it in the normal position.

> **NOTE** Reposition the flash head by pressing the flash head tilting/rotating lock release, and then moving the flash head up or down to the desired angle.

5. **Turn on your camera.**

6. **Turn on your Speedlite.** The On/Off switch for the Speedlite is located on the back panel.

7. **Check that the flash is ready.** The pilot lamp first glows green and then red when the flash is fully charged and ready.

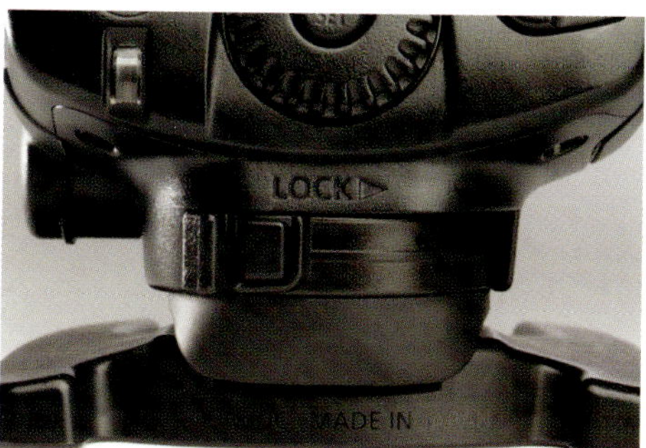

QT.1 The mounting foot's lock lever in the unlock position

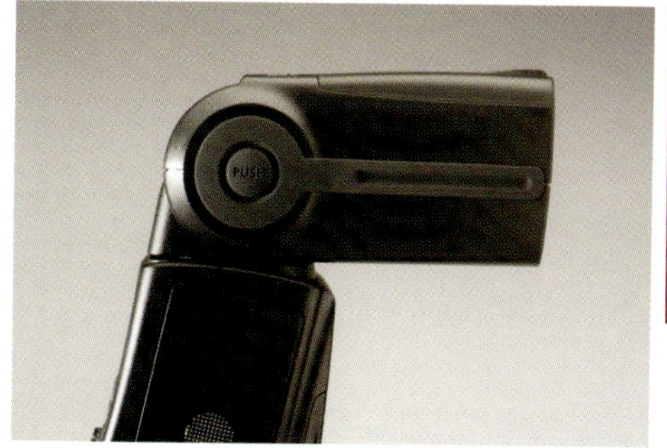

QT.2 The flash head in the normal horizontal position. Normal is the first click up from the down position.

NOTE When you're using the 580EX II, if the flash head is not in the normal horizontal position, the flash's LCD panel shows a blinking flash head icon to warn you that it's not in the normal position.

After you power up your Speedlite and camera with the flash head in the horizontal position, the flash and camera communicate with each other and automatic flash exposure is possible.

That's all there is to it, but it's just the tip of the iceberg of what's to come! You're now ready to begin your Speedlite journey and learn to light with amazing power and flexibility.

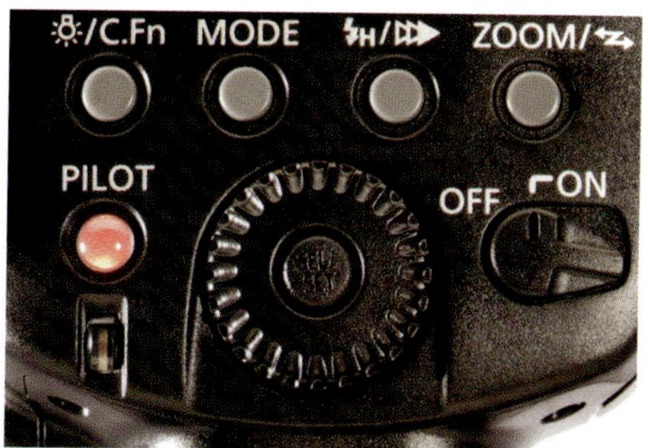

QT.3 The back of the 580EX Speedlite

Taking Your First Photos with the Speedlite

After you get your flash attached and powered on, the flash sets itself to either E-TTL or E-TTL II mode by default. The camera body in use determines which mode is chosen. This is a firmware/hardware compatibility decision and is not user-selectable.

E-TTL stands for Evaluative Through-the-Lens, which means that the light meter in the camera takes a reading through the lens and decides how much flash exposure you need, depending on your camera settings.

The primary difference between E-TTL and E-TTL II is that E-TTL is strongly biased toward the focus point and evaluates the flash exposure primarily at that focus point. E-TTL II does not have this high focus-point biasing, and the flash exposure is calculated using more of an evaluative metering pattern.

Depending on which of the following metering patterns your camera is set to, the flash will either add fill flash or expose only for the subject:

▶ When your camera meter is set to Evaluative metering mode (▣), the light meter takes a reading of the whole scene. The camera adjusts the flash exposure to match the ambient light, adding fill flash to create a more natural look.

▶ When your camera is set to Spot metering mode (▣) the camera's meter takes a reading of the subject and exposes just for that; it doesn't take into account any of the background light.

I recommend setting your camera to Evaluative metering mode (▣) and using the E-TTL II mode when you're getting started. When set to Evaluative metering, the camera measures the light intensity at several points in the scene and then combines the results to find the settings for the best average exposure.

> **TIP** When you're starting out, I recommend also trying your flash outside with sunlight. This is where E-TTL fill flash excels. The Speedlite fills in the harsh shadows created by the bright sun.

Understanding and controlling artificial light can be little intimidating at first, but try to simplify things and remind yourself that light is light, whatever the source. You may need a little more, a little less, some from the right, or some from the left. After you take all the technical jargon out of the equation, it really is that simple. With E-TTL, the camera/flash combination makes all the exposure adjustments for you and automatically adjusts the flash head zoom to match your lens. The flash head zoom is a feature of the Speedlite that adjusts the flash tube location to match the focal length of the lens you're using. You also have manual controls available that enable you to override what the camera has decided is best, but I get to that in Chapter 4.

Don't be concerned if you don't completely understand how E-TTL or E-TTL II flash works or why the flash head zoom is important — I get to all that with examples as you read through this book. In the meantime, this Quick Tour is meant to introduce you to basic flash photography concepts and terminology and get you comfortable with using your new flash equipment.

The best way to get comfortable is just go out and start taking pictures. Set your camera to Program (**P**), Aperture Priority (**Av**), or Shutter Priority (**Tv**) mode, and let the Speedlite and camera combination make the settings for you. This is the easiest way to begin, and it frees you up to learn about your flash.

People learn differently. Some want to jump right into Manual mode (**M**) and start experimenting with f-stops, ISO ratings, and shutter speeds as they relate to flash. Others prefer to let the camera help by reducing the number of settings they have to worry about when starting out. In any event, the more you can focus on lighting patterns and the ins and outs of your Speedlite, the quicker you'll be making the flash pictures you've always wanted. So try not to take on too much all at once.

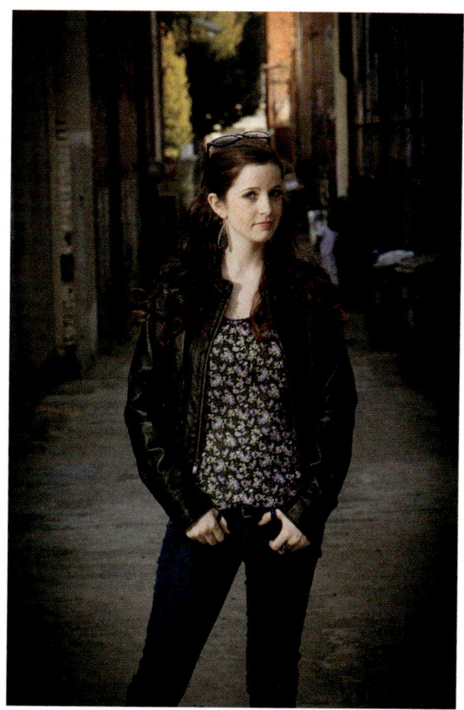

Courtesy of Dennis Urbiztondo

QT.4 Portrait of high school senior Alex using off-camera flash E-TTL II with evaluative metering. Exposure: ISO 400, f/11, 1/160 second with an EF 70-200mm f/2.8L USM lens.

Look for simple subjects that you would normally photograph, but this time use your Speedlite. They can be anything close by, such as your loved ones or pets. Get a feel for how the camera and flash system work together, and pay attention to how the flash illuminates subjects and fills and creates shadows. Think about the qualities of the light that you like and those you'd like to improve. Is the light to harsh; is it too weak or to bright? These are some of the judgments you'll be making as you proceed and learn to light.

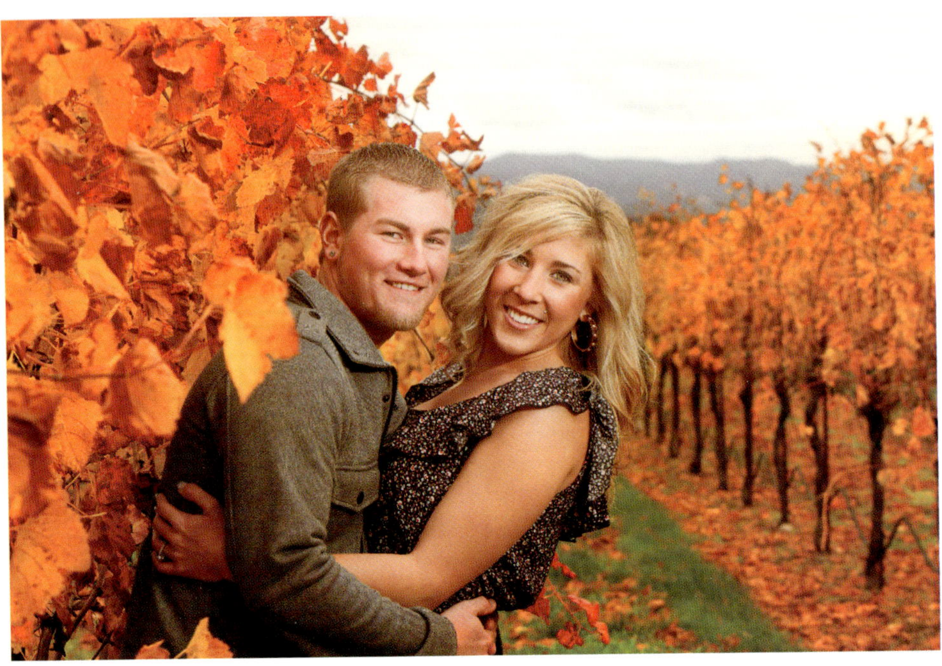

Courtesy of Dennis Urbiztondo

QT.5 Kayla and Travis's engagement session in Napa during the fall. Exposure: ISO 400, f/10, 1/200 second with an EF 70-200mm f/2.8L USM lens.

Get yourself a muse! This can be a spouse, a child, a parent, or even a mannequin. Preferably, you'll find someone interesting who is readily available for impromptu lighting experiments. Other photographers are a great source of models eager to learn more about lighting themselves. Photographers in most communities have monthly meetings where you can find willing victims! Connect with the local Strobist group in your area to find other photographers interested in handheld flash photography. Learn by doing — it's the quickest path to improvement and understanding.

Your first attempts at using flash may fall short and be disappointing, but don't worry. Just keep shooting and watching what the light does and how it reacts in different situations. Don't get too hung up on all the details at this point. Digital photography makes experimenting easy and affordable; the learning curve is considerably shortened by the ability to immediately review images on the camera's LCD. Keep in mind that you'll learn the most from your mistakes, so make as many as you can!

In the coming chapters, you learn about the quality of light and the different ways to shape and control it. As you become more comfortable with your Speedlite, note the impact that flash-to-subject, flash-to-background, and subject-to-background distances each play in the quality of light created. Keeping a notebook of lighting diagrams or using a diagram creation website like www.sylights.com is a great way to keep track of your ideas and take notes about lighting setups that worked and those that didn't. Remember, it's all about learning, so get out there and have fun with it.

QT

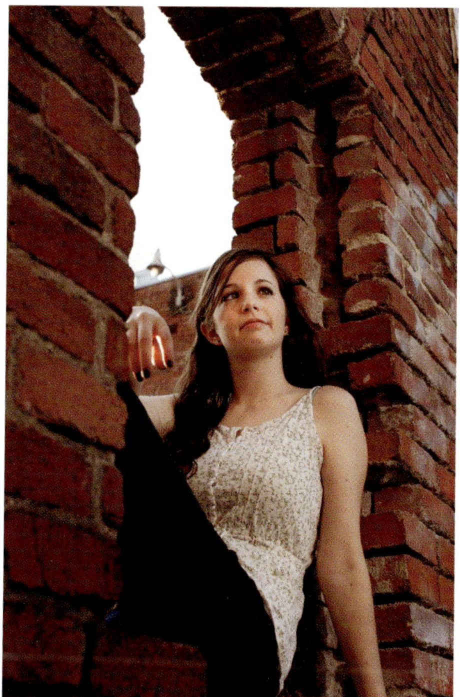

Courtesy of Dennis Urbiztondo

QT.6 An outdoor senior portrait of Alex. Notice the pleasing rim light created by placing the sun behind her. The sun is a free second light! One off-camera Speedlite is adding fill light from the front position. Exposure: ISO 125, f/7.1, 1/160 second with an EF 50mm f/2.8L USM lens.

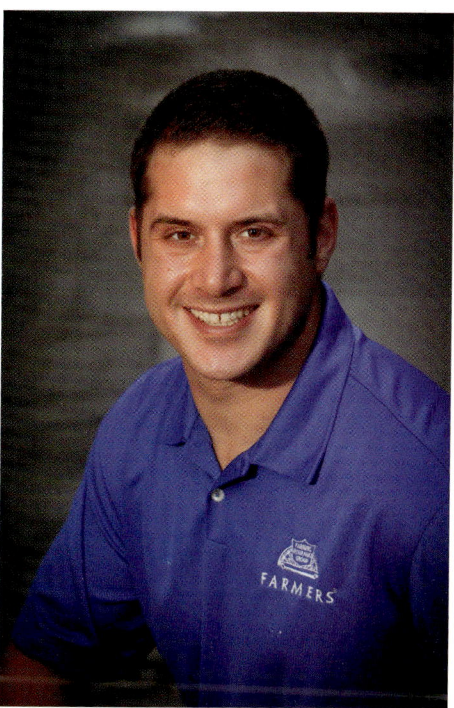

Courtesy of Dennis Urbiztondo

QT.7 Promotion portrait of Farmers Insurance agent Mike Witter. Shooting slightly down and placing the light slightly higher than the subject's head helps slim the face. Exposure: ISO 400, f/8, 1/60 second with an EF 70-200mm f/2.8L USM lens.

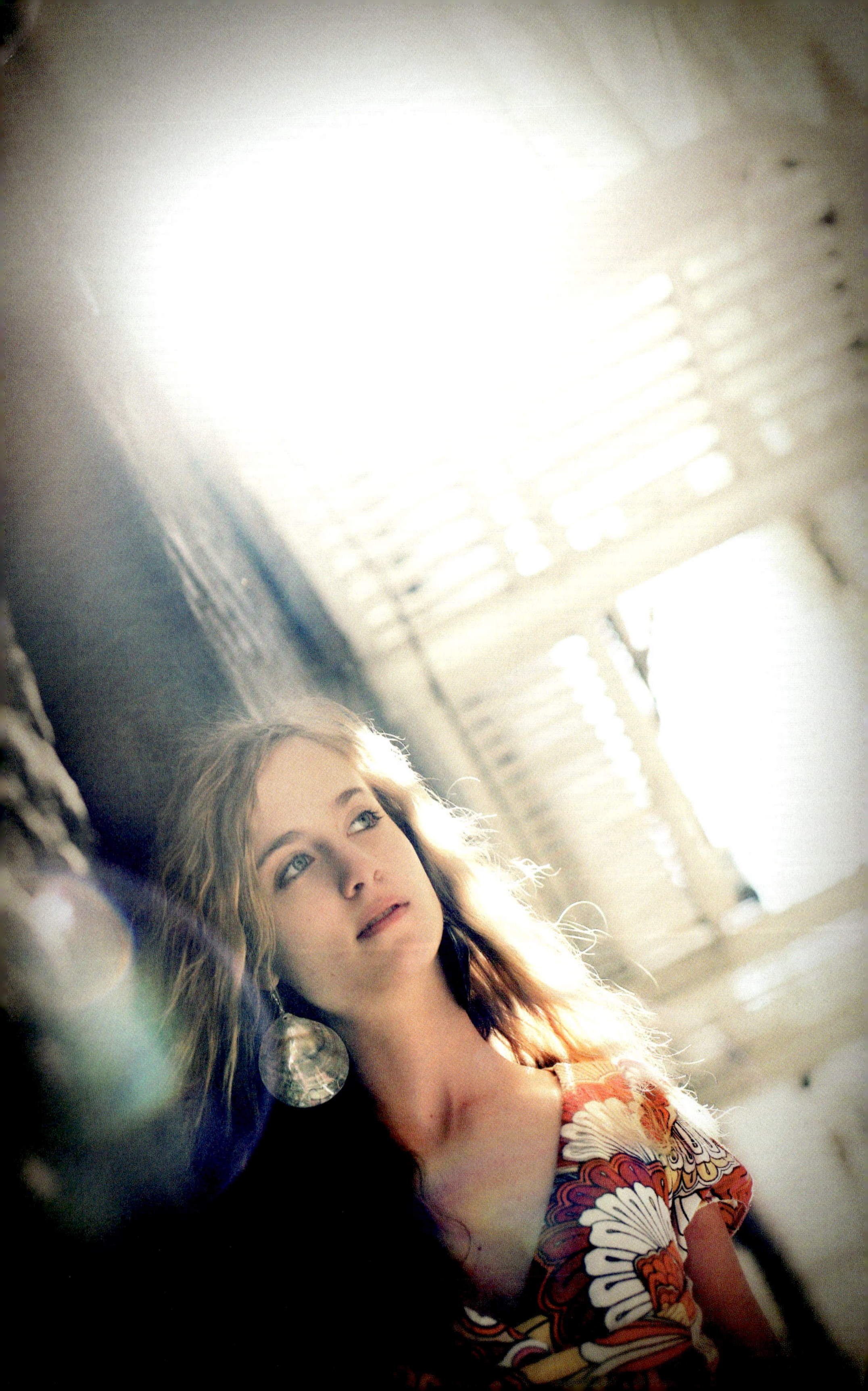

CHAPTER 1

Exploring the Canon Speedlite System

The 600EX, 600EX-RT, and 580EX II are the flagship models in the Canon Speedlite System and, combined with the E-TTL II metering system and a wide variety of lighting modifiers, they enable you to create extraordinary light in any situation.

This chapter acquaints you with the main features of the four major flash units in the Canon Speedlite System: the 600EX, 600EX-RT, 580EX II, and 430EX II. It also briefly touches on the 270EX II and 320EX. Sections covering the 600EX and radio-enabled 600EX-RT have been combined throughout the book because they are identical in all respects except for built-in radio wireless. Differences are noted where appropriate. I also cover all the functions of the other parts of the Canon Speedlite System, including the Speedlite transmitter ST-E3-RT and the ST-E2 wireless transmitter, along with an overview of a smaller entry-level Speedlite and the two macro Speedlite options.

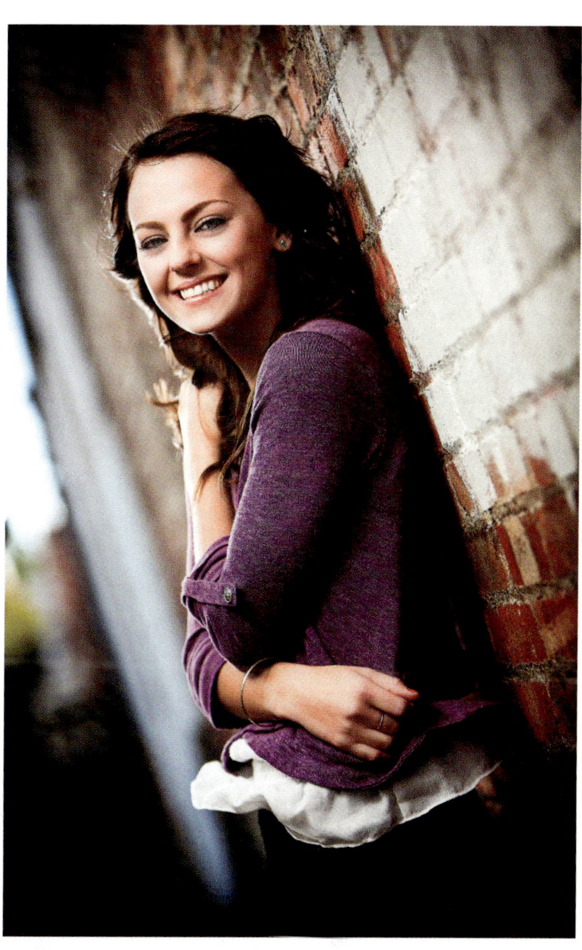

In this image of model Taylor Anderson, I had one 580EX II Speedlite positioned camera left and one positioned behind her and to the left to provide an accent light. Speedlites are triggered in High-speed sync mode using the RadioPopper PX system. Exposure: ISO 100, f/2.8, 1/320 second with an EF 70-200mm f/2.8L USM lens.

Features of the Canon Speedlite System

The main components of the Canon Speedlite System are any Canon dSLR camera and a compatible Speedlite such as the feature-rich 600EX/600EX-RT, 580EX II, and 430EX II Speedlites, which replace the 580EX and 430EX, respectively. Additional components include the OC-E3 Off-Camera Shoe Cord, the Speedlite transmitter ST-E3-RT and ST-E2, the Macro Twin Lite MT-24EX, the MR-14EX Ring Lite, the 270EX Speedlite (which replaces the 220EX flash), the 270EX II, and the 320EX. All Canon EOS dSLRs can be used with the Canon Speedlite System.

Here are some of the powerful features in the Canon Speedlite System:

- ▶ **E-TTL II.** Canon's most advanced flash metering system uses preflashes and flash metering algorithms to determine the proper flash exposure. The E-TTL II system reads information from all metering zones before and after the preflash. Areas with little change in brightness are then weighted for flash metering. This is done to prevent a highly reflective surface or overly bright area from creating a false reading, thereby causing underexposure. When you use certain EF lenses, distance information is also reported back to the flash and entered into the algorithm.

- ▶ **Flash Exposure Lock (FEL).** FEL enables you to fire the flash to meter the subject, get a reading for the proper flash exposure, and lock in that information. Pressing the FEL button allows you to meter the subject via a test flash and then recompose the shot while maintaining the proper flash exposure for that subject.

> **NOTE** Some Canon camera bodies have a separate FEL button (⚡*), while others have buttons that can be assigned to the FEL function.

- ▶ **Wireless lighting.** This feature allows you to use your Speedlites wirelessly using built-in optical or radio transmission. When using wireless lighting, you need to have either a 600EX, 600EX-RT (built-in radio), 580EX II, either of the Macro Speedlites, or a Speedlite transmitter ST-E3-RT (built-in radio) or ST-E2 wireless transmitter set as a master unit. A master unit fires a preflash, which then transmits information back and forth between the camera and any flashes set to Slave mode. The master unit can wirelessly control multiple Speedlites that are set as slaves, allowing really creative lighting setups. Many of the newer dSLRs in Canon's lineup have pop-up flashes that can be used as master flashes.

- ▶ **High-speed sync.** This feature allows you to use your flash at shutter sync speeds above those rated for your camera body. This setting is often used to freeze action or allow wider apertures (via higher shutter speeds) when shooting outdoor portraits.

▶ **AF-assist beam.** The 580EX II and 430EX II have a built-in red LED that projects a gridded light pattern onto a subject to aid the camera's autofocus (AF) system in very dark or low-contrast situations. This beam typically offers coverage for up to a specific number of AF points.

▶ **Flash color information communication.** As flash duration becomes longer, the color temperature changes slightly. The Canon Speedlites transmit this change to the camera body, ensuring a more accurate white balance.

600EX/600EX-RT

The 600EX and 600EX-RT, released in mid-2012, are the new flagship models of Canon's Speedlite lineup. Canon engineers and designers have been busy — these new Speedlites are a major leap forward. There are many significant improvements on both models, including a completely redesigned, context-sensitive menu/navigation system based on a 40-percent larger LCD panel and four Function buttons, a dedicated wireless button (no more digging through menus and holding multiple buttons), bigger and more legible dot matrix text on the LCD panel, Custom Function menus that are clear and understandable, a broader 20mm–200mm zoom range for more creative control, increased power output, beefed up weather sealing to match pro-series bodies like the 1D X, and an included gel filter set and carrying case. The redesigned menu/navigation system is straightforward, intuitive, and worth the upgrade alone. However, the real game changer is the 600EX-RT's built-in wireless radio capabilities. A non-radio-enabled version, the 600EX, is available exclusively in Europe where some countries prohibit use of the 600EX-RT's 2.4 GHz radio frequency.

Because the 600EX and 600EX-RT have many of the same components, inputs, and basic form factor as the 580EX II, I've pointed out the differences where necessary and kept figures to a minimum in this section to save space. Please refer to Figure 1.4–1.10 in the 580EX II section. Unless otherwise noted, these example figures are basically the same for the 580EX II and 600EX/600EX-RT.

600EX/600EX-RT specifications and features

This section covers some of the features available on the 600EX/600EX-RT Speedlites:

▶ **Guide number (GN).** The 600EX/600EX-RT's guide number is used to determine the proper exposure when shooting in Manual flash without a flash meter. With today's advanced flash systems, guide numbers are most often used to compare power output between flashes. Guide numbers are usually given for both feet and meters, so be sure that you use the right one in your calculations. The guide number varies with the zoom settings, from GN 26/85 (meters/feet) at 20mm to GN 60/197 (meters/feet) at 200mm. See your owner's manual for more information on GNs for specific zoom ranges.

- ▶ **Automatic zooming flash head.** This provides lens coverage from 20mm to 200mm. It supports up to 14mm coverage with the built-in wide-angle lens panel.

- ▶ **E-TTL.** The 600EX/600EX-RT supports E-TTL II, E-TTL, and TTL, along with full Manual flash output operation.

- ▶ **Wireless lighting.** Control up to three firing groups using ratio groups A, B, and C with the 600EX/600EX-RT in Optical Transmission Wireless Shooting mode or using a 600EX-RT set to Optical or Radio Transmission Wireless Shooting. Using a 600EX-RT in Radio Transmission Wireless Shooting mode with Group mode selected enables you to control Group mode (Gr). Control up to five different firing groups containing up to 15 Speedlites in either E-TTL II, Manual mode, or Auto external flash metering (Ext.A).

- ▶ **Group mode (Gr).** This is an exciting new feature available exclusively on the 600EX-RT Speedlite and Speedlite transmitter ST-E3-RT when used with 2012 or later EOS model cameras such as the 1D X and 5D Mark III. This feature not only allows radio-enabled wireless control of up to five groups containing up to 15 Speedlites but also permits use of mixed flash modes (E-TTL II/E-TTL, Manual, or Ext.A) for individual groups/Speedlites at the same time.

Understanding the Guide Number

The guide number (GN) is simply a measure of how powerful a flash is. In other words, a flash with a GN of 90 is more powerful than one with a GN of 40.

The GN is a number assigned by the manufacturer to assist you in obtaining the correct exposure. It is also a means of comparing light output among different Speedlites. Refer to your owner's manual for a table with the GN of the Speedlite at specific zoom ranges.

Although the actual power of the flash is fixed, the guide number (GN) of the flash changes with the ISO setting of the camera and also varies with the zoom setting of the flash. This is due to the increased sensitivity of the sensor and the actual dispersion of the light when set to a specific zoom range. When the ISO is at a higher setting, the sensor is more sensitive to light, in effect making the flash more powerful, hence a higher GN.

Also, when the zoom is set to a wide angle, the flash tube is positioned farther back in the flash head, spreading the light and giving it wider coverage. This makes the flash somewhat less bright, thereby warranting a lower GN.

▶ **Second-curtain sync (⧯▶).** This function fires the flash at the end of the exposure, rather than the beginning. This helps you capture more natural images when shooting long exposures because it causes a trail to appear behind a moving subject and not in front of it, which occurs when the flash is fired at the beginning of the exposure.

▶ **AF-assist beam.** To assist while focusing in low-light situations, the 600EX/600EX-RT emits a grid pattern of red light from its LED sensor.

▶ **High-speed sync (FP flash) (⧯).** This function enables you to shoot with a shutter speed higher than the top-rated sync speed of the camera. This feature is useful when shooting portraits in bright light using a wide aperture with fast shutter speeds.

▶ **Flash Exposure Lock (FEL).** You can use this feature to get a reading from your subject and then recompose the shot while retaining the original exposure.

▶ **Flash Exposure Compensation (⧯).** Similar to the way Exposure Compensation is set on the camera, this function allows you to adjust the light output up or down in 1/3-stop increments over a +/–3-stop range while still enjoying all the benefits of E-TTL II flash metering.

▶ **Modeling flash.** The 600EX/600EX-RT fires a short burst of flashes, allowing you to see what the light falling on your subject will look like. This is a battery drain and something I rarely use.

▶ **Multi-stroboscopic flash mode (MULTI).** The 600EX/600EX-RT fires a user-specified number of flashes per second, like a strobe light, for creative effect.

▶ **Tilting/rotating flash head for bouncing flash.** This allows you to tilt the flash head up to bounce light from the ceiling, or to the side to bounce light off a wall. The 600EX/600EX-RT also enables you to tilt the flash head downward –7 degrees for close-up subjects.

▶ **Wide panel.** A pull-out wide panel is included to extend flash output to 14mm lens coverage. This is a huge plus when doing group photography in tight quarters or using a wide-angle lens for flash work.

▶ **Catch-light panel.** Just above the wide panel is a retractable white panel. When it is extended, you can reflect light back into your subject's eyes, creating catch-lights and adding sparkle and vitality to the portrait.

▶ **PC terminal.** The 600EX/600EX-RT includes a receive-only PC sync terminal for triggering the Speedlite with radio frequency remotes like RadioPoppers, PocketWizards, or optical slave attachments.

▶ **External power supply socket.** For faster recycling times and longer flash shooting sessions, an external power supply socket is provided for use with the Canon CP-E4 Compact Battery Pack or third-party power supplies, such as those from Quantum.

▶ **External Speedlite control.** The latest Canon cameras include a menu option that enables you to set some or all of your Speedlites' controls directly from the camera depending on the model of Speedlite and camera. The benefit of this capability is that the camera's External Speedlite control menu provides more detail for the settings than the Speedlite's LCD.

Main components

The 600EX and, to a larger extent, the 600EX-RT Speedlite are a quantum leap forward in handheld flash technology. The 600EX-RT's built-in wireless radio as well as optical-transmission capabilities open up a whole new world of creative possibilities. These are fantastic tools for creating beautiful lighting with a new level of control and freedom. With so much amazing technology and so many options now literally at your fingertips, it's easy to be a little overwhelmed at first, but grasping how to use it gets easier. I start by covering the buttons and controls and describing what each does. In later chapters, I look at when to use certain settings for the best results.

▶ **Flash head/Wireless transmitter.** This is where the flash tube is housed. Inside is a mechanism that zooms the flash bulb forward and back to provide flash coverage for lenses of different focal lengths. The flash head is adjustable; it can be tilted upward to a full 90 degrees and downward to –7 degrees. It can also be adjusted horizontally 180 degrees to the left or to the right. Manual zoom adjustments can also be made independently of the lens's focal-length position when a narrower, more focused beam of light is desired for creative effects.

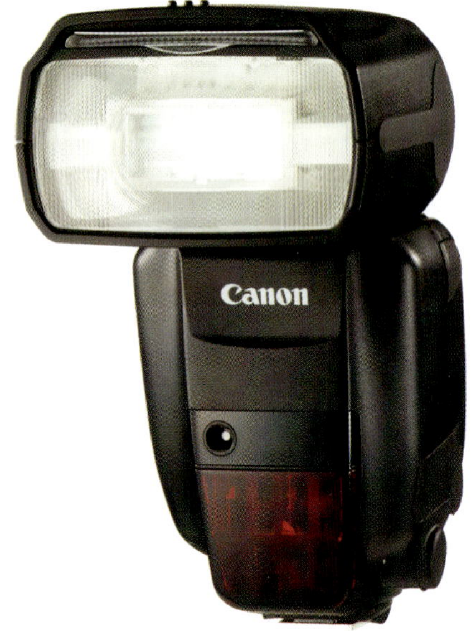

Courtesy of Canon

1.1 The front of the 600EX/600EX-RT Speedlite

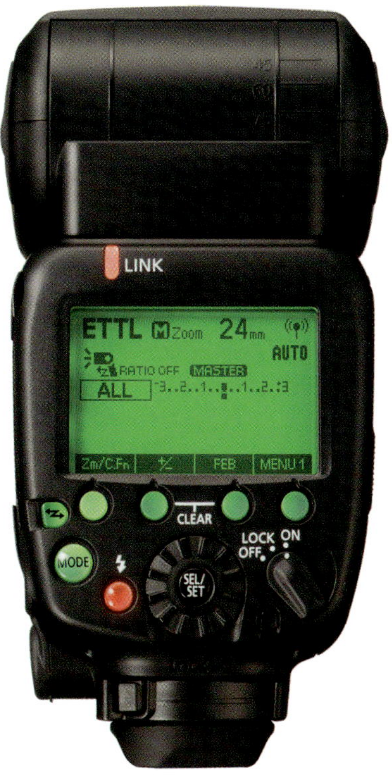

Courtesy of Canon

1.2 The back of the 600EX-RT Speedlite. Here the LCD panel shows the Speedlite in Radio Transmission Wireless Shooting mode and designated as a master.

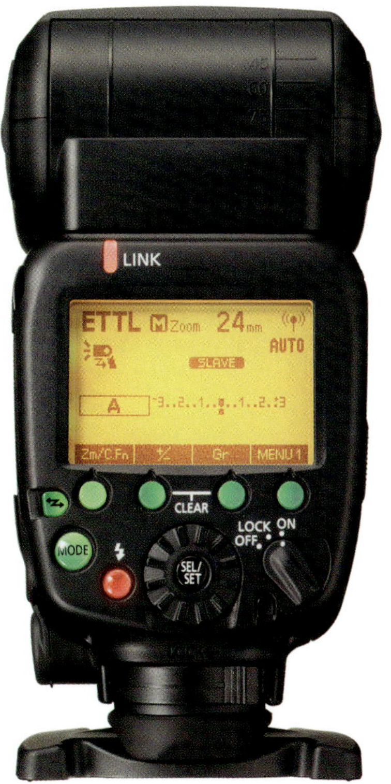

Courtesy of Canon

1.3 The back of the 600EX-RT Speedlite. Here the LCD panel shows the Speedlite in Radio Transmission Wireless Shooting mode set up as a slave. The optional orange LCD background color has been selected for use when the Speedlite is used as a slave.

▶ **Color filter holder attachment.** Located at the top of the flash head just behind the catch-light panel are three plastic nubs used to attach the included filter gel holder to the Speedlite.

▶ **Battery compartment cover.** Slide the center button left and then downward to open the spring-loaded battery compartment to load or change the batteries.

▶ **Wireless sensor for E-TTL and E-TTL II wireless flash.** This sensor reads signals from the master unit, enabling wireless flash operation.

- ▶ **External metering sensor.** The external metering sensor allows the flash to calculate its own light output without relying on the camera's metering system. The flash has to know camera settings (ISO, shutter speed, and aperture) to calculate the correct amount of output. External metering has to be set to Manual mode, and all the camera settings must be entered into the flash manually.

- ▶ **AF-assist beam emitter.** The 600EX/600EX-RT projects a red LED light grid onto the subject to allow the camera's autofocus system to operate successfully in low-light or low-contrast situations. The AF-assist beam is compatible with 28mm and longer lenses.

- ▶ **LINK (Radio transmission confirmation) lamp.** This lamp, located on the left side above the 600EX-RT LCD panel, changes from red to green when positive wireless radio communication has been confirmed between master and slave Speedlites.

- ▶ **Bounce angle scale.** This feature allows you to tilt the flash head from normal (0) to 45, 60, 75, or 90 degrees and to –7 degrees for close-ups. Although the flash head has detents at the values indicated on the scale, you can operate the flash at any angle between the detents.

- ▶ **Bounce Lock Release button.** This button releases the flash head lock, enabling you to adjust the angle of the flash head for bounce flash.

- ▶ **Flash head rotating-angle scale.** This feature denotes the horizontal rotation of the flash head from 0 to 60, 75, 90, 120, 150, and 180 degrees from the left. Although the flash head has detents at the values indicated on the scale, you can operate the flash at any angle between the detents.

- ▶ **LCD panel.** This is a display panel where you view and operate all the Speedlite settings, Custom Functions, and controls.

- ▶ **Function buttons.** Used in conjunction with the context-sensitive menu system, Function buttons specify settings and Custom Functions on the Speedlite.

- ▶ **Flash-ready lamp/Test flash button (⚡).** This light indicates that the Speedlite is ready to fire and can also be used to test-fire the master and any slaves. When you're working with 600EX-RT in Radio Transmission Wireless Shooting and using off-camera slaves, a red light confirms that all slaves are ready to fire. After the Speedlite is fired, this light glows green for Quick flash, then red when the Speedlite is fully recycled and ready to fire again. Quick flash allows the flash to be fired again before it has totally recycled to its full power capacity once the lamp glows green. Quick flash is limited to between 1/6 and 1/2 of the full light output and is ideal for close subjects and when you want a shorter recycling time. Quick flash does not operate in Continuous shooting (🖵), Flash Exposure Bracketing (FEB), Manual flash, or Multi-stroboscopic flash modes.

▶ **Flash exposure confirmation lamp.** This lamp glows green for about 3 seconds when standard flash exposure is attained.

▶ **Mounting foot lock lever.** This lever locks the Speedlite with a click into the camera's hot shoe or the included Speedlite stand.

▶ **Wide panel.** This built-in diffuser enables you to use the Speedlite with a lens as wide as 14mm without having light fall off at the edges of the image.

▶ **Catch-light panel.** This white plastic card reflects light back into the eyes, providing a catch-light when the flash is used in the bounced position.

▶ **External power source socket.** Canon's optional CP-E4 Compact Battery Pack external power source or a third-party power supply can be plugged into this socket.

▶ **Bracket mounting hole.** This is used to attach the Speedlite to the Canon SB-E2 Speedlite bracket. The SB-E2 allows the Speedlite to be attached to the side of the camera rather than to the hot shoe.

▶ **Hot shoe mounting foot.** Picking up on improvements made on the 580EX II, the 600EX/600RT has improved contacts, is made of metal, and has a lock lever that securely connects the flash with the camera. This connector slides into the hot shoe on your camera body, locks the Speedlite to the camera with the lock lever, and is the important electrical communication connection between the flash and the camera.

Function buttons, dedicated buttons, and Select dial

The 600EX/600EX-RT's redesigned user interface of buttons and menus provides a much easier, quicker, and more intuitive way to find what you're looking for. There are now four Function buttons that work in conjunction with the context-sensitive LCD panel readout. Button functions change depending on the flash mode being used and menu screen being viewed. The new navigation system is heads and shoulders above older models. Other improvements and additions include a larger flash mode button (Mode), a dedicated wireless/Linked shooting button (⇄) that makes switching to wireless shooting a one-button operation, and a LOCK position on the ON/OFF switch to help safeguard user settings. The Select dial and center Select/Set button function as they did previously, only now within the updated menu system. I describe the controls and how to use them in this and subsequent chapters. After reading through each section, I encourage you to spend time getting acquainted with the topics covered. This way, in the future you'll be able to quickly and easily make the adjustments you want.

▶ **Mode button.** The Mode button is used to cycle among the different flash exposure modes of the 600EX/600EX-RT Speedlite and during wireless operation to manually adjust flash output. These are the modes:

- **E-TTL.** The exposure is determined by a brief preflash before the main flash to obtain a more correct exposure and measure the light coming through the lens. The camera then uses this information to blend the flash output with the ambient light.

- **M (Full Manual mode).** You can use guide numbers or determine the flash output power by taking test shots and then reviewing them on the camera's LCD monitor. Output is adjustable in 1/3-stop power settings, allowing you to fine-tune your lighting or dial in each Speedlite individually in multi-flash lighting setups. You can also use a handheld flash meter to determine the flash and camera settings.

- **Group mode (Gr).** Group mode is available exclusively on the 600EX-RT Speedlite and Speedlite transmitter ST-E3-RT when used with 2012 or later EOS model cameras such as the 1D X and 5D Mark III. This feature allows radio-enabled wireless control of up to five groups containing up to 15 Speedlites and the use of mixed flash modes (E-TTL II/E-TTL, Manual, or Ext.A) for individual groups/Speedlites at the same time.

- **Multi-stroboscopic flash.** This mode allows you to fire the flash multiple times during a single exposure for creative effect.

▶ **Wireless button/Linked shooting button (⇆).** New on the 600EX/600EX-RT is a dedicated button for selecting the desired wireless mode. The 600EX permits Optical Transmission Wireless Shooting (⚡) with a master and slave flashes, and the 600EX-RT allows Optical or Radio Transmission Wireless Shooting (((•))) with a master and slave flashes.

▶ **Function button 1 – LCD Panel illumination, Zoom and Custom Functions (Zm/C.Fn).** Press this button once while in Menu screen 1 (the default screen) to manually change the flash head zoom by using the Select dial/Set button. Press and hold this button to enter the Custom Functions menus, and press again to enter Personal Functions menus. Pressing this button once also turns the LCD light on for about 10 seconds, useful for viewing settings in dim light.

CROSS REF See Chapter 2 for more on Custom Functions and their applications.

▶ **Function button 4 – FP flash (SYNC)/Second-curtain sync (⊳▶).** In E-TTL flash mode, pressing Function button 4 (SYNC) sets the Speedlite to

High-speed sync (⚡H). Pressing this button once enables you to set the flash to High-speed sync. A digital camera shutter is comprised of two *curtains,* one that opens the shutter to begin the exposure and one that closes it to end the exposure. At shutter speeds above the camera's top flash sync speed, the curtain that's closing starts moving before the curtain that's opening is fully open. This causes light from the flash to reach only a small portion of the sensor, resulting in an underexposed strip across the image. High-speed sync allows you to make flash exposures at higher-than-normal sync speeds by causing the Speedlite to repeatedly and perfectly pulse bursts of light as the shutter curtains move across the sensor instead of just one pop when the shutter first opens.

Pressing Function button 4 (**SYNC**) again turns on the Second-curtain sync (▷▶) feature. In standard flash photography, the normal operation sequence is the shutter opens and the flash fires immediately. In this mode, the flash fires at the very end of the exposure, just before the second curtain closes. To return to standard flash, push the button once again.

Both of these features work only in E-TTL and Manual flash modes, and not in the Multi-stroboscopic mode (**MULTI**).

▶ **Flash-ready lamp/Test flash button (⚡).** Press this button when lit to test-fire the 600EX/600EX-RT and any slaves to ensure they are functioning properly or to take a test reading using a handheld flash meter. This button also lets you know when the flash is fully charged and ready to fire. When the lamp glows green, the unit is ready for Quick flash; when it glows red, the flash is ready to fire at full power.

▶ **Select dial and Select/Set button.** Rotate the Select dial left and right, and confirm the settings by pressing the center Select/Set button.

   • **Left and right.** When scrolling left or right, you use this button to change the zoom of the flash, select Custom Functions settings, Flash Exposure Compensation, Manual flash output, wireless status, master/slave settings, multi-stroboscopic frequencies, or flash bracketing settings.

   • **Select.** After turning the Select dial to choose the desired settings, press the Select/Set button to commit to those settings.

▶ **ON/OFF/LOCK switch.** This switch controls whether the Speedlite is on or off and now includes a new Lock position to help safeguard user settings.

600EX/600EX-RT accessories

The 600EX/600EX-RT ships with a soft, ballistic nylon case for storing and carrying it, and it includes a tabletop Speedlite stand that enables you to mount your flash to a light stand or tripod. This new iteration of the case is more robust than the version included with the 580EX II. A color filter kit with two gel filters, filter wallet, filter holder and a carrying case is also included.

CROSS REF Third-party manufacturers, such as Honl Photo, ExpoImaging, and Lastolite, market many must-have Speedlite accessories discussed in detail in Chapter 5.

580EX II

The previous flagship of the Speedlite lineup, the 580EX II, debuted in May 2007 and has many improvements over its predecessor, the 580EX. It also includes many features that offer a great deal of versatility. These upgrades include a 20-percent-faster recycle time, metal mounting foot, mounting lock lever, power switch design, receive-only external PC terminal, and dust and water-resistant seals (a blessing for sports and photojournalism photographers). This is Canon's first weather-resistant flash.

580EX II specifications and features

This section covers some of the features available on the 580EX II Speedlite:

▶ **Guide number (GN).** A flash unit's guide number is used to determine the proper exposure when shooting Manual flash without a flash meter. With today's advanced flash systems, guide numbers are most often used to compare power output between flashes. Guide numbers are usually given for both feet and meters, so be sure that you use the right one in your calculations. The guide number varies with the zoom settings, from GN 28/92 (meters/feet) at 24mm to GN 58/190 (meters/feet) at 105mm. See your owner's manual for more information on GNs for specific zoom ranges.

▶ **Automatic zooming flash head.** This provides lens coverage from 24mm to 105mm. It supports up to 14mm coverage with the built-in wide-angle lens panel.

▶ **E-TTL.** The 580EX II supports E-TTL II, E-TTL, and TTL, along with full Manual flash output operation.

▶ **Wireless lighting.** You can control up to three different groups of Speedlites in E-TTL II or Manual mode.

▶ **Second-curtain sync.** This function fires the flash at the end of the exposure, rather than the beginning. This helps you capture more natural images when shooting long exposures, because it causes a trail to appear behind a moving subject and not in front of it, which occurs when the flash is fired at the beginning of the exposure.

▶ **AF-assist beam.** To assist while focusing in low-light situations, the 580EX II emits a grid pattern of red light from its LED sensor.

▶ **High-speed sync (FP flash).** This function allows you to shoot with a shutter speed higher than the rated sync speed of the camera. This feature is useful when shooting portraits in bright light using a wide aperture with fast shutter speeds.

▶ **Flash Exposure Lock (FEL).** You can use this feature to get a reading from your subject and then recompose the shot while retaining the original exposure.

▶ **Flash Exposure Compensation.** Similar to the way Exposure Compensation is set on the camera, this function allows you to adjust the light output up or down in 1/3-stop increments over a +/–3-stop range while still enjoying all the benefits of E-TTL II flash metering.

▶ **Modeling flash.** The 580EX II fires a short burst of flashes, allowing you to see what the light falling on your subject will look like. This is a battery drain and something I rarely use.

▶ **Multi-stroboscopic flash mode.** The 580EX II fires a user-specified number of flashes per second, like a strobe light, for creative effects.

▶ **Tilting/rotating flash head for bouncing flash.** This allows you to tilt the flash head up to bounce light from the ceiling, or to the side to bounce light off a wall. The 580EX II also allows you to tilt the flash head downward –7 degrees for close-up subjects.

▶ **Wide panel.** A pull-out wide panel is included to extend flash output to 14mm lens coverage. This is a huge plus when doing group photography in tight quarters or using a wide-angle lens for flash work.

▶ **Catch-light panel.** Just above the wide panel is a retractable white panel. When it is extended, you can reflect light back into your subject's eyes, creating catch-lights and adding sparkle and vitality to the portrait.

▶ **PC terminal.** The 580EX II includes a receive-only PC sync terminal for triggering the Speedlite with radio frequency remotes like RadioPoppers, PocketWizards, or optical slave attachments.

▶ **External power supply socket.** For faster recycling times and longer flash shooting sessions, an external power supply socket is provided for use with the Canon CP-E4 Compact Battery Pack or third-party power supplies, such as those from Quantum.

▶ **External Speedlite control.** The latest Canon cameras include a menu option that allows you to set some or all of your Speedlites' controls directly from the camera depending on the model of Speedlite. The benefit of this capability is that the camera's External Speedlite control menu provides more detail for the settings than the Speedlite's LCD.

Main components

The 580EX II Speedlite is a fantastic tool for creating beautiful lighting and to start you on your way to *making* pictures instead of *taking* them. This is all the more reason why this flash can at first seem a little overwhelming at first, but grasping how to use it gets easier. I'll start by going over all the buttons and controls and describing what each does. I'll get to the "why" in later chapters.

▶ **Flash head/Wireless transmitter.** This is where the flashtube is housed. Inside is a mechanism that zooms the flashbulb forward and back to provide flash coverage for lenses of different focal lengths. The flash head is adjustable; it can be tilted upward to a full 90 degrees and downward to –7 degrees. It can also be adjusted horizontally 180 degrees to the left or to the right. Zoom adjustments can also be made independently of the lens's focal-length position when a more narrow, focused beam of light is desired for creative effects.

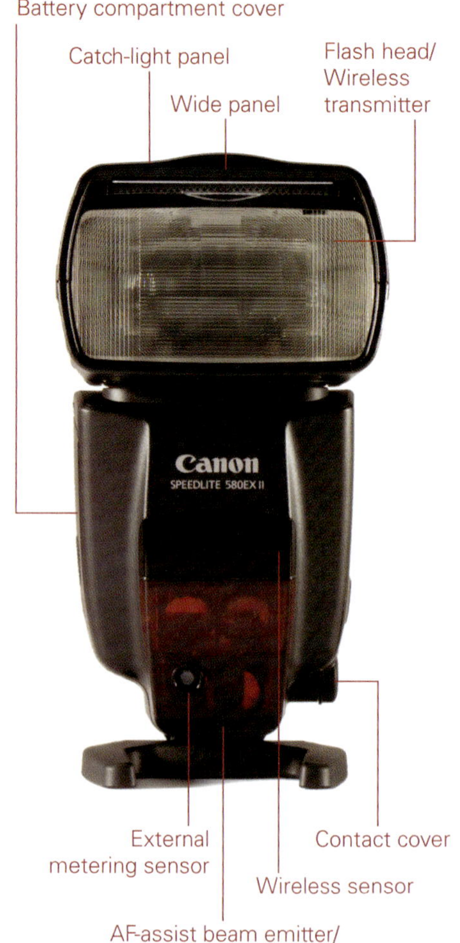

1.4 The front of the 580EX II Speedlite

▶ **Battery compartment cover.** This cover is a vast improvement over the old 580EX. Slide the center button left and then downward to open the spring-loaded battery compartment to load or change the batteries.

▶ **Wireless sensor for E-TTL and E-TTL II wireless flash.** This sensor reads signals from the master unit, enabling wireless flash operation.

▶ **External metering sensor.** The external metering sensor allows the flash to calculate its own light output without relying on the camera's metering system. The flash has to know camera settings (ISO, shutter speed, and aperture) to calculate the correct amount of output. External metering has to be set to Manual mode, and all the camera settings must be entered into the flash manually.

▶ **AF-assist beam emitter.** The 580EX II projects a red LED light-grid onto the subject to allow the camera's autofocus system to operate successfully in low-light or low-contrast situations. The AF-assist beam is compatible with 28mm and longer lenses.

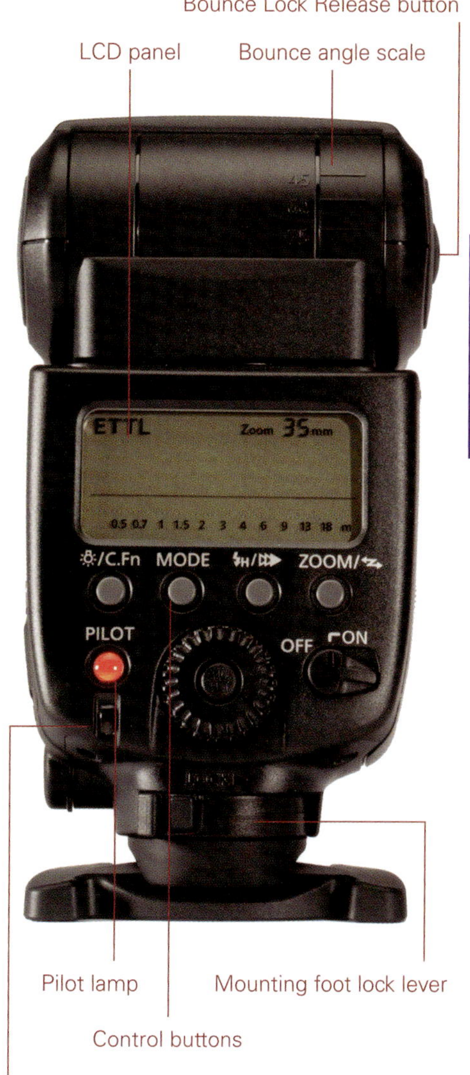

1.5 The back of the 580EX II Speedlite

▶ **Wireless remote ready light.** This operates as a ready light when the Speedlite is being used as a remote flash.

▶ **Bounce angle scale.** This feature allows you to tilt the flash head from normal (0) to 45, 60, 75, or 90 degrees and to –7 degrees for close-ups. Although the flash head has detents at the values indicated on the scale, you can operate the flash at any angle between the detents.

▶ **Bounce Lock Release button.** This button releases the flash-head lock, allowing you to adjust the angle of the flash head for bounce flash.

▶ **Flash head rotating-angle scale.** This feature denotes the horizontal rotation of the flash head from 0 to 60, 75, 90, 120, 150, and 180 degrees from the left. Although the flash head has detents at the values indicated

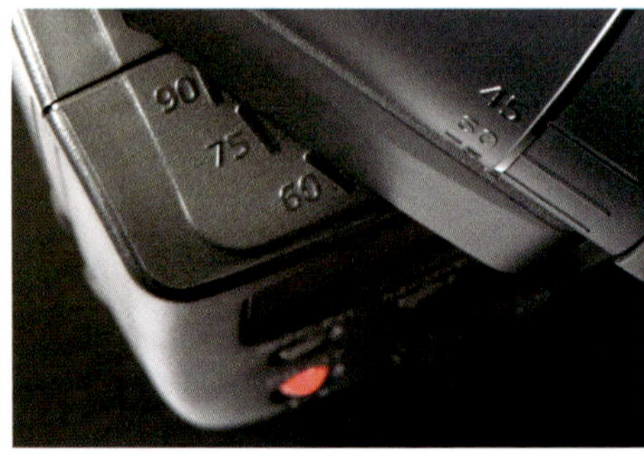

1.6 Bounce angle scale and flash head rotating-angle scale for bounce or creative flash

on the scale, you can operate the flash at any angle between the detents.

▶ **LCD panel.** This is a display panel where you view and operate all the Speedlite settings, Custom Functions, and controls.

▶ **Control buttons.** You can use the control buttons to specify settings and Custom Functions on the Speedlite.

▶ **Pilot lamp.** This light indicates that the Speedlite is ready to fire. After the Speedlite is fired, this light glows green for Quick flash, then red when the Speedlite is fully recycled and ready to fire again. Quick flash allows the flash to be fired again before it has totally recycled to its full power capacity once the lamp glows green. Quick flash is limited to between 1/6 and 1/2 of the full light output and is ideal for close subjects and when you want a shorter recycling time. Quick flash does not operate in Continuous shooting (⊒ᵢ), FEB, Manual flash, or Multi-stroboscopic flash modes.

▶ **Flash exposure confirmation lamp.** This indicator glows green for about three seconds when standard flash exposure is attained.

▶ **Mounting foot lock lever.** This is a huge improvement over the old 580EX. This lever locks the Speedlite with a click into the camera's hot shoe or the included Speedlite stand.

▶ **Wide panel.** This built-in diffuser enables you to use the Speedlite with a lens as wide as 14mm without having light fall off at the edges of the image.

▶ **Catch-light panel.** This white plastic card reflects light back into the eyes, providing a catch-light when the flash is used in the bounced position.

▶ **External power source socket.** Canon's optional CP-E4 Compact Battery Pack external power source or a third-party power supply can be plugged into this socket.

▶ **Bracket mounting hole.** This is used to attach the Speedlite to the Canon SB-E2 Speedlite bracket. The SB-E2 allows the Speedlite to be attached to the side of the camera rather than to the hot shoe.

▶ **Hot shoe mounting foot.** A major improvement over the mounting foot of the old 580EX, this new one is now made of metal and coupled with the new lock lever that securely connects the flash with the camera. This connector slides into the hot shoe on your camera body, locks the Speedlite to the camera with the lock lever, and is the important electrical communication connection between the flash and the camera.

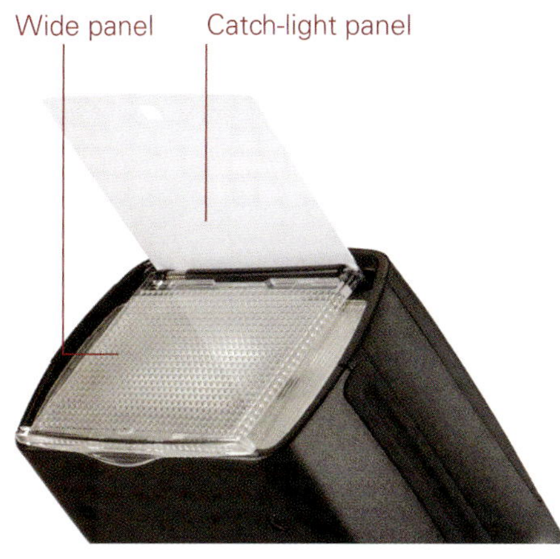

1.7 The wide panel and the built-in catch-light panel

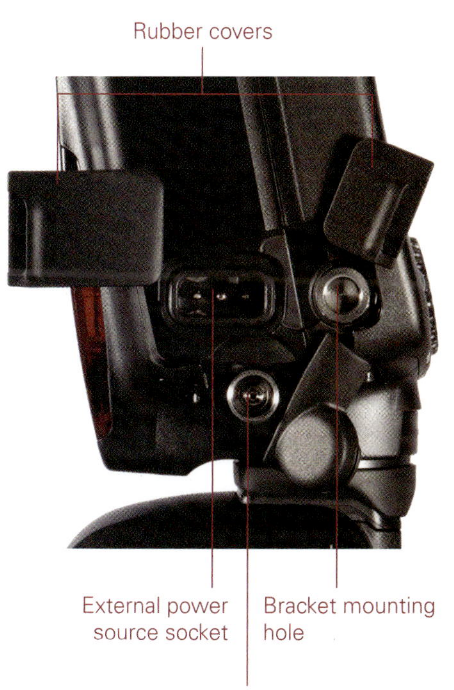

1.8 The side view of the flash

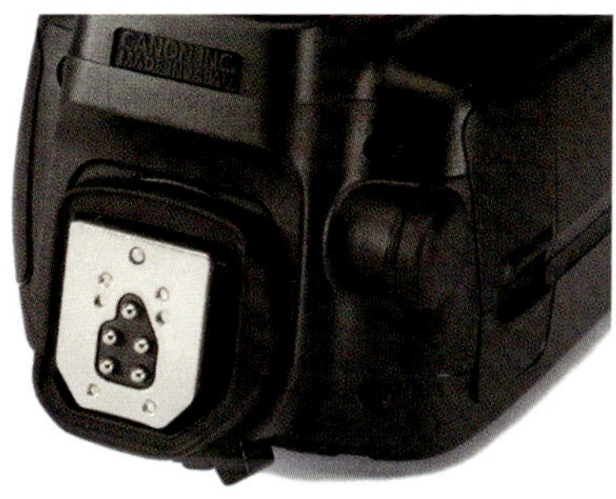

1.9 The hot shoe mounting foot

Control buttons and Select dial

There are several control buttons, a dial, and a switch on the back of the 580EX II, so I'll describe how each one operates in order to get the best results from your new Speedlite. Some of them are obvious, such as the On/Off switch, but others control the menus and settings that you select. Spend time getting acquainted with these controls; this way, in the future you'll be able to quickly and easily make the adjustments you want.

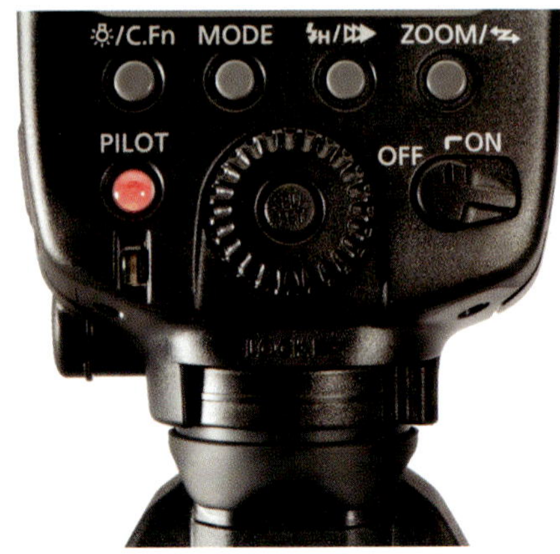

1.10 The 580EX II's main panel, showing the control buttons and Select dial

▶ **LCD Panel Illumination/Custom Functions (C.Fn) button.** Pressing this button once turns the LCD light on for about 10 seconds for viewing settings in dim light. Pressing and holding this button brings you to the Custom Functions menu. You can scroll through the Custom Functions by using the Select dial and choose them by pressing the Select/Set button.

CROSS REF See the tables in Chapter 2 for more on Custom Functions and their applications.

▶ **Mode button.** The Mode button is used to cycle among the different flash exposure modes of the 580EX II Speedlite and during wireless operation to manually adjust flash output. It has three modes:

- **E-TTL.** The exposure is determined by a brief preflash before the main flash in order to obtain a more correct exposure and measures the light coming through the lens. The camera then uses this information to blend the flash output with the ambient light.

- **M (full Manual mode).** You can use guide numbers or determine the flash output power by taking test shots and then reviewing them on the camera's LCD monitor. Output is adjustable in 1/3-stop power settings, allowing you to fine-tune your lighting or dial in each Speedlite individually in multi-flash lighting setups. You can also use a handheld flash meter to determine the flash and camera settings.

- **Multi-stroboscopic flash.** This mode allows you to fire the flash multiple times during a single exposure for creative effect.

- ▶ **High-speed sync (FP flash)/Second-curtain sync button.** Pressing this button once allows you to set the flash to High-speed sync. Pressing the High-speed sync (FP flash)/Second-curtain sync button a second time turns on the Second-curtain sync feature. In standard flash photography, the normal operation sequence is the shutter opens and the flash fires immediately. In this mode, the flash fires at the very end of the exposure, just before the second curtain closes. To return to standard flash, push the button once again.

  Both of these features work only in E-TTL and Manual flash modes, and not in the Multi-stroboscopic mode.

- ▶ **Zoom/Wireless Select/Set button.** Press this button to manually change the flash head zoom by using the Select dial/Set button. Press and hold this button to enter the wireless control menu, where you set master/slave status, channel number, group designations, and slave ratios.

- ▶ **Pilot Lamp button.** Press this button when lit to test-fire the 580EX II to ensure it is functioning properly or to take a test reading using a handheld flash meter. This button also lets you know when the flash is fully charged and ready to fire. When the lamp glows green, the unit is ready for Quick flash; when it glows red, the flash is ready to fire at full power.

- ▶ **Select dial and Select/Set button.** You rotate the Select dial left and right, and confirm the settings by pressing the center Select/Set button.

  - • **Left and right.** When scrolling left or right, you use this button to change the zoom of the flash, select Custom Functions settings, Flash Exposure Compensation, Manual flash output, wireless status, master/slave settings, multi-stroboscopic frequencies, or flash bracketing settings.

  - • **Select.** After turning the Select dial to choose the desired settings, press the Select/Set button to commit to those settings.

580EX II accessories

The 580EX II ships with a soft, ballistic nylon case for storing and carrying it, and includes a tabletop Speedlite stand that enables you to mount your flash to a light stand or tripod.

CROSS REF Third-party manufacturers, such as Honl Photo and ExpoImaging, market other accessories for your 580EX II, and these accessories are discussed in detail in Chapter 5.

430EX II

Introduced in the fall of 2008, the 430EX II is the middle child in the Canon Speedlite System; it includes many of the improvements built into the 580EX II, such as wireless control, a built-in wide-angle lens panel, and the very popular metal mounting foot and quick lock/quick release lever to securely mount it to your camera. The 430EX II is a step up for photographers accustomed to shooting with their camera's built-in flash, and offers more power, a higher guide number, and a tilting/rotating flash head for bounce-flash lighting techniques, which is not possible with the pop-up flashes.

430EX II specifications and features

As the intermediate flash in the Canon line, the 430EX II has less power, fewer features, a lower guide number range, and about 35-percent less reach than the 580EX II. Its major limitation for advanced use is that it cannot be used as a wireless controller in a multiple flash system. However, it can operate as a slave when combined with a Speedlite capable of master control, such as the 550EX, 580EX, or 580EX II, either of the Macro Speedlites, or the ST-E2 Speedlite transmitter. In all cases, the master controller must be mounted on the camera's hot shoe in order to use a 430EX II wirelessly off camera as a fill flash.

The 430EX II also cannot run from an external power source, which may be required to extend flash capacity and shorten recycle time in high-use situations, such as weddings.

This section provides a brief look at different features that are available on the 430EX II Speedlite. It is important to note, however, that some of its features may not be available, depending on the camera body you are using.

- ▶ **Guide number (GN).** The guide number varies with the zoom settings of the flash head, from GN 25/82 (meters/feet) at 24mm to GN 43/141 (meters/feet) at 105mm. See your owner's manual for more information on GNs for specific zoom ranges.

- ▶ **Automatic zooming flash head.** The 430EX II provides lens coverage from 24mm up to 105mm. It provides 14mm with the included wide panel.

- ▶ **E-TTL.** The 430EX II supports E-TTL II, E-TTL, TTL, and full manual operation.

- ▶ **AF-assist beam.** The 430EX II emits a grid of light from a red LED to assist in focusing in low-light situations.

- ▶ **High-speed sync (FP flash).** This function allows you to shoot with a shutter speed higher than the rated sync speed of the camera. This feature is useful when shooting portraits in bright light using a wide aperture with fast shutter speeds.

▶ **Flash Exposure Lock (FEL).** You can use this feature to get a reading from your subject and then recompose the shot while retaining the original exposure.

▶ **Flash Exposure Compensation.** Similar to the way Exposure Compensation is set on the camera, this function allows you to adjust the light output up or down in 1/3-stop increments over a +/– 3-stop range and still enjoy all the benefits of E-TTL II flash metering.

▶ **Modeling flash.** The 430EX II releases a short burst of flashes, allowing you to see what the light falling on your subject looks like.

▶ **Tilting/rotating flash head for bouncing flash.** This allows you to tilt the flash head up to bounce light from the ceiling, or to the side to bounce light off the wall.

▶ **Wireless sensor for E-TTL II wireless flash.** This sensor reads signals from the master unit, enabling wireless flash operation. The 430EX II can only be used as a slave unit in wireless flash operation.

Main components

The main controls of the 430EX II are located in the same configuration as the 580EX II with the exception of the Select/Set dial, which has been replaced with +/– buttons to the left and right of the Set button.

▶ **Flash head.** This is where the flashtube is housed. Inside is a mechanism that zooms the flashbulb forward and back to provide flash coverage for lenses of different focal lengths. The flash head is adjustable; it can be tilted upward to a full 90 degrees. It can also be adjusted horizontally 180 degrees to the left or 90 degrees to the right. Zoom adjustments can also be used independently of the lens's focal length position when a more narrow, focused beam of light is desired for creative effects.

▶ **Bounce Lock Release button.** This button releases the flash-head lock, allowing you to adjust the angle of the flash head for bounce flash.

▶ **Battery compartment cover.** You slide the cover downward to open the battery compartment to load or change the batteries.

▶ **Wireless sensor for E-TTL II wireless flash.** This sensor reads signals from the master unit, enabling wireless flash operation.

▶ **AF-assist beam emitter.** The 430EX II projects a red LED light-grid onto the subject to aid the camera's autofocus system to operate successfully in low-light or low-contrast situations. The AF-assist beam is compatible with 28mm and longer lenses.

► **Wireless remote ready light.** This operates as a ready light when the Speedlite is being used as a remote flash.

► **Bounce angle scale.** This feature allows you to tilt the flash head up from 0 (normal) to 45, 60, 75, or 90 degrees. While the flash head has detents at the values indicated on the scale, you can operate the flash at any angle between the detents.

► **Flash head rotating-angle scale.** This feature denotes the horizontal rotation of the flash head from 0 (normal) to 60, 75, 90, 120, 150, and 180 degrees from the left. To the right, it can be adjusted to 60, 75, and 90 degrees. While the flash head has detents at the values indicated on the scale, you can operate the flash at any angle between the detents.

► **LCD panel.** This is a display panel where you view and control all of the Speedlite settings, Custom Functions, and controls.

► **Control buttons.** You can use these buttons to specify settings and Custom Functions on the Speedlite.

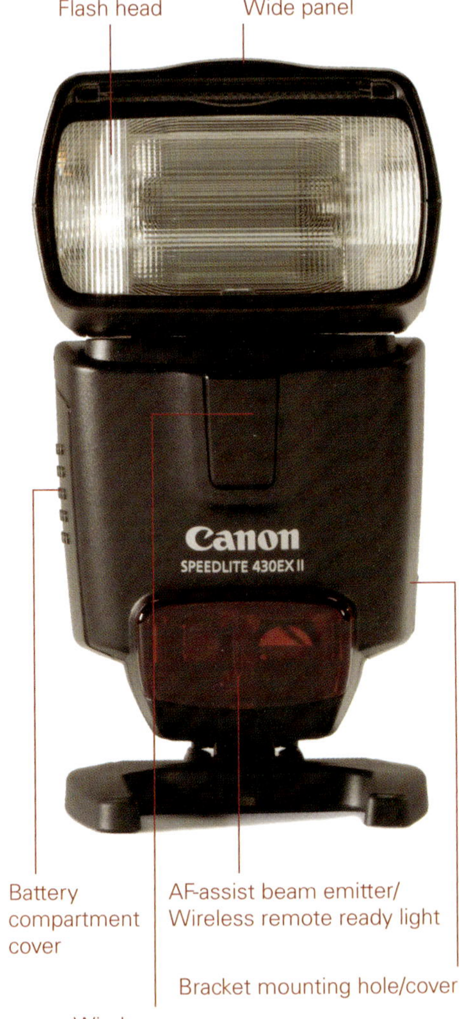

1.11 The front of the 430EX II Speedlite

▶ **Pilot Lamp button.** Press this button when illuminated to test-fire the 430EX II to ensure it is functioning properly or to take a test reading using a handheld flash meter. This button also lets you know when the flash is fully charged and ready to fire. When the lamp glows green, the unit is ready for Quick flash; when it glows red, the flash is ready to fire at full power.

▶ **Flash exposure confirmation lamp.** This indicator glows green for about three seconds when standard flash exposure is attained.

▶ **Hot shoe mounting foot.** A major improvement over the mounting foot of the old 430EX, this new one is made of metal and coupled with the new mounting lock lever that securely connects the flash with the camera. This connector slides into the hot shoe on your camera body and locks the Speedlite to the camera with the lock lever. It is the important electrical communication connection between the flash and the camera.

▶ **Wide panel.** This built-in diffuser enables you to use the Speedlite with a lens as wide as 14mm without having light fall off at the edges of the image.

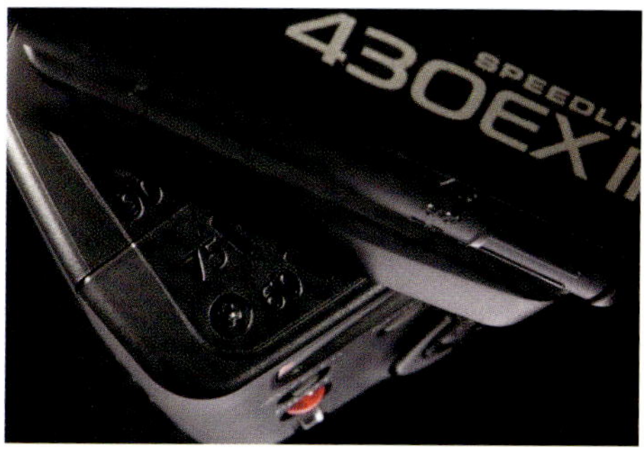

1.12 Flash head tilting/rotating-angle scale

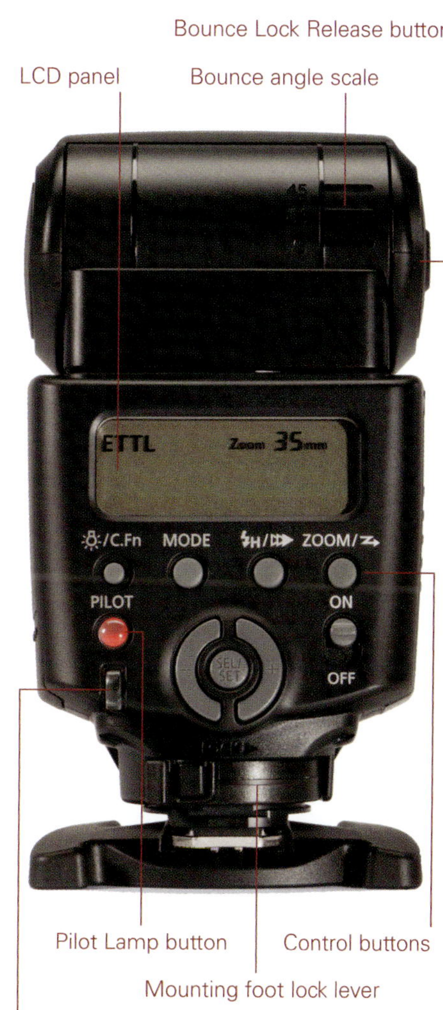

1.13 The back of the 430EX II Speedlite

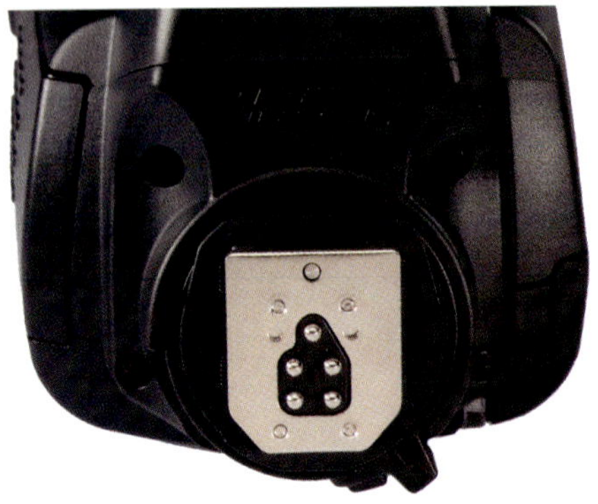

1.14 Hot shoe mounting foot and lock lever

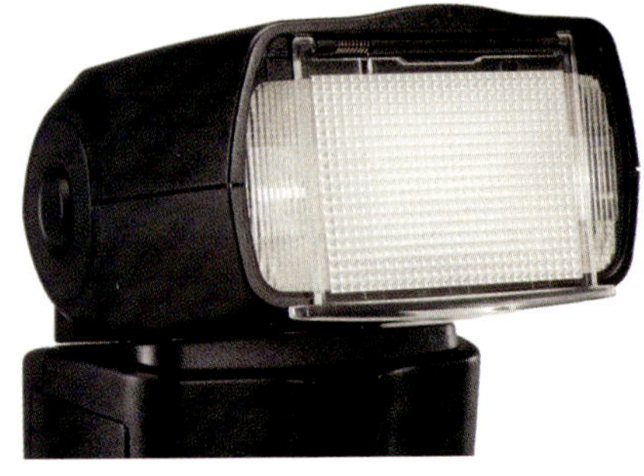

1.15 Wide panel

Control buttons

There are several control buttons and a switch on the back of the 430EX II, so I'll describe how each one operates so that you can get the best results from your new Speedlite. Some of them are obvious, such as the On/Off switch, but others control the menus and settings that you select. Spend time getting acquainted with these controls, this way in future you'll be able to quickly and easier make the adjustments you want.

▶ **LCD Panel Illumination/Custom Functions (C.Fn) button.** Pressing this button once turns the LCD light on for about 10 seconds for viewing settings in dim light. Pressing and holding this button brings you to the Custom Functions menu. You can access the Custom Functions by using the +/– buttons, and choose them by pressing the Select/Set button.

CROSS REF See the table in Chapter 2 for more on Custom Functions and their applications.

▶ **Mode button.** The Mode button is used to switch between the different flash exposure modes of the 430EX II Speedlite and in wireless operation is used to manually set flash output. The two modes are:

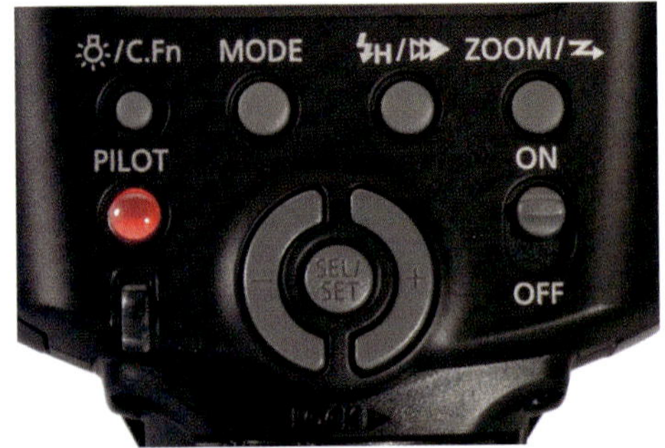

1.16 The 430EX II control panel

- **E-TTL.** The exposure is determined by a brief preflash before the main flash in order to obtain a more correct exposure and measures the light coming through the lens. The camera then uses this information to blend the flash output with the ambient light.

- **M (full Manual mode).** You determine the flash power by guide numbers or taking test shots and then reviewing on the camera's LCD monitor. Output is adjustable from 1/1 (full) to 1/64 power in 1/3-stop intervals, allowing you can fine-tune your lighting or dial in each Speedlite individually in multi-flash lighting setups. You can also use a handheld flash meter to determine the flash and camera settings.

▶ **High-speed sync (FP flash)/Second-curtain sync button.** Pressing this button once allows you to set the flash to High-speed sync. Pressing it a second time turns on the second-curtain sync feature. In standard flash photography, the normal operation sequence is the shutter opens and the flash fires immediately. In this mode, the flash fires at the very end of the exposure, just before the second curtain closes. To return to standard flash, push the button once again.

▶ **Zoom/Wireless Selection/Set button.** Press this button to manually change the flash head zoom using the +/– buttons. Press and hold this button to enter the wireless control menu, where you set slave status, channel number, and slave groups.

▶ **Pilot Lamp button.** Press this button when lit to test-fire the 430EX II to ensure it is functioning properly or to take a test reading using a handheld flash meter. This button also lets you know when the flash is fully charged and ready to fire. When the lamp glows green, the unit is ready for Quick flash; when it glows red, the flash is ready to fire at full power.

▶ **Select/Set and +/– buttons.** You press the right and left +/– buttons to change the settings, and confirm them by pressing the center Select/Set button.

  - **+/– buttons.** You use these buttons to change the zoom of the flash, Flash Exposure Compensation, Manual flash output, wireless status, slave settings, flash bracketing settings, or Custom Functions.

  - **Select/Set.** The center button is the Select/Set button. You use this button to confirm the flash settings that you have selected by turning the Select dial.

430EX II accessories

The 430EX II ships with a soft case for storing and carrying it, and includes a tabletop Speedlite stand that enables you to mount your flash to a light stand or tripod.

CROSS REF Third-party manufacturers such as Honl Photo and ExpoImaging market other accessories for your 580EX II, and these accessories are discussed in detail in Chapter 5.

Other Components of the Speedlite System

Becoming familiar with your new flash equipment is the first step in learning about lighting and understanding the creative possibilities of wireless flash. As exciting as that might seem, it's only the first phase of the complete Canon Speedlite System. There are additional items that round out the system, each designed for specific lighting tasks.

270EX

Released in May 2009, the Speedlite 270EX replaced the 220EX. Compact and lightweight, the 270EX expands your camera's capabilities over the on-board pop-up flash in a highly portable unit that fits in your shirt pocket. The 270EX is powered by two AA batteries instead of four, like most other Speedlites, seriously lightening the weight of this flash.

The biggest improvement over the 220EX is the bounce-capable flash head. Although the adjustment range is limited (90 degrees tilt, no rotation), the bounce capability is a big plus compared to a fixed flash head like the 220EX. Also important is the new two-position manual Tele-zoom option, which allows the 270EX to concentrate its light on

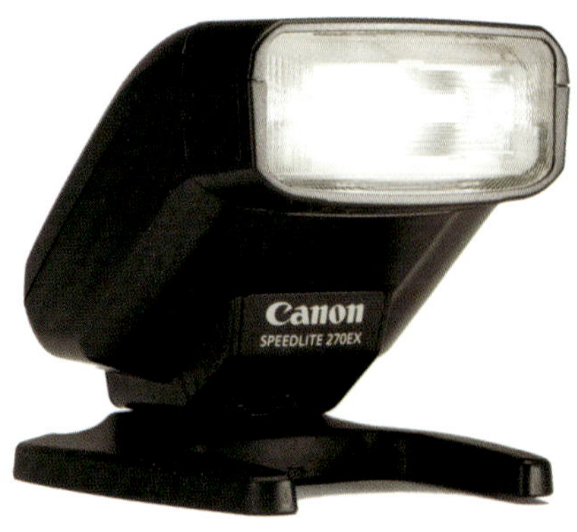

1.17 The Canon Speedlite 270EX

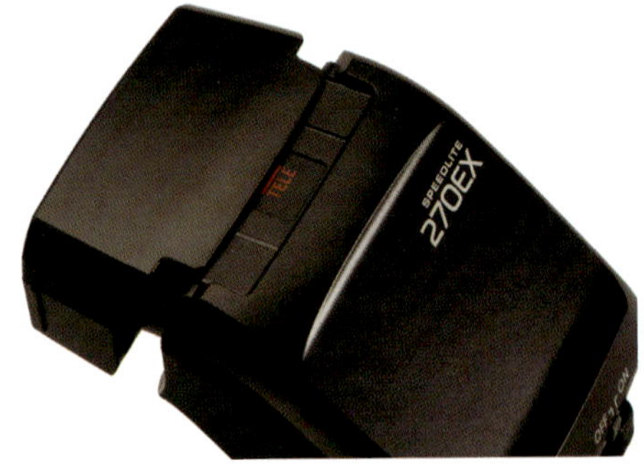

1.18 The Canon Speedlite 270EX Tele-zoom/bounce head

the subject, allowing creative choices not previously available with this model, making more efficient use of its power, and extending its useful distance.

Several features incorporated in Canon's newer flashes are inherited by the 270EX. These include the ability to control flash settings from a compatible camera's menu (including Manual flash mode settings), the communication of color temperature information with a compatible camera (for optimal white balance), and silent recycling. The lack of a slave function on this model may be a drawback for some.

270EX II

The 270EX II replaces the 270EX as Canon's entry-level, inexpensive, and lightweight flash. Compatible with all EOS and PowerShot cameras, its small size makes it a perfect mate for the PowerShot line.

One big difference between the 270EX and the upgraded 270EX II is that you can use this flash wirelessly off camera. The back of the Speedlite now has a slave switch. Being able to use this flash off camera, controlled by a line-of-sight master such as a 580EX II, ST-E2 Speedlite transmitter, or an integrated Speedlite controller included on some camera models (7D, 60D and Rebel T3i/600D) make the 270EX II a very useful little Speedlite. Add to that the bounce-capable tilting flash head (a carryover from the 270EX), and the benefits of this small, inexpensive flash are clear.

A cold shoe flash stand is now included as well, making it easy to position the Speedlite off camera where desired.

> **NOTE** A cold shoe is a receptacle for the flash's hot shoe foot that does not have a provide a wired connection between the camera and the Speedlite.

One interesting new feature on this model is its ability to remotely trigger the camera with a 2-second delay using the small Remote button on the side of the flash head. This feature works with all EOS model cameras compatible with the RC-6 Remote Controller.

A few of the things lacking on the 270EX II are the ability to use it as a master, a way to change settings from the flash itself (you have to use the camera's menu system on compatible models), and a flash head that swivels.

320EX

The 320EX is a newer model in the Canon Speedlite lineup. It fills the gap between the 270EX II and 430EX II. It is most similar to the 430EX II; however, it's smaller and slightly less powerful. Because it's so close in size, power, and price to the 430EX II, it's worth comparing the two and seeing which one meets your needs.

The 320EX and 430EX II are both midrange flashes, both medium priced, both medium power, both good starter flashes, and both function as remote slaves. One big difference between the two is the 320EX's LED light intended for video capture. The big difference between the 430EX II and 320EX is that the 320EX is not only a flash but also a continuous light source. Having the ability for continuous light sounds like a useful feature; however, there are some real drawbacks in its current iteration. The LED isn't very strong, and its small size is also an issue. You can only get a small amount of light from an LED the size of the one included on the 320EX. It's certainly not strong enough to overpower the sun in backlit situations. For practical purposes, any real-world video applications would require a much larger video light. In very dark situations, with the camera's ISO rating set to 800 or above and your widest available aperture selected, the LED does a fair job of illuminating subjects that are very close to the Speedlite.

When it comes to still photography, the 430EX II outshines the 320EX in the following areas: It's slightly more powerful (important for bounce flash where you need the power you can get) and the 430EX II can have manual power settings dialed in from the back of the flash while the 320EX lacks this ability. This means it can only be used in E-TTL mode or changed via the menu system on certain Canon dSLRs. One of the other big downsides of this flash is that you can't use it in full Manual (**M**) mode triggered wirelessly with radio triggers such as PocketWizards.

Another important difference between the 430EX II and 320EX is that the 320EX lacks a focus assist beam emitter that helps you focus in low-light situations. Instead, the 320EX uses a burst of preflashes from the flash head. Because this is annoying for subjects, it restricts my applications for this flash. For example, I wouldn't use it for event photography.

The 320EX lacks an automatic zoom head. When using a zoom lens, you have to manually adjust the flash head by pulling it out. This is easy to forget. Also absent from the 320EX is a pop-out wide panel diffuser and white bounce card.

Unfortunately, it seems like the 320EX tries to do too many things and ends up doing none of them well. I think the 430EX II is a better and more useful investment.

OC-E3 Off-Camera Shoe Cord

The Canon OC-E3 Off-Camera Shoe Cord supports all Speedlites and maintains all on-camera flash functions, including E-TTL II for Canon Speedlites used off-camera at distances up to 2 feet. It is compatible with all Canon EOS cameras, except for the 630 and RT.

One end of the cord mounts in the camera hot shoe, and the Speedlite mounts in the hot shoe foot at the other end of the cord. The foot is threaded so that it can be mounted on a tripod.

The OC-E3 has been improved with better sealing against dust and moisture, similar to the weather-resistant design of the EOS 1D Mark III and the 580EX II flash. It also now features a sturdier metal foot.

The Off-Camera Shoe Cord allows you to use your flash either handheld or with a flash bracket. Using the cord with a flash bracket allows the flash to stay above the lens axis and communicate with the camera whether in a horizontal or vertical position.

Shooting flash off axis from the lens allows you to light your subject directionally and adds three-dimensionality and modeling to your flash photos by having the light come from the side, thus creating highlights and shadows.

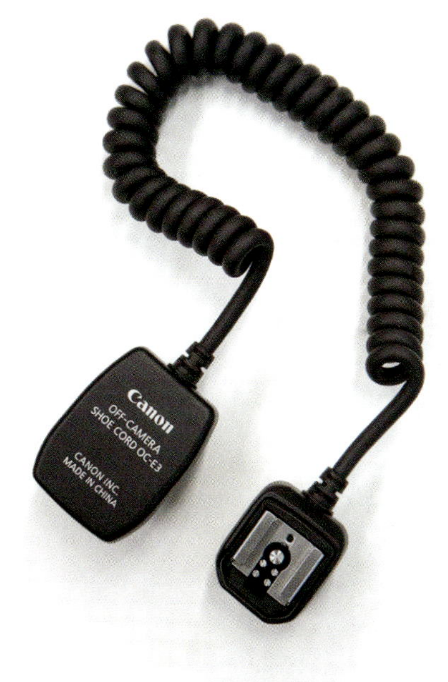

1.19 The Canon OC-E3 Off-Camera Shoe Cord

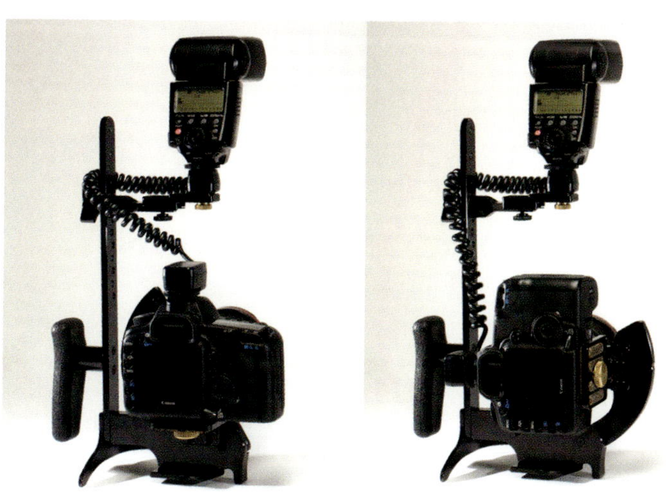

1.20 The Canon OC-E3 Off-Camera Shoe Cord used with a flash bracket

Speedlite transmitter ST-E3-RT

The radio-enabled Speedlite transmitter ST-E3-RT is a wireless controller that currently works exclusively with 600EX-RT Speedlites. This 2.4-GHz radio transmitter is exclusively radio based and therefore not backward compatible with Speedlites that communicate wirelessly using optical transmitters. In addition to built-in radio communication, the ST-E3-RT is lightweight, slimmer, and much lower in profile than the ST-E2. In a stroke of genius, the designers and engineers at Canon made the ST-E3-RT an almost exact duplicate of the 600EX-RT only without the flash head and an AF-assist beam. This makes learning how to use it a snap because once you've learned how to operate the 600EX-RT you've essentially learned how to use the ST-E3-RT, and vice versa.

When attached to your camera's hot shoe, the ST-E3-RT becomes the control center (master) for your radio-based wireless Speedlite use. Keep in mind that 2012 or later EOS camera models are required for full access to the camera's onboard external Speedlite menus and full radio-based functionality. However, everything you need is easily accessible using the improved interface and navigation on the new LCD panel located on top of the Speedlite transmitter ST-E3-RT.

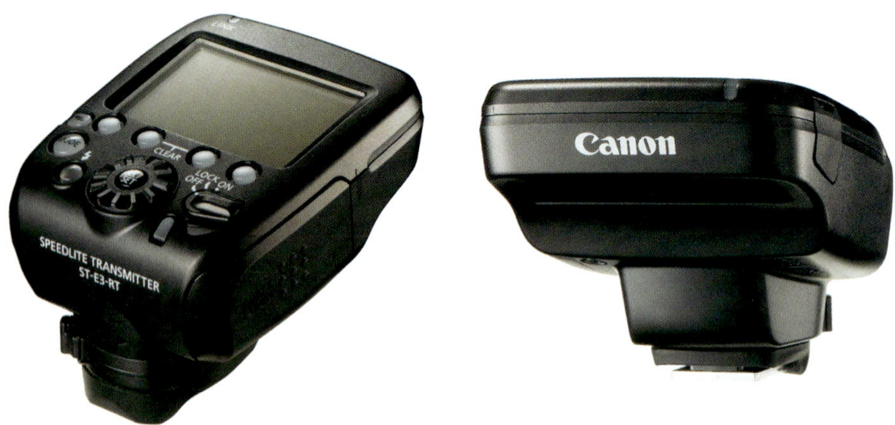

Courtesy of Canon

1.21 The Canon Speedlite transmitter ST-E3-RT

In E-TTL mode, using ratios, the ST-E3-RT can trigger three groups of flashes, A:B and C groups. One of the really exciting new features of the ST-E3-RT and 600EX-RT is Group mode (Gr). Using this mode, you can fire up to five slave groups containing up to 15 slave Speedlites. Each one of these groups can be independently controlled, their power output can be adjusted, they can be remotely powered on and off, and mixed flash modes can be assigned to each group. This a great feature because it allows you to shoot with a mixture of Speedlites in different flash modes, some in E-TTL and some in Manual, all at the same time and all controlled right from the ST-E3-RT. Having this capability provides tremendous flexibility, enabling you to leverage the best aspects of each flash mode in one exposure. The ST-E2's ratio, Flash Exposure Compensation, Flash Exposure Bracketing, and High-speed sync capabilities have been carried over to this model with a much improved navigation system for accessing and controlling them.

The ST-E3-RT's built-in radio-enabled transmitter is rated for a wireless radio communication range of up to 98 feet when used with 600EX-RT Speedlites. Because it is radio based, it suffers none of the limitations common with optically based communication systems such as limited distance and the necessity for an unobstructed line of sight between master and slave wireless sensors. Two-way radio communication between master and slaves is another first for the ST-E3-RT and 600EX-RT. This feature provides feedback on the master about whether slave units are communicating with the master and ready to fire. The master and each slave have a Link lamp above the LCD panel that switches from red to green when successful communication has been established. The Flash Test button (⚡) below the LCD displays a red light when all slaves are ready to fire. When shooting with slaves and using Group mode (Gr) or shooting using Speedlites in ratio groups, a lightning bolt symbol also appears next to each slave represented on LCD when it's ready to fire.

As mentioned previously, the ST-E3-RT is almost an exact duplicate of the 600EX-RT and therefore shares all its great new features such as a large LCD panel, optional LCD background colors, legible dot matrix LCD text, understandable language for Custom Functions (C.Fn) and Personal Functions (P.Fn), consistent menu item placement, intuitive navigation, and four Function buttons that work in conjunction with the context-sensitive LCD menu system.

For radio control of one or more off-camera Speedlites, the Speedlite transmitter ST-E3-RT is an indispensable tool that provides 98 feet of cable-free range without the limitations of optical systems. It's powered by 2 AA lithium batteries, a better choice than the less common and sometimes harder to find CR123 battery used in

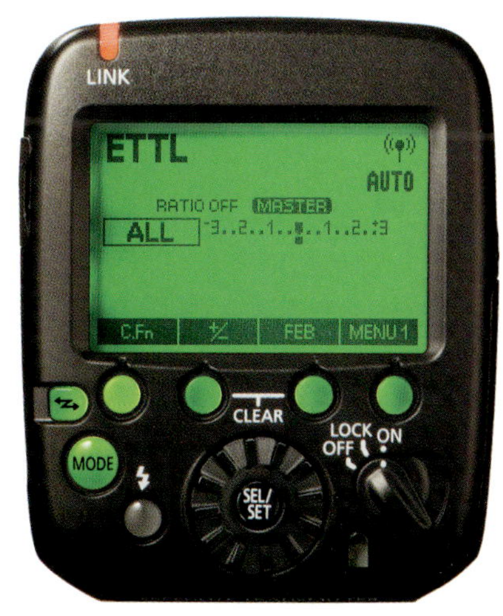

Courtesy of Canon

1.22 The ST-E3-RT LCD panel

the ST-E2. I prefer to use rechargeable AAs for the ST-E3-RT. The lack of an AF-assist beam is the one unfortunate omission on the ST-E3-RT and something Canon will hopefully address in the next version. At this point, low-light shooters will probably also want an additional 600EX-RT to help lock focus via the built-in AF-assist beam as well as communicate exposure information to the slaves.

Table 1.1 describes the ST-E3-RT Custom Functions and Table 1.2 reviews the ST-E3-RT Personal Functions.

Table 1.1 Speedlite Transmitter ST-E3-RT Custom Functions

Custom Function Number	Function	Settings and Description
C.Fn-01	Auto power off	0–Enabled/1–Disabled. Auto power off turns the flash off automatically after a certain period of inactivity (not user-specified, but between 1.5 minutes to 15 minutes) to save battery power. Press the shutter button or Pilot Lamp button to reactivate the Speedlite. I choose 1 to disable this function whenever I'm working with off-camera Speedlites.
C.Fn-02 (MODELING)	Modeling flash	0–Enabled (DOF preview button)/1–Enabled (Test-firing button)/2–Enabled (both buttons)/3–Disabled.
C.Fn-03 (AUTO CANCEL)	Flash exposure bracketing (FEB) auto cancel	0–Enabled/1–Disabled. This controls the FEB auto cancel feature. After three shots are taken, FEB is automatically canceled. Set to 1 to continue taking FEB photos in sets of three.
C.Fn-04	Flash exposure bracketing (FEB) sequence	0–minus exposure, plus exposure/1–minus exposure, on stop, plus exposure. I set this to 1 because on my computer, I like to see the pictures in exposure order sequence to pick the best one.
C.Fn-07 (TEST)	Test-firing with autoflash	0–1/32 power/1–full power. This allows the user to set the power level of the test flash. I use 0 to save battery life when I just want to check if the flash is working, and 1 when I'm metering the flash output with a handheld light meter.
C.Fn-13	Flash exposure metering setting	0–Speedlite button and dial/1–Speedlite dial only. Setting 1 saves you a step and time by not having to press the Select/Set button on the Speedlite to access FEC settings. You simply turn the dial to the desired FEC setting and shoot.

Custom Function Number	Function	Settings and Description
C.Fn-20 (◁)	Beep	0–OFF (disable)/1–ON (enable). Setting 1 enables a beep to sound when a Speedlite or slave in Radio Transmission Wireless Shooting is fully charged. The beep also sounds when the Speedlite is restricted from firing due to excessive heat in the flash head. I keep this set to 0 to be less intrusive when shooting.
C.Fn-22 (☼)	LCD panel illumination	0–On for 12 sec./1–OFF (Disable illumination)/2–On (Illumination always on). Change the amount of time the LCD illuminates when the dial or buttons are operated. I use 0–On for 12 sec.

Table 1.2 Speedlite Transmitter ST-E3-RT Personal Functions

Personal Function Number	Function	Settings and Description
P.Fn-01 (◖)	LCD panel display contrast	Five levels of LCD panel contrast adjustment
P.Fn-03 (☼)	LCD panel illumination color: Master	0–GREEN (green)/1–ORANGE (orange). Select an LCD panel illumination color for the master Speedlite used during radio or optical transmission linked shooting.
P.Fn-04 (☼)	LCD panel illumination color: Slave	0–GREEN (green)/1–ORANGE (orange). Select an LCD panel illumination color for the slave Speedlite(s) used during radio or optical transmission linked shooting. I set the LCD panel color for slaves to 1–ORANGE (orange) to help more easily distinguish them as slaves.

Custom and Personal Functions can be cleared using the menu system on compatible digital cameras and by pressing Function button 2 (CLEAR) and then Function button 1 (OK) on the 600EX/600EX-RT and Speedlite transmitter ST-E3-RT. Custom Functions that have been set are cleared.

ST-E2 wireless transmitter

For the ease of controlling multiple wireless Speedlites, or when the OC-E3 Off-Camera Shoe Cord is just not long enough, the Speedlite transmitter ST-E2 is an attractive option. Attached to the camera's hot shoe, the ST-E2 is an infrared wireless master control unit for the Canon Speedlite System. It functions in much the same way as the 580EX II does in master mode. This wireless flash controller transmits an infrared trigger, exposure information, and flash ratios to all EX-series Speedlites. The ST-E2 also includes a powerful infrared AF-assist beam, a welcome feature in nighttime shooting or for EOS cameras that lack one.

The ST-E2 transmitter slides into the hot shoe of your camera like any other Speedlite and is used to wirelessly control the Speedlites. It is smaller and lighter than any Speedlite, and its power source is a 2CR5 lithium battery, common in older EOS film cameras. It attaches to the camera with a plastic mounting foot much like older Speedlites, but it includes a very secure shoe lock slider switch instead of a mounting lock wheel.

Each channel can be used to control any number of flashes in two groups. From the ST-E2, you can control the output of each group individually in a ratio of up to a 3-stop range in 1/2-stop increments. The wireless range is greater indoors than outdoors, but I have achieved good communication results by turning the Speedlite's base to face the camera/transmitter and repositioning the flash head toward the subject.

The ST-E2 transmitter also has four independent channels, for those rare situations where you may be working near other photographers using ST-E2 wireless transmitters. You can change your wireless setup to a different channel so that someone else's transmitter won't fire your flashes and your transmitter won't fire theirs. I have never been in this situation, but it's nice to know the technology is there when you need it.

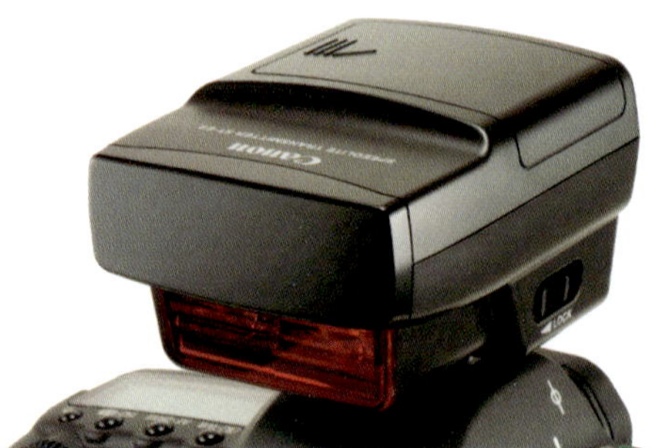

1.23 The Canon ST-E2 wireless transmitter

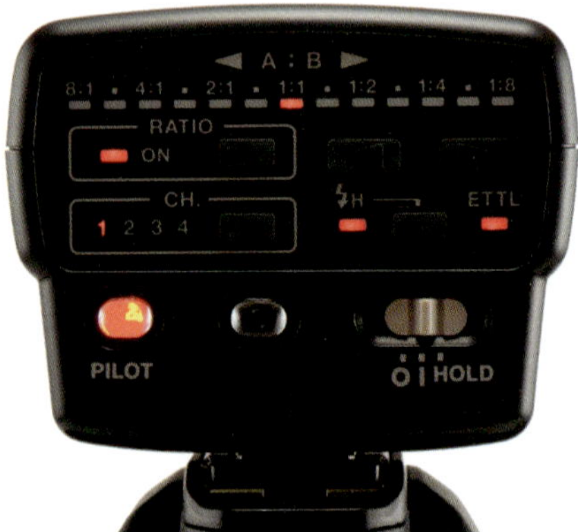

1.24 The rear control panel of the Canon ST-E2 wireless transmitter

The ST-E2 transmitter is a great tool for wireless control of Canon Speedlites, but it does have a few limitations. The main one for me is that it only allows you to shoot in E-TTL mode. This is fine for those setups where I'm only using a few Speedlites off camera and I want to control the flash output ratio of the flashes right from the camera. But when things really get creative out in the field, I switch to Manual exposure and replace the ST-E2 with PocketWizards for wireless control and full manual output. Secondly, the ST-E2 has a much shorter range and effectiveness outdoors. This is because the triggering signal is light based (infrared) rather than the radio frequency technology utilized by remotes, such as RadioPoppers or PocketWizards. It also only controls two groups of flashes, A + B, while the 580EX II set as the master can control three, A + B + C. One of the benefits of using the ST-E2 is not having to sacrifice one of your Speedlites for use on camera as a master controller.

Macro Twin Lite MT-24EX

Macro photography presents the photographer with specific problems to overcome. Often, the close subject distances of macro photography require smaller aperture openings to obtain adequate depth of field. Smaller f-stops require a lot of light or very slow shutter speeds, which is not always possible with subjects, such as swaying flowers or flying bees. Slower shutter speeds usually necessitate the use of a tripod and a stationary subject.

The Macro Twin Lite MT-24EX addresses these concerns in a compact and balanced unit. Its two small flash heads connect to a mounting ring that attaches directly to the front ring of the Canon EF 50mm f/2.5 Macro lens, Canon EF 100mm f/2.8 Macro USM lens, MP-E 65mm 1–5x f/2.8 Macro lens, or Canon's EF 100mm f/2.8L Image Stabilized USM lens.

To mount the Canon Macro Twin Lite on the Canon EF 180mm f/3.5 L USM Macro lens, you need the optional Canon Macro Lite Adapter 72C. These flash heads can be positioned, locked in place, individually turned on or off, or even removed from the mount ring and repositioned for greater creative control.

Two features are included to make focusing and illuminating your subject easy. On-board focusing lamps in each of the flash heads light up for 20 seconds or until you depress the shutter button. Modeling flash releases a short burst of flashes, allowing you to see what the light falling on your subject looks like.

The MT-24EX incorporates many of the features of the top-of-the-line Canon flashes, such as Flash Exposure Compensation, Flash Exposure Bracketing, High-speed sync, and adjustable output ratios between the two flashes by a 3-stop range in 1/2-stop increments.

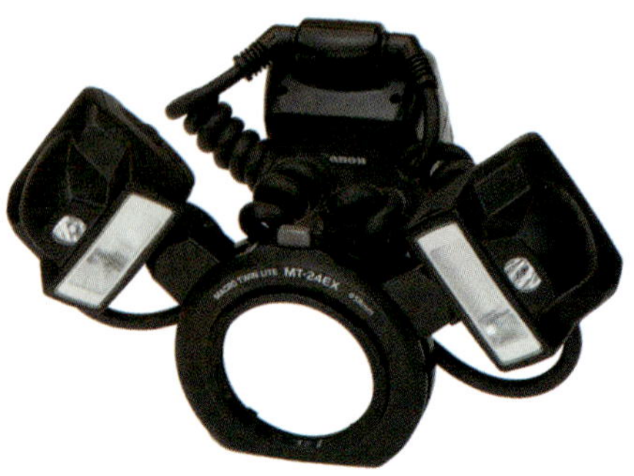

1.25 The Canon Macro Twin Lite MT-24EX

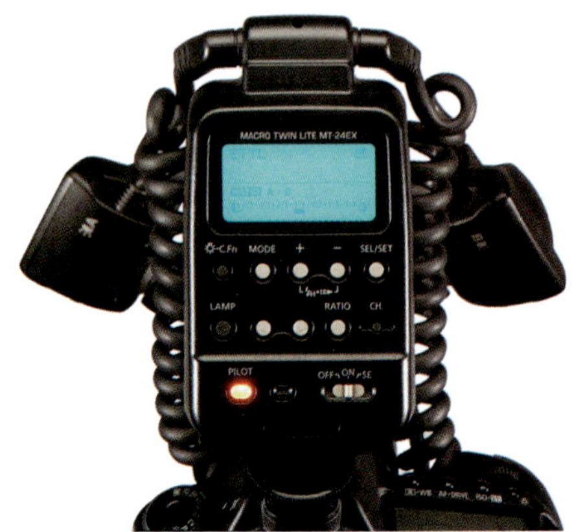

1.26 Control panel of the Macro Twin Lite MT-24EX

The MT-24EX supports wireless operation and can act as a master to trigger other compatible Speedlites for full E-TTL flash metering. It can also be set to work in conjunction with any number of other Speedlites on the same or different channels. To further fine-tune your macro lighting, you can set flash IDs A and B for the built-in flash heads and set any additional slave units to A, B, or C. Other convenient features include full E-TTL exposure, as well as M (Manual) for full control, incandescent focusing lamps, modeling flash operation via camera buttons, and many user-set Custom Functions.

The Macro Twin Lite MT-24EX is powered by four AA lithium, alkaline, or NiMH rechargeable batteries and includes a socket for Canon's optional CP-E4 Compact Battery Pack external power source or a third-party power supply.

For general macro photography, you may find the flash illumination to be a little harsh. To resolve this situation, you can change the ratios so that one flash is stronger than the other; Sto-Fen also makes a nice little set of frosted diffusers specifically for the MT-24EX to soften the light for a more natural look.

Macro Ring Lite MR-14EX

Similar in design to the Macro Twin Lite MT-24EX, the Macro Ring Lite MR-14EX is a Speedlite flash that is geared toward macro and close-up photography but yields a different look due to its unique construction. Two output-adjustable flash tubes encircle the lens and produce shadowless lighting of small subjects.

To make focusing and illuminating your subject easier, the Macro Ring Lite includes on-board focusing lamps between the flashtubes. These focusing lamps light up for

20 seconds or until you depress the shutter button. The modeling lamps release a series of short bursts of light, allowing you to preview what the light falling on your subject looks like.

Long a staple in the medical and dental industries for producing detailed before-and-after images of procedures, the ring light creates the most uniform lighting of small subjects. Because the light is emitted from all around the lens, shadows are eliminated and any reflective surfaces on your subject, such as an insect's covering or eyes, may reveal a round highlight similar to a lifesaver, an easy indicator of ring light use.

With an identical hot shoe–mounted control unit and similar features to the MT-24EX, the MR-14EX incorporates many of the functions of the top-of-the-line Canon flashes, such as Flash Exposure Compensation, Flash Exposure Bracketing, High-speed sync, and adjustable output ratios between the two flash tubes by a 3-stop range in 1/2-stop increments.

Like the ST-E2 and the MT-24EX, the MR-14EX can be used to trigger off-camera slave flashes, such as the 580EX II or the 430EX II, in multiple channels and groups. This feature is great if you need to illuminate the background separately from the subject to prevent the background from going completely black.

The Canon Speedlite System offers a variety of solutions for simple to complex lighting situations. The next chapter examines the different ways you can set up your Speedlites for different applications, explaining the techniques needed to take your flash photography to the next level.

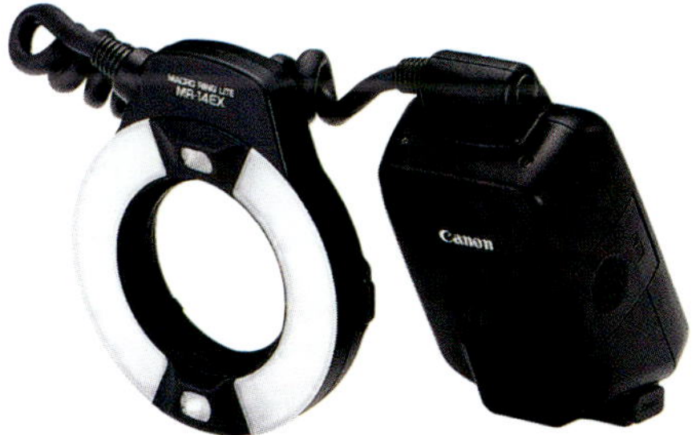

Image courtesy of Canon, Inc.

1.27 The Canon Macro Ring Lite MR-14EX

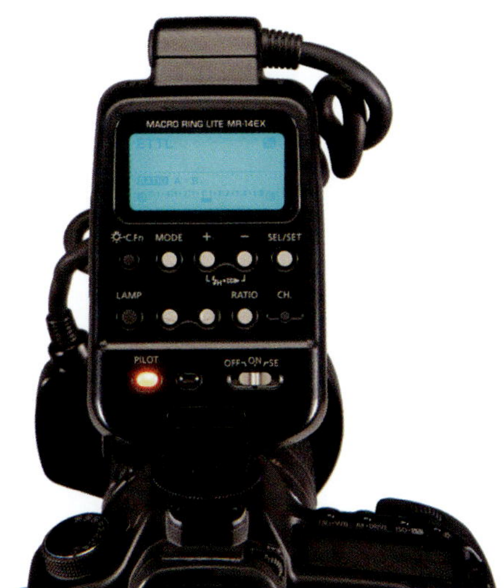

1.28 Control panel of the MR-14EX

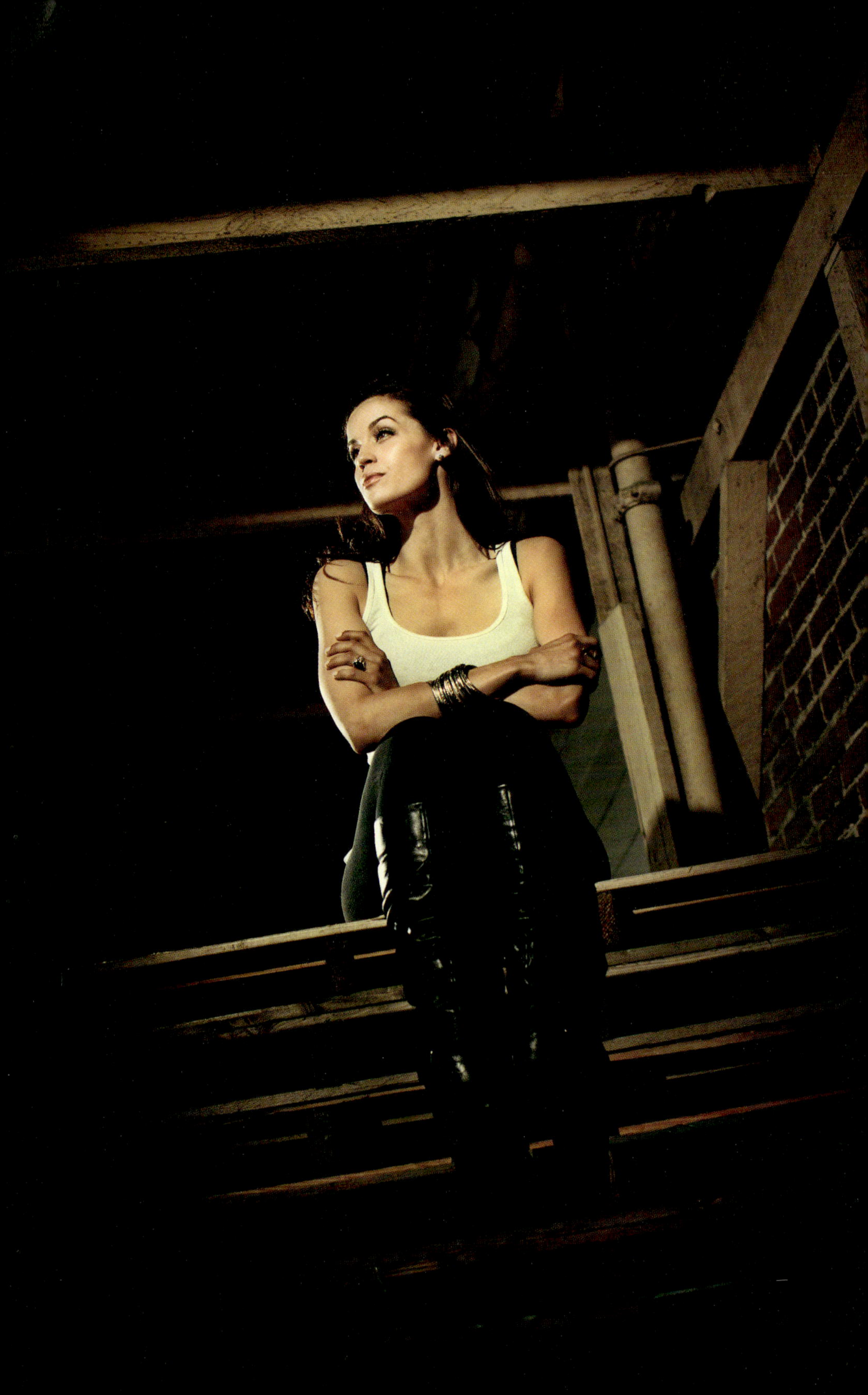

CHAPTER 2

Setting Up Your Speedlites

This chapter digs deeper and examines the nuts and bolts you need to understand to get your Speedlites set up for wireless off-camera operation as well on-camera use. Did you notice how I first mentioned *wireless off-camera* use? It's my not-so-subtle way of nudging you in that direction. Of course, I cover all the settings needed for on-camera flash as well, but for the best results, get your flash off your camera! (Sorry, I couldn't help myself.)

When you finish this chapter, you'll have a better understanding of the various menus, flash modes, and Personal/Custom Functions for your flash. You'll learn how to interact with your flash, access its settings, and quickly and easily set it up to do the things you want, when you want them!

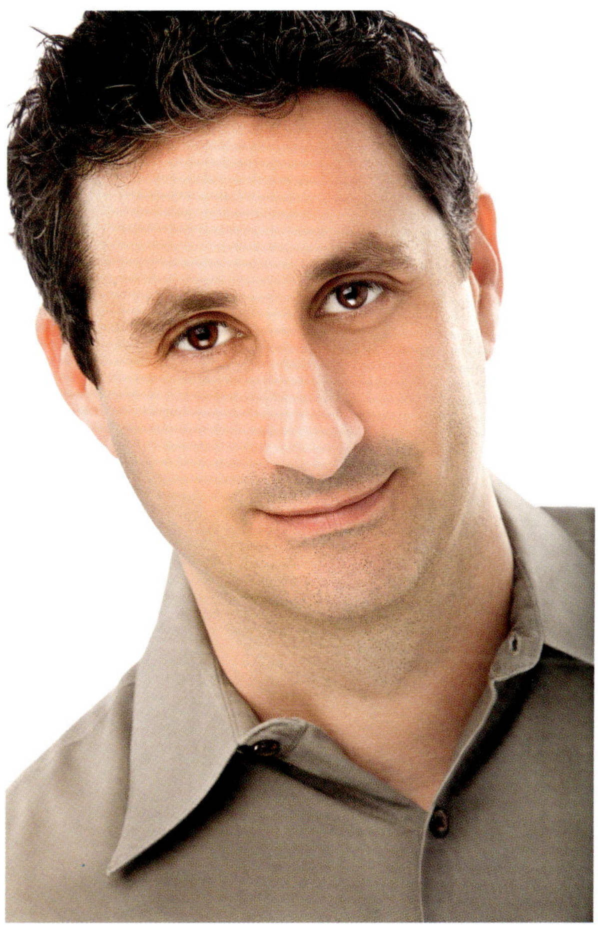

In this business portrait of Northern California chiropractor Jason Beck, a small octabank is used overhead, edge lights left (with a grid) and right (in a softbox), and a silver reflector from below. Exposure: ISO 100, f/11, 1/200 second with an EF 70-200mm f/2.8L USM lens.

Power Requirements

The 600EX/600EX-RT, 580EX II, and the 430EX II each use four AA-size batteries. Having additional fresh batteries on hand for your Speedlites is a must. I speak from personal experience when I tell you that batteries almost always die on you at the worst possible time. You should strongly consider packing at least one extra set of batteries for each Speedlite you'll be using.

Working with rechargeable batteries means that you're doing the right thing for the environment and also for your bottom line. The initial investment is higher than what you would pay for standard AA batteries, but in the long run, it pays off because you're not repeatedly purchasing expensive non-rechargeable batteries. I carry two sets of freshly charged batteries for each Speedlite I'm using. Five types of AA-size batteries are compatible with Canon Speedlites, and they fall into two categories: non-rechargeable and rechargeable.

Non-rechargeable

Primary, disposable, or one-use batteries have the dual advantages of having both a higher initial voltage and a longer life than secondary or rechargeable batteries of the same size. If you decide not to invest in a set or two of rechargeable batteries for your Speedlites, consider your choices within the non-rechargeable category. There are two types:

▶ **Alkaline.** This is your everyday, standard type of battery. Alkaline batteries are available just about everywhere, from your local supermarket to high-end camera stores. There are differences in quality, depending on the manufacturer. When buying these types of batteries, I suggest purchasing the batteries that are specifically designed for use with digital cameras and flash units. These batteries usually last longer and outperform less expensive brands.

▶ **Lithium.** Lithium batteries cost a little more than standard alkaline batteries, but they last a lot longer, and you get more flashes per set before you have to replace them. Professional photographers say they are worth every penny if they help you get the shot. You can find lithium batteries at office supply stores and camera shops.

Rechargeable

Rechargeable batteries require a greater initial investment, but you quickly get your money back by not having to repeatedly buy non-rechargeable batteries. There are two types of rechargeable batteries:

▶ **NiCd.** Nickel–cadmium batteries are the most common type of rechargeable batteries and are widely available. Although NiCd batteries are rechargeable, they do not last as long or fire as many flashes as the more expensive NiMH batteries. Another consideration is the so-called lazy battery effect, or battery memory effect. Certain NiCd batteries gradually lose their maximum energy capacity if they are repeatedly recharged after being only partially discharged. The battery appears to "remember" the lower capacity. The effect is caused by changes in the characteristics of the underused active materials of the cell.

▶ **NiMH.** Nickel–metal hydride batteries are more expensive, but they will last longer. AA NiMH batteries have two to three times the capacity of AA NiCd batteries, and therefore last longer on a single charge than NiCd batteries do, and the battery memory problem is not as significant. You can find NiMH batteries online, and in most office supply and photo stores. Sanyo's eneloop batteries are some of my favorites due to their ability to hold a charge over long periods.

With every battery, there are environmental concerns. The NiCd, in particular, is highly controversial because the element cadmium is considered one of the most toxic elements in the world. If the battery leaks or explodes, it could cause serious damage and endanger the lives of anyone around. The NiMH, on the other hand, has no known environmental concerns. When NiMH batteries came into the mainstream, people began to realize they far exceeded the performance of the older NiCd. Furthermore, the NiMH was also much safer than cadmium-based batteries and did not fall victim to the memory effect that was such an issue with NiCd batteries. In short, the technology in NiMH batteries is superior to NiCd and a better choice for your flash photography.

When purchasing rechargeable batteries for your Speedlite, always select batteries with the same mAh rating (milliamp hours) and be sure not to mix battery types. The higher the mAh rating, the longer it will last on a charge. Make sure that all the batteries are fully charged, and don't mix weaker batteries with freshly charged ones. A good practice is to number your batteries in sets that are always used together. Sanyo's eneloop batteries are designed to hold their charge over long periods, but all battery types slowly lose their charge when left in storage. Be sure to fully charge your batteries before every shoot.

Cold temperatures also affect battery life and performance. In cold weather shooting, I always keep a spare set inside my coat, close to my body to keep them warm.

RadioShack markets a great battery charger that recharges batteries in two hours and includes a Refresh option. This single feature is highly desirable in a battery charger. In Refresh mode, batteries that have not been used for a long time can have their charge depleted to zero to recover the optimum capacity of the rechargeable batteries. The charger then automatically switches back to Charge mode to fully charge the batteries. It recharges eight AA batteries at the same time (enough for two Speedlites) and works with AAA, C, D, and 9-volt batteries as well.

Canon also offers the CP-E4 Compact Battery Pack, which uses eight AA batteries, significantly reducing recycle time and doubling the working life of your Speedlite. Another option is the Canon Transistor Pack E, which holds six C-size batteries for extra-long battery life. These attach to the 600EX/600EX-RT, 580EX II, 430EX II, MT-24EX, and MR-14EX Speedlites via the external power source socket.

Flash Modes

Canon Speedlites come equipped with several different flash modes for complete creative control. Availability of these modes differs between Speedlite models. For instance, Group mode (Gr) is a Radio Transmission Wireless Shooting (((•))) option available only on the 600EX-RT. And Multi-stroboscopic mode (**MULTI**) cannot be set on the 430EX II (although it can be programmed that way by a master flash when it's used as a slave). All currently marketed Speedlites offer backward-compatible flash modes for use with pre-2004 Canon EOS dSLRs and even EOS SLR film cameras. The new Speedlite transmitter ST-E3-RT works exclusively with the 600EX-RT Speedlite and is not backward compatible.

E-TTL II

E-TTL II, commonly referred to simply as E-TTL, is the newest and most innovative flash mode from Canon. It was introduced in 2004 for use with the Canon EOS 1D Mark II, and it continues to be used with Canon's current lineup of EOS dSLR cameras. The camera gets most of the metering information from monitor preflashes that are emitted by the Speedlite. The camera also uses data from the lens, such as distance information and f-stop values.

The main improvement of E-TTL II over E-TTL is that it gives a more natural flash exposure by being able to handle difficult scenes where normally the old E-TTL system would be thrown off. Such improvements are possible because E-TTL II now incorporates lens-to-subject distance information in its calculation to assist in determining an appropriate guide number for flash output.

The flash metering system is also no longer linked to the AF system, where in the old E-TTL, metering bias was given to the selected AF point. Rather, E-TTL II compares the ambient and the preflash light levels of the scene to determine where the subject lies. This gives a photographer the flexibility to lock focus and recompose the scene without fooling the flash metering system. Hot spots that normally throw off the flash metering system are also ignored in the calculation. The results are more natural flash pictures and predictable results, even in many adverse lighting situations.

E-TTL

This is an older form of Canon's flash metering system. It functions very much like E-TTL II. This metering system was used on Canon camera bodies from 1995 to 2004, and it stopped being used with the introduction of E-TTL II.

The primary difference between E-TTL and E-TTL II is that E-TTL is strongly focus-point biased. E-TTL evaluates the flash exposure primarily at the active focus point. E-TTL II does not have this high focus-point biasing, and the flash exposure is calculated using more of an evaluative metering pattern.

E-TTL and E-TTL II appear as just "E-TTL" on the Speedlite LCD because, although the Speedlite functions in both of these modes, a camera body only uses one type of metering system. Whether it is E-TTL or E-TTL II depends on the particular camera with which you are using the Speedlite.

Canon's older film cameras used a flash metering system known as A-TTL. The 600EX/600EX-RT, 580EX II, and 430EX II flashes are not compatible with this older technology; they may work with these cameras, but they are not recommended because they do not share all communications with the camera. Canon series EZ Speedlites are the ones to use with EOS film cameras and are readily available for a good price on eBay.

Manual

E-TTL and E-TTL II are great for any number of picture-taking situations or those times when you want to get the best results possible when shooting on the fly. Then you just set the camera on Program (**P**), Aperture Priority (**Av**), or Shutter Priority (**Tv**) mode and shoot away. The sophisticated camera/flash communications take care of

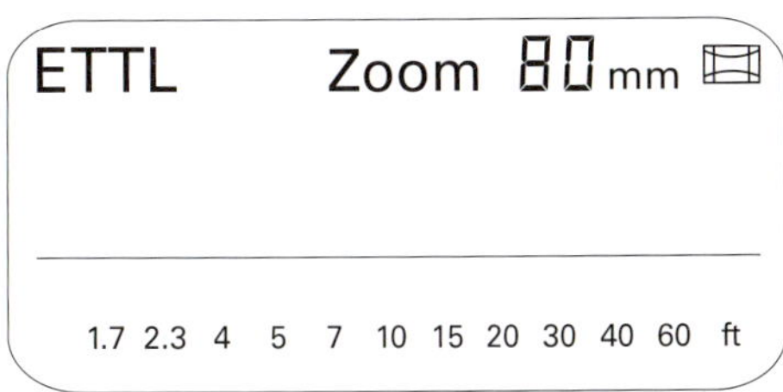

2.1 The 580EX II LCD menu set to E-TTL

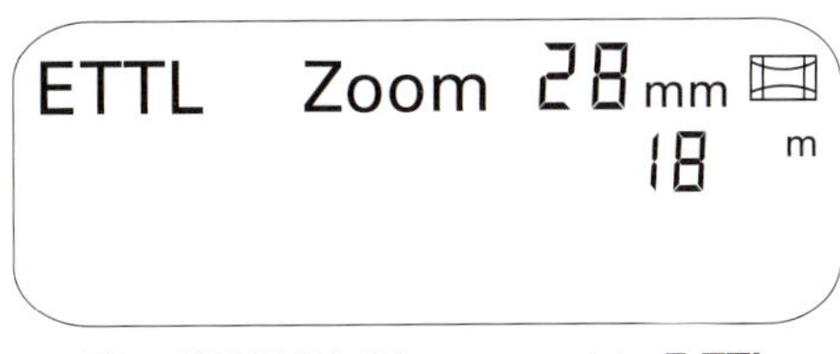

2.2 The 430EX II LCD menu set to E-TTL

many lighting problems and produce well-lit images. In the old days, photographers had to figure out a guide number and do a few calculations that took their eye away from the viewfinder. Now, it's as easy as shooting a test shot, judging the results on your camera's LCD monitor or tethered computer screen, and making corrections and adjustments before shooting again.

In certain circumstances, the E-TTL II system, while still awesome, may begin to feel a little limiting and rigid, considering you are locked into only a 3-stop range among all Speedlites and groups. Working with the 600EX/600EX-RT, 580EX II, and 430EX II Speedlites in full Manual mode may take some getting used to, but it offers you the greatest amount of creative control, especially in multiple-flash setups where you want individual control or each light. However, I have seen amazing results when utilizing eight Speedlites in E-TTL II mode for sports photography or two sets of four Speedlites each fired into a shoot-through umbrella for group shots at weddings. The beauty of E-TTL II is that it gives you freedom of movement and the flexibility to work quickly. With the 600EX/RT, you can now easily mix E-TTL and Manual mode Speedlites in multiple-flash setups.

Many photographers consider it confusing or intimidating to work with their flashes set to Manual output, but nothing could be further from the truth when it comes to off-camera flash set-ups. Don't be afraid of Manual flash mode — it's your friend! When you use a non-radio-enabled Speedlite or need additional range, many great

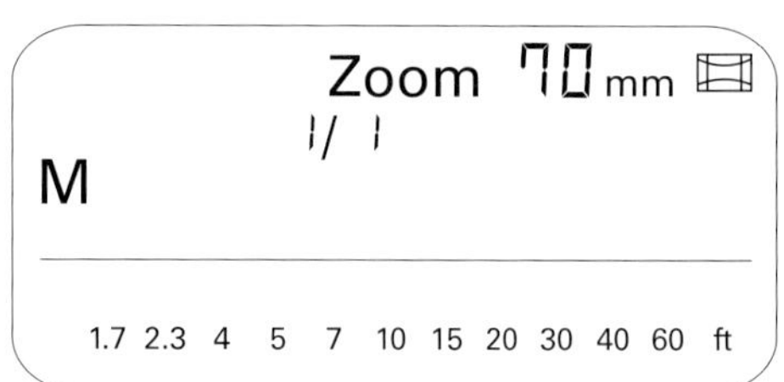

2.3 The 580EX II LCD menu set to Manual full power

products are available to facilitate wireless communication in both E-TTL and Manual modes, such as the RadioPopper PX and JrX systems. A wide range of lighting modi-fiers, such as those from Honl Photo, ExpoImaging, and Lastolite, are also available to help photographers mold, shape, and filter the light just the way they want it. All these tools add up to limitless creative possibilities.

CROSS REF For more information on the many different light modifiers, see Chapters 5 and 6.

Multi-stroboscopic flash

In this mode, the flash fires repeatedly, similar to a strobe light, during a single expo-sure. You may have seen multiple images of dancers, tennis players, or gymnasts that are achieved by using this flash mode. You decide the frequency and the number of times you want the flash to fire by specifying the Hz numbers, which correspond to the number of flashes per second. The slower the shutter speed, the more flashes you are able to capture. This mode works best in low-light situations or locations where the background is predominantly very dark or black.

600EX/600EX-RT

To set up Multi-stroboscopic mode on the 600EX/600EX-RT, follow these steps:

1. **Press the Mode button on the Speedlite until Multi appears in the upper-left corner of the Speedlite's LCD.**

2. **Press Function button 4 (Hz) to highlight the frequency setting.** The frequency is set in hertz (Hz). Use the Select dial to change the frequency from 1 to 199 Hz. Press the center Select/Set button again to confirm your selection and set the frequency level.

   NOTE Hertz is simply a measurement of cycles per second. 1 Hz is one cycle (flash burst) per second.

3. **Press Function button 3 (MULTI) to highlight the input field on the LCD for the number of flashes per frame.** Use the Select dial to set how many times you want the flash to fire during the exposure. Press the center Select/Set button again. This confirms the number of flashes just selected.

4. **Set your shutter speed.** Your shutter speed depends on the firing frequency of the flash per second (measured in Hz) and the number of flashes (also called the repeat rate). Your shutter speed is equal to the number of flashes divided by the firing frequency. For example, say you set the frequency to 5 Hz, and you want the flash to fire 20 times in a single frame; in this case, you divide 20 by 5. This tells you that you need at least a 4-second exposure to accomplish this.

5. **Check the Flash ready lamp/Test flash button (⚡) for ready status and shoot the photo.**

After 10 multi-stroboscopic frames, allow the flash tube to rest and cool down for at least 15 minutes, or, if you continue to shoot, it may automatically shut down for 15 minutes.

580EX II

To set up Multi-stroboscopic mode on the 580EX II, follow these steps:

1. **Set the camera to Manual exposure mode (M).**

2. **Press the Mode button on the Speedlite until the Multi menu appears in the upper-left corner of the Speedlite's LCD.**

3. **Press the 580EX II's Select/Set button in the middle of the dial to highlight the frequency setting.** The frequency is set in hertz (Hz). Use the dial to change the frequency from 1 to 199 Hz. Hertz is simply a measurement of cycles per second. 1 Hz is one cycle (flash burst) per second.

4. **Press the center Select/Set button again to confirm your selection.** This sets the frequency level and highlights the number of flashes per frame. Use the dial to set how many times you want the flash to fire during the exposure.

5. **Press the center Select/Set button again.** This enters the number of flashes selected in the previous step.

6. **Set your shutter speed.** Your shutter speed depends on the firing frequency of the flash per second (measured in Hz) and the number of flashes (also called the repeat rate). Your shutter speed is equal to the number of flashes divided by the firing frequency. For example, say you set the frequency to 5 Hz, and you want the flash to fire 20 times in a single frame; in this case, you divide 20 by 5. This tells you that you'll need at least a 4-second exposure to accomplish this.

7. **Check the pilot lamp for ready status and shoot the photo.**

After 10 multi-stroboscopic frames, allow the flash tube to rest and cool down for at least 15 minutes, or, if you continue to shoot, it may automatically shut down for 15 minutes.

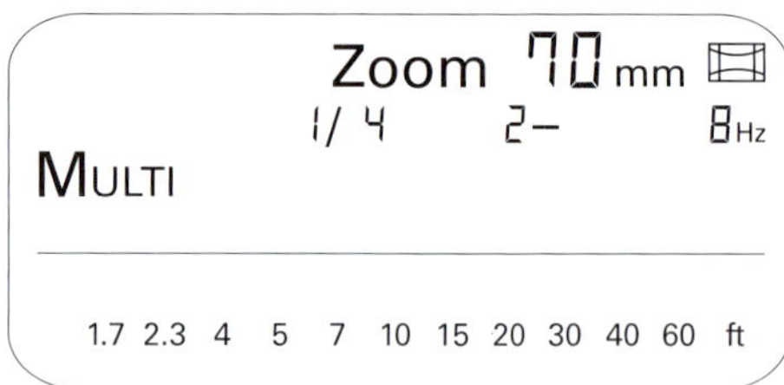

2.4 The 580EX II LCD menu set to Multi-stroboscopic flash

Zoom position

The zooming feature of the Speedlite focuses the light from the flash in order to match the angle of coverage of your lens. To facilitate the wider coverage that wide-angle lenses require, the flash tube is zoomed forward, diffusing the light through the Speedlite's Fresnel lens and dispersing it to a wider area. When a longer lens is used, the flash tube is pulled back, and coverage is diminished, but intensity picks up and output is focused through the Fresnel to allow a farther distance to be lit.

When the 600EX/600EX-RT, 580EX II, or 430EX II is mounted on the camera, by default it automatically sets the zoom to match the lens. When I'm shooting quickly or in E-TTL mode with the flash on camera, 90 percent of the time I'm in flash Auto Zoom mode. However, during photo shoots, when I am setting up multiple wireless off-camera flashes, I am nearly always working the Manual Zoom settings to contain light spill for creative control.

600EX/600EX-RT

To set the zoom manually on the 600EX/600EX-RT, follow these steps:

1. **Press Function button 1 (Zm/C.Fn) on the Speedlite.** This highlights the zoom value input field at the top of the LCD.

2. **Use the Select dial to choose a Zoom setting from 20mm–200mm.**

3. **Press the Select/Set button to confirm the setting.**

580EX II

To set the zoom manually on the 580EX II, follow these steps:

1. **Press the Zoom button on the back of the flash.** The Zoom setting flashes when it is ready to be changed.

2. **Scroll the dial left or right to change the Zoom setting.**

3. **When finished, press the Zoom button again to save the setting.** You can also just tap the shutter button to resume shooting.

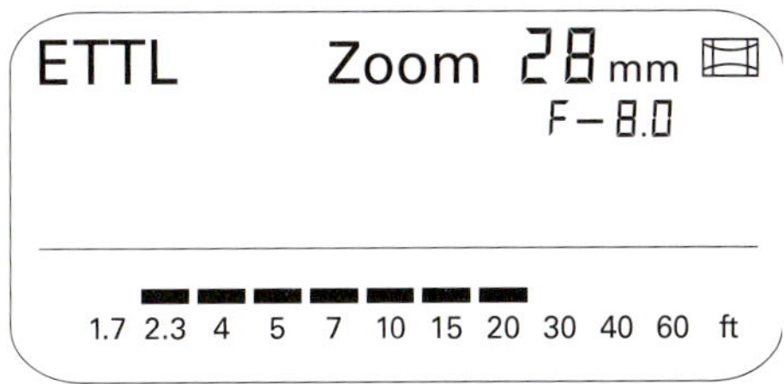

2.5 The 580EX II LCD menu zoom setting at 28mm

430EX II

To set the zoom manually on the 430EX II, follow these steps:

1. **Press the Zoom button on the back of the flash.** The Zoom setting flashes when it is ready to be changed.

2. **Use the + or – button to change the Zoom setting.**

3. **When finished, press the Zoom button again to save the setting.** You can also just tap the shutter button to resume shooting.

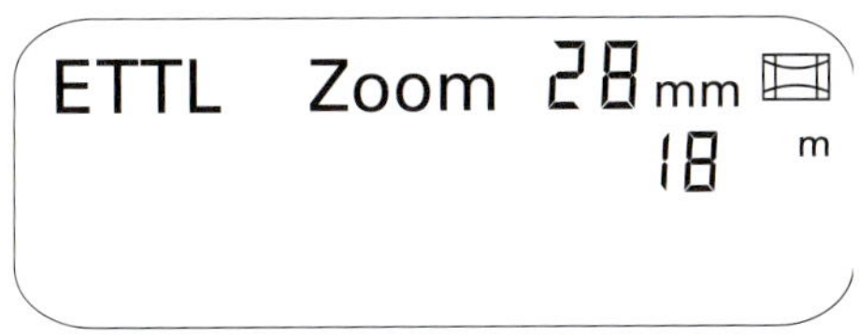

2.6 The 430EX II LCD menu zoom setting at 28mm

Auto Zoom Adjustment for APS-C Sensors

Certain Canon camera bodies, such as the 5D, 5D Mark II, and 1Ds Mark III, have a full-frame sensor. This means the digital sensor is exactly the same size as a frame of 35mm film. Canon currently makes three dSLR sensor sizes and utilizes them in many different dSLR camera models.

Canon's professional and consumer dSLRs are equipped with APS-H and APS-C sensors, respectively, which are a bit smaller than a 35mm frame of film by certain percentages. With this smaller sensor, the actual coverage area of the lens is larger than the sensor because it doesn't cover the same area as it would on a full-frame sensor or a piece of 35mm film. This brings up the lens conversion factor.

Simply stated, you take the actual focal length of the lens and multiply this number by the sensor's conversion factor to find the equivalent focal length of the lens in terms of 35mm film. For example, on a full-frame 5D Mark III camera, a 28mm lens is considered wide angle and yields the standard image that a 28mm lens produces. However, when you multiply it by the lens conversion factor for your particular camera's sensor, you get a different angle of view. For APS-C cameras, the conversion factor is 1.6x and for APS-H cameras, it is 1.3x. Doing the math, it would yield the same coverage as a 44.8mm lens when using the same 28mm lens on a camera with an APS-C size sensor, and the equivalent of a 36.4mm lens with an APS-H sensor.

Canon Speedlites automatically recognize the EOS digital camera's sensor size, adjust the flash head zoom automatically, and set the flash coverage for the converted lens focal lengths from 24mm to 105mm. When the Speedlite is connected, an icon appears in the upper-right corner of the Speedlite's LCD monitor.

Adjusting Flash Exposure Compensation

E-TTL and E-TTL II are great for producing well-lit images in difficult lighting situations; I use E-TTL II all the time. However, when you can anticipate how the camera will see certain areas of your image or don't care for the results of a test exposure, it can be very helpful to have creative control over how much light the flash is contributing to the exposure. Flash Exposure Compensation (FEC) involves adjusting the flash output higher or lower than what the camera chose. You reduce the flash's power by specifying a minus FEC setting, making the flash weaker, contributing less light to the exposure, and possibly creating a more natural balance between the ambient light in the scene and the light from the flash. Specify more FEC with a positive number, and the flash will dominate the ambient light. FEC can be adjusted in 1/3-stop increments over a 6-stop range (3 under, 3 over normal).

You can adjust the output of your Speedlite in a number of ways. When the Speedlite is mounted on your camera, you can adjust the output on the camera body itself. Most Canon dSLRs have a button for setting Flash Exposure Compensation that works with Speedlites as well as the on-board pop-up flash. Some of the newer Canon cameras, such as the 5D Mark III, also have an External Speedlite Control menu where you can adjust the flash settings by using the camera's buttons and dials.

Finally, you can also adjust the FEC on the Speedlite itself.

600EX/600EX-RT

To set Exposure Compensation on the 600EX/600EX-RT, follow these steps:

1. **Press Function button 2 (+/–) to highlight the FEC value scale, number field, and icons.**

2. **Use the Select dial to choose a FEC value from +/–3 stops in 1/3-stop increments.**

3. **Press the Select/Set button to confirm the settings.**

580EX II

To set Exposure Compensation on the 580EX II in E-TTL mode, follow these steps:

1. **Press the Select/Set button for about one-half second.** The Flash Exposure Compensation (FEC) icon begins to blink.

2. **Scroll the Select dial left or right to make the adjustments.**

3. **After your adjustments are made, press the Select/Set button again to save the setting.**

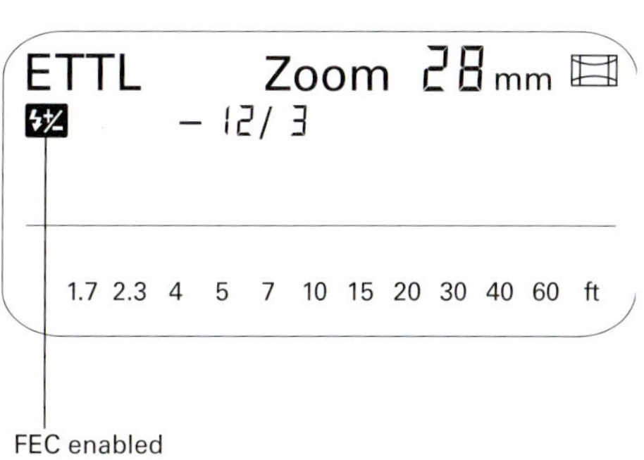

2.7 The 580EX II LCD menu FEC-enabled by –1 2/3 stop

430EX II

Follow these steps to set the flash output on the 430EX II in E-TTL mode:

1. **Press the Select/Set button for about one-half second.** The Flash Exposure Compensation (FEC) icon begins to blink.

2. **Press the + or – button to adjust the settings accordingly.**

3. **Press the Select/Set button to save the setting.**

When Exposure Compensation is selected, the settings appear on the Speedlite's LCD. When the FEC is returned to normal, the FEC icon does not appear.

ETTL   Zoom 35 mm
⚡   —   2/3

2.8 The 430EX II LCD menu FEC-enabled by –2/3 stop

To return the FEC to normal, follow the same procedure as in the previous set of steps, and set the Speedlite accordingly.

Red-eye Reduction

Everybody's seen red-eye in a picture at one time or another. It's that red glow in the eyes of people and pets that leaves you wondering if they're really possessed by evil spirits. Well, of course they're not; this is just an annoying anomaly caused by the reflection of the light from the flash off the eye's retina. Most cameras that have flash compatibility have a Red-eye Reduction function to correct this, which consists of a preflash or an LED that produces a light bright enough to constrict the pupils prior to the exposure, therefore reducing the amount of light reflecting off the retina.

Red-eye Reduction cannot be set on the 580EX II or 430EX II. Camera bodies control this function. Consult the owner's manual for your camera for instructions on how to set it up.

AF-Assist Beam

When you're photographing in a dark environment, it can be very hard for your camera's autofocus sensor to find something to lock on to. When you're using a 600EX/600EX-RT, 580EX II, or 430EX II in a low-light situation, the flash emits an LED pattern to give your camera sensor a red grid to focus on. For this feature to operate correctly, you must be using an AF lens and the camera's focus mode must be set to Single-shot (☐) or AI Focus (**AI FOCUS**).

600EX/600EX-RT

To turn the AF-assist illuminator on and off on the 600EX/600EX-RT, follow these steps:

1. **Press Function button 1 (Zm/C.Fn) for 2 seconds to enter the Custom Functions menu.**

2. **Use the Select dial to choose C.Fn 08.** Press the Select/Set button in the middle of the Select dial to enter the settings area for the AF-assist Custom Function (AF).

3. **Scroll the Select dial left or right to change the setting to either 0 or 1.** The 0 indicates that the AF-assist beam is enabled. Changing the setting from 0 to 1 disables the AF-assist beam by activating the disabled function and causing it not to illuminate. Press Function button 4 (↰) to go back in the menus if necessary.

4. **Press the Select/Set button to save the settings.**

5. **Press the Function button 4 (↰) to return to the main menu.**

On newer Canon EOS cameras like the 5D Mark III, 7D, and others, all the latest Speedlites controls and Custom Functions can be set from the camera's External Speedlite control menu.

580EX II

To turn the AF-assist illuminator on and off on the 580EX II, follow these steps:

1. **Press the C.Fn button for two seconds to enter the Custom Functions menu.**

2. **Scroll the dial left or right to select the C.Fn number.** The C.Fn number for AF-assist beam firing is F08. After you select C.Fn F08, press the Set button in the middle of the dial; the setting digit blinks.

3. **Scroll the dial left or right to change the setting to either 0 or 1.** The 0 indicates that the AF-assist beam is enabled. Changing the setting from 0 to 1 will disable the AF-assist beam by activating the disabled function and causing it not to illuminate.

4. **Press the Set button to save the setting.**

5. **Press the Mode button to return to the main menu.**

On newer Canon EOS cameras like the 5D Mark II, 7D, and others, all the latest Speedlites controls and Custom Functions can be set from the camera's External Speedlite control menu.

430EX II

To turn the AF-assist illuminator on and off on the 430EX II, follow these steps:

1. **Press the C.Fn button for 2 seconds to enter the Custom Functions menu.**

2. **Press the + and – buttons to select the C.Fn number.** The C.Fn number for AF-assist beam OFF is F08. After you select C.Fn F08, press the Select/Set button; the setting digit blinks.

3. **Press the + or – button to change the setting to either 0 or 1.** The 0 indicates that the AF-assist beam is enabled. Changing the setting from 0 to 1 will disable the AF-assist beam activating the disabled function and causing it not to illuminate.

4. **Press the Select/Set button to save the setting.**

5. **Press the Mode button to return to the main menu.**

LCD Panel Illumination

The LCD panels of both the 580EX II and 430EX II have an LCD backlight built in to help viewing in low-light situations. To turn on this backlight, simply press the Custom Functions (C.Fn) button. This LCD backlight turns off when you press the button a second time, or it will automatically turn off after approximately 10 seconds. This is an invaluable feature when you're trying to change a setting quickly shooting in dark environments. I also carry a small Maglite flashlight to help illuminate the buttons on the back of the Speedlite. This is a very useful tool to have on hand for all sorts of low-light situations.

The 600EX/600EX-RT and Speedlite transmitter ST-E3-RT have two LCD background colors to choose from. These options are found in the Personal functions (P.Fn) menu and can be set by pressing Function button 1 (**Zm/C.Fn**) for 2 seconds to enter the Custom Functions menu and then pressing it again to switch to the Personal Functions (P.Fn) menu. P.Fn 02, 03, and 04 control this feature on the 600EX/600EX-RT and P.Fn 03 and 04 control it on the Speedlite transmitter ST-E3-RT.

Custom Functions

Similar to your Canon EOS camera, the 600EX/600EX-RT, 580EX II, and 430EX II Speedlites all come with user-adjustable Custom Functions (C.Fn) to offer you greater flexibility and control over their performance. As mentioned previously, the 600EX/600EX-RT also now includes a set of Personal Functions (P.Fn) to further customize the Speedlite. The 600EX has 18 Custom Functions and five Personal Functions (P.Fn 06-07 are unavailable on this model), the 600EX-RT has 18 Custom Functions and seven Personal Functions. The 580EX II has 14 Custom Functions, and the 430EX II has nine. They are accessed by using the same instructions as for the AF-assist beam. The Speedlite transmitter ST-E3-RT has eight Custom Functions and three Personal Functions.

Setting Custom Functions on the flash

Setting the Custom Functions (C.Fn) on Speedlite models prior to the 600EX/600EX-RT is as easy as pushing the Backlight/C.Fn button, turning a dial, and pushing some buttons to make adjustments. The hard part is remembering what all the C.Fn numbers correspond to, and what each of the settings means in terms of performance. Most users set up their Custom Functions when they first get their flashes and leave them set that way. Occasionally, a situation will arise where you need to operate your Speedlite differently than you normally do; these cases will often involve changing one of your Speedlite's preset Custom Functions.

Accessing Custom and Personal Functions on the 600EX/600EX-RT Speedlites and Speedlite transmitter ST-E3-RT is equally easy and can be done by pressing and holding Function button 1 (**Zm/C.Fn**) for 2 seconds.

Prior to the 600EX and 600EX-RT Speedlites, Custom Function (C.Fn) menus didn't provide much information. Menus displayed just the function number and setting number, making it difficult to know what each setting did without referring to the manual or the camera's External Speedlite control menus. This has changed dramatically with the introduction on 600EX/600EX-RT Speedlites and new Speedlite transmitter ST-E3-RT. All have a Custom/Personal Function menu with easy-to-understand descriptions and icons. These menus are accessible from the built-in LCD panels on these units and External Speedlite control menus available on recent EOS digital camera models. I prefer to use the camera's External Speedlite control menu that includes the function's description whenever possible, especially when working with 580EX II and 430EX II Speedlites. Also feel free to download the Custom Function and Settings tables for use with smartphones and tablets at www.wiley.com/go/canon slsdfg3e. I created these for handy, backlit, in-the-field reference. Tables 2.1 through 2.4 list the C.Fn or P.Fn number of the respective Speedlites, what the settings are, and why you'd want to use them.

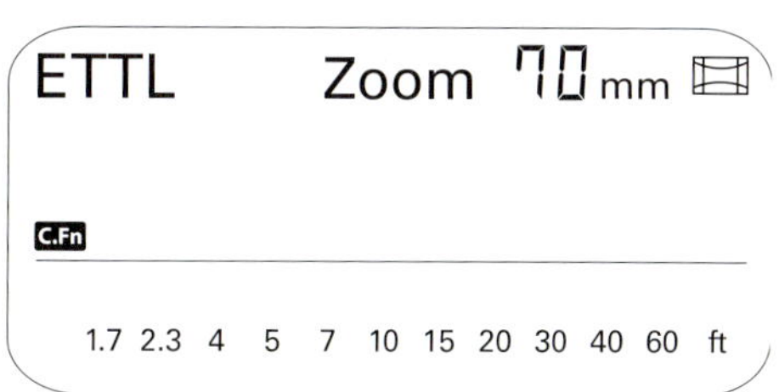

2.9 Any time a Custom Function has been changed from the default settings, the C.Fn icon appears on the Speedlite's LCD panel.

Table 2.1 600EX/600EX-RT Custom Functions

Custom Function Number	Function	Settings and Description
C.Fn-00 (⎩⎍⎍⎍⎭ m/ft)	Distance indicator display	0–meters/1–feet. Depending upon where you live, set this to the most common distance designation.
C.Fn-01 (🔦ᶻ)	Auto power off	0–Enabled/1–Disabled. Auto power off turns the flash off automatically after a certain period of inactivity (not user-specified, but between 1.5 minutes to 15 minutes) to save battery power. Press the shutter button or Pilot Lamp button to reactivate the Speedlite. I choose 1 to disable this function whenever I'm working with off-camera Speedlites.
C.Fn-02 (ᴱ🔦MODELING)	Modeling flash	0–Enabled (DOF preview button)/1–Enabled (Test-firing button)/2–Enabled (both buttons)/3–Disabled.
C.Fn-03 (📷 AUTO CANCEL)	Flash exposure bracketing (FEB) auto cancel	0–Enabled/1–Disabled. This controls the FEB auto cancel feature. After three shots are taken, FEB is automatically canceled. Set to 1 to continue taking FEB photos in sets of three.
C.Fn-04 (📷)	Flash exposure bracketing (FEB) sequence	0–minus exposure, plus exposure/1–minus exposure, on stop, plus exposure. I set this to 1 because on my computer, I like to see the pictures in exposure order sequence to pick the best one.
C.Fn-05 (**MODE**)	Flash metering mode	0–E-TTL II & E-TTL/1–TTL/2–External metering: Auto/3–External metering: Manual. This enables the user to choose between several advanced metering systems of the Speedlite along with two modes of external metering, Auto and Manual. In external Auto mode, the camera's ISO and aperture are set automatically by the Speedlite. In External Manual mode, this information must be entered into the Speedlite for the function to operate properly.
C.Fn-06 (🔦 QUICK)	Quick flash with continuous shooting	0–Disabled/1–Enabled. In situations where you don't need a lot of flash power output, if you choose 1, Quick flash can be employed for continuous shooting but operates only with the camera in Single-shot mode (☐). This enables you to shoot flash photos faster in Quick mode and not to have to wait for the Speedlite to fully power up. However, it can deliver underpowered flash pops.
C.Fn-07 (🔦 TEST)	Test firing with auto-flash	0–1/32 power/1–full power. This enables the user to set the power level of the test flash. I use 0 to save battery life when I just want to check if the flash is working, and I use 1 when I'm metering the flash output with a hand-held light meter.

Custom Function Number	Function	Settings and Description
C.Fn-08 (⚡ AF)	AF-assist beam firing	0–Enabled/1–Disabled. Use this setting when you don't need the AF-assist beam to focus the camera or in situations, such as performance photography, where the beam would be distracting to others.
C.Fn-09 (▦)	Auto zoom for sensor size	0–Enabled/1–Disabled. EOS digital cameras have one of three different sensor sizes. The Speedlite automatically recognizes the sensor size and adjusts the flash zoom for proper coverage. I leave this on.
C.Fn-10 (⚡ᶻ)	Slave auto power off timer	0–60 minutes/1–10 minutes. This enables the user to set the time interval the Speedlite stays active when used as a slave. I prefer the longer setting to make adjustments to the set, model, or lighting without having the slave flash power down and have to be reset.
C.Fn-11 (⚡ᶻ→⚡)	Slave auto power off cancel	0–Within 8 hours/1–Within 1 hour. You can specify the time range in which the slave unit's auto power off feature can be cancelled by the master. Again, I prefer the longer time setting.
C.Fn-12 (⚡1)	Flash recycle with external power source	0–Flash and external power source/1–External power source. When the Speedlite is in its default mode, it draws power from both sets of batteries. Switching to 1 allows the flash to be recycled only by the external power source; therefore, the internal batteries last longer. When I'm using the CP-E4, I prefer to set Custom Function 12 for the Speedlite to the 1 setting to draw power from the battery pack only. That way I still have a fully charged set of internal batteries available if the pack runs low on power. If the internal batteries become exhausted, shooting might not be possible. Even with the flash set to 1, the Speedlite still requires internal batteries to operate.
C.Fn-13 (⚡)	Flash exposure meter setting	0–Speedlite button and dial/1–Speedlite dial only. Setting 1 saves you a step and time by not having to press the Select/Set button on the Speedlite to access FEC settings. You simply turn the dial to the desired FEC setting and shoot.
C.Fn-20 (◁)	Beep	0–OFF (Disable)/1–ON (Enable). 1–Enable a beep to sound when a Speedlite or slave in Radio Transmission Wireless Shooting is fully charged. The beep also sounds when the Speedlite is restricted from firing due to excessive heat in the flash head. I keep this set to 0 to be less intrusive when shooting.

continued

Table 2.1 600EX/600EX-RT Custom Functions *(continued)*

Custom Function Number	Function	Settings and Description
C.Fn-21	Light distribution	Change the flash coverage of the Speedlite in relation to the shooting angle of view when flash coverage is set to Automatic. 0–(Standard): ideal flash coverage determined automatically 1–(Guide number priority): flash coverage set automatically and slightly more telephoto than the actual angle of view. Gives priority to flash output. 2–(Even coverage): Automatically set flash coverage, slightly wider than actual shooting angle of view. Helps reduce light falloff.
C.Fn-22	LCD panel illumination	0–On for 12 sec./1–OFF (Disable illumination)/2–On (Illumination always on). Change the amount of time the LCD illuminates when the dial or buttons are operated. I use 0–On for 12 sec.
C.Fn-23	Slave flash battery check	0–Enable AF-assist beam blinking /1–Disable AF-assist beam blinking. When shooting with wireless flashes, slave flash AF-assist beams blink to indicate they're fully charged. Most often I leave this enabled.

Table 2.2 600EX/600EX-RT Personal Functions

Personal Function Number	Function	Settings and Description
P.Fn-01	LCD panel display contrast	Five levels of LCD panel contrast adjustment.
P.Fn-02	LCD panel illumination color: Normal shooting	0–GREEN (green)/1–ORANGE (orange). Select an LCD panel illumination color to use during on-camera shooting.
P.Fn-03	LCD panel illumination color: Master	0–GREEN (green)/1–ORANGE (orange). Select an LCD panel illumination color for the master Speedlite used during radio or optical transmission linked shooting.
P.Fn-04	LCD panel illumination color: Slave	0–GREEN (green)/1–ORANGE (orange). Select an LCD panel illumination color for the slave Speedlite(s) used during radio or optical transmission linked shooting. I set the LCD panel color for slaves to 1–ORANGE (orange) to help more easily distinguish them as slaves.

Personal Function Number	Function	Settings and Description
P.Fn-05 (🎞️)	Color filter auto detection	0–AUTO (Auto)/1–OFF (Disable). Set to 0 for auto detection when using the filter set included with the 600EX/600EX-RT. Set to 1 when using commercially available filters so they are not auto detected.
P.Fn-06 (⚡)	Wireless button toggle sequence	Change the sequence of options displayed when pushing the Linked shooting button. 0–Normal (off), Radio, Optical 1–Normal (off), Radio 2–Normal (off), Optical Use 0 when working with a mix or 600EX-RT/600EX and older optically based Speedlites. Use 1 when working exclusively with 600EX-RT and the Speedlite transmitter ST-E3-RT. Use 2 when working exclusively with optical transmission. P.Fn-06 is not available on the 600EX.
P.Fn-07 (⚡ LINKED SHOT)	Flash firing during linked shooting	0–OFF (Disabled)/1–ON (Enabled). Set flashes mounted to cameras used during Linked shooting to fire or not fire. Set this function on each flash used. P.Fn-07 is not available on the 600EX.

> **NOTE** Custom and Personal Functions can be cleared using the menu system on compatible digital cameras and by pressing Function button 2 (CLEAR) and then Function button 1 (OK) on the 600EX/600EX-RT and Speedlite transmitter ST-E3-RT. Custom Functions that have been set are cleared.

Table 2.3 580EX II Custom Functions

Custom Function Number	Function	Settings and Description
C.Fn-00	Distance indicator display	0–meters/1–feet. Depending upon where you live, set this to the most common distance designation.
C.Fn-01	Auto power off	0–Enabled/1–Disabled. Auto power off turns the flash off automatically after a certain period of inactivity (not user-specified, but between 1.5 minutes to 15 minutes) to save battery power. Press the shutter button or Pilot Lamp button to reactivate the Speedlite. I choose 1 to disable this function whenever I'm working with off-camera Speedlites.

(continued)

Table 2.3 580EX II Custom Functions *(continued)*

Custom Function Number	Function	Settings and Description
C.Fn-02	Modeling flash	0–Enabled (DOF preview button)/1–Enabled (Test-firing button)/2–Enabled (both buttons)/3–Disabled. You can choose which buttons you want to use to fire the modeling flash.
C.Fn-03	Flash exposure bracketing (FEB) auto cancel	0–Enabled/1–Disabled. This controls the FEB auto cancel feature. After three shots are taken, FEB is automatically canceled. Set to 1 to continue taking FEB photos in sets of three.
C.Fn-04	Flash exposure bracketing (FEB) sequence	0–minus exposure, plus exposure/1–minus exposure, on stop, plus exposure. I set this to 1 because on my computer, I like to see the pictures in exposure order sequence to pick the best one.
C.Fn-05	Flash metering mode	0–E-TTL II & E-TTL/1–TTL/2–External metering: Auto/3–External metering: Manual. This allows the user to choose between several advanced metering systems of the Speedlite along with two modes of external metering, Auto and Manual. In external Auto mode, the camera's ISO and aperture are set automatically by the Speedlite. In External Manual mode, this information must be entered into the Speedlite for the function to operate properly.
C.Fn-06	Quick flash with continuous shooting	0–Disabled/1–Enabled. In situations where you don't need a lot of flash power output, by choosing 1, Quick flash can be employed for continuous shooting but operates only with the camera in Single-shot (☐) mode. This allows you to shoot flash photos faster in Quick mode and not to have to wait for the Speedlite to fully power up, but can deliver underpowered flash pops.
C.Fn-07	Test firing with autoflash	0–1/32 power/1–full power. This allows the user to set the power level of the test flash. I use 0 to save battery life when I just want to check if the flash is working, and 1 when I'm metering the flash output with a handheld light meter.
C.Fn-08	AF-assist beam firing	0–Enabled/1–Disabled. Use this setting when you don't need the AF-assist beam to focus the camera or in situations, such as performance photography, where the beam would be distracting to others.
C.Fn-09	Auto zoom for sensor size	0–Enabled/1–Disabled. EOS digital cameras have one of three different sensor sizes. The Speedlite automatically recognizes the sensor size and adjusts the flash zoom for proper coverage. I leave this on.

Custom Function Number	Function	Settings and Description
C.Fn-10	Slave auto power off timer	0–60 minutes/1–10 minutes. This allows the user to set the time interval the Speedlite stays active when used as a slave. I prefer the longer setting to make adjustments to the set, model, or lighting without having the slave flash power down and have to be reset.
C.Fn-11	Slave auto power off cancel	0–Within 8 hours/1–Within 1 hour. You can specify the time range in which the slave unit's auto power off feature can be cancelled by the master. Again, I prefer the longer time setting.
C.Fn-12	Flash recycle with external power source	0–Flash and external power source/1–External power source. When the Speedlite is in its default mode, it will draw power from both sets of batteries. Switching to 1 allows the flash to be recycled only by the external power source; therefore, the internal batteries will last longer. When I'm using the CP-E4, I prefer to set Custom Function 12 for the Speedlite to the 1 setting to draw power from the battery pack only. That way I still have a fully charged set of internal batteries available if the pack runs low on power. If the internal batteries become exhausted, shooting might not be possible. Even with the flash set to 1, the Speedlite will still require internal batteries to operate.
C.Fn-13	Flash exposure meter setting	0–Speedlite button and dial/1–Speedlite dial only. Setting 1 saves you a step and time by not having to press the Select/Set button on the Speedlite to access FEC settings. You simply turn the dial to the desired FEC setting and shoot.

Table 2.4 430EX II Custom Functions

Custom Function Number	Function	Settings and Description
C.Fn-00	Distance indicator display	0–meters/1–feet. Depending upon where you live, set this to the most common distance designation.
C.Fn-01	Auto power off	0–Enabled/1–Disabled. Auto power off turns the flash off automatically after a certain period of inactivity (not user-specified, but between 1.5 minutes and 15 minutes) to save battery power. Press the shutter button or Pilot Lamp button to reactivate the Speedlite. I choose 1 to disable this function whenever working with off-camera Speedlites.

(continued)

Table 2.4 430EX II Custom Functions *(continued)*

Custom Function Number	Function	Settings and Description
C.Fn-02	Modeling flash	0–Enabled (DOF preview button)/1–Enabled (Test-firing button)/2–Enabled (both buttons)/3–Disabled. You can choose which buttons you want to use to fire the modeling flash.
C.Fn-07	Test firing with autoflash	0–1/32 power/1–full power. This allows the user to set the power level of the test flash. I use 0 to save battery life when I just want to check if the flash is working, and 1 when I'm metering the flash output with a handheld light meter.
C.Fn-08	AF-assist beam firing	0–Enabled/1–Disabled. Use this setting when you don't need the AF-assist beam to focus the camera or in situations such as performance photography, where the beam would be distracting to others.
C.Fn-09	Auto zoom for sensor size	0–Enabled/1–Disabled. EOS digital cameras have one of three different sensor sizes. The Speedlite automatically recognizes the sensor size and adjusts the flash zoom for proper coverage.
C.Fn-10	Slave auto power off timer	0–60 minutes/1–10 minutes. This allows the user to set the time interval during which the Speedlite stays active when used as a slave. I prefer the longer setting to make adjustments to the set, model, or lighting without having the slave flash power down and have to be reset.
C.Fn-11	Slave auto power off cancel	0–Within 8 hours/1–Within 1 hour. You can specify the time range during which the slave unit's auto power off feature can be cancelled by the master. Again, I prefer the longer time setting.
C.Fn-14	Flash range/ Aperture info	0–Maximum distance/1–Aperture display. This allows the LCD display of the Speedlite to give you different information. When you press the shutter button down halfway, the maximum effective range (distance) of the flash will be displayed with setting 0, and the aperture range will be displayed with setting 1.

Note that Custom Functions 03, 04, 05, 06, 12, and 13 from the 580EX II are missing from the list for the 430EX II. They are not available on the 430EX II. The MT-24EX and MR-14EX Speedlites also include slightly limited Custom Function menus.

Setting Custom Functions via the camera

Several Canon camera models now allow you to control the Speedlites' exposure modes, settings, and Custom Functions right from the camera's LCD monitor. Using this larger menu screen is a much more intuitive and easier way to interact with your Speedlites' available settings. It's also a huge time-saver when you can make all the settings for both pieces of equipment in one place, not having to use another gadget's menu, buttons, and dials. It's hard enough of just trying to get the shot! So any time-savers are appreciated.

Currently, the 1Ds Mark III, 1D Mark III, 1D Mark IV, 5D Mark II, 7D, 40D, 50D, 60D, the latest Rebels, and the new 1D X and 5D Mark III support this feature and offer External Speedlite control. Canon plans to offer this feature with all future dSLR cameras.

Auto Off mode

The 600EX/600EX-RT, 580EX II, and 430EX II have an Auto Off or standby mode. The Auto Off function puts the flash to sleep when not in use, which helps conserve battery power. When the Speedlite goes into standby mode, tap the shutter button or switch the Speedlite off and then on. When using the Speedlite transmitter ST-E3-RT with a 600EX-RT or the ST-E2 Speedlite transmitter with the 600EX, 580EX II, and 430EX II, simply push the Test fire button on your Speedlite to wake up the slaves.

Speedlites are set by default for an automatic standby time. This is fine when you're shooting with a Speedlite connected to the camera. However, when you're using Speedlites remotely, this setting can quickly become an annoyance, especially when you're working in combination with third-party remotes, such as RadioPoppers or PocketWizards. Because the Auto Off default setting for the flash is to switch to a power-saving sleep state when not in use, and the Speedlites not being physically connected to the camera, the flashes will sleep at the most in inopportune times, like right in the middle of a shoot when your Speedlite is buried inside a softbox. This has freaked me out more than once until I learned how to disable this feature. I keep the Auto Off standby function turned off all the time. To do this on your Speedlites (and I recommend you do), enter the Custom Function menu and disable C.Fn 01 ( ) on the 600EX/600EX-RT, 580EX II, and 430EX II. Change Custom Function settings using the same steps used to change the settings for the AF-assist beam, described earlier in this chapter.

As you get more comfortable with small-flash lighting, you'll be getting those flashes off your camera and using the adjustments described in this chapter to create the kind of images you've always wanted!

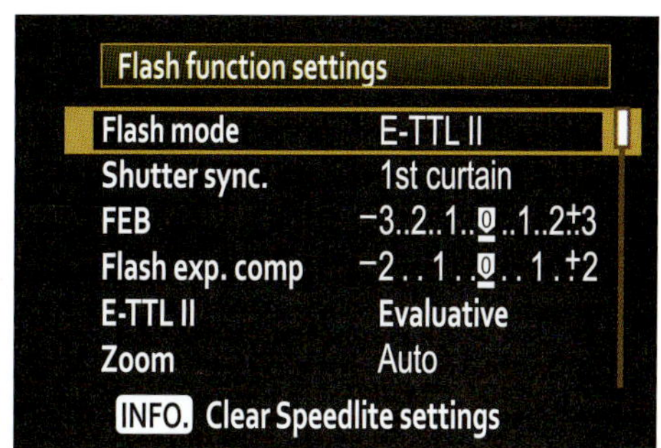

2.10 The External Speedlite menu of the Canon 5D Mark II with a 580EX II attached

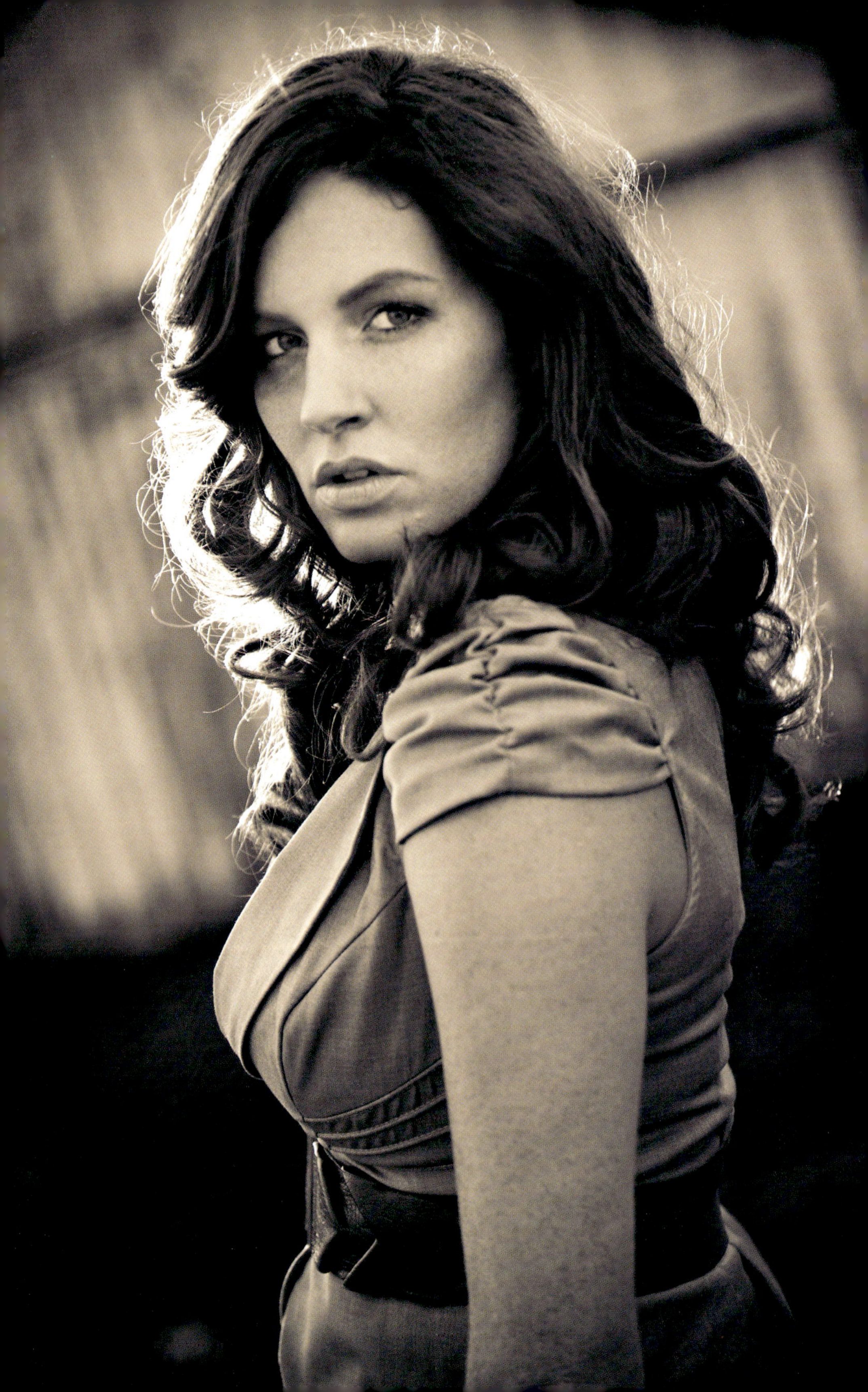

CHAPTER 3

Flash Photography Basics

Flash photography can be intimidating. Many photographers only shoot with available light and confine their outdoor shooting to when the light is just right. This is very limiting! Available light is just that — it's the light that you have available. If that happens to be a Canon 600EX or 600EX-RT Speedlite, great. If it happens to be the sun, that's great too. And if it's a combination of both a Speedlite and the sun, that's also great. The goal is to take creative control and not be held captive by the existing lighting conditions. It's valuable to develop the skills and confidence necessary to create the light you need when you need it.

This chapter helps demystify flash photography and encourages you to experiment. Invest time to develop the skills to effectively incorporate Speedlites into your photography. Learning how to use Speedlites and strobes is a tremendous asset both creatively and financially.

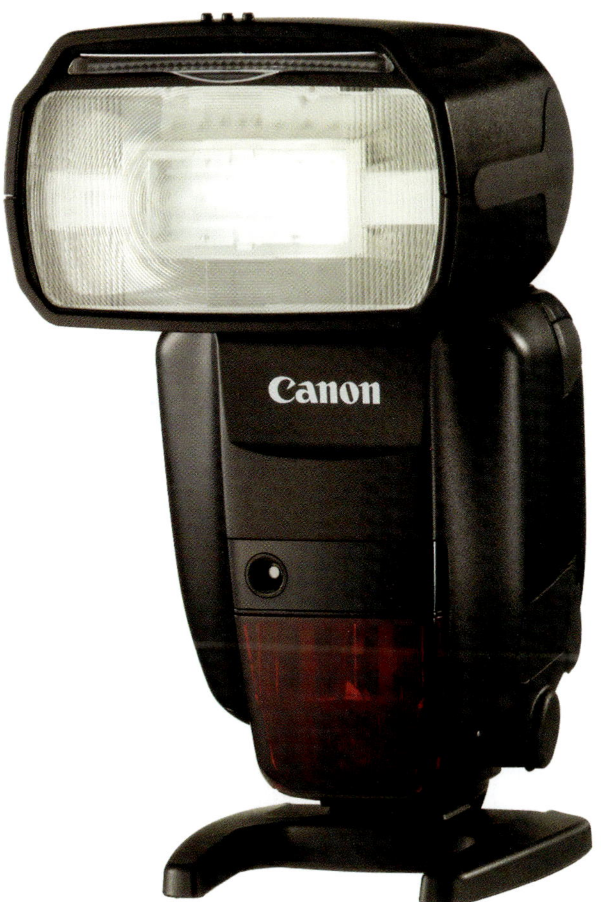

Courtesy of Canon

The Canon 600EX-RT Speedlite with its included tabletop stand, a powerful ally in your creative lighting arsenal

Studio Strobes or Speedlites?

Studio lighting systems fall into two main categories — continuous lighting and flash lighting. Here I concentrate primarily on flash lighting. Whether you're using Speedlites or studio strobes, lighting with flash is convenient because the light output can be adjusted in specific increments and shaped with numerous modifiers. Furthermore, flashes can freeze action, can be triggered wirelessly, and can sometimes deliver the watt-seconds necessary to overpower the sun.

Continuous lights, such as fluorescents, HMI's (Hydrargyrum medium-arc iodide lamps), and hot lights, are a great addition to any studio's equipment list and worth mentioning briefly. Keep in mind that the quality of light produced by continuous lights differs from that produced by Speedlites and strobes. Continuous light can, in some situations, cause the pupils of a subject's eyes to become small when they adjust to the light. This can easily be remedied in post-processing but is something to keep in mind, as larger pupils are considered more flattering. Don't get me wrong — I love continuous lights for many, many things. F.J. Westcott's fluorescent Spiderlites produce gorgeous, soft, glowing light. Incandescent hot lights and HMI's can be used to great effect producing dramatic portraits reminiscent of the 1940s Hollywood style made famous by George Hurrell. They're great in situations when you want a "what you see is what you get" lighting setup. They're also terrific because they never make you wait like strobes or Speedlites do while they recycle, and they never flash, which can make some subjects self-conscious.

There are three main types of flash lighting systems that you should consider before you start to outfit your studio and purchase equipment. The first and most powerful is the pack-and-head system, which includes individual flash heads connected by cables to a single power pack. For this type of flash, I use a 1200 watt-second Profoto Pro-7b pack with two air-cooled heads. It can be used in the studio with an AC power adapter or in the field with its DC battery. Profoto and other systems have a large number of light modifiers, such as softboxes, grids, and snoots, available and are well suited to every-day studio or location use. However, when compared with Speedlites, they tend to be rather large. Even those packs that can operate on battery power can be cumbersome when working alone. One new entry in this category worth mentioning is Elinchrom's Ranger Quadra. At 400 watt-seconds, battery powered, and extremely portable, this setup is a versatile hybrid between Speedlites and higher powered strobes.

NOTE A watt-second is a unit of energy, equal to a watt of power expended for 1 second. It's precisely equal to a newton meter or a joule. The name *joule* is used with devices other than photographic strobes. All other things being equal, twice the number of watt-seconds delivers twice the light output. In other words, it gives you a 1-stop increase in exposure value.

The second type of flash lighting equipment is the monolight. Monolights combine the power supply and flash head into one lightweight, easy-to-transport unit. They allow a full range of output adjustments independent of one another and accept the same modifiers as their pack cousins. However, they still require AC power or a portable battery to operate. Many pack-and-head systems have symmetric/asymmetric power distribution between their light heads, meaning that the output of the lights is always divided into a variable power ratio set by the user, such as 1:1 or 2:1. The independent power control over each light head with monolights provides more fine-tuning control on a head-by-head basis and is appealing to many for this reason.

The last type is, of course, small handheld flashes, or in this case, Speedlites. Although lower in power output than the previously discussed systems, their portability, E-TTL capabilities, and ease of use make them great solutions for travel, location, and entry-level studio work.

Each system is meant for different purposes and, therefore, has different strengths and weaknesses. No one size fits all. To make an informed decision concerning what type of flash system to purchase, you should consider your needs. Ideally, as a working photographer, you have a few different systems at your disposal for the different situations that arise. Keep in mind that you don't have to purchase everything all at once. Pros often rent equipment from photographic supply houses, such as Calumet and others. The following list looks at some of the pros and cons of the three different lighting systems:

- ▶ **Cost.** Without a doubt, Speedlites and monolights are the most economical of the three systems mentioned. Many times, the cost of pack-and-head systems is beyond the reach of a casual photographer's budget. Speedlites are more financially feasible in the short run and can last for years of regular use.

- ▶ **Portability.** Speedlites win in this category. You still need stands and light modifiers for many types of shooting, but the Speedlites themselves are small and very portable, and offer a good range of power output. You can also use gorilla pods or small clamps to easily mount Speedlites, which is not something you can do with monolights or studio flash heads.

- ▶ **Power supply.** Speedlites run on AA batteries. You don't have to rely on AC current and long extension cords to power these small flashes. For location work, you can power studio flashes with auxiliary batteries, but the battery can sometimes weigh more than the actual flash heads. That's one more piece of equipment that you have to purchase, carry, and maintain.

> **TIP** The night before a photo shoot, I always put a freshly charged set of rechargeable batteries in the Speedlites I'll be using the next day. One set of batteries can last for hundreds of exposures. You should always have at least two sets of extra batteries on hand for each Speedlite you bring with you.

▶ **Ease of use.** After you arrange and configure your Speedlites, you're ready to shoot, and you're able to control flash output from a central location. With many older style studio flash systems, you make all of your adjustments either at the flash head (if using monolights) or at the power pack. Tricky lighting setups can involve a lot of walking back and forth from the camera, changing the flash output settings. Recent wireless systems, such as the Profoto Air and Elinchrom Skyport have solved this problem. These systems allow the power output of each light to be adjusted directly from a wireless controller mounted on your camera's hot shoe.

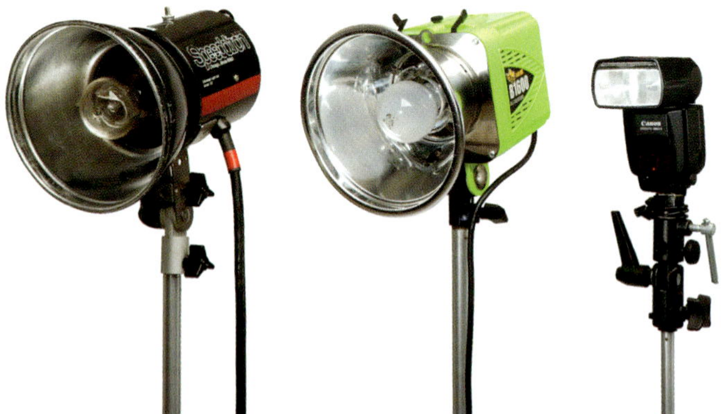

3.1 Three different types of flash lighting equipment. From left to right, a Speedotron 102 flash head that connects to a 2403B power pack, an AlienBees B1600 monolight, and a Canon 580EX II Speedlite.

▶ **TTL.** This one's a biggie! With studio flash systems, you don't have the advantage of Through-the-Lens (TTL) metering. When using Canon's version of TTL metering, E-TTL (E-TTL II), the camera automatically adjusts the flash output according to the desired exposure and measures the distance to the subject as calculated from the lens distance reading. This automatic adjustment is a huge advantage of using Speedlites — you can just set your Speedlites to E-TTL mode, set the groups and channels, and start shooting. The Canon Speedlite System and your camera do all the rest. Add to that the benefits of being able to shoot in High-speed sync mode (**⚡H**), and E-TTL becomes very compelling.

CROSS REF For information on setting groups and channels, see Chapter 4.

Most often, the determining factor in equipment purchases is budget. It's likely that a set of Speedlites is a good option, especially if you like to shoot quickly, don't need a ton of power (to overpower the sun), and need portability. After you cross the threshold of four or more Speedlites in an attempt to build up enough power for things like overpowering the sun, the Elinchrom Ranger Quadra is probably a better bet for the money and power output. Studio units have cords that people can trip over, and they contain high voltage electronics that can be dangerous when not properly maintained. However, studio flash systems offer several advantages over Speedlites in many shooting situations:

- ▶ **Power.** For sheer raw light output, pack-and-head and monolight systems can't be beat. They offer stable light sources as long as there is a receptacle to plug in to or a battery available. They also allow you to shoot in controlled environments at higher f-stops, resulting in greater depth of field. There is, however, a price to pay for all that flash power, usually in the form of portability and cost.

- ▶ **Recycling time.** Recycling time refers to the amount of time it takes the flash to be powered up fully to make another exposure. Speedlites typically take 0.1 to 6 seconds between shots, and as batteries lose power, they take longer to recharge the flash. Power packs connected to wall outlets don't have this issue but still need time to recycle.

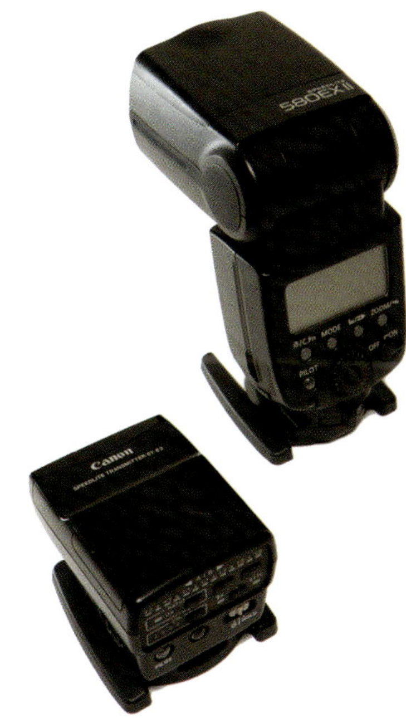

3.2 A 580EX II or an ST-E2 (or one of the macro Speedlites) is all you need to control lighting output of multiple Speedlites right from your camera.

▶ **Modeling lights.** Studio flashes usually have the capability to illuminate a subject using a modeling light. A modeling light is a secondary lighting element in the flash head that, once turned on, simulates the light output of the flash, allowing the photographer to model highlights and shadows and adjust the lighting output and placement. Although the 600EX/600EX-RT, 580EX II, and 430EX II have a modeling light feature, the modeling light isn't continuous (only 2.5 seconds) and is of limited use to help you preview the lighting effect on the subject.

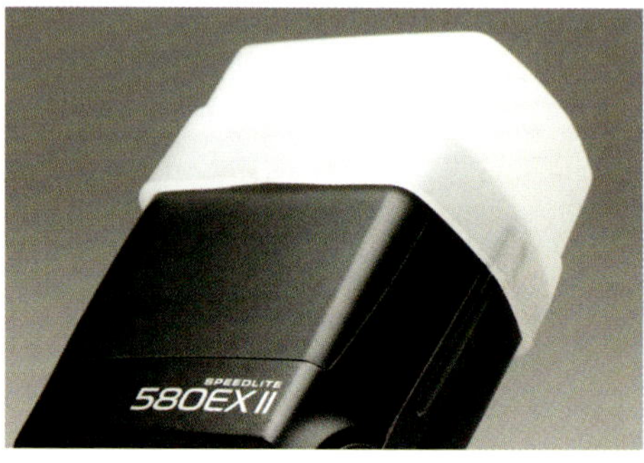

3.3 Your first light modifier should be this Sto-Fen diffusion dome. This custom-made, frosted-plastic dome scatters the light emitted from a Speedlite to soften it, and it protects the flash face. Sto-Fen manufactures a large assortment of these diffusion domes — make sure you get the right one for your Speedlite model.

NOTE The modeling light from a Speedlite fires a 2.5-second series of flashes. It doesn't provide constant lighting so that you can see where the highlights and shadows fall. It also rapidly depletes your battery power and can overheat your flash tube if you keep using it, requiring a costly repair. For these reasons, I never use this feature.

▶ **Accessories.** Studio flash systems have long offered a wide array of light modifiers and accessories. Diffusion panels, grids, snoots, barn doors, gobos, gel holders, umbrellas, octabanks, beauty dishes, and softboxes are common accessories for all commercial studio systems. In the past, small flash users often had to create their own accessories, but with the recent groundswell of small flash popularity, many vendors such as Honl Photo, ExpoImaging, and Lastolite now make modifiers specifically for these small flashes.

Only you can decide which system best meets your shooting needs. Speedlites are much less expensive than the other two types of lighting discussed, and when used correctly, they offer the photographer a powerful, lightweight option that provides beautiful light in a wide variety of shooting situations.

Color Temperature and White Balance

Light, whether it is sunlight, moonlight, fluorescent light, or light from a Speedlite, has a color that can be measured using the Kelvin scale. This measurement is also known as color temperature. Although our vision can automatically adjust for changes in the color temperature, a digital camera has to measure and approximate it in any number of lighting situations through white balance adjustments. If your Canon digital camera is set to an Automatic white balance (**AWB**), it automatically adjusts the white point for the exposure you are taking because white is most dramatically affected by the color of the light source. The result of using a correct white balance setting with your digital camera is correct color in all of your photographs.

TIP If you shoot JPEG images, the white balance is set in the camera by the preset you choose. If you shoot RAW images, the white balance setting is only "noted," and you can set or adjust the white balance in a RAW conversion program after the image is captured.

What is Kelvin temperature?

Similar to Fahrenheit and Celsius, Kelvin (K) is a temperature scale, normally used in the fields of physics and astronomy, where absolute zero (0K) denotes the absence of all heat energy and molecular movement.

Kelvin is a scale for measuring temperature. Zero degrees Kelvin corresponds to –459.67 degrees Fahrenheit. The relationship between color and Kelvin temperature is derived from heating a *black body radiator* (a piece of black metal) until it glows. The particular color seen at a specific temperature is the color temperature. When the black body is hot enough and begins to glow, it is dull red. As more heat is applied, it glows yellow, and then white, and ultimately blue.

For most people, Kelvin and color temperature are opposite of what you generally think of as warm and cool colors. You respond to colors and light on an emotional level that does not correspond to the Kelvin temperatures. On the Kelvin scale, what you think of as hot or warm colors represents the lowest temperatures. Blues and greens that are perceived as cool or cold colors actually represent the highest temperatures.

Choosing the white balance

Canon dSLRs offer four methods for setting white balance. Having these choices gives you flexibility to use different approaches in different shooting situations. Here are some examples that provide a starting point for using each of the three methods:

▶ **Auto white balance (AWB).** When you're shooting quickly and there is no time to perform a custom white balance, choose Auto white balance (AWB). The camera takes into account the various ambient lighting sources and does its best to provide neutral colors.

▶ **Custom white balance (✍).** Setting a custom white balance produces very accurate color because the white balance is set precisely for the light temperature of the scene. To use this option, shoot a white or gray card (or use the ExpoDisc discussed in Chapter 5) and select that image as your desired white balance. The camera imports the color data and uses it as a new custom white balance until you change it.

CROSS REF See Appendix D for more information on how to use the gray card and color checker included in this book.

You can use the custom white balance as long as you're shooting in the same light, but if the light changes or you add a Speedlite, you have to repeat the process to set a new custom white balance.

▶ **White balance presets.** For outdoor shooting, especially in clearly defined lighting conditions such as bright daylight, an overcast sky, or fluorescent light, using a preset white balance setting produces accurate color in most cases. The exception is shooting in tungsten light and using the Auto white balance (AWB) option, which I feel produces less-than-ideal color reproduction. It's in situations like this that the ExpoDisc really shines. Otherwise, the preset white balance settings have very good color and hue accuracy, and acceptable color saturation.

▶ **Manual Kelvin temperature settings.** If you happen to know the specific Kelvin temperature of the lighting equipment you're using, go ahead and choose the Kelvin (K) setting and select the temperature to match them. Please note that not all Canon dSLRs have a manual white balance setting.

The file format you choose determines whether the images are stored on the memory card in JPEG or in RAW format, and the quality level you choose determines the number of images you can store on the card, as well as the overall image quality and the sizes at which you can enlarge and print images while still maintaining quality. RAW format also allows you to set the white balance after the fact, when you are processing the images. With JPEG, you are locked in to the white balance settings you chose, so choose wisely.

Your choice of file format and quality will also be determined by the situation and intended output. For example, I shoot RAW images during portrait sessions and environmental location shoots with mixed lighting, but then I might switch to Large/Fine JPEG format (◢ L) for the reception images during a wedding or luncheon because I know these images will likely be printed no larger than 8 × 10 inches. However, the majority of my work is shot in RAW (RAW) to capture the most information, to be assured of the highest image quality, and to have the widest latitude for converting and editing the images.

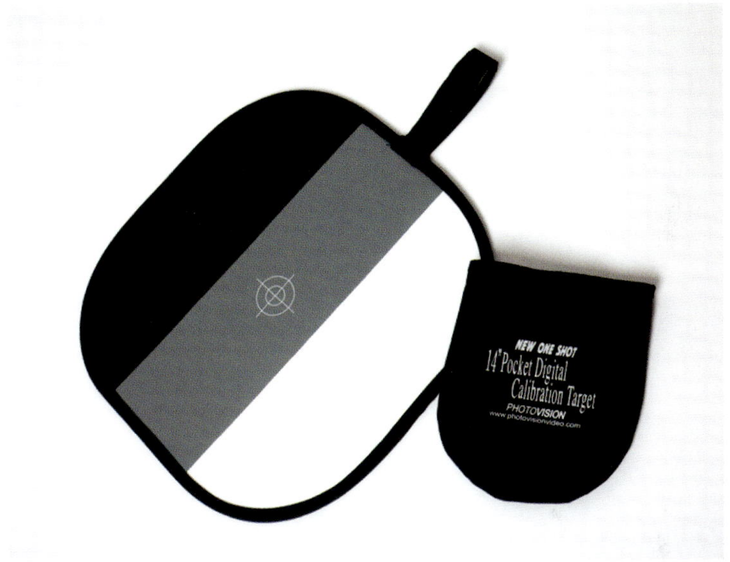

3.4 PhotoVision's 14-inch calibration target

When it comes to white balance for RAW capture, several techniques are available. For my work, I prefer the ease of use and consistent results provided with the ExpoDisc. I simply cover the lens with the ExpoDisc, point the camera toward the dominant light source, make an exposure, and then select that exposure as my custom white balance. I sometimes use an alternate method in the studio where I shoot a calibration target from PhotoVision, which has three sections of black, gray, and white, and then I color-balance a batch of images during RAW conversion in Adobe Photoshop Lightroom. Both techniques work in the same general way; they only differ in when you set the white balance.

With one, you set the white balance (**WB**) before shooting, and with the other, the click-balance technique, you set the white balance during RAW image conversion. However, if you are shooting a wedding and plan on presenting a JPEG slide show of your images from the day during the reception, then setting a custom white balance (⌲) as you shoot is the way to go. This will assure you correct white balance as you shoot and save you precious time when preparing your show.

Even with RAW and its ability to change white balance after the fact, it's always a good practice to try to get an accurate white balance when shooting. By doing this, you won't be distracted by off colors while shooting or while making selections during image editing.

White balance presets

White balance presets give you a variety of ways to ensure color that accurately reflects the light in the scene. You can set the white balance by choosing one of the

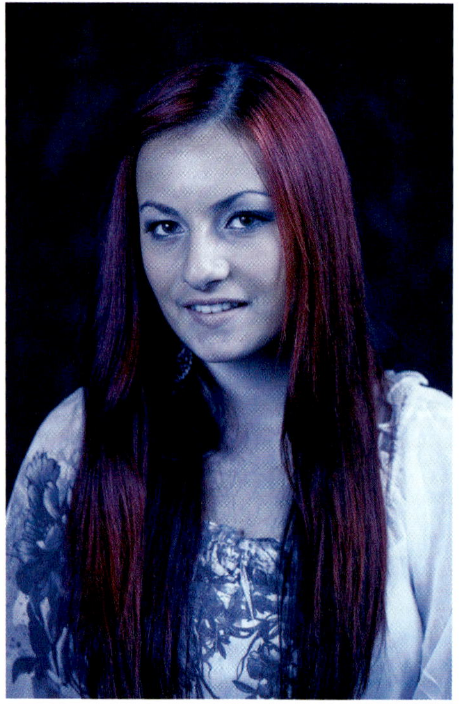

3.5 Tungsten white balance, 2850K

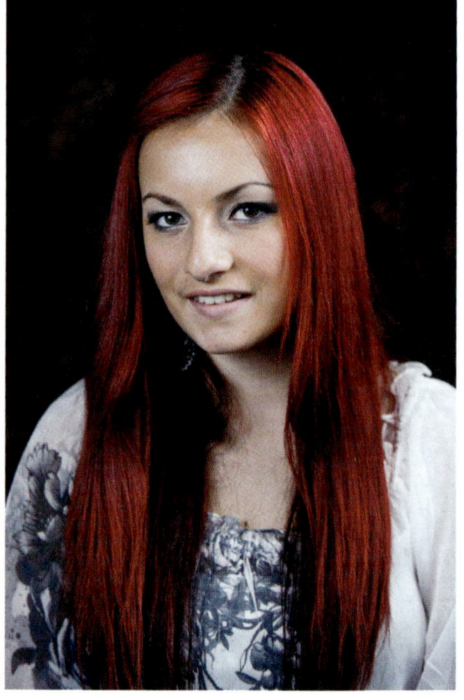

3.6 Auto white balance, 3750K

preset options, by setting a specific Kelvin color temperature, by setting a custom white balance (◣◿) that is specific to the scene, or by selecting Auto white balance (**AWB**). These settings may not be possible on all EOS cameras. The next series of images shows the difference in white balance settings from a photo shot with multiple Speedlites. This image was captured in RAW format after performing a custom white balance off a target, and then exported as shot in each of the color presets. Each photo represents a different white balance setting, with color temperatures ranging from 2850K to 6500K. The lower the color temperature, the more blue appears in the image. The higher the color temperature, the more red and yellow appear in the image.

TIP Don't fall into the habit of always relying on the Automatic white balance settings, because **AWB** can't always solve mixed light situations, especially when adding Speedlites. After your camera and flash are set up, it takes less than a minute to perform and set a custom color balance.

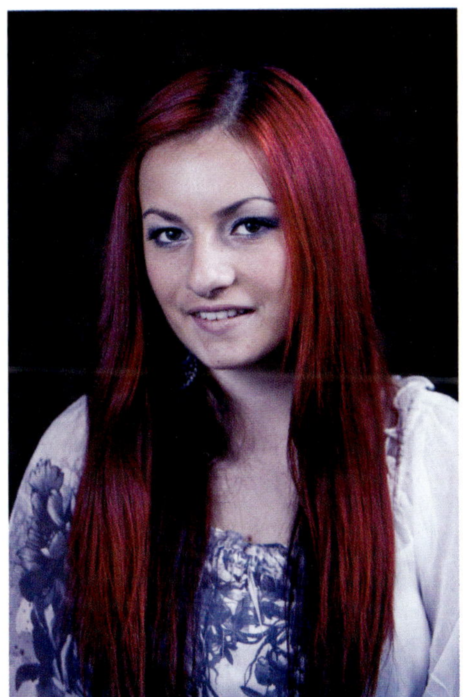

3.7 Fluorescent white balance, 3800K

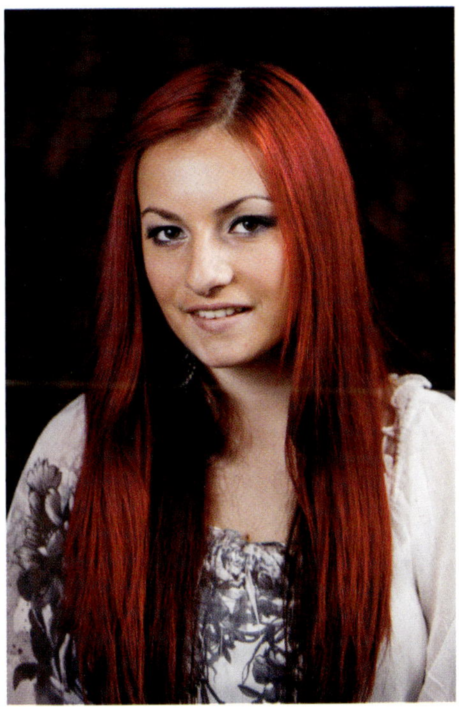

3.8 Custom white balance from a calibration target, 5050K

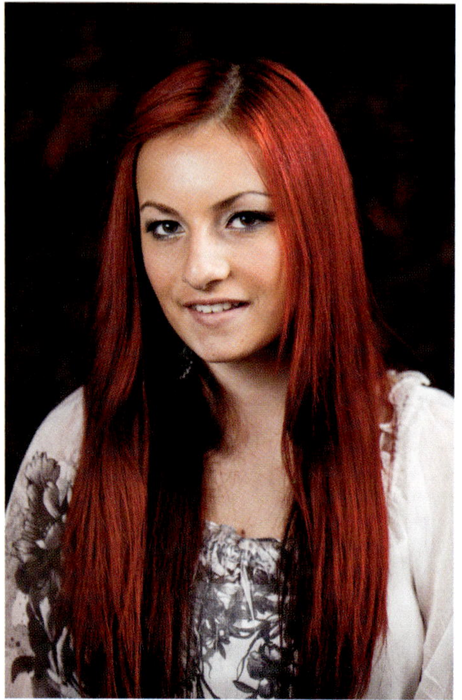

3.9 Daylight/Flash white balance, 5500K

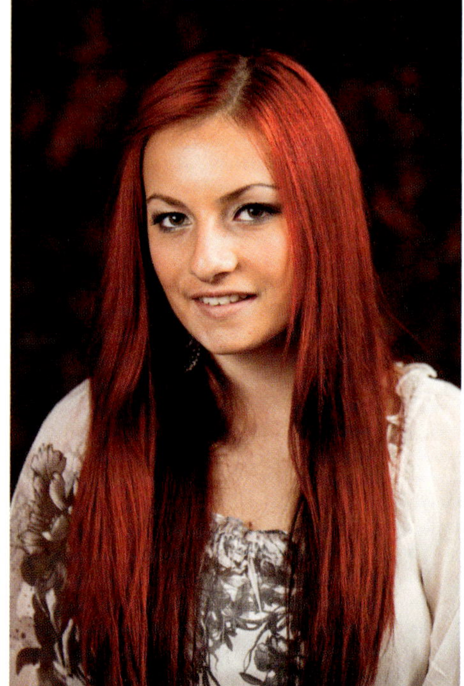

3.10 Cloudy white balance, 6500K

Consider these approaches regarding white balance and the use of Speedlites:

▶ **Speedlites are 5500K.** Speedlites produce light with a color temperature of 5500K, which is also the same color temperature as the Daylight white balance setting (☀). The decision about which color balance is best when shooting subjects with a lot of ambient light and Speedlites is yours, so try the different white balance presets on your digital camera to see which ones you like, gel the flashes to match the ambient light if necessary, or just keep your camera on the Auto white balance (AWB) or the Flash (⚡) preset.

▶ **Cooler color temperatures appear blue.** If your digital camera is set to a white balance setting that represents lower color temperatures (below 5000K), your images appear bluer, or cooler. For a creative twist, try using a Tungsten preset (💡) and gelling your Speedlite with a tungsten-colored gel (full CTO) when you're shooting outdoors. This will cause the background to go blue while whatever the flash is illuminating will have the correct tungsten white balance.

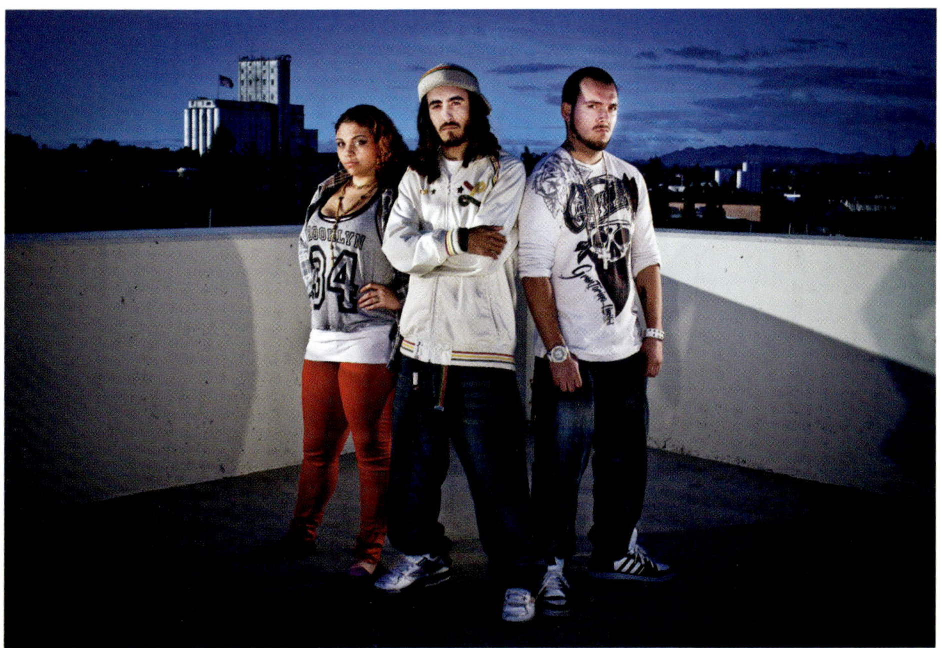

3.11 Creative use of color balance. Setting the camera's white balance preset to tungsten and adding full color temperature orange (full CTO) gels to each of the six Speedlites keeps the subjects daylight balanced while everything else, especially the sky, becomes a deep moody blue tone. Refer to Chapter 6 for a lighting diagram and technical notes about this image. Exposure: ISO 100, f/10, 1/200 second with an EF 50mm f/1.2L USM lens.

▶ **Warmer color temperatures appear orange.** Setting your digital camera to a white balance setting that represents higher color temperatures (above 5000K) makes your images appear more orange, resulting in a much warmer appearance to skin tones.

▶ **Automatic white balance settings can be very accurate.** Today's digital cameras measure a subject's white balance very accurately. Setting your digital camera to an Automatic white balance (AWB) setting often results in images with the correct color temperature balance. When using Auto white balance (AWB) and a Speedlite with an E-TTL II–compatible digital camera, the Speedlite sends color temperature information to the camera, usually resulting in a more accurate white balance than when it is set to Flash white balance (⚡).

By keeping your digital camera set to the Automatic white balance (AWB) setting, you can shoot quickly in RAW mode (RAW) and not worry about incorrect color temperatures. You'll probably want to get it as close as possible, but you don't need to be as accurate as you do when shooting JPEGs. Remember with JPEGs the color temperature is baked into the file at the time of capture. You may find that your camera's ability to evaluate and produce a pleasing white balance is more accurate than adjusting white balance settings manually.

▶ **Shoot in RAW format for ultimate control of white balance.** All Canon dSLR models offer you the ability to shoot your images in RAW mode. When shooting your images in RAW format instead of JPEG, you can adjust the white balance of your images while or after you transfer the files to your computer. By using the RAW conversion software that is included with your digital camera or using Adobe Camera Raw or Adobe Photoshop Lightroom, you can adjust the white balance of an image after you've imported it into the computer.

Balancing for the ambient light

The Speedlite's small size and high flash output make it ideal for professional location lighting when your scene is of a manageable size. Speedlites can be placed almost anywhere and set to produce just the right amount of light that you need to create a dramatic portrait or interior shot. The exposure controls of the camera in tandem with the settings of a compatible Speedlite make it simple to balance both ambient light and the flash light.

Sometimes you'll find yourself shooting in locations or situations where you need all the ambient light you can get, but you still need your Speedlite to add some snap and punch to the colors. In these situations, I set my camera to the appropriate white balance preset and add a colored gel to my flash to match the ambient light. Gel kits are available from Honl Photo and ExpoImaging that provide quick and easy mounting solutions. You can also buy larger gel sheets from theatrical supply houses and cut your own.

There are three main color-correcting gels that I use on my flash:

▶ **CTO.** Color Temperature Orange gels are used to color-match the flash to tungsten light, resulting in a more realistic look. These are the gels I use most, as I often shoot in indoor locations and need to match the Speedlite color temperature to the ambient light. CTO gels come in 1/8, 1/4, 1/2, and full-strength versions. One full-strength CTO will usually get you back to neutral, but I often add another full- or half-strength CTO to warm up my subject.

▶ **CTB.** Color Temperature Blue gels are used less frequently in situations when you need to balance tungsten to daylight, for example when there is a window in the scene. CTBs come in the same strengths as CTOs.

▶ **Green.** For fluorescent conversion, green gels color-match the flash to fluorescent light and are great when you are shooting in office situations. There are so many flavors of fluorescent light out there now that it has become more difficult to get an exact match with gels.

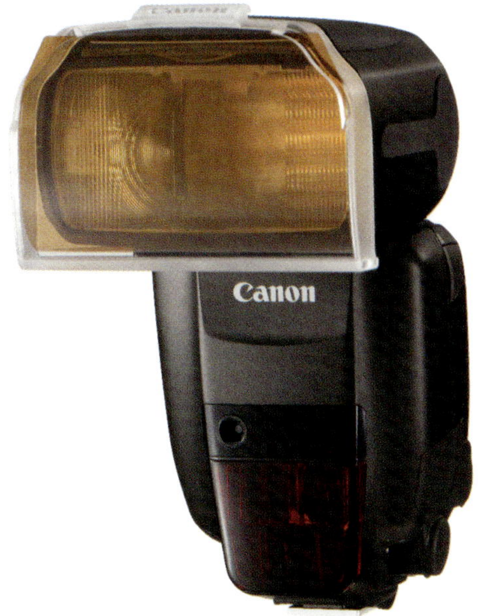

Courtesy of Canon

3.12 The Canon 600EX-RT pictured with its included filter holder (SCH-E1) and filter from the SCF-E1 filter set attached

The Canon 600EX/600EX-RT comes with a basic filter kit. The kit includes a padded case with two CTO filters (low and high), a color filter case, and a color filter holder for attaching filters to the Speedlite. If you're using other commercially available filters, be sure to disable the automatic filter detection function by setting Personal Function P.Fn-05 (📷) to 1 (disable).

CROSS REF More gel options are discussed in Chapter 5.

Using Bounce Flash

You can create a softer quality of light when shooting with a Speedlite, either on or off camera, by bouncing its light. This means aiming the Speedlite at a ceiling (preferably a white one, as color will also reflect) or a reflector (silver, white, or gold), causing its light to be reflected back onto your subject. Bounce flash provides not only softer light but also more evenly lit images.

Bounce flash is a technique used both indoors and out in many situations and can be accomplished in a couple different ways. Most commonly, your flash head needs to

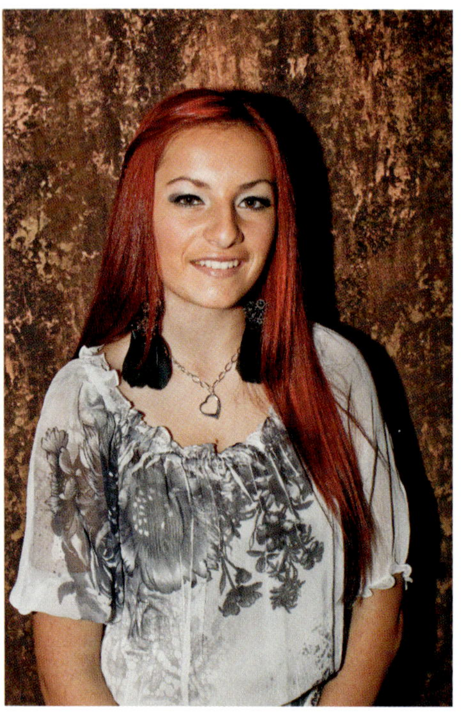

3.13 Standard portrait taken using a 580EX II on camera and pointed at the subject

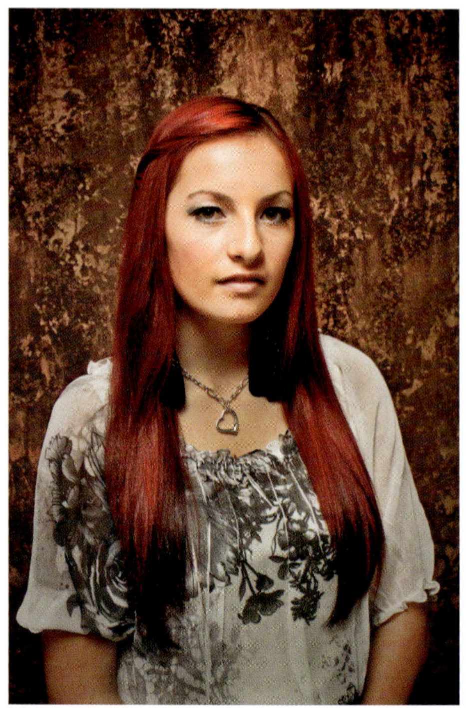

3.14 Portrait taken using a 580EX II on camera and bounced off a white ceiling

be positioned so the light is pointed away from the subject and toward a ceiling, wall, or reflector that bounces the light from that surface back onto your subject. If a ceiling or wall isn't close by, you can use attachable bounce reflectors such as those by ExpoImaging, Honl Photo, F.J. Westcott, and others. ExpoImaging (www.expo imaging.com) makes an entire line of bounce flash reflectors and accessories. When I'm working with a Speedlite off the camera, one of my favorite tools for bouncing the light back onto subjects is California Sunbounce's handheld Micro-Mini reflector with a Sunbounce flash bracket (www.californiasunbounce.com).

Why and when to use bounce flash

Bounce flash is useful when you need to soften the light falling on the subject, spread out the light to cover a larger area, or produce a more natural lighting effect. These situations can include the following:

▶ **When the camera is close to the subject.** If you're positioned close to your subject when taking photos, having your Speedlite pointed directly at the subject can result in a blown-out or overlit photo. Bouncing the flash off a ceiling, wall, or reflector can help soften the light.

▶ **When even illumination is desired.** If you're capturing a scene where you want more even lighting throughout the frame, bounce flash helps more evenly illuminate the entire area. For example, it helps when you're taking photos where you want both the foreground and background evenly lit.

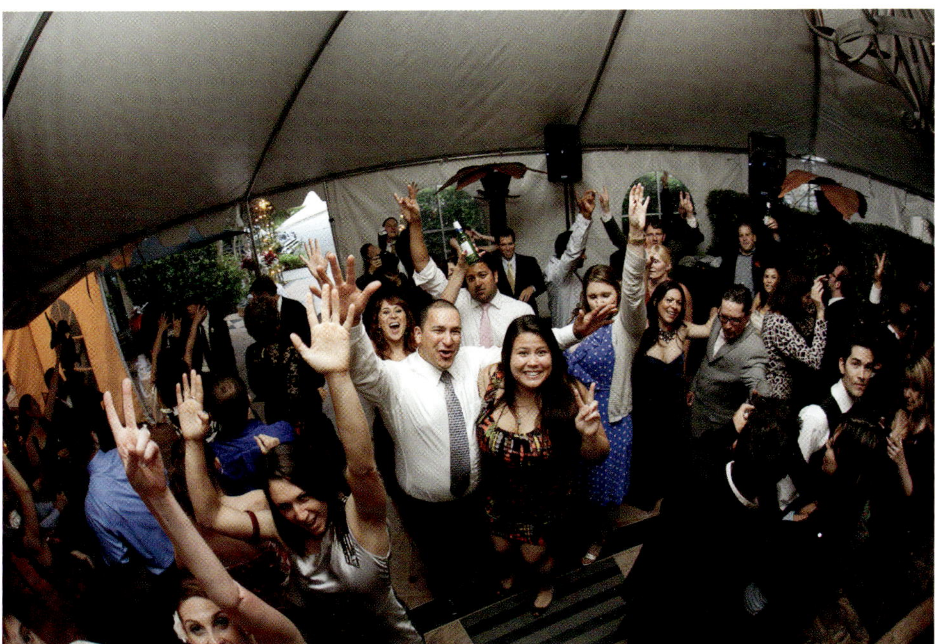

Courtesy of Dennis Urbiztondo

3.15 Wedding reception guests enjoy themselves on the dance floor and mug for the camera. Bouncing the flash on a white surface, in this case the roof of the venue's tent, provides wide coverage, soft white light, and no off colorcasts. Taken with the 580EX II. Exposure: ISO 1250, f/4.5, 1/60 second with an EF 15mm f/2.8L USM lens.

▶ **When shooting portraits.** Directly lit portrait subjects can result in harsh skin tones, heavy shadows, and flat, unattractive lighting. Straight-on flash can create the undesirable effect of making skin look plastic, increasing skin shine, and blowing out highlights. To soften the light, you can bounce your Speedlite off a ceiling, wall, reflector, bounce accessory attachment, or an opaque umbrella. In certain situations, I use a diffusion technique where rather than bouncing the flash I shoot it through a translucent white umbrella or diffusion panel. This produces a similar effect but allows additional light to reach the subject.

Camera and Speedlite settings

When you have the 270EX II, 320EX, 430EX II, 580EX II, or 600EX/600EX RT mounted securely on your camera, you can tilt the flash head up to bounce the light off the ceiling or walls. For a solo portrait, use a longer lens somewhere in the 85-150mm range to keep you a nice distance away from the subject so that the bounced light doesn't create shadows in the eye sockets. When bouncing light off the ceiling, adjust the flash head position and find the best angle. Shoot. Review. Adjust. Depending on the height of the ceiling or distance from the wall, angles play a major role in the direction of the light.

When using bounce flash, you need to position your Speedlite flash head, make camera settings, and then make some adjustments to your Speedlite. Follow these steps:

1. **Set your camera's exposure mode to the desired setting.** Whether you prefer using Aperture Priority (**Av**), Program (**P**), Full Auto (⌶⁺), or Shutter Priority (**Tv**) mode, make sure you have your desired exposure mode set in your camera.

2. **Set the white balance.** Set your camera's white balance setting to Custom (⊿), Flash (⚡), or Auto (AWB). If you are using a custom white balance, remember to create the target by also using bounce flash. Many different whites are out there, and the bounce surface will also influence the color.

3. **Set the flash mode.** Make sure that the flash mode on your Speedlite is set to E-TTL. You can toggle to the desired flash mode by pressing the Mode button on your 600EX/600EX-RT, 580EX II or 430EX II Speedlite.

4. **Position the flash head.** Tilt or rotate the Speedlite's head by pressing the Bounce Lock Release button and moving the flash head to the desired position. The 600EX/600EX-RT and 580EX II Speedlite can tilt up 90 degrees (straight up) and rotate horizontally 180 degrees to the left and right. The 430EX II can tilt up 90 degrees and rotate horizontally 180 degrees to the left and 90 degrees to the right. The 270EX II can tilt up to 90 degrees but does not rotate. The 320EX rotates a total of 270 degrees: 90 degrees to the right and 180 degrees to the left.

5. **Take a test shot.** Capture an image and review the results on your camera's LCD screen. If the image appears under- or overexposed, you can adjust the output of the flash by adjusting the Flash Exposure Compensation (FEC) or by adjusting the aperture setting on your camera. FEC only applies to the light output of the flash. Exposure Compensation values dialed into the camera, plus or minus, affect only the ambient light values in the scene. When using bounce

flash, you typically lose approximately 2 to 3 stops of light. This is because bouncing the light results in less illumination on the subject than when using normal, direct flash.

Explaining Flash Exposure and Specifications

If you want to go old-school style and figure out the flash exposure yourself, it's really not that difficult once you know how. After you know what the numbers mean and where to apply them, it becomes relatively easy. This can be a huge time-saver if you've been creating lighting diagrams (using a notepad or diagram-creation site such as www.lightingdiagram.com), and need to create repeatable lighting setups.

If you are using your Speedlite in the E-TTL mode, all these calculations are done for you, but it's always good to know how to achieve the same results in Manual shooting (**M**) mode. When you know this information, you can use any flash and get solid, repeatable results.

In the following sections, I discuss how to use the guide number, the distance from the Speedlite to the subject, and the aperture to determine the proper flash exposure.

Guide number

The guide number (GN) for a Speedlite measures its ability to illuminate the subject to be photographed at a specific ISO and angle of view. A higher GN indicates a more powerful flash. You can find the GN for your specific Speedlite in the owner's manual, and I've also included tables of GNs for the 600EX/600EX-RT, 580EX II, and 430EX II. The GN changes with the ISO sensitivity, so that the GN at ISO 400 is greater than the GN of the same Speedlite when set to ISO 100. The GN also differs, depending on the zoom setting of the Speedlite. Tables 3.1, 3.2, and 3.3 break down the guide numbers according to the flash output setting and the zoom range selected on the Speedlites.

If you have access to a flash meter, you can determine the GN of your Speedlite at any setting by placing the light meter 10 feet away and firing the flash. Then take the aperture reading from the flash meter and multiply by ten. This is the correct GN for your flash.

Table 3.1 600EX/600EX-RT Guide Numbers (at ISO 100)

Flash Coverage (meters/feet)										
Flash Output	14	20	24	28	35	50	70	80	105	135	200
1/1	15/ 49.2	26/ 85.3	28/ 91.9	30/ 98.4	36/ 118.1	42/ 137.8	50/ 164	53/ 173.9	58/ 190.3	59/ 193.6	60/ 196.9
1/2	10.6/ 34.8	18.4/ 60.4	19.8/ 65	21.2/ 69.6	25.5/ 83.7	29.7/ 97.4	35.4/ 116.1	37.5/ 123	41/ 134.5	41.7/ 136.8	42.4/ 139.1
1/4	7.5/ 24.6	13/ 42.7	14/ 45.9	15/ 49.2	18/ 59.1	21/ 68.9	25/ 82	26.5/ 86.9	29/ 95.1	29.5/ 96.8	30/ 98.4
1/8	5.3/ 17.4	9.2/ 30.2	9.9/ 32.5	10.6/ 34.8	12.7/ 41.7	14.8/ 48.6	17.7/ 58.1	18.7/ 61.4	20.5/ 67.3	20.9/ 68.6	21.2/ 69.6
1/16	3.8/ 12.5	6.5/ 21.3	7/ 23	7.5/ 24.6	9/ 29.5	10.5/ 34.4	12.5/ 41	13.3/ 43.6	14.5/ 47.6	14.8/ 48.6	15/ 49.2
1/32	2.7/ 8.9	4.6/ 15.1	4.9/ 16.1	5.3/ 17.4	6.4/ 21	7.4/ 24.3	8.8/ 28.9	9.4/ 30.8	10.3/ 33.8	10.4/ 34.1	10.6/ 34.8
1/64	1.9/ 6.2	3.3/ 10.8	3.5/ 11.5	3.8/ 12.5	4.5/ 14.8	5.3/ 17.4	6.3/ 20.7	6.6/ 21.7	7.3/ 24	7.4/ 24.3	7.5/ 24.6
1/128	1.3/ 4.3	2.3/ 7.5	2.5/ 8.2	2.7/ 8.9	3.2/ 10.5	3.7/ 12.1	4.4/ 14.4	4.7/ 15.4	5.1/ 16.7	5.2/ 17.1	5.3/ 17.4

Table 3.2 580EX II Guide Numbers (at ISO 100)

Flash Coverage (meters/feet)								
Flash Output	**14**	**24**	**28**	**35**	**50**	**70**	**80**	**105**
1/1	15/ 49.2	28/ 91.9	30/ 98.4	36/ 118.1	42/ 137.8	50/ 164	53/ 173.9	58/ 190.3
1/2	10.6/ 34.8	19.8/ 65	21.2/ 69.6	25.5/ 83.7	29.7/ 97.4	35.4/ 116.1	37.5/ 123	41/ 134.5
1/4	7.5/ 24.6	14/ 45.9	15/ 49.2	18/ 59.1	21/ 68.9	25/ 82	26.5/ 86.9	29/ 95.1
1/8	5.3/ 17.4	9.9/ 32.5	10.6/ 34.8	12.7/ 41.7	14.8/ 48.6	17.7/ 58.1	18.7/ 61.4	20.5/ 67.3
1/16	3.8/ 12.5	7/ 23	7.5/ 24.6	9/ 29.5	10.5/ 34.4	12.5/ 41	13.3/ 43.6	14.5/ 47.6
1/32	2.7/ 8.9	4.9/ 16.1	5.3/ 17.4	6.4/ 21	7.4/ 24.3	8.8/ 28.9	9.4/ 30.8	10.3/ 33.8
1/64	1.9/ 6.2	3.5/ 11.5	3.8/ 12.5	4.5/ 14.8	5.3/ 17.4	6.3/ 20.7	6.6/ 21.7	7.3/ 24
1/128	1.3/ 4.3	2.5/ 8.2	2.7/ 8.9	3.2/ 10.5	3.7/ 12.1	4.4/ 14.4	4.7/ 15.4	5.1/ 16.7

Table 3.3 430EX II Guide Numbers (at ISO 100)

Flash Coverage (meters/feet)								
Flash Output	14	24	28	35	50	70	80	105
1/1	11/ 36.1	25/ 82	27/ 88.6	31/ 101.7	34/ 111.5	37/ 121.4	40/ 131.2	43/ 141.1
1/2	7.8/ 25.6	17.7/ 58.1	19.1/ 62.7	21.9/ 71.9	24/ 78.7	26.2/ 86	28.3/ 92.8	30.4/ 99.7
1/4	5.5/ 18	12.5/ 41	13.5/ 44.3	15.5/ 50.9	17/ 55.8	18.5/ 60.7	20/ 65.6	21.5/ 70.5
1/8	3.9/ 12.8	8.8/ 28.9	9.5/ 31.2	11/ 36.1	12/ 39.4	13.1/ 43	14.1/ 46.3	15.2/ 49.9
1/16	2.8/ 9.2	6.3/ 20.7	6.8/ 22.3	7.8/ 25.6	8.5/ 27.9	9.3/ 30.5	10/ 32.8	10.8/ 35.4
1/32	1.9/ 6.2	4.4/ 14.4	4.8/ 15.7	5.5/ 18	6/ 19.7	6.5/ 21.3	7.1/ 23.3	7.6/ 24.9
1/64	1.4/ 4.6	3.1/ 10.2	3.4/ 11.2	3.9/ 12.8	4.3/ 14.1	4.6/ 15.1	5/ 16.4	5.4/ 17.7

Aperture

Another factor that determines the proper flash exposure is the aperture setting. The wider the aperture (smaller f-stop number), the more light hits the sensor. The aperture or f-stop number is actually a ratio showing the fractional equivalent of the opening of the lens compared to the focal length. Confused? Really it's not that bad; read on.

All math aside, all you really need to know is this: if your Speedlite output is going to remain the same, in order to lessen the exposure, you need to stop down the lens to a narrower aperture or move the Speedlite farther away from the subject. Bear in mind, the aperture controls the light intensity from the flash falling on your subject, and the shutter speed controls the amount of the ambient light in the exposure.

Distance

The third factor that determines the proper flash exposure is the distance from the light source to the subject. The closer the light is to your subject, the more flash exposure you have. Conversely, the farther away the light source is, the less illumination your subject receives. The amount of light falloff is based on the Inverse Square Law, which states that the quantity or strength of the light (coming from the Speedlite) landing on your subject is inversely proportional to the square of the distance from the subject to the Speedlite.

Okay — deep breath — that means you divide 1 by the distance and then square the result. So if you double the distance, you get 1/2 squared, or 1/4 of the total light; if you quadruple the distance, you get 1/4 squared or 1/16 of the total light. This factor is important because if you set your Speedlite to a certain output, you can still accurately determine the exposure by moving the Speedlite closer or farther as needed.

Guide number ÷ Distance = Aperture

Here's where it all makes sense. Take the GN of your flash, divide by the distance the flash is away from the subject, and you get the aperture at which you need to shoot. Because you can express an equation in a few different ways, you can change this equation based on the information you already have to find out what you want to know specifically.

- ▶ Aperture × Distance = GN

- ▶ Distance = GN ÷ Aperture

The guide number represents an exposure constant for the flash unit. A guide number of 80 feet at ISO 100 means that a subject 20 feet away will be correctly illuminated with an aperture of f/4 (80 = 20 × 4) using ISO 100. For the same guide number and an aperture of f/8, the flash should be 10 feet from the subject (80 = 10 × 8).

Sync speed

The recommended sync speed of your camera is the fastest shutter speed you can shoot with and still capture the full exposure of the flash. The sync speed is based on the limitations of the shutter mechanism, usually around 1/200 to 1/250 second. The sync speed on different camera bodies differs with the type of shutter mechanism used.

When you use Canon Speedlites, the camera body prevents you from selecting a shutter speed faster than the rated sync speed, but you can select any of the slower ones. This is important when you need to bring up the value of the ambient light, often referred as *dragging the shutter* or when you want to shoot with wider apertures and faster shutter speeds during portrait work. When a nondedicated flash or an external flash is used via the PC terminal, there is no mechanism to make the camera aware of this, so it is possible to set a shutter speed higher than the rated sync speed. The disappointing result of this is usually a partially exposed image due to the shutter already closing while the flash is reaching its peak output. E-TTL compatible Speedlites like the Canon 600EX/600EX-RT and 580EX II allow you to override this limitation by using High-speed sync mode ($\sharp$H).

Second-curtain sync

All Canon EOS cameras have two moving *curtains* in the shutter mechanism. One curtain of the shutter opens, and the other closes after the correct exposure time. The normal operation of the shutter and flash causes the flash to fire immediately when the first curtain opens. This is called first-curtain sync, and it is fine for most general flash applications. So what's wrong with that? Say your subject is moving and you are tracking the subject using a slow shutter speed to pick up some ambient light. You press the shutter button, the shutter opens, the flash fires, and then the shutter remains open to complete its exposure. When you review the image, you see motion trails out in front of the subject you tracked, and it looks like it's moving backward. The proper technique is to get the flash to fire right before the shutter closes, thereby showing the motion trails behind the subject, and this is exactly what second-curtain sync does. You can set this feature either on the camera or on the Speedlite, but the Speedlite will take precedence over the camera settings.

Fill flash

When shooting outdoors on a sunny day using the sun as your main light source, you usually get images that are very high in contrast. As a result, the shadows are invariably much darker than they should be. To overcome this, a technique called *fill flash* is used.

When your camera is set to Shutter Priority (**Tv**) or Aperture Priority (**Av**), the camera meter exposes for the ambient light and the Speedlite is used as a fill. When using the Manual setting on your Speedlite, you can also use fill flash but will want to reduce the power output to something below the ambient levels.

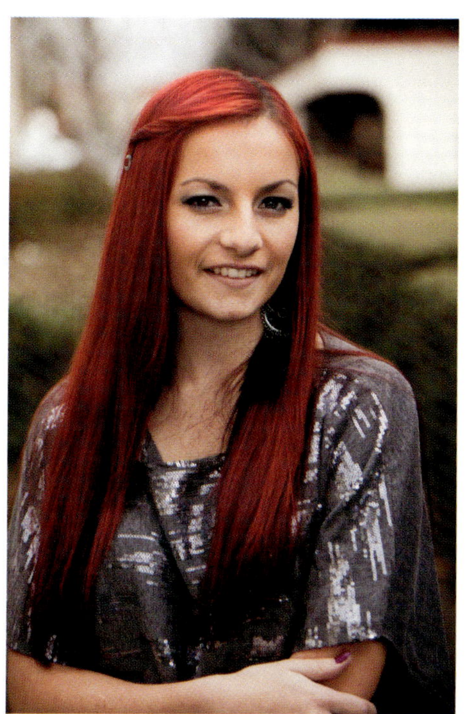

3.16 Model Samantha Hagle photographed outside with no fill flash

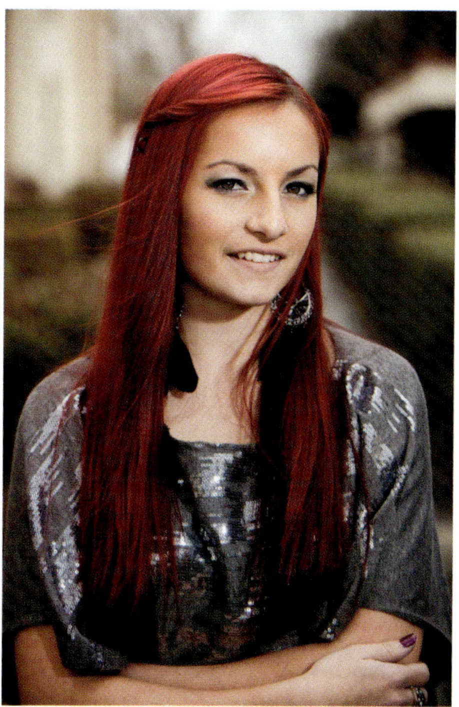

3.17 Model Samantha Hagle photographed outside with fill flash provided from two Canon 580EX II Speedlites bounced into a California Sunbounce Micro Mini reflector with silver fabric. The flashes were triggered in E-TTL II mode using the RadioPopper PX system.

NOTE When working on bright sunny days, you may find yourself needing very fast shutter speeds to shoot at wider apertures, as is sometimes desired. Activating the High-speed sync mode (⚡H) from the back of the flash will allow you to use your Speedlite with shutter speeds above the camera's normal maximum sync setting.

For realistic-looking fill flash, I decide what ISO setting I want to use based on the time of day and ambient lighting conditions, taking into consideration whether my subjects are going to be moving. I then set my Speedlite to expose just under the ambient level, somewhere between −1 and −2 stops. Exactly matching the ambient level with the Speedlite creates flat and artificial results in my opinion, and often my goal is to try to mask the fact that I used flash at all.

To use fill flash in E-TTL mode with the camera set to Manual (**M**), follow these steps:

1. **Position your subject so that the background looks just right.** Avoid having the sun shine directly in your subject's eyes and causing the dreaded the squint effect.

2. **Use your camera's light meter to determine the correct exposure.** A typical exposure for a sunny day at ISO 100 is f/16 at 1/100 second.

3. **Determine the proper exposure for your Speedlite by making test exposures or by using the GN ÷ Distance = Aperture formula.** Remember to take into account the focal length of the lens and the flash's zoom head position. You can also determine the approximate distance to your subject by looking at the distance scale on the lens if your lens has one, or simply using a tape measure to determine the distance.

4. **Once you have determined the exposure, set the flash to expose at 1/3 to 2/3 stop under the proper exposure.** The actual amount of underexposure needed depends on the brightness of the sun and the relative darkness of the scenes.

5. **On the 580EX II and 430EX II in E-TTL mode, press the Select/Set button.** Turn the select dial on the 580EX II or the minus button on the 430EX II to reduce the flash output.

6. **On the 600EX/600EX-RT in E-TTL mode, press Function button 2.** The FEC icon (⚡) and FEC +/– scale will appear on the LCD panel. Turn the select dial on the 600EX/600EX-RT to reduce the flash output.

7. **Take the picture and review it on the LCD.** This helps you to decide if you need more or less flash exposure to render the scene properly. Change the Exposure Compensation value and reshoot.

NOTE When shooting manual fill flash, be sure the flash head is zoomed to the same focal length as the lens in use.

Practice Makes Perfect

In this chapter, I've covered some of the essentials. Consider these the building blocks of your flash photography foundation. I'll keep adding concepts and techniques in the chapters that follow. Before you proceed, take some time and try the following practice lessons:

▶ **White balance presets.** With your Speedlite attached and powered on, cycle through each of your camera's white balance presets and capture one exposure for each. Notice the color shifts that occur.

▶ **Creative use of white balance presets.** Pick up one small sheet gel material known as a full color temperature orange (full CTO) and attach it to the front of your Speedlite so that it covers the flash element. Change your camera's white balance to the Tungsten setting (☀) and photograph a subject in an exterior setting, mixing both the natural ambient light and the light from the flash. Notice how the subject's white balance appears correct (daylight balanced) while the background shifts to a deep blue color.

▶ **Bounce flash.** In this exercise, you learn about two important aspects of bounce flash. First, have a model stand in a room with a white ceiling for you. Then make a flash exposure with a bare Speedlite pointing straight your subject. Next aim your Speedlite at the ceiling and make a test exposure. Notice the different, softer, broader quality of light. The light has no color shift because you bounced it onto a white surface. Next, take the same model to a room with a colored ceiling and make another bounce exposure. Now you can see distinct colorcast affecting the image and model's skin; this colorcast has been picked up from the color of the ceiling. Therefore, always look for white surfaces to bounce into.

▶ **Fill flash.** Grab a piece of white foam core or find a white wall to work with. Have a model pose for you in a position opposite the foam core or white wall. Rotate your Speedlite to the side and slightly back, away from the model, pointing it toward the white foam core or wall. This will cause the light to bounce back off the white surface and cast soft fill light on the model.

▶ **Sto-Fen.** Your first light modifier experiment — this is big! Either inside or out, make an exposure of a model or relatively close object with bare direct flash pointed at the subject. Next, apply a Sto-Fen cap to flash and repeat the process. Notice how the light is less harsh because it has been scattered by the Sto-Fen cap's diffusion material.

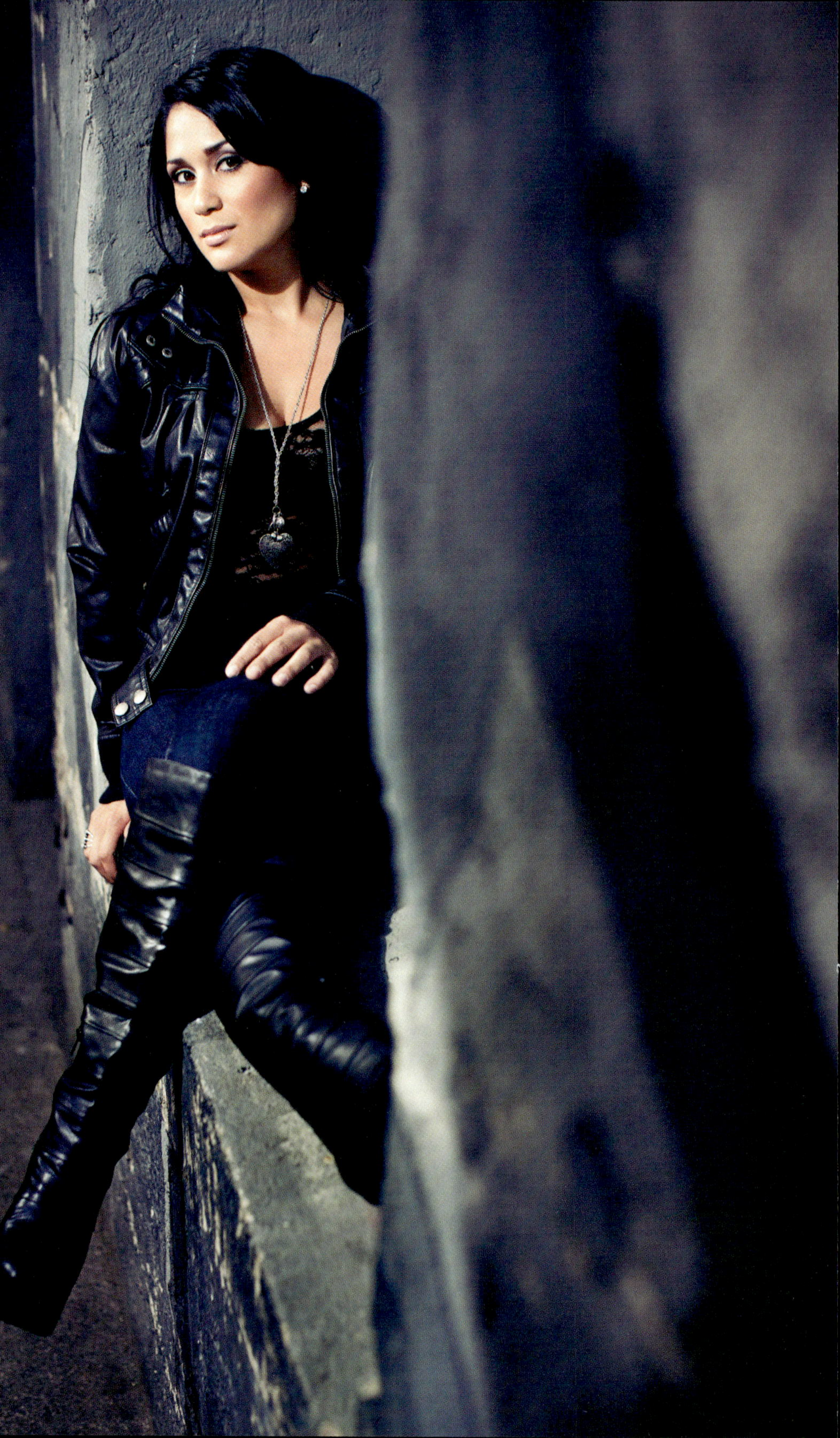

CHAPTER 4

Using Your Flash Off Your Camera

Most, if not all, professional images are produced with off-camera flash. When people ask me how to improve their flash photography, the one piece of advice I give is to get the flash off their camera as soon as possible. This means using the flash with a little knowledge so that you can produce stunning images.

The Canon Speedlite System allows you the flexibility to set up your flashes in groups, individually control flash exposure on your subject and background, and add a hair light or backlight. This chapter examines how the Canon Speedlite System uses the camera in conjunction with a Speedlite designated as a master unit to communicate with remote Speedlites designated as slaves. Understanding these concepts and putting them into practice opens up a whole new world of creative possibilities for your flash photography.

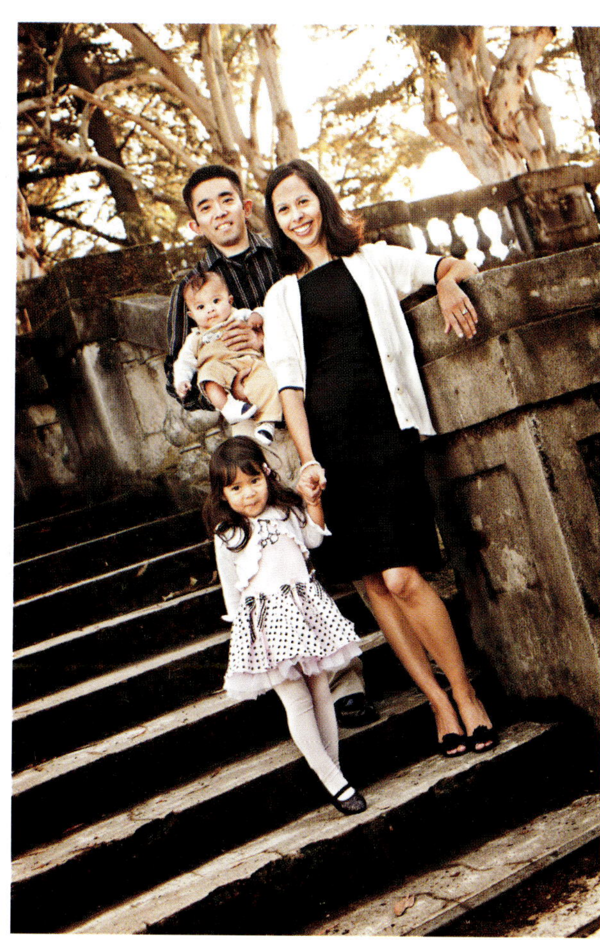

Two Speedlites were fired wirelessly through a 7-foot octabank positioned camera left for this portrait of the Shinzato family. Exposure: ISO 160, f/2.8, 1/80 second with an EF 500mm f/1.2L USM lens.

How the Speedlite System Works Wirelessly with Your Camera

The ingenious thing about the Canon Speedlite System is that Speedlites don't have to be physically connected to the camera to be triggered or to utilize the myriad benefits of E-TTL II communication between the camera and flash. You can make all your adjustments using the External Speedlite control menu on some of Canon's newer cameras, the 600EX/600EX-RT and 580EX II's LCD monitor, or the back panel of the ST-E2 or ST-E3-RT Speedlite transmitter. When the flash is set to E-TTL, the Speedlite relays information to the camera, and the camera body relays information back to the Speedlite. You begin the conversation by pressing the shutter button and making the exposure. In a fraction of a second, the Speedlite fires a preflash and, along with the ambient light metering, determines what it thinks the correct flash output should be based on the metered zones. Zones that differ greatly in brightness are given less weight in the equation, as they are most likely to be reflections from small, highly reflective objects.

Modern lenses that return distance information to the camera also figure into the equation. It becomes even more complex (but easier for you) when you add slave flashes to the mix. The Speedlite, set to master, sends out a signal to the remotes to fire a series of preflashes to determine the exposure level. These preflashes are read by the camera's TTL metering sensors, which combine readings from all the separate groups of Speedlites along with a reading of the ambient light.

The camera then tells the master unit what the proper exposure needs to be. The master unit then relays specific information to each group about how much exposure to give the subject. The camera then tells the master unit when the shutter is opened, and the master unit instructs the remote flashes to fire at the specified output.

All this is done in a millisecond, and for the most part, the results are superb. All these calculations go on behind the scenes so quickly that you don't even notice they are happening. Swing your camera around to frame a different scene, and the whole process begins again — rapidly, wirelessly, and with amazing results.

When set as a master, wireless controllers like Speedlites or the ST-E3-RT and ST-E2 Speedlite transmitters communicate to slave flashes through an arrangement of channels, groups, and ratios. They use these controls to organize and set the light output for multiple Speedlites.

Overview of Wireless Flash Setup with the Canon Speedlite System

It is more than likely that you'll begin your foray into the world of wireless flash photography with only one or two Speedlites, an ST-E3-RT or ST-E2 Speedlite transmitter, and possibly a pop-up flash if your camera has one. The pop-up flash can be used as a master on the latest EOS cameras that include them. Working this way, you can use one of the larger and more powerful Speedlites, such as the 600EX/600EX-RT or 580EX II, as an independent light source for background, hair light, or rim lighting from the side. The more lights you add, the more you think of creative ways to use them.

In the past, when photographers worked with studio strobe units, four heads were considered a standard kit and could handle most commercial assignments. Heavy and time consuming to set up and tear down, they were the price photographers had to pay for all that awesome location power. Granted they were capturing images on large pieces of low-ISO film at f/32 and f/64, and needed all that raw power. Nowadays, with digital technology and the ability to get great results with higher ISOs, that power is no longer as much of an issue.

Step 1: Choose a flash mode

Begin by deciding which flash mode you want to use. The main flash modes available when using the Speedlite System are E-TTL Automatic flash and Manual (M) mode, or Group mode (Gr) when using the 600EX-RT Speedlite. I usually just go with the E-TTL unless I need more precise control of individual Speedlites. A Speedlite set to Manual at 1/1 power delivers all the output that the Speedlite has to offer. E-TTL can sometimes be fooled by what the camera is seeing and vary the flash output. Keep in mind that the system is making all sorts of adjustments and computations based on the information it is receiving in real time, and every once in a while, all that incoming data just doesn't add up. It's up to you, the thinking human, to make the creative and technical judgment calls necessary to achieve the desired results. This is where Exposure Compensation and Flash Exposure Compensation can play an important role.

CROSS REF For more information on using the flash modes, see Chapter 2.

Step 2: Choose a wireless mode

Determine which wireless mode to select: Optical Transmission Wireless Shooting or Radio Transmission Wireless Shooting. This depends on the Speedlites and transmitter you're working with as well as the shooting conditions. If you're using a 600EX, 580EX II, or ST-E2, then the choice is simple because only optical wireless is available with those models. The 600EX-RT has a built-in radio transmitter as well as optical wireless capabilities, while the Speedlite transmitter ST-E3-RT has only built-in radio functionalty. Optically based systems require an unobstructed line of sight between the master and slave Speedlites and/or transmitter sensors to perform correctly. They have a limited range of approximately 30 feet outdoors and can fail in shooting conditions containing bright or direct sunlight.

Radio-based systems such as the 600EX-RT and ST-E3-RT have no such limitations. The 600EX-RT has a 98-foot range and the radio signal can easily pass through walls, through people, around corners, and so on. In Optical mode, the 600EX-RT is backward compatible with the 580EX II, 430EX II, and ST-E2. Note that when mixing 600EX-RTs, 600EXs, 580EX IIs and 430EX IIs together, you must choose either all Optical Transmission Wireless Shooting or all Radio Transmission Wireless Shooting, and you cannot use a mixture of both. Only Optical Transmission Wireless Shooting is comptible with the 600EX, 580EX II, and 430EX II.

Step 3: Choose a channel

After you select a flash shooting mode, the next step is to decide which channel to use. I usually just pick channel 1. In the rare times you are working near other photographers using Canon Speedlites wirelessly, find out which channel they're using and just switch to a different one. In commercial settings, from time to time you may

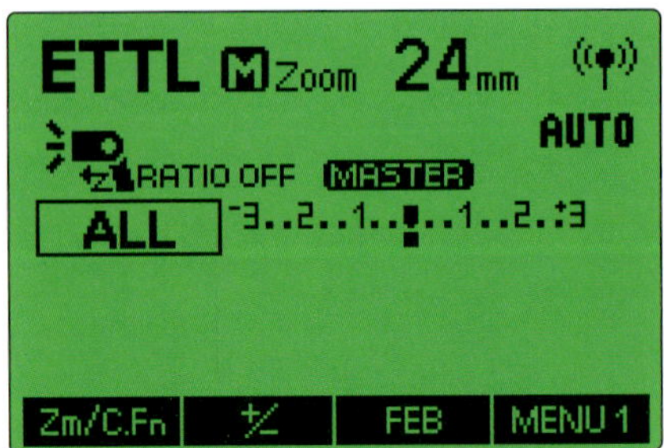

Courtesy of Canon

4.1 The 600EX-RT and Speedlite transmitter ST-E3-RT display the Radio Transmission Wireless Shooting symbol in the upper-right corner. This screen also shows what the 600EX/600EX-RT Speedlites and ST-E3-RT look like when set as a master.

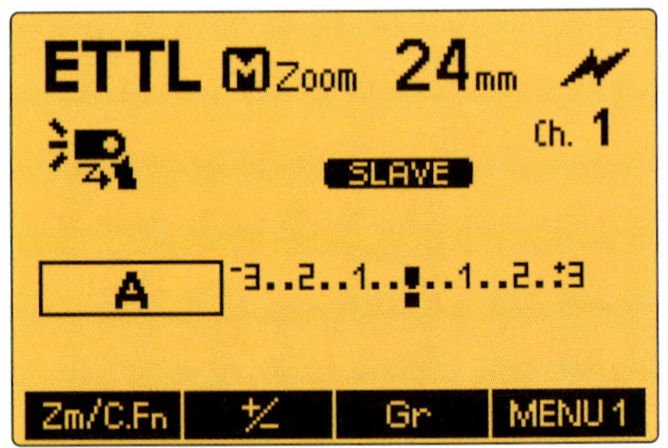

Courtesy of Canon

4.2 The 600EX/600EX-RT screen in Optical Transmission Wireless Shooting and Slave mode. Also shown is the option orange background color for the LCD screen. This can be set using Personal Function P.Fn 02-04 on the 600EX/600EX-RT and P.Fn 03-04 on the Speedlite transmitter ST-E3-RT.

encounter interference problems with the channel you're using, but switching to another channel usually solves this issue.

When using Radio Transmission Wireless Shooting mode ((ᵠ)), the 600EX-RT and Speedlite transmitter ST-E3-RT default to Auto Channel Select mode. This mode chooses the best channel to use. There is also a Channel Scan feature to assist in finding the channel with the strongest signal. Based on the scan results, the channel can then be set manually. These units also allow input of a personal pin number for the channel, further minimizing the chance of radio interference.

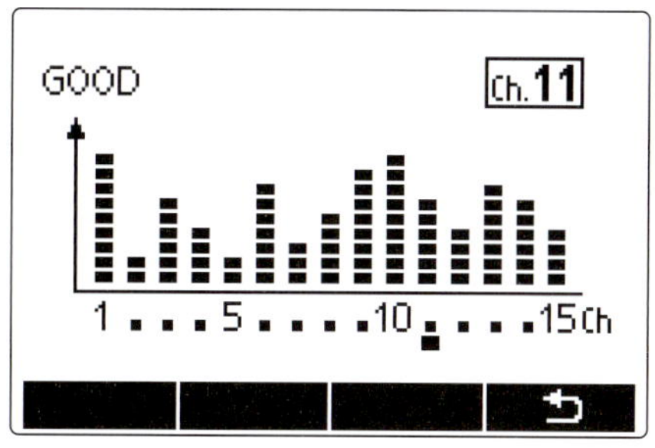

Courtesy of Canon

4.3 The channel scan results screen on the 600EX-RT Speedlite and Speedlite transmitter ST-E3-RT

NOTE Be sure all your Speedlites are set to the same channel, or they won't function properly.

Step 4: Set up groups or slave IDs

For more complex lighting scenarios, the next step is setting up groups, also known as slave IDs. Generally, I set my main lights to group A; the fill lights to group B; and any peripheral lights, such as hair and background lights, to group C. This way you can adjust the output of the specific lights. The fill lights could be a little under what the E-TTL reading is, so by setting them to group B, you can adjust the ratios without altering the exposure of your main light. The background lights may or may not need to be adjusted, depending on the darkness or lightness of the background, whether you're shooting high key or low key, and so on. I set these lights to group C so that I can make the necessary adjustments without affecting the other two exposures.

In addition to increasing the number of available groups from 3 to 5 and being able to work with up to 15 Speedlites wirelessly, the 600EX-RT Speedlite allows wireless mixing and control of E-TTL and manual flash all from the camera, master, or Speedlite transmitter ST-E3-RT. This opens up many new creative possibilities!

Step 5: Adjust the flash ratio levels

Last, I adjust the flash ratio levels. After the Speedlites are set up and the channels and groups are set, it's time to take some test shots. If I have everything set to E-TTL flash mode right from the start, I'm pretty close to the proper exposure. I might just need to make some minor adjustments to the flash ratios, make any zoom head adjustments to tailor the light coverage and color of the light, and then I can start shooting. Adjustments can be made right on the flash on the camera, or on the ST-E3-RT or ST-E2 Speedlite transmitter, so there's no need to visit each flash to make minor changes, a huge time-saver when working by yourself.

In the following sections, I go step by step through setting up your flashes for master and remote (slave) use, choosing a flash mode, setting channels and groups, and adjusting the output ratios for your specific needs.

Setting Up Master and Slave Flashes

This next part is a little technical, but don't be alarmed. The really technical stuff goes on behind the scenes with algorithms and mathematics you don't need to worry about; all you need to do is follow the action through your viewfinder and capture images. I cover how to set up the Speedlite as a master flash or a wireless remote (slave) flash, how to adjust the exposure, and how to set up groups of lights. I also give you some advice from the field. By now you are beginning to see just how multitalented and powerful the Canon Speedlite System can be.

You can control up to 15 Speedlites (600EX-RT), all from your camera. You don't even need to have a light meter (although it is a useful tool); the camera meters for you. If you don't like the way the lighting looks, you can change the flash output between the groups and/or individual Speedlites (in the case of the 600EX-RT and Speedlite transmitter ST-E3-RT) right from the camera or Speedlite transmitter. This is very convenient when you need to work quickly, such as when it's getting dark out and you're rapidly losing your ambient light or when you're working without an assistant.

Masters

Start by setting up a Speedlite to serve as your control center or master flash. The master flash is what controls all the wireless slaves and sends them the instructions about what to do. A master flash can be a 600EX/600EX-RT, 580EX II, 580EX, 550EX, either of the Macro Speedlite flashes, or the ST-E3-RT or ST-E2. The 430EX II, older 430EX, 320EX, 270EX, and 270EX II cannot be used as masters, only as slaves during wireless remote operation.

> **NOTE** The MR-14EX and the MT-24EX Macro flashes can also be used as masters to control off-camera remote slaves.

Setting up the 600EX/600EX-RT as a master

To use the 600EX/600EX-RT as a master flash, follow these steps:

1. **Turn on the Speedlite and select E-TTL mode.** Slide the OFF/LOCK/ON switch to the On position. Use the Mode button to toggle through modes and choose E-TTL mode.

2. **Select Radio or Optical Transmission Wireless Shooting.** Press the Linked Shooting button (⇄) to select Radio Transmission Wireless Shooting (((•))) or Optical Transmission Wireless Shooting ( ). Pressing the Linked Shooting button toggles though the master/slave Optical Transmission Wireless Shooting (600EX) and Radio Transmission Wireless Shooting (600EX/600EX-RT) modes on the LCD screen. Pressing the Linked Shooting button once selects Radio Transmission Wireless Shooting and sets the Speedlite as a master. Pressing the Wireless button three times selects Optical Transmission Wireless Shooting and sets the Speedlite as a master.

   NOTE When your Speedlite is set for wireless master/slave functions, the flash remembers where you are in the sequence of choices. If you make a selection and then do nothing, after 10 seconds the settings are confirmed.

3. **Set the zoom value.** Press Function button 1 (Zm/C.Fn) once. By default, the 600EX/600EX-RT is already on the Menu 1 screen. The zoom value is highlighted. If the Speedlite is connected to the camera's hot shoe, you can reset the auto zoom feature using the Select dial. If the flash is used off camera, depending on the look you wish to create with flash, use the Select dial to set the zoom designation to match the focal length of the lens you're using. Or use different zoom settings to cover larger or smaller areas of the scene for creative effect. Press the Select/Set button to enter your zoom setting. The zoom head feature allows you to set how much of the scene you want to cover with the flash.

   NOTE Function button 4 allows access to the Speedlite's four menus. The sequence of the menus is as follows: Menu 1: Function button 1 controls zoom and accesses Custom Functions, Function button 2 sets FEC, and Function button 3 sets FEB. Menu 2: Function button 1 disables/enables Speedlite output and Function button 2 accesses ratio settings. Menu 3: Function button 1 sets channel selection, Function button 2 sets ID selections (600EX-RT), Function button 3 accesses channel scanning (600EX-RT). Menu 4: Function button 2 sets High-speed sync and Function button 3 saves or loads memory settings.

> **NOTE** When you work with Speedlites off-camera, the auto zoom function is disabled.

4. **Set a ratio if desired.** Press Function button 4 once to enter Menu 2. Use Function button 2 in E-TTL mode to toggle between ALL (Ratio Off), A:B Ratio, or A:B and C Ratio for Speedlites or groups of Speedlites. Press Function button 3 (**Gr**) or the Select/Set button to toggle between A:B and the ratio scale. Function buttons are context sensitive and the name of Function button 3 on the LCD screen temporarily changes to A:B+/–. When the ratio value scale is highlighted, use the Select dial to choose the desired ratio. If you've selected the A:B and C ratio option, when you're in the Ratio Setting mode (Function 3 button — **Gr**), you can switch from A:B to C by using the Select dial. This temporarily changes Function button 3's title on the LCD screen to C +/–. Press the Select/Set button or Function button 3 to access the Ratio value scale for C. Set your desired ratio. In all cases, once the desired ratio is selected, press the Select/Set button to confirm, or do nothing and the Speedlite confirms your ratio selection after 5 seconds.

In Manual mode, press Function button 2 on Menu screen 1 to access Ratio settings for A, B, and C. Press Function button 3 to select A, B, or C and press it again or use the Select/Set button to access the ratio value scale for the desired group. Use the Select dial to set the desired ratio value on the scale, press the Select/Set button to confirm, or do nothing and the Speedlite confirms your ratio selection after 5 seconds.

In Multi mode, use Function button 4 on Menu screen 1 to advance to Menu screen 2. Use Function button 2 (**RATIO**) to set the desired groups, ALL (Ratio Off), A, B, or C. Once the groups are set, press Function button 3 (**Gr**) to select the group and adjust its power. With group A, B, or C highlighted, use either Function button 3 or the Select/Set button to access to the ratio scale for the selected group. Function 3's title on the LCD temporarily changes to indicate which group is selected and displays A +/–, B +/–, or C +/–. Use the Select dial to set the desired ratio value on the scale, press the Select/Set button to confirm, or do nothing and the Speedlite confirms your ratio selection after 5 seconds.

> **NOTE** When you're using only one group of Speedlites and you want them all to fire at the same power output, set the master ratio group setting to ALL. This disables any ratio settings. The master flash is always A group. When using two groups, choose ratio A:B. When using three groups of different Speedlites, the C group won't fire unless you choose ratio A:B C.

5. Set up Group mode (Gr) if desired. Exclusive to the 600EX-RT and Speedlite transmitter ST-E3-RT is the new Group mode, accessed on both using the Mode button. This mode allows control with the master of up to five groups in Wireless Radio mode. To access Groups A, B, C, D, and E, use Function button 3 (**Gr**) on Menu screen 1 in the Group mode. Use the Select dial to toggle

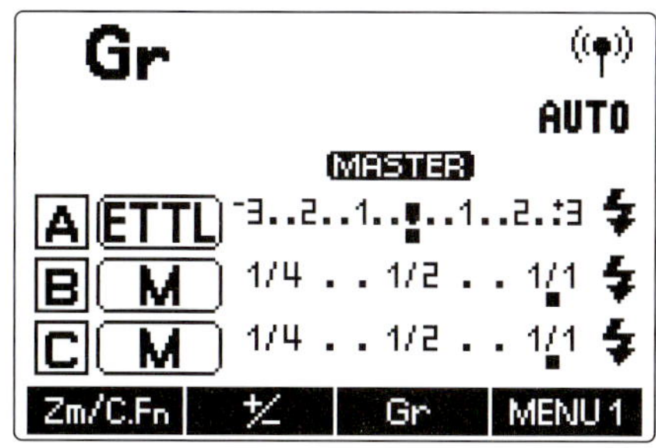

Courtesy of Canon

4.4 Group mode (Gr). Note the mixture of Manual and E-TTL modes used on different groups at the same time.

through the groups, each highlighted when selected. Press the Select/Set button or Function button 3 (which now indicates which group is selected) to access the power scale for that Speedlite or group. Use the Select dial to choose a power setting in 1/3-stop increments up to +/– 3 stops for the selected group, press the Select/Set button to confirm, or do nothing and the Speedlite confirms your ratio selection after 5 seconds.

Definitely worth mentioning are the ON/OFF and A/MODE options in Group mode. Once you are in Group mode, press Function button 3 (**Gr**). Note that the names on the LCD screen for Function buttons 1 and 2 have changed to ON/OFF and A/MODE. These are really awesome additions and open up many new creative possibilities. After you press Function button 3 (**Gr**), one of the Speedlite's groups is highlighted. Using Function buttons 1 and 2, you are able to individually turn off or on a group (Speedlite or group of Speedlites) or change the mode of that group from E-TTL to Manual or Ext.A. This means two things: First of all, you can power on one Group at a time to see its effect. This is a tremendous aid when building light patterns. Second, you are now able to mix and match E-TTL and manual flash at the same time and control them all from the master or camera (2012 or later EOS camera model required). Once a group is selected, press Function button 1 (ON/OFF) to toggle the group on or off. Use Function button 2 (A/MODE) to toggle between available modes for that group (E-TTL, M, Ext.A). If a group is in Manual (M) mode, the group can be adjusted from 1/1–1/128 power by pressing Function button 3 (**Gr**) in Menu 1, using the Select dial to choose the group you've set to (M) mode, pressing Function button 3 or the Select/Set button to enter the power value scale, and rotating the Select dial to the desired power setting. Press the Select/Set button to confirm.

6. **Use Auto Channel Selection or manually select a channel.** When using the 600EX-RT in Radio Transmission Wireless Shooting mode (((•))), press Function button 4 (Menu 1) twice to enter Menu 3. Press Function button 1 (**CH**), and the selected channel number or Auto (600EX-RT radio mode) appears in the upper-right corner of the LCD. Use the Select dial to choose the desired channel. The same channel must be selected for the master and all slaves to function properly. The 600EX-RT is in Auto channel select mode by default. Pressing function button 2 (**ID**) enables you to enter a personal pin number ID to further reduce the chances of radio interference in the event someone nearby is using the same channel. When using channels 1–15 in radio mode, pressing Function button 3 (**SCAN**) scans signal strength and displays a screen where you can select the strongest channel using the Select dial to move between channels. If you need to go back in the menu system, use Function button 4 (**⤺**). Press the Select/Set button to confirm your choice.

   When you're using the 600EX/600EX-RT in Optical Transmission Wireless Shooting mode (**⚡**), press Function button 4 (Menu 1) twice to enter Menu 2. Press Function button 1 to highlight the channel in the upper-right corner of the LCD and use the Select dial to choose channels 1–4. Press the Select/Set button to confirm your choice.

7. **Set master flash output.** Press Function button 4 (Menu 1) once until its LCD name changes to Menu 2. Press Function button 1 to toggle the flash output on (⚡) or off (⚡). Typically, when you're working with a master flash mounted on the camera's hot shoe and with slave flashes in remote positions, you want to turn this to the Off (⚡) position. When you do this, the master flash does not fire or contribute to the exposure, but it does continue to communicate the necessary instructions to the slave flashes being used.

8. **Choose High-speed sync if desired.** Press Function button 4 (Menu 1) three times to display Menu 4. Press Function button 2 (**SYNC**) to toggle High-speed sync (⚡H) on and off.

9. **Turn off wireless Master mode if desired.** Press the Linked Shooting button to toggle through the various wireless modes and turn off the wireless system.

> **NOTE** The first number in each ratio always refers to Speedlites in group A, and the second number of the ratio always refers to Speedlites in group B.

Setting up the 580EX II as a master

To use the 580EX II as a master flash, follow these steps:

1. **Turn on the Speedlite and select E-TTL mode.** Flip the On/Off switch to the On position. Use the Mode button to toggle through modes and choose E-TTL.

2. **Press and hold the Zoom/Wireless button to enter the Wireless setup menu.** Both Off and the wireless icon blink on the Speedlite's LCD.

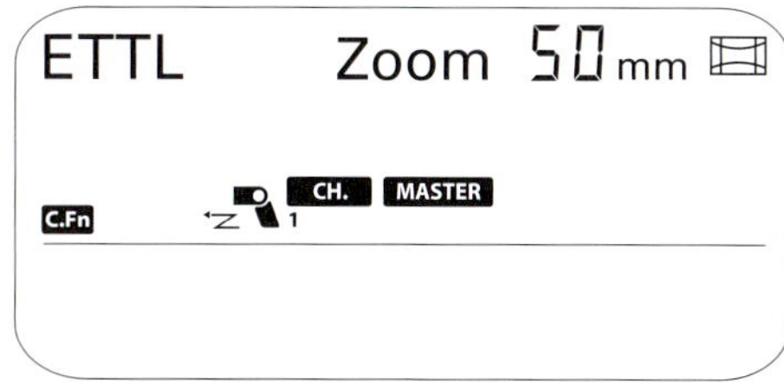

4.5 580EX II set to master

3. **Turn the Select dial so that On, Master, and the wireless icon blink on the Speedlite's LCD.** The auto zoom icon switches to manual. If you do nothing, after 5 seconds the display stops blinking.

4. **Press the Zoom button once.** The zoom designation blinks. If the Speedlite is connected to the camera's hot shoe, you can reset the auto zoom feature using the Select dial. If the flash is used off-camera, depending on the look you wish to create with flash, set the zoom designation to match the focal length of the lens you're using or use different zoom settings to cover larger or smaller areas of the scene for creative effect. The zoom head feature allows you to set how much of the scene you want to cover with the flash.

NOTE When your Speedlite is set for wireless master/slave functions, the flash remembers where you are in the sequence of choices and cycles to the next one every time you push the Zoom button. If you make a selection and then do nothing, after 5 seconds the display stops blinking, and the settings are confirmed. The next time you push the Zoom button, the next item starts to blink, allowing you to change it. The sequence order is zoom head setting, ratio on/off setting, channel setting, flash firing on/off, and, if ratio was turned on, the settings for that.

NOTE When you work with Speedlites off-camera, the auto zoom function is disabled.

5. **Press the Zoom button so that both Off and the Ratio icon blink.** Set your desired ratio. Use the Select dial to change the setting. Choose from ratio off, ratio A:B, or ratio A:B C. Again, you can press the Select/Set button to confirm, or do nothing and the Speedlite will confirm your ratio selection after 5 seconds.

NOTE When you're using only one group of Speedlites, or if you want all the Speedlites to fire at the same power output, just use one group and choose the ratio off setting. The master flash is always A. When using two groups, choose ratio A:B. When using three groups of different Speedlites, the C group won't fire unless you choose ratio A:B C. The power output of C group flashes can only be controlled using a master flash and not the ST-E2 transmitter with is limited to A:B groups. The Speedlite transmitter ST-E3-RT is not compatible.

6. **Press the Zoom button until the channel settings blink.** Use the Select dial to change the setting from channels 1 through 4.

7. **Press the Zoom button until the master flash output setting blinks.** Use the Select dial to turn the flash output on or off. Typically when working with a master flash mounted on the camera's hot shoe and slave flashes in remote positions you'll want to turn this to the Off position. By doing this, the master flash will not fire or contribute to the exposure but it will continue to communicate the necessary instructions to the slave flashes being used.

8. **Press the Zoom button to finish, or set the A:B ratio numbers if ratio was selected.** Scroll the dial left or right to set the flash ratio. You can set the flash ratio from 8:1 to 1:1 to 1:8. To set the output level for group C when using three groups of Speedlites, set the ratio to A:B C. When everything else is set, press the Select/Set button in the center of the Select dial until ratio C is blinking, and then scroll the dial left or right to adjust the Flash Exposure Compensation (FEC). This can be adjusted in 1/3 stops to +/–3 stops of light. With no Exposure Compensation, group C fires at the same output as group B.

9. **If desired, press and hold the Zoom/Wireless button again to turn off the wireless system by selecting Off with the Select dial.**

NOTE The first number in each ratio always refers to Speedlites in group A, and the second number of the ratio always refers to Speedlites in group B.

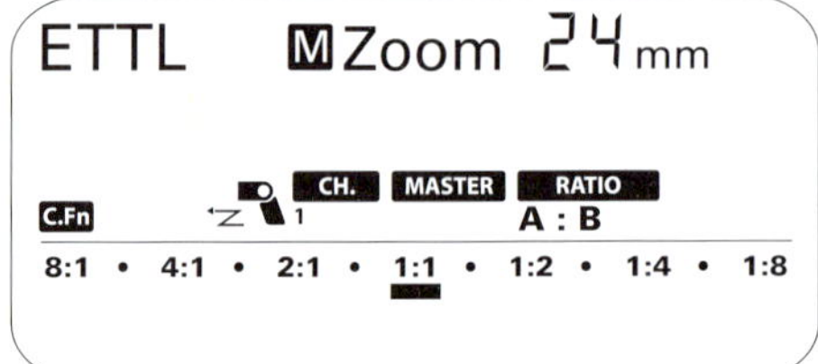

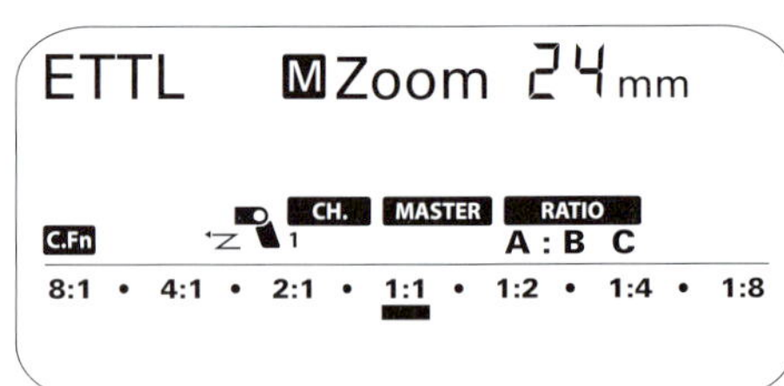

4.6 The 580EX II channel, master, and ratio settings. Ratio settings are shown using an A:B combination in the first image and an A:B C combination in the second image.

Understanding Flash Ratios in the Canon Speedlite System

When setting the ratios for your wireless Speedlites, you are given quite a few options. The ratios are adjustable in increments of 1/2 stop, allowing you 13 different settings. This allows you a total of +/–3 stops of light, enough latitude for most situations.

In the center position is the ratio 1:1. This means that the Speedlites in group A and the Speedlites in group B both fire at the same output. Adjusting the ratio to 2:1 means that the Speedlites in group A fire at twice the output as group B. Conversely, adjusting the ratio to 1:2 means that group A fires at half the power of group B.

Group C fires at the same output as group B when used in ratio A:B C. Use Flash Exposure Compensation to adjust group C to fit your specific lighting requirements.

Setting up the ST-E3-RT

The Speedlite transmitter ST-E3-RT is a new radio-enabled wireless controller, and at this point, it is exclusively compatible with the 600EX-RT Speedlite. Fantastic in many ways, this lightweight, slimmer, and much lower profile transmitter than ST-E2 is an almost exact duplicate of the 600EX-RT in every way except it has no flash head or AF-assist beam. This makes learning how to use it a snap. Once you've learned how to operate the 600EX-RT, you've essentially learned how to use the ST-E3 and vice versa.

When attached to your camera's hotshoe, the ST-E3 becomes the control center (master) for your radio-based wireless Speedlite use. Keep in mind that 2012 or later EOS camera models are required for full access to the camera's onboard external Speedlite menus and full radio-based functionality. However, everything you need is easily accessible using the improved interface and navigation on the new LCD screen located on top of the Speedlite transmitter ST-E3-RT. Keep in mind also that in E-TTL mode the Speedlite transmitter ST-E3-RT can trigger three groups of flashes. A:B and C groups fire if ratios are set. In Group mode (Gr), up to five groups containing up to 15 Speedlites can be independently controlled using E-TTL, Manual (M), Ext.A, or a mixture of each. The ST-E2's ratio, FEC, FEB, and High-speed sync capabilities have been carried over to this model with a much improved navigation system for accessing and controlling these features. See more information earlier in this chapter on setting the 600EX/600EX-RT as a master.

Here are some of the new features of the Speedlite transmitter ST-E3-RT:

▶ Built-in radio-enabled transmitter. Up to 98 feet of wireless radio communication range with 600EX-RT Speedlites and no line-of-sight limitations.

▶ Independent control of the mode setting and light output of up to 5 slave groups containing up to 15 slave Speedlites.

▶ Dot Matrix LCD screen, understandable language for Custom Functions (C.Fn) and Personal Functions (P.Fn), consistent menu item placement, and intuitive navigation.

▶ Four Function buttons that change their function depending on the mode being displayed via a context-sensitive LCD menu system.

▶ Two-way radio communication between the master and slaves. The master and each slave have a Link lamp above the LCD screen switches from from red to green when successful communication has been established. The Test flash button below the LCD displays a red light when all slaves are ready to fire.

▶ When you shoot with a slave using Group mode (Gr) or shoot using Speedlites in ratio groups, a lightning bolt symbol appears next to each slave represented on the LCD when it's ready to fire.

For radio control of one or more off-camera Speedlites, the Speedlite transmitter ST-E3-RT is invaluable because it gives you cable-free operation unencumbered by optical system line-of-sight restrictions, with 98 feet of range. The unit is powered by 2 AA lithium batteries. I prefer to use rechargeable AAs for the ST-E3-RT. The lack of an AF-assist beam is an unfortunate omission and something Canon will hopefully address in the next version. Low-light shooters shouldn't have to rely on an additional 600EX-RT solely for this purpose.

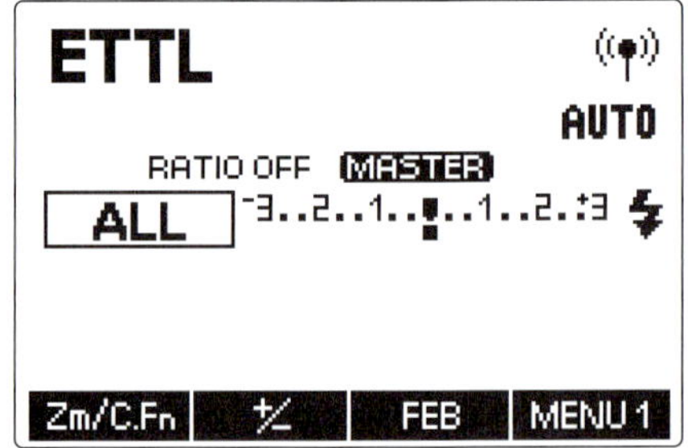

Courtesy of Canon

4.7 The Speedlite transmitter ST-E3-RT and 600EX-RT Speedlite share similar menus. This screen shows the ST-E3-RT in Radio Transmission Wireless Shooting mode set to E-TTL. Note the lightning bolt symbol next ALL indicating slave flashes are ready to fire.

To set up the ST-E3-RT Speedlite transmitter, do the following (the ST-E3-RT is exclusively a master commander):

1. **Attach the Speedlite transmitter ST-E3-RT.** Mount the ST-E3-RT on your camera's hot shoe. Slide the hot shoe locking switch on the bottom of the transmitter to the right to lock it into position.

2. **Turn on the Speedlite transmitter ST-E3-RT.** Slide the OFF/LOCK/ON switch to the On position.

3. **Select a mode using the Mode button.** Choose E-TTL, Manual (M), Stroboscopic (Multi), or Group (Gr).

4. **Set up Group mode (Gr) if desired.**

> **NOTE** For details on how to complete Steps 4 through 7, see the instructions earlier in this chapter on setting up the 600EX/600EX-RT as a master.

5. **Set a ratio if desired.**

6. **Use Auto Channel Selection or manually select a channel.**

7. **Select a personal pin number ID for your channel.**

8. **Choose High-speed sync if desired.** Press Function button 4 (Menu 1) three times to display Menu 4. Press Function button 2 (Sync) to toggle High-speed sync (⚡H) on and off.

> **NOTE** To lock the settings on the Speedlite transmitter ST-E3-RT and prevent them from being changed, slide the Power switch to the Lock position.

4

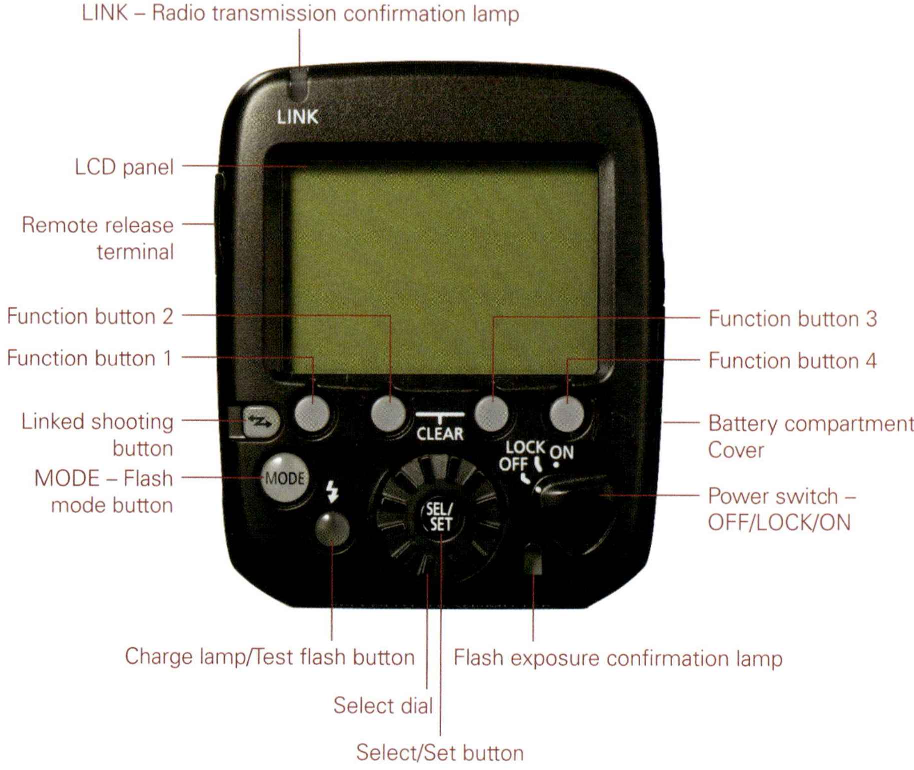

Courtesy of Canon

4.8 Control panel of the Speedlite transmitter ST-E3-RT

Setting up the ST-E2

The ST-E2 Speedlite transmitter is a joy to work with. Lightweight, compact, and very balanced when it's connected to the camera's hot shoe, it becomes the control center for your wireless shooting. All the necessary changes can be made right from the back panel. Keep in mind that while the ST-E2 can trigger three groups of flashes, only the A:B groups will fire if ratios are set.

Here are some of the features of the ST-E2:

▶ Control of three groups of Speedlites with the ability to control the slave's light output.

▶ An AF-assist beam that is compatible with 28mm and longer lens focal lengths. The AF-assist beam has an effective range of approximately 2.0 to 32 feet along the periphery (in total darkness). The ST-E2 can come in handy as an AF-assist tool, even if you aren't using flash, in low light situations where locking focus can be a challenge.

▶ Flash ratio control and adjustment and channel control. The flash ratio control for the A:B ratio is 1:8 to 8:1, in 1/2-step increments or 13 steps.

▶ FE Lock, Flash Exposure Bracketing, Flash Exposure Compensation, Stroboscopic flash, and High-speed sync (FP flash) in High-speed sync mode for flash synchronization at all shutter speeds. Flash Exposure Confirmation during FE Lock is indicated when the flash exposure level icon is lit in the viewfinder. If the flash exposure is insufficient, the icon blinks. After the flash fires, the ST-E2's flash confirmation lamp lights in green for 3 seconds.

▶ Infrared pulse transmission system with a range of approximately 12 to 15 meters (39.4 to 49.2 feet) indoors, and approximately 8 to 10 meters (26.2 to 32.8 feet) outdoors. The flash transmission coverage is +/–40 degrees horizontal and +/–30 degrees vertical.

For multiple off-camera Speedlite shooting, the ST-E2 is invaluable because it gives you cable-free operation and precise flash ratio control. The unit is powered by CR5 lithium batteries. I prefer to use rechargeable CR5s for the ST-E2, which provide approximately 1,000 to 1,500 transmissions per charge.

To set up the ST-E2 Speedlite transmitter, follow these steps:

1. **Attach the ST-E2 to your camera's hot shoe and lock with the switch on the lower-left side of the transmitter.**

2. **Turn the ST-E2 on using the power switch.**

3. **Select the proper channel using the Channel button.** The channel number is illuminated when selected. Keep pressing the Channel button to select different channels.

4. **To turn on the ratio feature, press the Ratio button.** The Ratio On lamp lights up when activated.

5. **Adjust the flash ratio settings using the left and right arrow buttons.** The lamps under the ratio designations are illuminated when selected.

6. **Press the High-speed sync button to turn this feature on or off.**

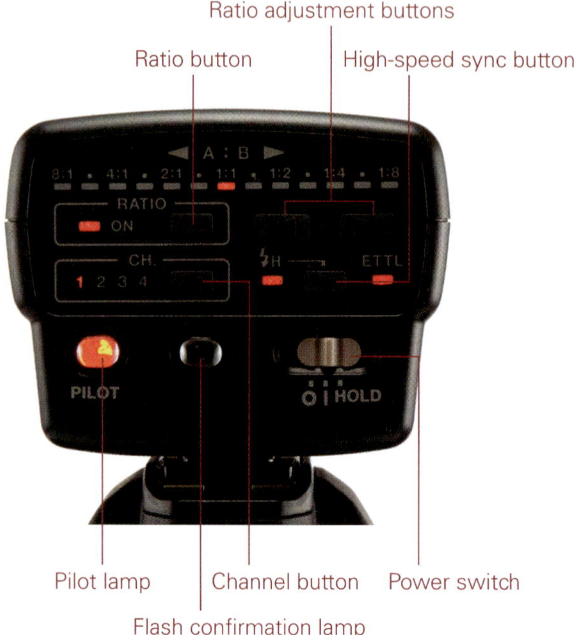

4.9 Control panel of the ST-E2

NOTE To lock the settings on the ST-E2 and prevent them from being changed, slide the Power button to the Hold position.

Slaves

There is perhaps no more fun in flash photography than when you use multiple wireless Speedlites to create colorful, stunning photographs. I use the 600EX/600EX-RT and the Speedlite transmitter ST-E3-RT or the 580EX II and the ST-E2 transmitter with Speedlites, and I add light modifiers depending on the subject and the mood I'm trying to create. As stated previously, the two systems differ in the way they commnicate wirelessly and their resulting range and capabilities. When you use optically based wireless systems like the 580EX II and ST-E2 outdoors, you have to ensure that the signal between the Speedlites and or transmitter is direct, or in a line of sight. In an interior setting, you have a bit more flexibility in setting up the flashes. Systems that are enabled for radio communication like the 600EX-RT and Speedlite transmitter ST-E3-RT have a much greater range and no line-of-sight restrictions.

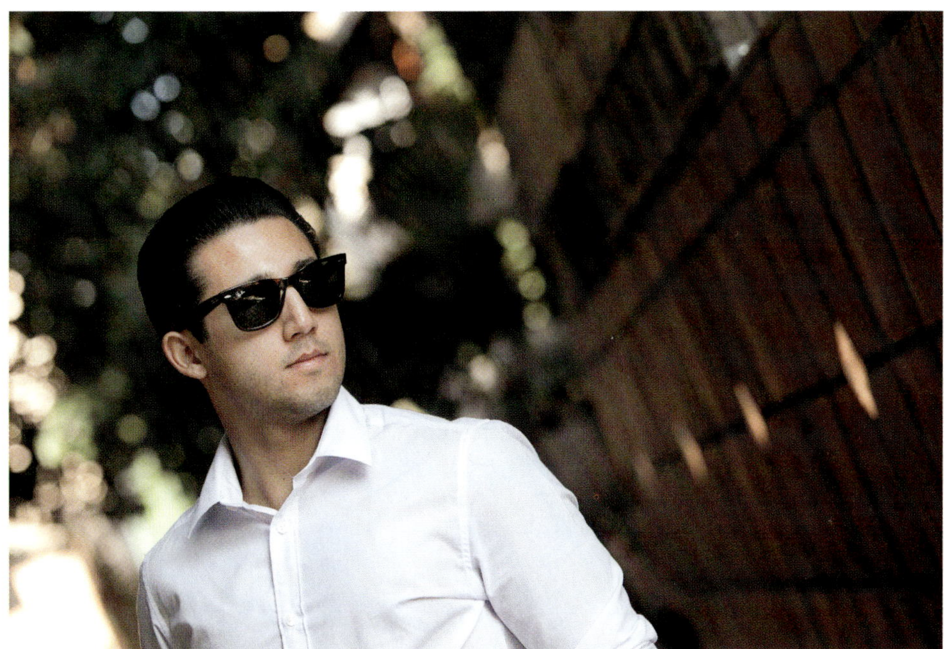

Courtesy of Dennis Urbiztondo

4.10 Here the slave flash, fired wirelessly, was placed camera left and bounced into a Hanson Fong bounce card that was attached. Exposure: ISO 400, f/4.5, 1/250 second with an EF 70-200mm f/2.8L USM lens.

Setting up the 600EX/600EX-RT as a remote slave

To set up the 600EX/600EX-RT for use as a wireless remote slave flash, follow these steps:

1. **Turn on the Speedlite and select Radio or Optical Transmission Wireless Shooting.** Slide the OFF/LOCK/ON switch to the On position. Press the Linked Shooting button (⇆) repeatedly until either Radio Transmission Wireless Shooting (((⸙))) Slave mode or Optical Transmission Wireless Shooting (⚡) Slave mode is selected. In Radio Transmission Wireless Shooting mode, the master can either be a 600EX-RT or Speedlite transmitter ST-E3-RT. If the master and slave are communicating, the green Link lamp on both will be lit. In Optical Transmission Wireless Shooting mode, the master can be a 600EX/600EX-RT, 580EX II, 580EX, 550EX, either of the Macro Speedlite flashes, the ST-E2 Speedlite transmitter, or the pop-up flash on the newest EOS cameras.

2. **Set up Group mode (Gr).** In Radio Transmission Wireless Shooting (((📶))) Slave mode, press Function button 3 to select the slave group A, B, C, D, or E. By default the 600EX-RT is set to the A slave group. Press Function button 2 (**+/−**) to activate the FEC value scale and use the Select dial to choose the desired +/− 3 stops of power in 1/3-stop increments. In Optical Transmission Wireless Shooting mode (⚡), the 600EX/600EX-RT also defaults to the A slave group. Press Function button 3 to select slave group A, B, or C. Press Function button 2 (+/−) to activate the FEC value scale and use the Select dial to choose the desired +/− 3 stops of power in 1/3-stop increments. Press the Select/Set button to confirm your choice.

3. **Set the zoom value.** Press Function button 4 again to return to Menu 1. Press Function button 1 (**Zm/C.Fn**) to highlight the manual zoom value in the upper-right corner of the LCD screen. Use the Select dial to scroll left or right to set the flash head zoom to match the focal length of the lens you're using or to use a different zoom amount (20mm–200mm) for creative effect. Press the Select/Set button to confirm your choices. The zoom head feature allows you to set how much of the scene you want to cover with the flash.

4. **Use Auto Channel Selection or manually select a channel.** In Radio Transmission Wireless Shooting (((📶))) Slave mode (600EX-RT), press Function button 4 until you access Menu 3. Press Function button 1 (**CH**) to highlight the channel indicator in the upper-right of the LCD screen. The default is Auto Channel Selection mode. Use the Select dial to choose channels 1–15, and press the Select/Set button to confirm your choice. Note that the channel scanning feature is only available on radio-enabled masters. Press Function button 4 until Menu 3 is selected and press Function button 2 (**ID**) to enter a personal pin number ID. This is intended to help reduce the chance of radio interference from people nearby using the same channel.

When you're using the 600EX/600EX-RT in Optical Transmission Wireless Shooting Slave mode (⚡), press Function 4 button (Menu 1) twice to enter Menu 2. Press Function button 1 to highlight the channel in the upper-right corner of the LCD and use the Select dial to choose channels 1–4. Press the Select/Set button to confirm your choice.

NOTE In both Radio (((📶))) and Optical (⚡) Wireless modes, both the master and the slave must share the same channel setting for wireless flash to function.

Setting up the 580EX II as a remote slave

To set up the 580EX II for use as a wireless remote slave flash:

1. **Turn on and set the master unit to E-TTL.** The master can be a 580EX II, 580EX, 550EX, either of the Macro Speedlite flashes, the ST-E2 Speedlite Transmitter or the pop-up flash on the newest EOS cameras.

2. **Press and hold the Zoom/Wireless button to enter the Wireless setup menu.** Both Off and the wireless icon blink on the Speedlite's LCD. These settings include the flash head zoom range (24mm–105mm), the communication channel (1–4), and the slave group (A, B, or C). When the specific setting is ready to be changed, it blinks.

3. **Set the flash status to Slave.** Press and hold the Zoom/Wireless button until the display blinks, then turn the Select dial until Slave blinks, and then press the Select/Set button to confirm.

4. **Set the zoom.** Press the Zoom/Wireless button again and scroll the dial left or right to set the flash head zoom to match the focal length of the lens you're using or use different zoom settings for creative effect. The zoom head feature allows you to set how much of the scene you want to cover with the flash.

5. **Set the channel.** Scroll the dial left or right to set the channel on which the flashes communicate with each other.

   NOTE Both the master and the slave must be set to the same channel number for wireless flash to work.

6. **Set the slave group.** You can have up to three different groups of Speedlites: A, B, or C.

   NOTE The slave ID only needs to be set when you're using two or more groups of flashes.

Setting up the 430EX II as a remote slave

To set up the 430EX II for use as a wireless remote slave flash, follow these steps:

1. **Turn on and set the master unit to E-TTL; this will be either another Speedlite or an ST-E2 transmitter.**

2. **Press and hold the Zoom button for two seconds or more to set the flash for wireless slave operation and additional settings.** These settings include the flash head zoom range (24mm–105mm), the communication channel (1–4), and the slave ID (A, B, or C). When the specific setting is ready to be changed, it starts blinking.

3. **Set the zoom.** Press the + or – button to set the flash head zoom to match the focal length of the lens you're using or use different zoom settings for creative effect. The zoom head feature allows you to set how much of the scene you want to cover with the flash.

4. **Set the channel.** Press the + or – button to set the channel on which the flashes communicate with each other.

NOTE Both the master and the slave must be set to the same channel for wireless flash to work.

5. **Set the slave group.** You can have up to three different groups of Speedlites: A, B, or C.

Setting Up a Wireless Manual Flash

Changing from E-TTL mode to Manual mode is not as scary as it sounds. Sure, photographers in the old days had to figure out some guide numbers charts that used to be on flashes and set their flashes accordingly. They also had to wait a few days to get their results back from the lab. In that amount of time, camera settings and flash-to-subject distances could be forgotten, replaced by other details in life unless they were written down. However, today, with digital cameras and the ability to review your results on the camera's LCD monitor immediately (chimping), more time is spent shooting than figuring out manual flash output settings.

Getting a handle on manual flash output is as easy as turning on a water faucet when you consider the similarities. If you need a lot of water in a hurry, you turn it on full blast. If you only need a tiny bit of moisture to seal an envelope, you release only a drop or two.

Manual flash output works in a similar fashion. I rarely use the two extremes — 1/1 to full power or 1/128 for the 600EX/600EX-RT and 580EX II or 1/64 for the 430EX II — and I find myself nearly always in the middle of the range, 1/16, 1/8 power settings, and so on. In fact, that's where I start, somewhere in the middle of the range, and much like a chef, I add a little bit of power here and take away some there. It's all about molding and shaping the light to perform the way you want it to.

Another consideration in my lighting setup is that the full power setting uses up batteries faster, which produces slower recycle times. Conversely, using low power or adding more Speedlites so that you can adjust them to lower power settings individually speeds up recycle times and extends battery life. You can also adjust the effect of the Speedlite's contribution to the scene by physically moving the flash closer or farther away from the subject to control the amount of light hitting the scene.

600EX/600EX-RT in Manual mode

To set up for manual wireless flash on the 600EX/600EX-RT in Master mode, follow these steps:

> **NOTE** In the previous section's steps you were in Slave mode. The Speedlite can't be in Slave mode for this step. If the unit is in Slave mode, use the Linked Shooting button to switch to Manual (M) Master mode in either Radio or Optical modes.

1. **Turn on the Speedlite.** Slide the OFF/LOCK/ON switch to the On position.

2. **Select Radio or Optical Transmission Wireless Shooting.** Press the Linking Shooting button (⭪) repeatedly and choose either Radio Transmission Wireless Shooting (⦙) Master mode or Optical Transmission Wireless Shooting (↗) Master mode.

3. **Set the 600EX/600EX-RT to Manual.** Press the Mode button to change the flash from E-TTL to Manual (M).

4. **Set master flash output.** Press Function button 4 (Menu 1) once until its LCD name changes to Menu 2. Press Function button 1 to toggle the flash output on (⚡) or off (⚡). Typically, when you're working with a master flash mounted on the camera's hot shoe and with slave flashes in remote positions, you want to turn this to the Off (⚡) position. When you do this, the master flash does not fire or contribute to the exposure but it does continue to communicate the necessary instructions to the slave flashes being used.

5. **Set Flash Exposure Compensation (FEC).** By default, the Speedlite is in the ALL group, meaning the power settings you assign for the master (if firing) and the slaves apply uniformly to all linked Speedlites. Press Function button 2 (▮+⁄−▮) to highlight the FEC value scale and use the Select dial to choose +/− 3 stops of power in 1/3-stop increments. Press the Select/Set button to confirm your settings.

6. **Set a ratio if desired.** Press Function button 2 (**RATIO**), once to change ALL to A and B groups. Press Function button 2 again to add the C group. Press Function button 3 (**Gr**) to highlight the group's power you want to adjust. Function button 3 temporarily changes to indicate the selected group and display either A +/–, B +/–, or C +/–. Press Function button 3 again (or the Select/Set button) to highlight the output power scale, and use the Select dial to choose the desired setting from 1/1 (full power) to 1/128 power. Press Function button 4 to go backward in the menus if necessary. Press the Select/Set button to confirm your settings.

7. **Set up Group mode (Gr) if desired.** Press the Mode button to toggle modes and choose the Group mode (Gr). This mode allows control with the master of up to five groups in Wireless Radio mode (((•))). To access Groups A, B, C, D, and E, use Function button 3 (**Gr**) on Menu screen 1 in the Group mode. Use the Select dial to toggle through the groups, each highlighted when selected. Press the Select/Set button or Function button 3 (which now indicates which group is selected) to access the power scale for that Speedlite or group. Use the Select dial to choose a power setting in 1/3-stop increments up to +/– 3 stops for the selected group, press the Select/Set button to confirm, or do nothing and the Speedlite confirms your ratio selection after 5 seconds.

   Once you are in Group mode, press Function button 3 (**Gr**). Note that the names on the LCD screen for Function buttons 1 and 2 have changed to ON/OFF and A/MODE. After you press Function button 3 (**Gr**), one of the Speedlite's groups is highlighted. Using Function buttons 1 and 2, you are able to individually turn off or on a group (Speedlite or group of Speedlites) or change the mode of that group from E-TTL to Manual or Ext.A. You are now able to mix and match E-TTL and manual flash at the same time and control them all from the master or camera (2012 or later EOS camera model required). Once a group is selected, press Function button 1 (ON/OFF) to toggle the group on or off. Use Function button 2 (A/MODE) to toggle between available modes for that group (E-TTL, M, Ext.A). If a group is in Manual (M) mode, the group can be adjusted from 1/1– 1/128 power by pressing Function button 3 (**Gr**) in Menu 1, using the Select dial to choose the group you've set to (M) mode, pressing Function button 3 or the Select/Set button to enter the power value scale, and rotating the Select dial to the desired power setting. Press the Select/Set button to confirm.

8. **Set Zoom value.** In Menu 1, press Function button 1 (**Zm/C.Fn**) to highlight the manual zoom value in the upper-right corner of the LCD screen. Use the Select dial to scroll left or right to set the flash head zoom to match the focal length of the lens you're using or to use a different zoom amount (20mm–200mm) for creative effect. Press the Select/Set button to confirm your choices.

9. **Use Auto Channel Selection or manually select a channel and ID.** In Radio Transmission Wireless Shooting Slave mode (600EX-RT), press Function button 4 until you access menu 3. Press Function button 1 (**CH**) to highlight the channel indicator in the upper-right of the LCD screen. The default is Auto Channel Selection mode. Use the Select dial to choose channels 1–15, and press the Select/Set button to confirm your choice. Channel scanning is only available on the master. Press Function button 4 until Menu 3 is selected and press Function button 2 (**ID**) to enter a personal pin number ID. This is intended to help reduce the chance of radio interference from people nearby using the same channel.

   When using the 600EX/600EX-RT in Optical Transmission Wireless Shooting (⚡) Slave mode, press Function button 4 (Menu 1) twice to enter Menu 2. Press Function button 1 to highlight the channel in the upper-right corner of the LCD and use the Select dial to choose channels 1–4. Press the Select/Set button to confirm your choice.

10. **Choose High-speed sync if desired.** Press Function button 4 (Menu 1) three times to display Menu 4. Press Function button 2 (**SYNC**) to toggle High-speed sync (⚡H) on and off.

11. **Confirm communication.** If you've also powered on and set up your slaves, the green Link lamp on the master and slave(s) should be lit, indicating successful communication.

12. **Turn off wireless Master mode if desired.** Press the Linked Shooting button (⇆) to toggle through the various wireless modes and turn off the wireless system.

580EX II in Manual mode

To set up for manual wireless flash on the 580EX II in Master mode, follow these steps:

1. **Turn on the Speedlite.** Slide the On/Off switch to the On position. Press the Mode button to change the flash from E-TTL to Manual (M). Confirm that the flash is set to Master mode.

NOTE In the previous steps you were in Slave mode. The Speedlite can't be in Slave mode for this first step. If the unit is in Slave mode, you can't switch out of E-TTL unless you press and hold the Mode button.

2. **Set the 580EX II to Master.** Press and hold the Zoom/Wireless button until the display blinks and then turn the Select dial until Master blinks. Press the Select/Set button to confirm your selection.

3. **Press the Select/Set button.** The manual flash output setting will blink. Use the Select dial to set the flash's desired output. You have 21 different power levels available in 1/3-stop increments.

4. **Press the Zoom button.** This selects the flash head zoom range so that it can be changed. When the 580EX II is ready to change, it blinks. Set the flash head zoom to match the focal length of the lens you are using.

5. **Press the Zoom button again.** This sets the zoom and highlights the ratio setting so that it can be changed. Use the Select dial to choose from ratio off, ratio A:B, or ratio A:B C.

   When using only one group of Speedlites, set the ratio to ratio off. When using two groups, set the ratio to ratio A:B. When using three groups, set the ratio to ratio A:B C.

6. **Press the Zoom button to highlight the channel settings.** Use the Select dial to choose from channels 1 through 4.

7. **Press the Select/Set button in the center of the dial to choose the group.** When the group letter is blinking, use the dial to set the desired output level. Press the Select/Set button to cycle through the groups.

8. **Turn the Select dial to set the desired light output.** Then press the Select/Set button to confirm or do nothing, and after a few seconds the display will stop blinking.

Setting slaves for manual flash

You can also set your slave units to function entirely manually. Changes need to be made on the slave unit itself; any changes made on the master unit do not affect the power output of the slaves. This takes a little more effort, but remember, you're *making* pictures, not just taking them.

When setting up my Speedlites for manual remote use, I start by setting all the masters and slaves to the same power output settings, placing them where I want them, and working from there. After my lights are situated, I add any light modifiers I'm planning on using such as such as diffusers, snoots, gobos, grids, and colored gels. Light modifiers reduce the light output of the Speedlites they're attached to in varying degrees, so if I start with all the Speedlites set the same in manual, I know how far from that baseline they are and can begin adjusting as needed.

600EX/600EX-RT

To set the 600EX/600EX-RT as a manual slave, follow these steps on the master:

1. **Turn on the Speedlite and set it as master or use the Speedlite Transmitter ST-E3-RT.** Slide the OFF/LOCK/ON switch to the On position. This is your master. If you're using the Speedlite transmitter ST-E3-RT, it is a master by default. If you're using the 600EX/600EX-RT, press the Linked Shooting button (↰) to toggle through the wireless modes and select either Radio Transmission Wireless Shooting (((•))) Master mode or Optical Transmission Wireless Shooting (↗) Master mode.

2. **Switch the master to Manual.** Using the Mode button, select Manual (M) mode on the device you're using as your master.

3. **Select the Wireless Transmission mode on the slave Speedlite(s).** Press the Linked Shooting button (↰) to toggle through the wireless modes and select either Radio Transmission Wireless Shooting (((•))) Slave mode or Optical Transmission Wireless Shooting (↗) Slave mode.

4. **Set the number of groups.** On the master, in Menu 1, press Function button 2 (RATIO) to switch from ALL (RATIO OFF) to A and B groups. Press Function button 2 again to add the C group.

5. **Set the power level output of each group.** On the master, press Function button 3 (Gr) to highlight the group with the flash output you want to adjust. Function button 3 temporarily changes to indicate the selected group and displays either A +/–, B +/–, or C +/–. Press Function button 3 again (or the Select/Set button) to highlight the output power scale. Use the Select dial to choose the desired setting from 1/1 (full power) to 1/128 power. Press Function button 4 (↰) to go backward in the menus if necessary. Press the Select/Set button to confirm your settings.

6. **Set Zoom value.** On the slave, in Menu 1, press Function button 1 (Zm/C.Fn) to highlight the manual zoom value in the upper-right corner of the LCD screen. Use the Select dial to scroll left or right to set the flash head zoom to match the focal length of the lens you're using or use different zoom amount (20mm–200mm) for creative effect. Press the Select/Set button to confirm your choices.

7. **Set the channel and ID.** In Radio Transmission Wireless Shooting (((•))) Slave mode (600EX-RT), press Function button 4 until you access Menu 3. Press Function button 1 (CH) to highlight the channel indictor in the upper-right of the LCD screen. The default is Auto Channel Selection mode. Use the Select dial to choose channels 1–15, and press the Select/Set button to confirm your choice. Channel scanning is only available on the master. Press Function button

4 until Menu 3 is selected and press Function button 2 (█ ID █) to enter a personal pin number ID. This is intended to help reduce the chance of radio interference from people nearby using the same channel.

When using the 600EX/600EX-RT in Optical Transmission Wireless Shooting (⚡) Slave mode, press Function 4 button (Menu 1) twice to enter Menu 2. Press Function button 1 to highlight the channel in the upper-right corner of the LCD and use the Select dial to choose channels 1–4. Press the Select/Set button to confirm your choice.

8. **Confirm communication.** The green Link lamp on the master and slave(s) is lit if they are successfully communicating.

580EX II

To set the 580EX II as a manual slave, follow these steps:

1. **Turn on the Speedlite.**

2. **Set the 580EX II to Slave.** Press the Zoom/Wireless button for two seconds or longer until the display blinks. Turn the Select dial until Slave blinks and press the Select/Set button to confirm.

3. **Press the Mode button for two seconds.** This sets the flash to Manual mode. You see a blinking M on the LCD and the power level indicated.

4. **Press and hold the Select/Set button.** The M and the power level blink.

5. **Set the power level output using the Select dial.** The power level can be set to 1/1 or full power, all the way down to 1/128 power.

6. **Press the Select/Set button to save the power setting.**

430EX II

To set the 430EX II as a manual slave, follow these steps:

1. **Turn on the Speedlite.**

2. **Set the 430EX II to slave by holding down the Zoom/Wireless button for two seconds or longer.**

3. **Press and hold the Mode button for 2 seconds.** This sets the flash to Manual Slave mode. You see a blinking M on the LCD.

4. **Press and hold the Select/Set button for 1 second.** The M and the power level blink.

5. **Set the power level output using the + or – button.** The power level can be set to 1/1 or full power, all the way down to 1/64 power.

6. **Press the Select/Set button to save the power setting.**

Using Wireless Multi-Stroboscopic Flash

You can use your 600EX/600EX-RT and 580EX II to fire a slave using the Multi-stroboscopic flash mode. Although the 430EX II does not have the ability to do multi-stroboscopic flash on its own, when you use it as a slave with the 600EX/600EX-RT (optical transmission wireless shooting) or 580EX II as a master, this function does become available to you.

Setting Up Channels and Groups or Slave IDs

In this section, you look at how to set channels and slave IDs to be used with wireless flash.

Channels

When using a Speedlite in the wireless mode, you can decide which channel your master unit uses to communicate with the slave. In Optical Transmission Wireless Shooting mode ( ), you have four channels numbered 1 through 4 to choose from, and it doesn't really matter which one you use. This feature is included because professional photographers sometimes shoot alongside each other using similar equipment, such as at a sporting event or stage performance. To prevent another photographer's Speedlites from setting off your own (and vice versa), you can set your master flash or transmitter to a different channel.

When you use the 600EX-RT in Radio Transmission Wireless Shooting mode ( ) and the Speedlite Transmitter ST-E3-RT (which is always in Radio Transmission Wireless Shooting mode), you have additional channel options available, including 15 channels (1–15), Auto channel select mode, Channel Scan mode, Manual channel selection, and personal pin number IDs for channels.

As previously described, channels are different than groups. All the Speedlites you wish to use can be set to different groups but must all be set to the same channel.

Groups

When you use more than one Speedlite, set up your Speedlite's slave in separate groups in order to adjust the lighting for each group to produce different quantities of light, unless you are shooting in Manual power mode. Setting each group to different output levels enables you to creatively control the light that falls on your subject. For many shooting situations, I like to vary the light output to show texture, some color, and contouring.

Your subject in relation to the background determines the lighting setup. In an ideal world, there would be excellent backgrounds everywhere, but in much of the location portrait work I do, there aren't. You still have to come back with results, and so I often use different groups to light stubborn areas of my shot that are going too dark. The size of the light source, distance to subject, diffusers, grids, light modifiers, and gels are the tools I use to fine-tune the light and get the shot.

> **NOTE** The channel and slave group setting must be set on each individual Speedlite for them to function properly.

600EX/600EX-RT

To set channels, personal pin number IDs for channels, groups, and ratios using the 600EX/600EX-RT, follow these steps:

1. **Select a channel and personal pin number ID.** Use Auto channel selection (600EX-RT) or manually select a channel. When using the 600EX-RT in Radio Transmission Wireless Shooting mode ((( )), press Function button 4 (Menu 1) twice to enter Menu 3. Press Function button 1 (**CH**), and the selected Channel number or Auto (600EX-RT radio mode) appears in the upper-right corner of the LCD. Use the Select dial to choose the desired channel. The same channel must be selected for the master and all slaves to function properly. The 600EX-RT is in Auto channel select mode by default. Pressing function button 2 (**ID**) enables you to enter a personal pin number ID to further reduce the chances of radio interference in the event someone nearby is using the same channel. When using channels 1–15 in Radio mode, pressing Function button 3 (**SCAN**) scans signal strength and displays a screen where you can select the strongest channel using the Select dial to move between channels. If you need to go back in the menu system, use Function button 4 (⤺). Press the Select/Set button to confirm your choice.

   When you use the 600EX/600EX-RT in Optical Transmission Wireless Shooting mode (⚡), press Function 4 button (Menu 1) twice to enter Menu 2. Press

Function button 1 (**CH**) to highlight the channel in the upper-right corner of the LCD and use the Select dial to choose channels 1–4. Press the Select/Set button to confirm your choice.

2. **Set up Group modes (Gr).** Press the Mode button to toggle modes and choose the Group mode (**✳ MODE**). This mode allows control with the master of up to five groups in Wireless Radio mode. To access Groups A, B, C, D, and E, use Function button 3 (**Gr**) on Menu screen 1 in the Group mode. Use the Select dial to toggle through the groups; each is highlighted when selected. Press the Select/Set button or Function button 3 (which now indicates which group is selected) to access the power scale for that Speedlite or group. Use the Select dial to choose a power setting in 1/3-stop increments up to +/– 3 stops for the selected group, press the Select/Set button to confirm, or do nothing and the Speedlite confirms your ratio selection after 5 seconds.

Once you are in Group mode, press Function button 3 (**Gr**). Note that the names on the LCD screen for Function buttons 1 and 2 have changed to ON/OFF and A/MODE. After you press Function button 3 (**Gr**), one of the Speedlite's groups is highlighted. Using Function buttons 1 and 2, you are able to individually turn off or on a group (Speedlite or group of Speedlites) or change the mode of that group from E-TTL to Manual or Ext.A. You are now able to mix and match, E-TTL and manual flash at the same time and control them all from the master or camera (2012 or later EOS camera model required). Once a group is selected, press Function button 1 (ON/OFF) to toggle the group on or off, use Function button 2 (A/MODE) to toggle between available modes for that group (E-TTL, M, or Ext.A). If a group is in Manual (M) mode, the group can be adjusted from 1/1–1/128 power by pressing Function button 3 (**Gr**) in Menu 1, using the Select dial to choose the group you've set to (M) mode, pressing Function button 3 or the Select/Set button to enter the power value scale, and rotating the Select dial to the desired power setting. Press the Select/Set button to confirm.

3. **Set up a Ratio.** Press Function button 4 once to enter Menu 2. Use Function button 2 to in E-TTL mode to toggle between ALL (Ratio Off), A:B Ratio, or A:B and C Ratio for Speedlites or groups of Speedlites. Press Function button 3 (**Gr**) or Select/Set button to toggle between A:B and the ratio scale. Function buttons are context sensitive and the name of Function button 3 on the LCD screen will temporarily change to A:B+/–. When the ratio value scale is highlighted, use the Select dial to choose the desired ratio. If you've selected the A:B and C ratio option, when you're in the Ratio Setting mode (Function 3 button — (**Gr**)), you can switch from A:B to C by using the Select dial. This temporarily changes Function button 3's title on the LCD screen to C +/–. Press the Select/Set button or Function button 3 to access the Ratio value scale for C.

Set your desired ratio. In all cases, once the desired ratio is selected, press the Select/Set button to confirm, or do nothing and the Speedlite confirms your ratio selection after 5 seconds.

In Manual mode, press Function button 2 on Menu screen 1 to access Ratio settings for A, B, and C. Press Function button 3 to select A, B, or C and press it again or use the Select/Set button to access the ratio value scale for the desired group. Use the Select dial to set the desired ratio value on the scale, press the Select/Set button to confirm or do nothing and the Speedlite confirms your ratio selection after 5 seconds.

In Multi mode, use Function button 4 on Menu screen 1 to advance to Menu screen 2. Use the Function button 2 (**RATIO**) to set the desired groups, ALL (Ratio Off), A, B, or C. Once the groups are set, press Function button 3 (**Gr**) to select the group and adjust its power. With group A, B or C highlighted, use either Function button 3 or the Select/Set button to access to the ratio scale for the selected group. Function 3's title on the LCD temporarily changes to indicate which group is selected and displays A +/–, B +/–, or C +/–. Use the Select dial to set the desired ratio value on the scale, press the Select/Set button to confirm, or do nothing and the Speedlite confirms your ratio selection after 5 seconds.

NOTE When you're using only one group of Speedlites and you want them all to fire at the same power output, set the master ratio group setting to ALL. This disables any ratio settings. The master flash is always A group. When using two groups, choose ratio A:B. When using three groups of different Speedlites, the C group won't fire unless you choose ratio A:B C.

580EX II

To set channels and slave IDs using the 580EX II, follow these steps:

1. **Set the 580EX II to Slave.** Press the Zoom/Wireless button for two seconds or longer until the display blinks. Turn the Select dial to select Slave, and then press the Select/Set button to choose.

2. **Press the Zoom button.** This selects the flash head zoom range so it can be changed. When it is ready to change, it blinks. Set the flash head zoom to match the focal length of the lens you are using.

3. **Press the Zoom button again.** This sets the zoom and highlights the channel setting so it can be changed. Use the Select dial to choose from channel 1, 2, 3, or 4, matching your selected channel on the master.

4. **Press the Zoom button again.** This highlights the slave ID setting so it can be changed. Use the Select dial to choose from slave ID A, B, or C.

5. **Press the Select/Set button to save the settings.**

430EX II

To set up channels and slave IDs using the 430EX II, follow these steps:

1. **Set the 430EX II to Slave.** Press and hold down the Zoom/Wireless button for two seconds or longer.

2. **Press the Zoom button.** This selects the flash head zoom range so it can be changed.

3. **Press the Zoom button again.** This sets the zoom and highlights the channel setting so it can be changed. Press the +/– buttons to choose from channels 1, 2, 3, or 4.

4. **Press the Zoom button again.** This highlights the slave ID setting so it can be changed. Press the +/– buttons to choose from slave ID A, B, or C.

5. **Press the Select/Set button between the +/– buttons to save the settings.**

Setting Flash Exposure Compensation

Occasionally, you may find yourself in interesting lighting situations where you read the scene and just know that it's going to trick the camera. For example, you may be shooting strongly backlit scenes, or you may have reduced the ambient exposure on the camera by adjusting Exposure Compensation and now want to boost the flash a little.

Photographers use the terms *plus* or *minus EV* (exposure value) to describe any time they purposely override the camera's E-TTL shutter speed/aperture combinations that would yield the same exposures. Taking away EV reduces the exposure while adding EV increases it.

You use Flash Exposure Compensation (FEC) to fine-tune the settings to achieve the desired brightness of the overall image, much like adjusting the manual settings, although you have less range to choose from. The FEC can be adjusted in 1/3-stop increments, up to +3 and down to –3 stops of light.

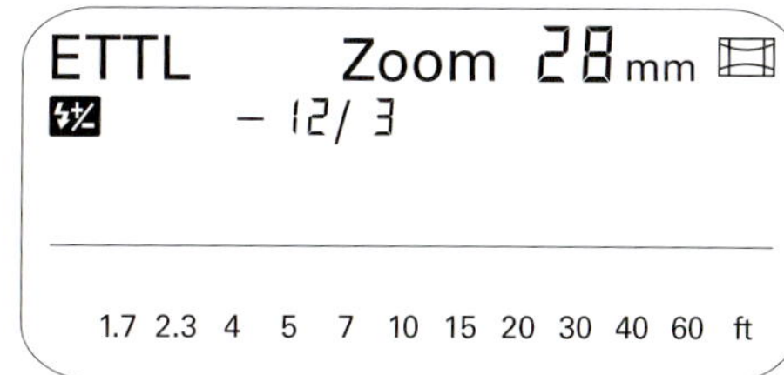

4.11 The 580EX II with Flash Exposure Compensation set to underexpose by –1 2/3 f-stops

Setting FEC with the 600EX/600EX-RT set to Master

To set Flash Exposure Compensation, follow these steps:

1. **Turn on the Speedlite.** Slide the OFF/LOCK/ON switch to the On position.

2. **Select Radio or Optical Transmission Wireless Shooting.** Use the Linked Shooting button (⇄) to choose the desired wireless Master mode.

3. **Set the desired FEC.** Use Function button 4 to navigate to Menu 1 if you aren't already there, and press Function button 2 (⚡) to highlight the FEC value scale. Use the Select dial to choose from +/– 3 stops of power in 1/3-stop increments. Note the FEC +/– and value icons appearing in the upper-left of LCD screen.

4. **Press the Select/Set button to confirm settings.**

Setting FEC with the 580EX II set to Master

To set Flash Exposure Compensation, follow these steps:

1. **Turn on the Speedlite.**

2. **Be sure the 580EX II is set to Master.**

3. **Press the Select/Set button in the middle of the Select dial.** This brings up the FEC compensation factor. It blinks when it is ready to change.

4. **Scroll the Select dial left or right to adjust the amount of FEC.**

5. **Press the Select/Set button in the middle of the Select dial to confirm the settings.**

Setting FEC slave flashes

When you're using a 580EX II Speedlite as the master, this technique works well. But when you're triggering wirelessly with the ST-E2 wireless transmitter, the FEC must be set on the slave flash.

600EX/600EX-RT

To change FEC on the 600EX/600EX-RT in Slave mode, follow these steps:

1. **Turn on the Speedlite.** Slide the OFF/LOCK/ON switch to the On position.

2. **Select Radio (((ꝉ))) or Optical Transmission Wireless (⚡) Shooting.** Use the Linked Shooting button to choose the desired wireless Master mode.

3. **Set desired FEC.** Use Function button 4 to navigate to Menu 1 if you aren't already there, and press Function button 2 (⚡) to highlight the FEC value scale. Use the Select dial to choose from +/– 3 stops of power in 1/3-stop increments. Note the FEC +/– and value icons appearing in the upper-left of LCD screen.

4. **Press the Select/Set button to confirm settings.**

580EX II

To change FEC on the 580EX II in Slave mode, follow these steps:

1. **Press the Select/Set button.** The FEC icon flashes when changes are ready to be made.

2. **Scroll the Select dial left or right to make the adjustments.**

3. **After your adjustments are made, press the Select/Set button again to set them.**

430EX II

To change FEC on the 430EX II in Slave mode, follow these steps:

1. **Press the Select/Set button.** The FEC icon begins to blink.

2. **Press the + or – button to adjust the settings accordingly.**

3. **Press the Select/Set button again to save the setting.**

Testing and Modeling Flash from a Slave Unit

In Radio Transmission Wireless Shooting (((•))) with the 600EX-RT set as a slave unit, you can perform a test flash and modeling flash.

> **NOTE** Model flash from a 600EX-RT slave unit in Radio Transmission Wireless Shooting mode is possible on 2012 or later EOS camera models.

To perform a test flash or modeling flash using a 600EX-RT Radio Transmission Wireless Shooting Slave mode, do the following:

1. **Press Function button 4 to navigate to Menu 2.**

2. **To fire a test flash, press Function button 3 (TEST).**

3. **To fire a modeling flash, press Function button 2 (Model).**

> **NOTE** When you're using more than one master, model flash is performed by the master whose Link lamp is green.

Remote Release from a Slave Unit

In Radio Transmission Wireless Shooting with the 600EX-RT set as a slave unit, it is possible to perform remote control shooting. EOS digital camera models released prior to 2012 require an SR-N3 release cable to connect the camera and mater unit.

Follow these steps to perform remote release from a 600EX-RT slave unit in Radio Transmission Wireless Shooting mode (((•))):

1. **Connect the master unit to the camera that will be used remotely.** On pre-2012 camera bodies, use the SR-N3 release cable to connect the master to the camera's N3 remote control terminal.

> **TIP** Connect the SR-N3 cable while power is off on both the remote camera and master unit.

2. **On a 600EX-RT set as a Radio Transmission Wireless Shooting (((•))) slave unit, press Function button 4 to navigate to Menu 2.**

TIP Turn off autofocus. Focus the lens on the remote camera manually. The camera's shutter won't release if autofocus fails.

3. **Press Function button 1 (REL) on the slave to send a release signal to the master unit.** The shutter releases.

TIP If you're using more than one master, release is performed by the master whose Link lamp is green.

Linked Shooting with Radio Transmission

Linked shooting allows automatic shutter release of remote cameras that have a 600EX-RT or Speedlite transmitter ST-E3-RT attached (in Radio Transmission Wireless Shooting (((ᵠ))) Slave mode) via a 600EX-RT (in Radio Transmission Wireless Shooting Master mode (((ᵠ))) or a Speedlite transmitter ST-E3-RT.

This feature supports up to 16 units including the master and slave, and it is intended for shooting a subject from multiple angels at the same time.

To perform linked shooting with radio transmission, follow these steps:

1. **Attach a 600EX-RT or Speedlite transmitter ST-E3-RT to the master camera.**

2. **Set the master to Radio Transmission Wireless Shooting (((ᵠ))).**

NOTE EOS digital camera models released prior to 2012 (with an N3 remote control terminal) require an SR-N3 release cable to connect the slave flash and slave camera unit.

3. **Attach a 600EX-RT or Speedlite transmitter ST-E3-RT to each camera being used for linked shooting.**

NOTE In Linked shooting the Speedlite transmitter ST-E3-RT can be used either as master or slave unit.

4. **Press the Linked Shooting button (⇆) to set the flash or transmitter to the normal (nonwireless) E-TTL mode.** Make sure wireless operation is off.

5. **Press the Linked Shooting button (⇆) repeatedly until LINKED SHOT appears in the upper-left corner of the LCD screen.** The slave unit is now set.

6. **Press the Linked Shooting button (⇆) again to set the master unit for the Linked Shooting mode.**

7. **Choose the channel and ID.** Press Function button 2 (**CH**) and using the Select dial to choose a channel. Press Function button 3 (**ID**) to enter a personal pin number ID for the channel.

8. **Set up the camera's shooting functions.**

9. **Set up all the Speedlites.** Repeat Steps 4–8 and set all Speedlites to Linked Shooting mode master or slave unit. If you're using the Speedlite transmitter ST-E3-RT, set it the same way.

10. **Set up the cameras being used as slave units.** Check the slave Speedlite or Speedlite transmitter's Link lamp to make sure it's green, indicating successful communication.

11. **Release the shutter on the master unit camera (with the master Speedlite or Speedlite transmitter attached) and the slave unit camera shutter is released.**

Here are some tips on linked shooting:

▶ Turn off autofocus on slave unit cameras and focus their lenses manually; they won't release their shutters if autofocus fails.

▶ After a linked shooting exposure is made, the Link lamp on slave units briefly becomes orange.

▶ A slight lag between the master camera unit and slave unit cameras is normal. In order for linked shooting to function, Flash Firing in Flash function settings must be enabled.

▶ The range for linked shooting is 98 feet depending on conditions such as position, environment, and weather.

▶ When using Live View with the master camera unit, Silent Live View shoot must be disabled in Personal Functions. Set P.Fn-07 to 0 to disable.

▶ Linked shooting may be performed without the master Speedlite or Speedlite transmitter being attached to the camera. Press Function button 1 (**REL**) on the master Speedlite or Speedlite transmitter to trigger all slave unit cameras.

▶ Speedlites are able to fire in Linked Shooting mode.

Using Your Speedlites with Radio Triggers

When I'm using Speedlites other than the 600EX-RT or ST-E3-RT transmitter, I rely on radio triggers. The way I set up my Speedlites for use with remote triggers depends entirely on the kind of triggers I'll be using, the controls I want, the number of lights in play, and the things I want to accomplish. If I'm using manual triggers, such as the RadioPopper JrX, PocketWizard Plus, or MultiMAX, I start by attaching the transmitter/transceiver to the camera's hot shoe and the receivers/transceivers to each Speedlite. Next, I place my remote Speedlites where I want them, select groups and channel settings, and determine the power settings for each Speedlite in the scene.

If I'm working with E-TTL triggers such as RadioPopper PX or PocketWizard's MiniTT1 transmitter and FlexTT5 Transceiver, it's simply a matter of connecting the radio transmitter to my Speedlite and mounting it on my camera's hot shoe. Typically I disable the light output of the master flash and use it only for communicating exposure information to all the remote slave flash units. Next, I set my remote Speedlites as slaves and attach the receiver triggers to each one. Once these steps are taken, I'm free to place the lights where I want them and add any light modifiers I'm planning on using, such as diffusers, snoots, gobos, grids, and colored gels.

Using your Speedlites with PocketWizards

PocketWizards have earned a reputation for reliability and outstanding range. The PocketWizard remote triggering system was developed in a secret electronics lab in Burlington, Vermont, in the late '80s and has attracted a growing legion of loyal professional photographers ever since. For the Speedlite System, PocketWizard radio systems enable greater working distances and more reliability outdoors than Speedlites do but complement them perfectly. Unlike Speedlites, PocketWizards use radio frequencies to communicate with flashes instead of infrared (IR), as the Speedlites and ST-E2 transmitter do.

The Canon Speedlite System uses infrared light (IR) to trigger the flashes to fire. This works well indoors because there are lots of surfaces for the IR signal to bounce off to be picked up by the Speedlite's sensor. Outdoors there usually are not readily available surfaces for this to happen, and the IR has to compete with higher ambient light levels to operate properly. PocketWizards solve this wireless problem. Early PocketWizards had no E-TTL capability, but new models such as the MiniTT1 and FlexTT5 provide wireless E-TTL.

PocketWizards have a very generous 1600-foot range of use, fast sync speeds, locking shoe mount, and a fast FPS (frames per second) rating (up to 12 FPS on capable cameras), and they run on two AA batteries. They also include status-ready and connect LEDs that let you know they are communicating successfully.

In the late 1990s, the PocketWizard line of precision wireless-control devices introduced the Plus and the MultiMAX products. These two products have evolved significantly since then, and I can say from experience that they are extremely reliable and easy to use. The trade-off with this generation of PocketWizards was the lack of TTL or E-TTL capabilities, something photographers came to rely on when using the Speedlite System indoors. PocketWizard addressed this issue with the MiniTT1 and FlexTT5, which include full E-TTL II capability.

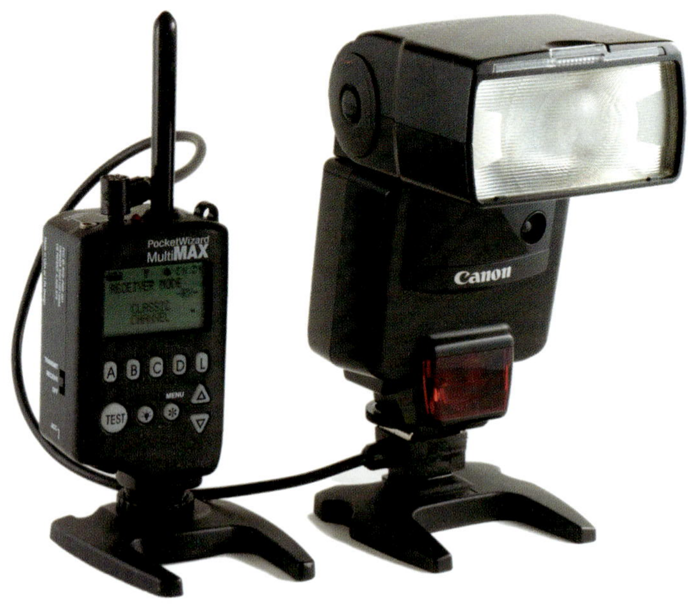

4.12 PocketWizards afford the photographer unlimited possibilities of flash units to use manually, as is the case of this older EZ series Speedlite being triggered remotely.

Setting channels

Because of their popularity, PocketWizards also come with different channel settings to prevent triggering the flashes of other photographers who might be using the same system. These channel settings have no relation to the same numbered Canon channels.

Plus II transceivers and MultiMAXes

PocketWizard Plus II transceivers are the easiest to use and the less expensive than MultiMAX. They are called *transceivers* because they both transmit and receive radio signals so that you can use them attached to the camera and at the remote flash. Plus IIs also include a Mode switch that allows you to fire locally (flash connected to the PocketWizard), remotely (PocketWizard connected to a remote flash), or both.

MultiMAX transceivers are far more sophisticated. They offer a range of 32 different frequency channels and much more timing and firing control. They also offer a Quad-triggering mode that allows you to fire four different flashes separately, together, or in any combination of the four.

PocketWizard now has a new era of PocketWizard E-TTL triggering devices featuring the MiniTT1 transmitter and the FlexTT5 transceiver for Canon. With the ControlTL software platform, these new E-TTL II–capable radio slaves make using off-camera flash as effortless as sliding the unit in, turning it on, and shooting.

Using your Speedlites with RadioPoppers

RadioPoppers are the new kids on block and have quickly established themselves as favorites among serious photographers. Known for their reliability, ease of use, and 1,500-foot range, they consist of two systems: the E-TTL PX system and the less expensive manual JrX system. Each is ready to use straight out of the box, requires no complicated programming, and has 16 channels (all with different frequencies), assuring a good, clean channel no matter what the environment.

The X family of products also plays well with each other. So, whether you are just starting to experiment with your lighting or have six off-camera Speedlites, the RadioPopper X family will accommodate.

The RadioPopper PX System

The PX system has two units: the transmitter and receiver. The PX transmitter converts the electronic pulses from the master flash or ST-E2 on your camera and sends the radio command to the PX receiver on the remote flash. The PX receiver then converts the radio into infrared and feeds that to the flash. The result is that your flash fires, no matter where you position it. The PX system gives you the flexibility to shoot in either E-TTL or Manual, to use groups or ratios, and to sync at shutter speeds up to an incredible 1/8000 second.

To use this system, I set up one Speedlite (550EX, 580EX, or 580EX II) as my master flash and disable the light output of that flash so that it serves only as a device that

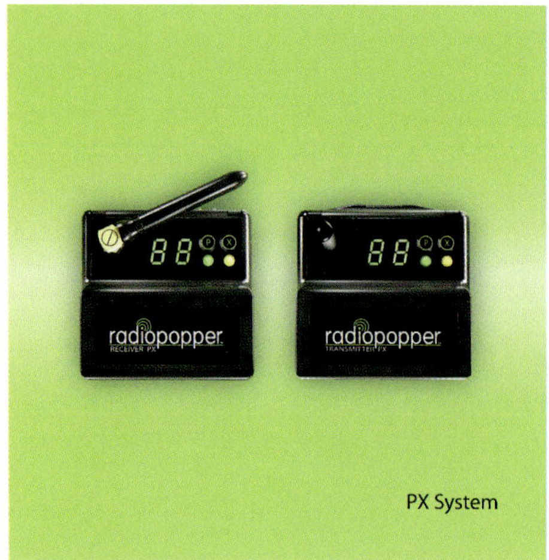

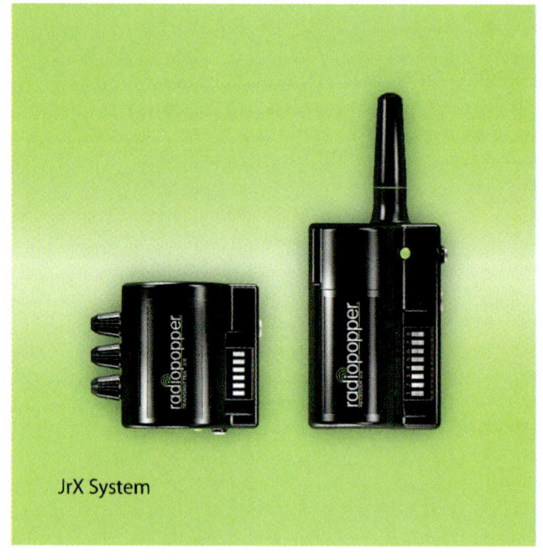

Courtesy of RadioPopper

4.13 The RadioPopper JrX System

Courtesy of RadioPopper

4.14 The RadioPopper PX System

communicates exposure information to the slave flash units. I then attach the RadioPopper transmitter to the top of the Speedlite and mount it on the camera's hot shoe. Then I set flashes as slaves (430EX, 430EX II, 550EX, 580EX, or 580EX II), which I position in the RadioPopper bracket/receiver units, attach to light stands, and place where desired. I'm now ready to shoot wirelessly with full E-TTL communication between the camera, master, and slave flashes. It's that simple!

The RadioPopper JrX System

The JrX system is a less expensive manual trigger that is effortless, plug-n-play technology offering unmatched reliability. Using the RPCube (a hot-shoe accessory), the JrX Studio system also allows power adjustment of up to three groups of Speedlites right from the transmitter mounted on your camera's hot shoe. No more running across the room — turn your lights up and down with a turn of the JrX transmitter dial.

CHAPTER 5

Setting Up a Wireless Studio

The beauty of Speedlites is their small size and portability. You can easily fit several Speedlites, stands, remote triggers, gels, extra batteries, umbrellas, and additional light modifiers into one gear bag.

In this chapter, I show you what equipment you need to set up a home studio suitable for portrait and small product photography. Because not everyone can come to your studio, location work makes up a good part of what photographers do. Being able to quickly grab your gear and go is key. This chapter covers what you need to make your studio mobile. With continuing advances in Speedlite technology and equipment getting smaller and more powerful every day, many tasks previously handled by cases of heavy studio lights can now be achieved with one bag of lightweight Speedlite gear.

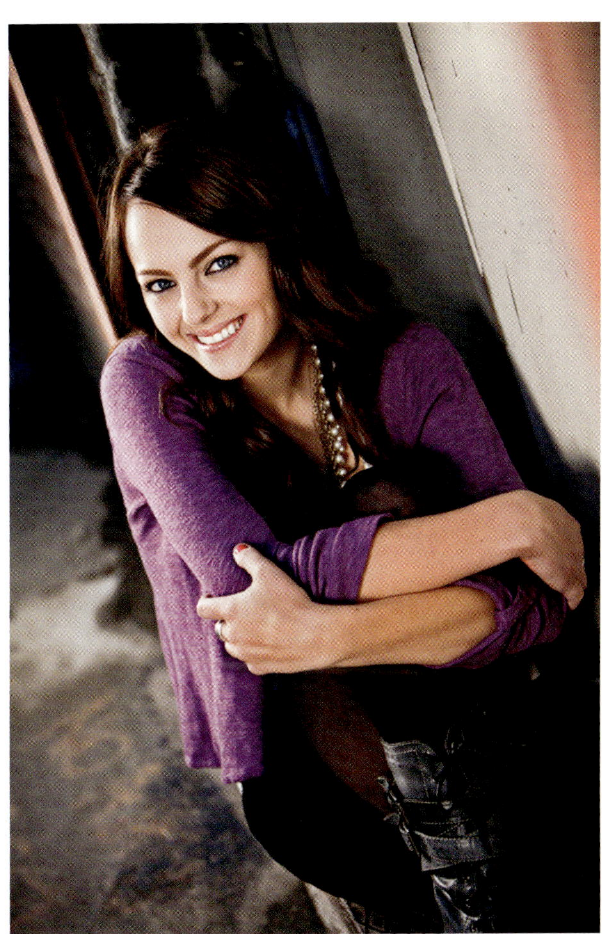

With a few basic tools and an understanding of Speedlites, you can create images like this one. Here, I'm using two off-camera Speedlites, RadioPopper PX receivers/transmitters to provide E-TTL control between the camera and flashes, and two Lastolite EzyBox hot-shoe softboxes. Exposure: ISO 200, f/2.8, 1/200 second with an EF 70-200mm f/2.8L USM lens.

Introduction to the Portable Studio

In addition to a well-equipped studio, most photographers also find that they need a portable lighting kit. This kit should be compact, lightweight, and ready to go whenever you need it. Having a checklist of equipment to pack when you're heading out can be very useful, or even better, a packed bag of gear for location shooting that's always ready and waiting.

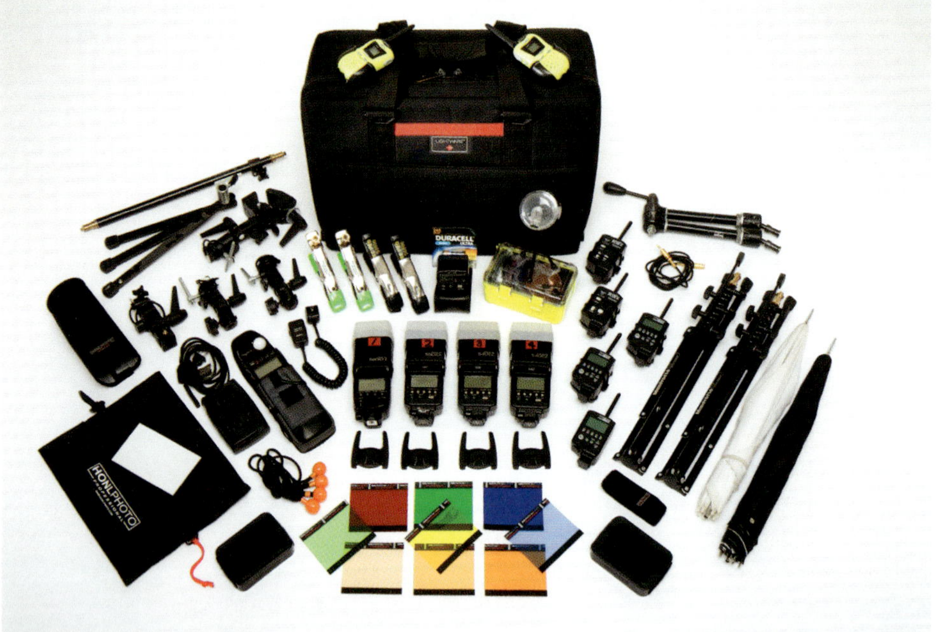

5.1 Everything you need to create beautiful location lighting can easily fit into one bag such as this 22 × 16 × 8-inch Lightware MF 1420 Multi-Format Case. For many assignments, this and a camera bag are all you need.

Ideally, a portable lighting kit should include the following items:

- ▶ At least one Speedlite, preferably radio enabled

- ▶ An E-TTL cord (to get the flash off your camera)

- ▶ One or two collapsible reflectors to fill in shadows created by the flash

- ▶ A collapsible diffuser to filter the sun

- ▶ A compact umbrella or small softbox to soften light from the flash

- ▶ One or more light stands

- ▶ An empty sandbag for each light stand

As your lighting knowledge grows and your technique develops, you'll likely want to add additional equipment to your kit. This includes the following:

- ▶ More Speedlites (ten is excellent, four is great, and you can do a lot with just one or two)

- ▶ Wireless radio transmitters/receivers to remotely trigger these flashes

- ▶ Various grip heads to put in places where stands won't work

- ▶ Brackets for attaching multiple Speedlites to one stand or modifier

- ▶ Softboxes with different shapes and reflective interior surfaces to create different qualities of light

The following sections examine some of the extra equipment to consider as you build your own location lighting kit.

Cables, Cords, and Triggers

Obviously, using cables and cords doesn't fall into the category of working wirelessly. However, I've included them here because they're inexpensive solutions and a great way to get started using your flash off of the camera. If they're long enough, cables and cords can offer plenty of flexibility and portability. There are cables, cords, and accessories of all stripes and colors. Here are the ones I feel are worthwhile.

Extra-long E-TTL cords

Getting your flash off the camera is the single biggest step you can take to dramatically improve the look of your flash photography. However, accomplishing this can seem like an expensive proposition when you're first starting. You have many options at your disposal, including optical slaves, master flash and slave flash arrangements, infrared (IR) E-TTL transmitters (those that maintain a connection with the camera's metering system), radio transmitters and receivers, both manual and E-TTL, and E-TTL cables.

One of the least expensive ways I know to get your flash off the camera while still remaining connected to the camera's metering system is by using an E-TTL cable.

Until recently, these cables have been very short and sold in coiled configurations that caused them to retract, possibly pulling your gear in unwanted directions.

Photographer Syl Arena has recently created an extra-long and uncoiled E-TTL cable, available online at http://ocfgear.com in 16- and 33-foot lengths, for $49 and $65, respectively, at the time of printing. So think about it: If you've got only one Speedlite, you can start taking your flash photography to an entirely different level for about 50 bucks! If you've got two Speedlites, with this extra-long E-TTL cable you'll be able to shoot with not just one but both flashes off the camera in either manual or full E-TTL mode! All you have to do is have the Speedlite that's connected to your camera with the OCR gear E-TTL cable set as the master flash and the second flash set as a slave.

These settings were covered in Chapter 1, but here's a quick refresher. On the 580EX II, just hold down the Zoom button for four seconds and choose the Master Flash option, and then do the same thing on the second flash but set that one to Slave Flash. Now both flashes are connected to the camera's metering system and will fire at the same time. Refer to Chapter 4 for 600EX/600EX-RT instructions.

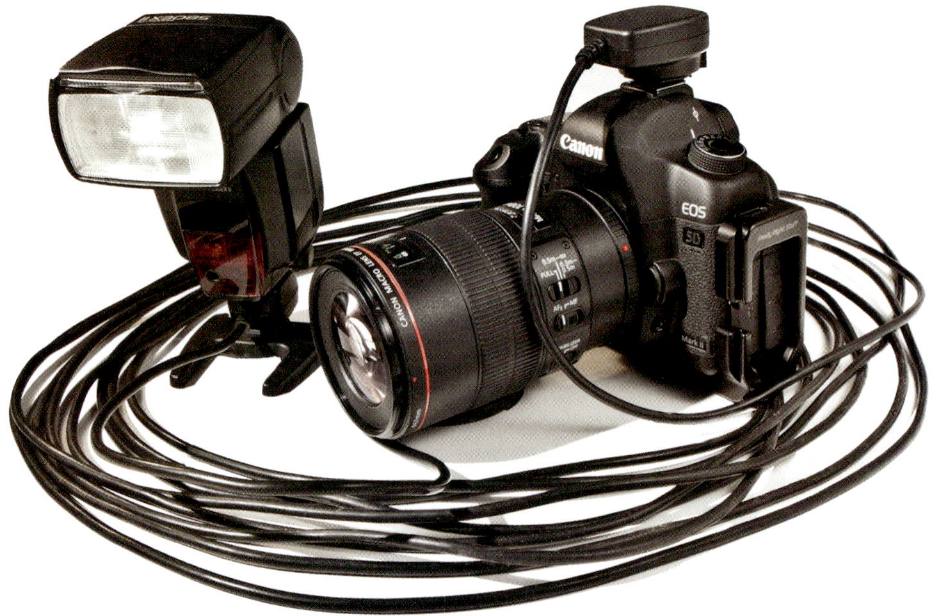

Courtesy of OCF Gear
5.2 OCF Gear's extra-long E-TTL cable pictured with a camera and Speedlite

Custom cables

If you're a tinkerer, jerry-rigger, and do-it-yourselfer like I am, you'll definitely want to know about Michael Bass Designs. Michael Bass is a practicing dentist who also designs custom cables, signal splitters, and brackets.

As you descend into the rabbit hole of multiple Speedlites, E-TTL and non-E-TTL signal splitters, and do-anything-you-want cables, you'll definitely want Michael Bass Designs along as your guide. I use his cables to trigger four Speedlites in full E-TTL mode with only one trigger transmitter and one of Michael's amazing splitters! You can find cool stuff and more information at www.michaelbassdesigns.com.

Cable releases

Cable releases allow you to trigger your camera's shutter remotely while it's mounted on a tripod without ever touching it. This eliminates the possibility of unintended camera shake that can cause blurry images.

Wired and wireless cable releases are a great solution for low-light photography, where long shutter speeds are required. Using a cable release helps you freeze the action with your flash while providing a shake-and-blur-free way to capture the rest of ambient light during long exposures. This is a great way to add some motion to your flash photography.

I use the Vello Wireless ShutterBoss Timer Remote RCW-C2 and ShutterBoss Timer Remote RC-C2. Both have tons of features and are very reliable. More information is available at http://vellogear.com.

Tethered shooting

Tethered shooting, connecting the camera to a computer via a cable or wireless device, is not only a great way to preview images on a much larger, more accurate screen than the camera's small LCD, but also gets your images onto your computer where you want them.

Popular software titles, such as Adobe Photoshop Lightroom, Apple Aperture, and Capture One, allow tethered shooting and remote camera control. Several options are available for connecting your camera to your computer. The simplest, least expensive, and best way to get started with tethered shooting is to use a USB cable to connect your camera and computer. (Check your camera and computer manuals to confirm cable requirements.) As always, when using cables of any kind, exercise caution to avoid injuries from tripping. I recommend taping down cords and cables with gaffers tape whenever possible. Wireless options include camera grips, transmitters, and memory cards that use radio frequencies to transmit the camera's files to a computer. For iPhone and iPad owners, OnOne Software's (www.ononesoftware.com) DSLR Remote app works wirelessly with many cameras over a Wi-Fi network, letting you control the camera remotely and preview exactly what's being captured.

To effectively shoot tethered either in the studio or on location, you'll want some additional hardware specifically for this purpose, for this I recommend a company called Tether Tools (www.tethertools.com). A relatively new and innovative company, Tether Tools manufactures an array of useful equipment that makes tethered shooting much easier.

Radio triggers

Radio triggers allow flashes to be fired wirelessly from the camera. They function in pairs, requiring a transmitter and least one receiver, provide a range of approximately 1600 feet and are available in manual and full E-TTL versions from companies such as RadioPopper (what I use) and PocketWizard. Canon's new flagship Speedlite, the 600EX-RT, and the Speedlite transmitter ST-E3-RT have built-in radio transceivers.

Radio triggers operate by using radio waves and, therefore, are not constrained by the range and line-of-sight limitations of the infrared (IR) technology. IR sensors work well when there is a direct line of sight between both the master flash and slave flash and distance between the two is relatively short. Direct sunlight can also cause problems when using IR sensors.

White Balance and Filters

Controlling white balance and exposure are two of the most important aspects of working with Speedlites. I examine both in the following sections.

White balance and the ExpoDisc

Obtaining the correct white balance in mixed lighting situations can be challenging. An example of this is when flash is your main light source and tungsten (household bulbs), fluorescent, or other kinds of light are also contributing to the exposure. This is a challenge because handheld flash units and studio strobes are balanced for daylight at a color temperature of 5500 Kelvin (K) while tungsten light is between 2700 and 3200 K and fluorescent lights are anywhere from 3400 to 6300 K. When the color temperatures of the light sources present aren't all the same, the result is a different colorcast from each kind of light contributing to an exposure — flash, tungsten, fluorescent, and so on.

> **NOTE** The numbers followed by a "K" in this section are taken from the Kelvin scale, which measures the color temperature of different light sources. Unlike traditional temperature measurements, on the Kelvin scale, the lower the temperature number, the warmer (yellower) the color of the light source, and conversely, the higher the temperature on the scale, the colder (bluer) the color of the light source.

It's when you throw in mercury lamps, xenon short-arc, high-pressure sodium, halogen, and metal halide light sources that your head really starts spinning. Identifying these lights on location and knowing their color temperatures can be difficult even for an expert. In this scenario, it's hard to correctively gel your Speedlites because you're unsure of the temperature to correct for.

Fixing color balance issues in post-production when shooting RAW files can be a time-consuming task and sometimes very challenging. If you're shooting JPEG files, then your white balance is fixed once the exposure is made and cannot be altered after capture. Neither scenario is ideal, so why not get it right in the camera in the first place?

This is where a fantastic tool from ExpoImaging (www.expoimaging.com) called the ExpoDisc saves the day. This simple tool allows you to quickly and easily create a custom white balance for your camera to use that is based on the dominant (main) light source in your scene. I use the ExpoDisc on nearly every shoot, and it saves me a ton of time and unnecessary headaches in post-production.

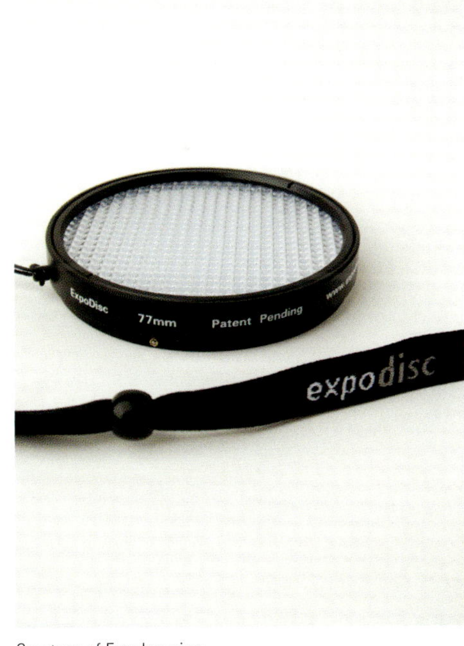

Courtesy of ExpoImaging

5.3 ExpoImaging's ExpoDisc

The big white balance takeaway is this: your camera can only set white balance for a single color temperature. It's that simple. You'll want that temperature to be the same as your main light source (flash) and preferably your ambient light sources as well. If you know the color temperature of the ambient light sources, ideally you'd gel your Speedlites to match them so that all your light is the same temperature. The second step is to use the ExpoDisc to create a custom white balance based on main light source (your gelled Speedlite). If you're unsure of the color temperature of the ambient light (industrial settings, and so on) just use the ExpoDisc to create a custom white balance based on output from your Speedlite (your dominant source) and you're good to go. Please refer to Chapter 3 for additional information about white balance.

Neutral density filters for wider apertures

Shooting with wider apertures is great way to add drama to your images by blurring the background and keeping the focus on what's happening in the foreground. Shooting with Speedlites can present a challenge for this technique because, once at your maximum sync shutter speed, you'll need to stop down your lens to create a balanced exposure, thereby losing those much-sought-after blurred backgrounds. High-speed sync hardware solutions exist and are also discussed in this chapter. However, there is a simple, effective, and inexpensive solution for this problem — neutral density (ND) filters! These filters, available in various densities, attach directly to the front of your lens or to a filter holder and cut the amount of light reaching your camera's meter and sensor in varying degrees. This then allows you to open up your aperture again and get those lovely blurred backgrounds. I use the LEE Filters Gel Snap 4 × 4-inch Filter Holder and 4 × 4-inch Neutral Density Polyester Filter Set (www.bhphoto video.com).

Light Modifiers

Light modifiers are tools you add to your light source(s) to focus, bend, shape, direct, diffuse, color, and reflect light. These tools allow photographers to create the light they want, where and when they want it. If the light you need isn't available, you have to be able to create it. Light modifiers help you do just that.

With the help of accomplished professional photographers like Joe McNally, Syl Arena, and David Hobby of Strobist.com leading the way, the understanding and popularity of Speedlites is increasing every day. If you're the do-it-yourself type or on a tight budget, then the Internet should be your first stop. It's chock-full of tutorials showing you how you can construct your own light modifiers from common household items. If you'd rather get right to shooting instead of tinkering, there's no shortage of amazing light modifiers commercially available for your specific flash.

The Honl Photo Professional Speed system is one such line of products. It's a collection of lightweight, durable, and affordable light modifiers. Designed to universally fit all shoe-mount flashes, these versatile light modifiers provide photographers with an assortment of very useful light-shaping tools.

The Honl Photo Professional Speed system is an assortment of grids, snoots, bounce card reflectors, and gels that attach quickly and easily to any shoe-mount flash via the Speed Strap, a simple, nonslip Velcro strap that wraps around any flash head without the use of annoying adhesives.

Lastolite's Strobo Kit is a clever new addition into the field of lightweight modifiers for Speedlites. This versatile system, designed around a series of magnets, allows grids, gels, and gobos to be attached directly to a flash either individually or in combination. Optional barn doors (four movable panels, mounted top, bottom, left, and right) used to control the shape and spill of light are also available.

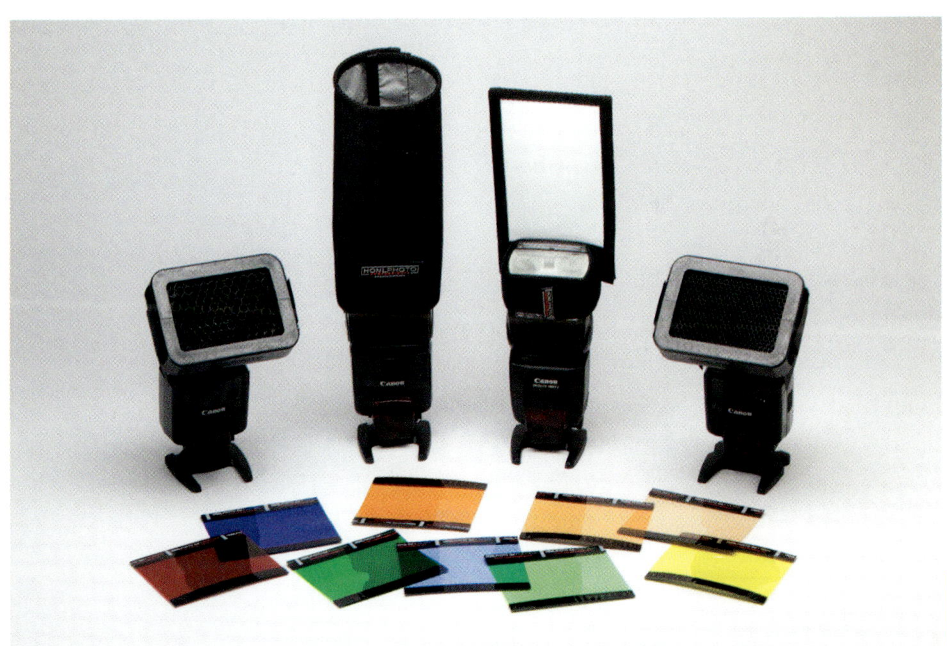

5.4 The Honl Photo Professional Speed system includes gels, grids, a snoot, and a bounce card reflector, each attached using the Speed Strap mounting design.

Both of these systems allow you to bring studio-style lighting control into the field. You can find out more at www.lastolite.us and www.honlphoto.com.

All of these items, as well as what they do and when to use them, are covered in the following sections.

Reflectors

Reflectors do what their name implies: they reflect light. They're primarily used to reflect light back onto a subject and help open up shadow areas, but they also can be used to block harsh light from the sun. If there's one piece of lighting equipment to invest in when you're starting out, this is it. Good quality, inexpensive commercial reflectors are readily available and essentially like having an additional light source without having to pay for one.

That said, almost anything with a white, silver, or gold surface can be used as a reflector — a piece of white foam core, insulation boards with reflective metallic facing, or a white wall. I've even seen pillowcases used in a pinch. If you go the foam core route, try to find a piece that has white on one side and black on the other. That way, you'll be able to add as well as subtract light with the one board!

When using 4 × 8-foot sheets of foam core board in the studio as reflector panels and V-flats (two 4 × 8-foot sheets taped together along the center seam to form a V), you'll want a way to easily position and move these large panels around your studio. Foamcorestands.com makes inexpensive wooden foam core board stands that are perfect for this.

Portable reflectors with multiple reflective surface fabrics are available from many top-quality manufacturers, such as California Sunbounce, Lastolite, F.J. Westcott, and Photoflex. Most of these are either aluminum or PVC tube frames that fit together and then have reflective fabric stretched over them. These types of reflectors, generally available in 4 × 4, 4 × 6, and 4 × 8 feet, break down into portable carrying cases for transport.

When it comes to location shooting, collapsible reflectors are a great option. These super portable reflectors are twistable frames with fabric stretched over them. They are perfect for photographers on the go. The Lastolite 33-inch TriFlip 8-in-1 kit is my tool of choice. It comes with eight different surface skin fabrics (2-stop diffuser, Gold, Sunfire, Sunlite, Silver, SoftSilver, White, Black) and a very useful molded handle for handheld use (an optional mounting bracket for a light stand is also available). It also twists down to a third of its size into a disc-shaped carrying case. Learning how to twist down the reflectors to their compact size can take a little getting used to, but after you get the hang of it, you'll wonder how you ever got along without these great tools.

The surface skin fabrics provided with the TriFlip and other reflectors each create a different quality of light when reflecting it. White produces the softest light, Silver adds more specularity/contrast (a slightly harder edge), Gold adds warmth to the shadowed areas, Sunfire and Sunlite are combinations of Silver and Gold, and the fully opaque Black blocks light entirely.

California Sunbounce reflectors and scrims are also very portable and some of the sturdiest on the market. They're built to last and stand up to the demands of windy location shoots. The 2 × 3-foot Micro Mini is a reflector kit I use (with white and silver and gold and silver fabrics) in combination with the Sunbounce Flash Bracket. This arrangement allows me to handhold or stand mount the reflector with a Speedlite attached to it and bounce the light back onto my subjects. This is a very portable and flexible solution that produces a beautiful, soft light. The entire kit packs into a small shoulder bag that's included. (See Chapter 6 for example images of these tools in action.)

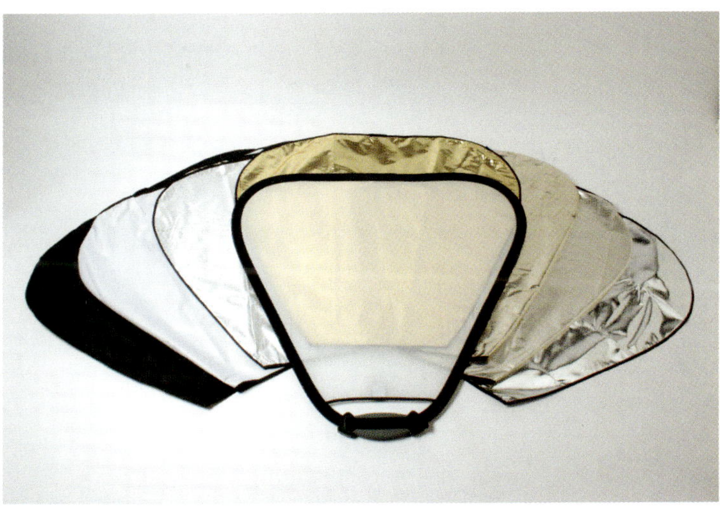

Courtesy of Lastolite

5.5 The Lastolite TriFlip 8-in-1 reflector kit. This 33-inch collapsible reflector comes with eight different surface skin fabrics, has a very useful molded handle, and folds down to a third of its expanded size.

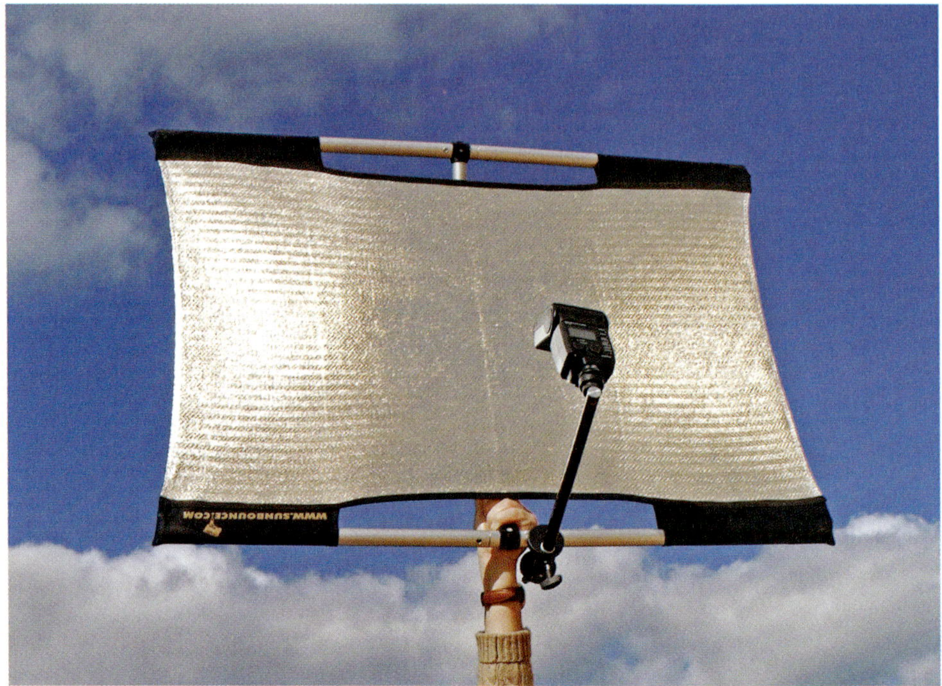

Courtesy of California Sunbounce

5.6 The California Sunbounce Micro-Mini and Sunbounce Flash Bracket provide a portable bounce reflector for location work.

Gels

Gels are thin sheets of polycarbonate or polyester placed in front of a light source, in the path of its beam. They're used in theater, photography, videography, and cinematography to color light either for a creative effect or for color correction.

In photography, gels are used for two reasons: color-correcting the light output of your flash to match the ambient light temperature or adding color to create an effect. Adding gels to a flash diminishes the amount of light reaching the subject from that flash, depending on the flash's strength. This is no problem when shooting E-TTL because the camera and flash processors take the loss of light into account and change the exposure or output accordingly.

When used correctively, gels are a great way to fix color balance in situations such as those where tungsten light and daylight-balanced flash are used together. In this scenario, you know that the color temperature of tungsten light is approximately 2700 K, so you can simply add what's known as a *CTO* (color temperature orange) gel in front of your flash and all the light sources will be the same color temperature.

Gels can be obtained in various sheet sizes from professional camera supply houses like B&H Photo, Adorama, and Calumet. Complimentary gel swatch-books are often available from these vendors, and with a little bit of effort they can easily be removed from the swatchbook and attached to the front of your Speedlite. Top manufacturers include LEE (www.leefilters.com), Rosco (www.rosco.com), Honl Photo (www.honlphoto.com), and Lastolite (www.lastolite.com).

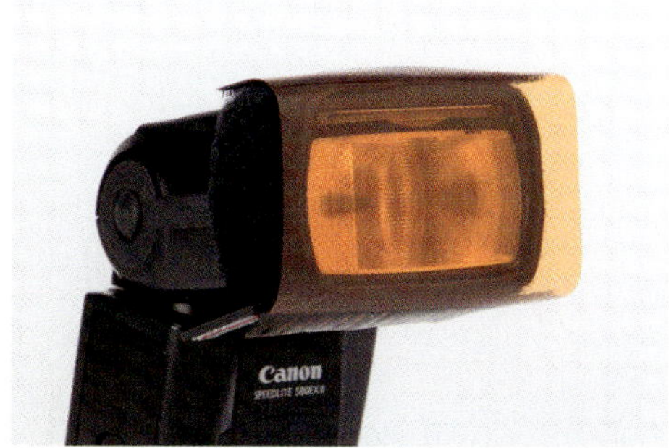

5.7 A Canon 580EX II with a Honl full Color Temperature Orange (CTO) gel mounted to the Speed Strap

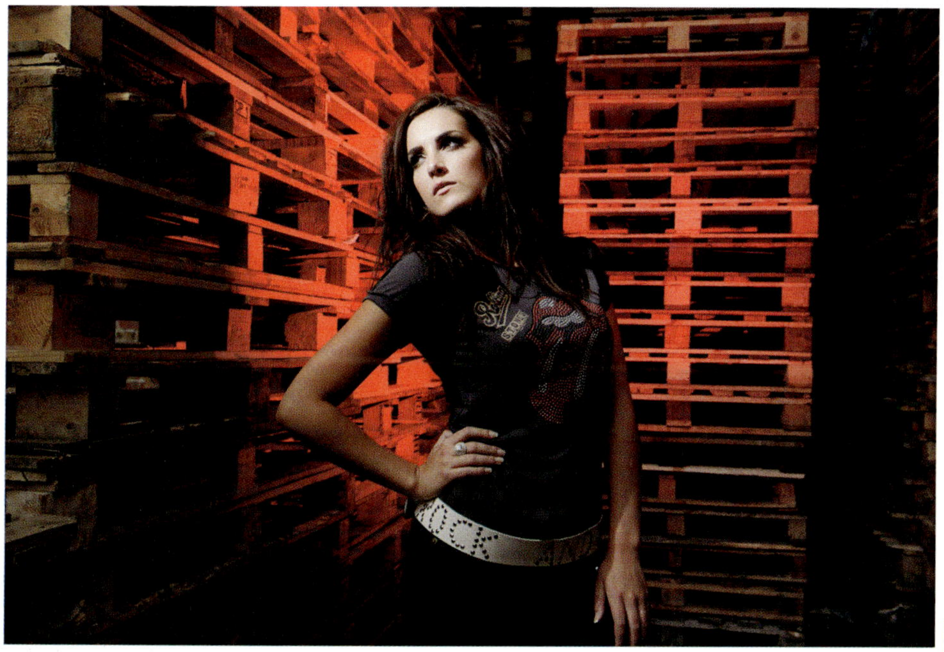

Courtesy of Adam Duckworth

5.8 A red gel is used to add a large area of color to the background of this environmental portrait.

Grids and snoots

Grids and snoots are both used to focus and concentrate light exclusively on specific areas of a subject while excluding others. They help create drama and mood by focusing the viewer's attention exactly where you want it. Using a snoot is an easy way to create a natural in-camera vignette with gradual light falloff. Adding a snoot to the front of your flash concentrates the light into a narrow beam. When using a snoot, you also want to set the Speedlite's zoom setting to the maximum focal length. Because of this reduced spread of light, you want to pay special attention to your aim to assure the light falls exactly where you want it. A few test shots and you should be in business.

Snoots for Speedlites are commercially available from many sources, including Honl Photo, and can also easily be made from common household items. I've seen snoots made from all kinds of things including empty round oatmeal containers! I've also made them out of large round coffee containers that have a silver interior and a translucent plastic cap that can used as a diffuser.

Grids, which also fit over the front of the flash head, are typically either round or rectangular blocks with holes arranged in a honeycomb pattern cut through them, like looking through a handful of cut straws about an inch long. In fact, you can make do-it-yourself versions with everyday drinking straws! They are available in varying degrees of grid pattern tightness. The smaller the honeycomb grid pattern, the tighter or more narrow the resulting pattern of light from the flash. The results can be very dramatic and stylized. Using multiple Speedlites with grids, a technique often used to create an even more dramatic effect, is discussed in Chapter 6.

> **NOTE** When you use gels and grids in combination, the gel should always occupy the first position in front of your Speedlite in your modifier stack. The grid would then have the second position in front of the gel.

A recent entry into the Speedlite grid market is ExpoImaging (www.expoimaging. com). Its Rogue line of grids and corresponding gels are unique due to their patent pending stackable design and the desirable round light pattern they produce. Interchangeable and stackable honeycomb grids provide 16-, 25-, and 45-degree spot lighting control. Their quality of light and systemized approach to adding and subtracting modifiers make this a worthwhile product to have in your bag.

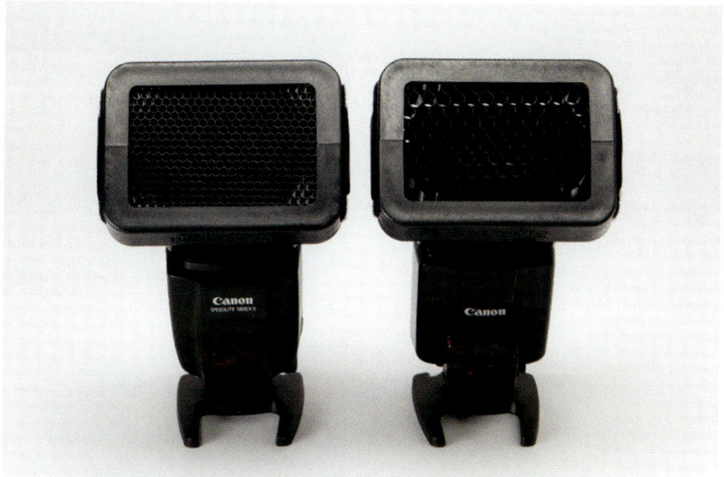

5.9 Grids produce concentrated areas of light that quickly falls off. They're typically available in round or rectangular honeycomb patterned grid material. The tighter the grid pattern, the tighter the pattern of light produced.

Diffusers, small flags, and bounce cards

Diffusers are another must-have tool. They break up light rays and scatter them into different lengths and different directions, producing soft lighting effects, less contrast, and greater *falloff* (the transition between highlights, diffused highlights, and shadows). As discussed earlier in this chapter, the Lastolite line of collapsible reflectors and diffusers are my tools of choice.

Ideally, you want to have one Lastolite 8-in-1 TriFlip and one Lastolite TriGrip, both the same size. This combination allows you maximum flexibility and creative options. The Lastolite TriGrip is a 33-inch collapsible panel that functions as both a diffusion panel and reflector, as described earlier. When the sun is directly overhead, with no cloud cover to help filter the light, a diffusion panel's ability to soften the light is your best friend. Additional models, sizes, and diffusion fabrics are available in larger panel formats (discussed earlier in the reflectors section) from manufacturers such as F.J. Westcott, Photoflex, California Sunbounce, and others.

The ability to block light from the camera's lens and sensor can be very useful when trying to eliminate unwanted lens flare caused by the sun or a light. Flare can be a desirable effect, but in some cases it can degrade image quality. It's a creative choice, and diffusion fabric gives you control over when you want it and when you don't. Black blocking devices, known as *flags,* can be as simple as a piece of cardboard or as complex as large stand-mounted fabric scrims. Whatever gets the job done of shading the lens from the offending light source will do the trick. When used with black fabric, the TriFlip can also be employed as a blocking scrim to completely shade the overhead sun. Black fabric or the 2-stop diffusion fabric is useful for controlling ambient light to varying degrees when using a Speedlite as your main source of illumination.

The next tool you want in your bag is the Sto-Fen. This custom molded cap of frosted plastic fits over the flash head and helps scatter and soften light. It's compact, lightweight, and inexpensive. The Sto-Fen also works well when bouncing light onto surfaces by softening the light prior to it reaching the surface.

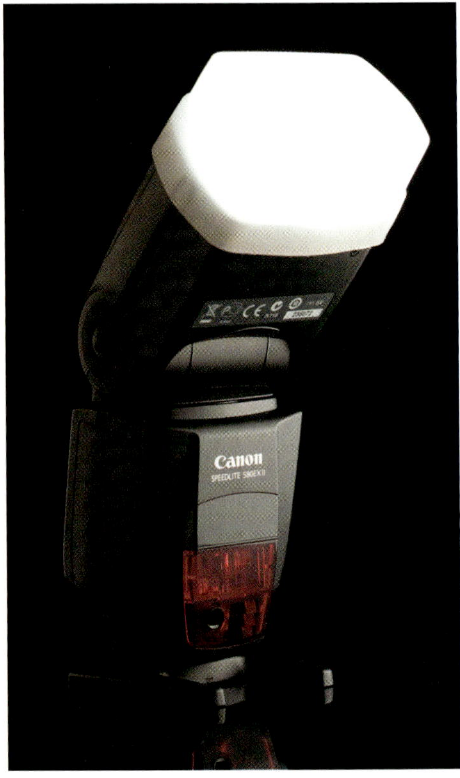

5.10 The Sto-Fen pop-on diffuser. Be sure to get the one that is specific to your model flash.

Another great way to modify light on the go is with the use of small flags, bendable bounce cards, snoots, and light modifiers that mount directly to your Speedlite. These small and very portable tools help shape, focus, and soften the light much like their larger cousins. ExpoImaging's Rogue system (www.expoimaging.com) and Honl Photo's Speed system (www.honlphoto.com) are two of my go-to tool sets. (See Chapter 6 for example images of these tools in action.)

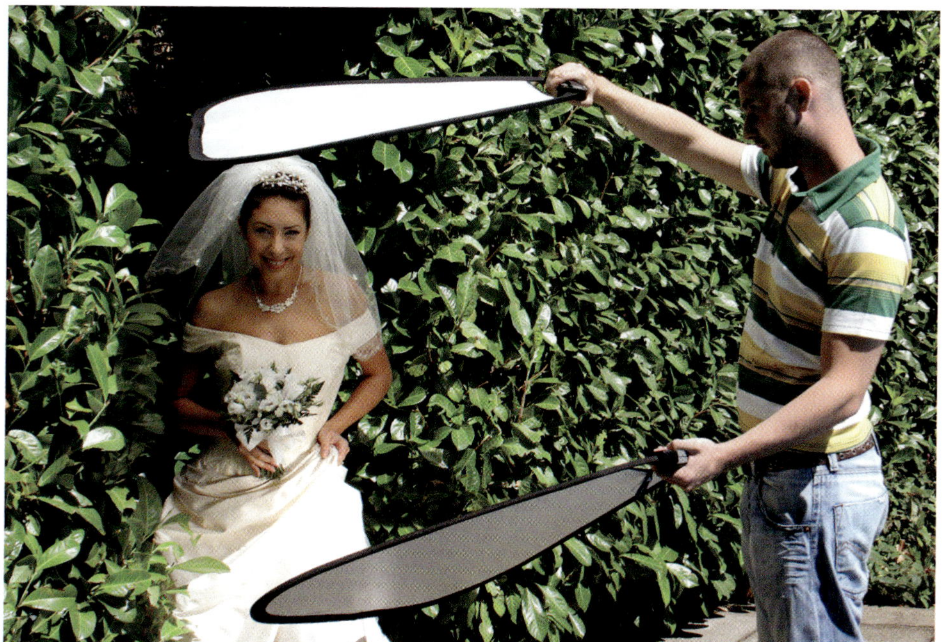

Courtesy of Lastolite

5.11 The Lastolite TriGrip collapsible reflector can be used as either a diffusion panel or a reflector, has a very useful molded handle for handheld use, and twists down to a third of its full size.

Umbrellas

Photographic umbrellas are one the easiest light modifiers to use and should be the first choice for photographers looking to take their lighting technique to the next level. They're lightweight, inexpensive, and included in nearly every lighting kit sold. Photographic umbrellas come in many different sizes and operate just like umbrellas used to keep you dry in the rain. The difference with photography umbrellas is they come with reflective or translucent coverings. Countless brackets allowing umbrellas, Speedlites, and stands to be joined together are readily available from various manufacturers. Note the just-released handheld flash and umbrella bracket at the end of this section for a cool new entry in the bracket category.

Typically, you place the umbrella to the left or right of your subject, aim the flash head directly into it, and point the inside of the umbrella directly toward the subject from above at an approximately 45-degree angle. As counterintuitive as it sounds, the closer an umbrella is to your subject, the softer the resulting light is, and the farther away the umbrella (or any other light source for that matter), the harder the light. Multiple umbrellas can be used to achieve broader lighting coverage for larger groups and various other lighting patterns (see Chapter 6 for examples).

You can choose from three types of umbrellas:

▶ **Standard.** The most common type of umbrella has a black outside covering to keep light from getting through the fabric, with an inside surface coated with a reflective material that is usually white, silver, or gold. These are designed so that you can point your Speedlite into the inside or concave side of the umbrella and bounce the light back onto the subject, resulting in a nondirectional, soft light source. These types of umbrellas can also be very effective when trying to achieve a bright white background (see Chapter 6 for examples).

▶ **Shoot-through.** Manufactured out of translucent nylon material, these umbrellas enable you to fire your Speedlite through them, producing a softer light similar to that of a softbox. As the name indicates, with shoot-through umbrellas, the back or convex side of the umbrella faces your subject, and the flash is fired through the translucent material onto your subject. Because the light source is being

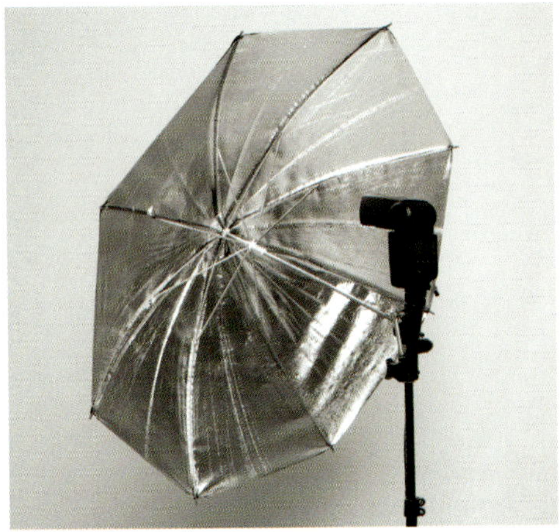

5.12 Stand-mounted, 30-inch, silver umbrella with Speedlite attached

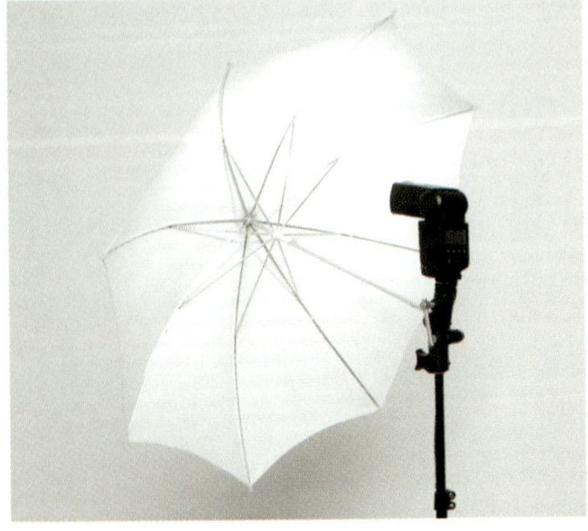

5.13 Stand-mounted, 30-inch, white shoot-through umbrella with Speedlite attached

diffused, the light is softer than that produced by using a standard umbrella.

▶ **Convertible.** Convertible umbrellas have a white, silver, or gold lining inside and a removable black cover outside. You can use these umbrellas to bounce light back toward your subject or, with the backing removed, as a shoot-through. If have only one type of umbrella, this is the one I'd recommend because it's economical and versatile. It's like getting two umbrellas in one. Lastolite recently released an 8-in-1 convertible umbrella that I love, which, as the name implies, is like getting eight umbrellas in one.

Choosing the right umbrella really depends on its intended use. Photographic umbrellas come in various sizes, usually ranging from 25 inches all the way up to 12½ feet. For standard headshots, portraits, and small to medium products, umbrellas ranging from 25 inches to about 40 inches supply plenty of coverage. For full-length portraits and larger products, a 60 to 72-inch umbrella (with two Speedlites inside for maxium power) is generally recommended. If you're photographing groups of people or especially large products, you may need to go beyond the 72-inch umbrella or add a second light with an umbrella of the same size. Generally, the small-to-medium umbrellas lose about 1½ to 2 stops of light over straight-on flash. Larger umbrellas generally lose 2 or more stops of light because the light is being spread out over a larger area. Smaller umbrellas tend to have a much more directional light than do larger umbrellas.

It's important to note that keeping umbrella-to-subject distance as a constant, the larger the umbrella, the softer the light falling on the subject will be. This can be counterintuitive when you are starting out, but it is such an important concept that I think it bears repeating. By moving a light modifier closer, an umbrella in this case, you are also making it larger in relation to your subject. The larger the light source, the softer the light will be. The smaller the light source in relation to the subject, the harder the light.

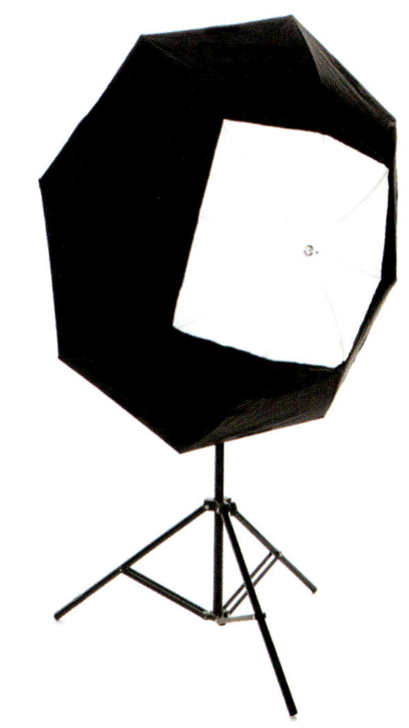

Courtesy of Lastolite

5.14 Lastolite 8-in-1 umbrella. This convertible umbrella offers eight possible variations in one umbrella!

NOTE The closer and larger a light source is to a subject, the softer the light will be and conversely, the farther away and smaller a light source is from a subject, the harder the light will be. Repeat that last sentence out loud until you know it cold!

For studio applications or location work where an assistant is available, larger umbrellas are a great choice for their soft quality of light. Keep in mind that these are large and cumbersome when set up and can take off like a sail if you're working outside on a windy day. So be sure and have a few sand-bags on hand, and an assistant is always a plus.

For on-the-go, light-on-your-feet shooting, smaller is definitely the way to go. There are many options in this category, but my personal favorite for compact umbrellas is the F.J. Westcott collapsible and coverable umbrella style 2011. This umbrella expands to 43 inches, which provides plenty of coverage for standard headshots, portraits, and small to medium product shots, and it folds down to an impressive 14.5 inches for easy transport. Convertible umbrellas are definitely your best bet when traveling because they can do more than one thing and minimize the equipment you need to carry.

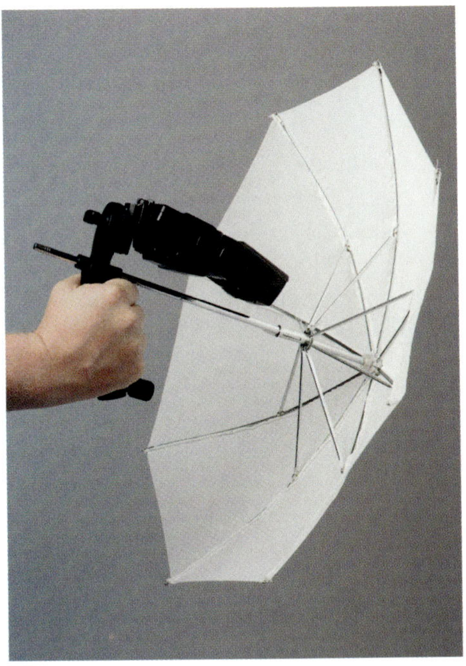

Courtesy of Lastolite

5.15 Lastolite Brolly Grip. This handheld bracket for a Speedlite and umbrella can also be mounted on a standard light stand.

The Softlighter II by Photek (www.photekusa.com) is a bounce-back umbrella with a front diffusion panel. Your Speedlite is mounted and fired pointing into it, away from your subject. The softened light is then reflected back from its white interior panels and softened again as it passes through a diffusion panel on the front of the umbrella. Uniquely constructed of ten reflective panels rather the usual eight, it produces a perfect circle of light as well as pleasing catch-lights and can be easily converted into a shoot-through umbrella. This tool is the perfect choice when beautiful, soft, diffuse light is what you're after. I first saw this modifier used by Annie Leibovitz, and the results were nothing short of amazing. I had to have a set of my own. They're available in three sizes, 36, 46, and 60 inches. I use them with an optional shoe mount light stand/umbrella adapter to accommodate Speedlites.

If you are just getting started with light modifiers, umbrellas are the way to go. They're compact, simple to use, inexpensive, and attach to a light stand with a small bracket available at any photography store for around $20. Starting with a convertible umbrella is a great way to get your feet wet and experiment with the various kinds of light different umbrellas can produce. Find the quality of light you like and expand your collection of umbrellas from there.

Softboxes

As with umbrellas, softboxes are used to diffuse and soften light from a strobe to create a more flattering, natural result. Softboxes range in size from small, 6-inch versions that you mount directly onto the flash head to large boxes that usually mount directly to a studio strobe. Softboxes also come in a variety of shapes, such as large, rectangular softboxes to long, narrow stripbanks that produce thin highlights and directional beams of light.

Softboxes are usually closed around the light source with Velcro tabs, thereby preventing unwanted light from being bounced back toward the camera. The diffusion material evens out the light and reduces the possibility of creating hotspots on your subject. A *hotspot* is an overly bright spot on your subject, usually caused by bright or uneven lighting.

Many softboxes also offer versatility in the way the front panel attaches to it, which enables the photographer to control the spill rate from the light. A large Velcro strip on the front edge of the softbox allows you to mount the front panel either flush or recessed. Flush mounting creates a gradual falloff to the light, while recessed mounting tightens the edge of the light.

In the past, softboxes were generally made to be used with larger studio strobes. With so much innovation in the Speedlite space recently, photographers have many options for Speedlite dedicated softboxes from vendors, including Lastolite, F.J. Westcott, and Photoflex. F.J. Westcott's Apollo line of Speedlite softboxes is a great set of modifiers.

Softboxes designed for studio strobes attach via a device called a *speedring*. A speedring is specific to the type of lights to which it is meant to attach. F.J. Westcott has eliminated the need for speedrings in its Apollo line of softboxes and octabanks (octagonally shaped softboxes), which are designed specifically for use with handheld flashes. These light modifiers open just like an umbrella and, along with a Speedlite, can be mounted to a light stand with the use of a swivel head bracket.

Most photographers use square, octagon, or rectangular softboxes and stripbanks, and, like any accessory, some perform better than others in certain shooting situations. Choose your modifier based on the task at hand. As with umbrellas, the size of the softbox you need to use is dependent on the subjects you plan on photographing. Softboxes can be taken apart and folded up pretty conveniently, and many of them come with storage bags that you can use to transport them. Don't be disappointed when you struggle to squeeze your softbox back into its storage bag. It happens to everyone!

Flash-mounted softboxes

Small, flash-mounted softboxes are very economical and easy to use. You just attach the softbox directly to the flash head and use it with your flash mounted on the camera or on a flash bracket. That said, I always advocate getting your flash off the camera whenever possible for the best possible results. These small flash-mounted softboxes also work well with the flash attached to a camera bracket that incorporates an E-TTL cable and elevates the Speedlite above and to the left or right of the lens. Go this route when you can, and your images will be much better looking. This type of softbox is good to use while photographing an event, informal portraits, or candid wedding shots, or anytime you'd like to increase the quality of your flash's light. You generally lose

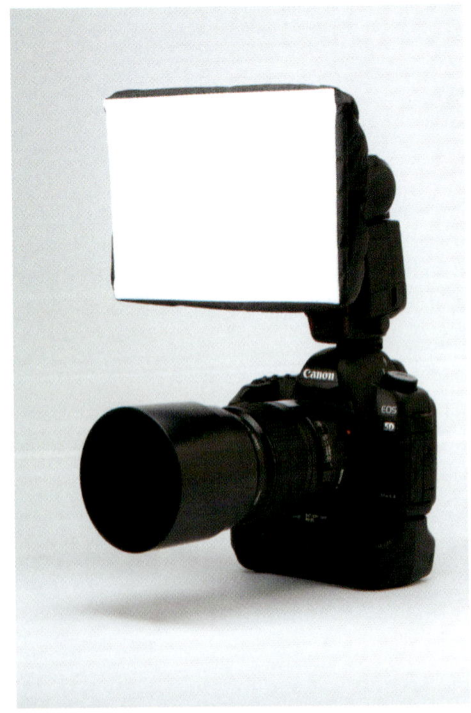

5.16 Flash-mounted softboxes, such as this Micro Apollo from F.J. Westcott, are small and collapsible, eliminate red-eye, and produce better light than just a straight flash.

about 1 stop of light with a softbox when shooting with your flash set to manual power, but E-TTL takes this into account and compensates accordingly. For shooting small still-life subjects or simple portraits, this may be all you need to get started with your wireless or portable studio.

There are many compact mini softboxes available for Speedlites from manufacturers, such as Luminquest and others. However, one modifier that has recently caught my attention and become a quick favorite is the Traveller line of softboxes from Honl Photo. Available in two sizes, these softboxes mount to your Speedlite like other miniatures, but unlike the others, they're round! This conical shape makes a difference, providing not only a more natural catch-light in the eyes but a beautiful soft quality of light, as well. The desire for more natural-looking catch-lights precipitated the advent of the hugely popular octabank softboxes discussed later. More info is available at www.honlphoto.com.

Stand-mounted softboxes

As previously stated, my advice is that you get your flash off your camera as soon as you possibly can to start achieving a vastly superior quality of light. After you do this, you'll need a way to support the Speedlite and a modifier to control the output quality. You might consider a medium-sized softbox that is mounted, along with your Speedlite, onto a suitable light stand. The Lastolite EzyBox hot shoe is one such choice. This line of collapsible softboxes is fantastic. The softboxes travel in a small bag that is about a third of their expanded size and pop into a fully expanded size in seconds. They attach directly to Speedlites with an included universal bracket, they're available in sizes ranging from 15 × 15 inches to 30 × 30 inches, and they are incredibly portable given their expanded size. I use two 24 × 24-inch EzyBox hot shoe softboxes and love them. These unique softboxes have a wire frame design similar to the collapsible reflectors discussed earlier. They're a real godsend when you want to achieve a sophisticated quality of light but still travel light.

When working with just the flash and a Sto-Fen or a small softbox or umbrella, the Manfrotto 5001B Nano Retractable Compact light stand is a sturdy, reliable, and very compact stand to have at your disposal. For medium- and larger-sized softboxes, you need a sturdier stand to prevent the lighting setup from tipping over, especially outside, where even the slightest breeze can send a softbox flying. F.J. Westcott and Manfrotto manufacture a range of stands that work well, set up easily, and are highly portable.

Shooting on location presents certain considerations that don't exist when shooting in a studio. Many cities and towns prohibit the use of light stands in public areas without a permit. Add to this the possible liability incurred if someone trips over your light stand, and you see how using one on location can be problematic. One great way around these issues is to use monopods and extension poles. These one-legged stands, also known as light on a stick, keep one to several Speedlites, a remote trigger, external battery packs, and a light modifier off the ground. With the help of an assistant (what photographers jokingly

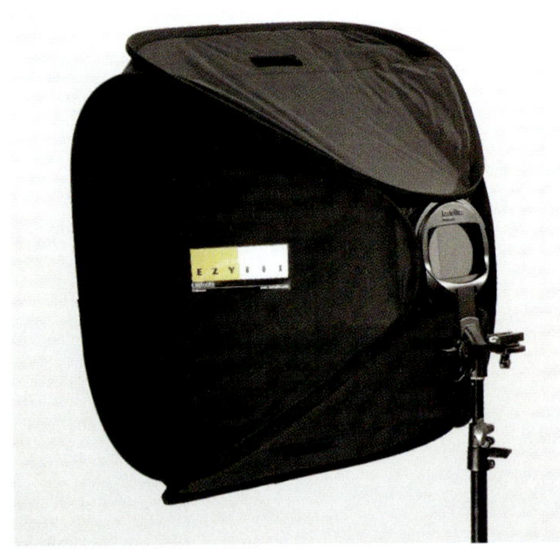

Courtesy of Lastolite

5.17 Stand-mounted Lastolite EzyBox hot shoe

refer to in this case as a "voice-activated light stand"), these can be easily positioned exactly where you need them. One of my favorites is the Lastolite EzyBox HS Long Extending Handle (www.lastolite.us). A retractable paint pole paired with a Kacey Pole Adapter (www.kaceyenterprises.com) and a swivel mount bracket is also a great option.

Octabanks

Gaining in popularity recently is another type of softbox called an octa-bank, named for its somewhat circular, eight-sided construction. Larger studio units often contain an elaborate mounting system, while those developed to work with Speedlites look and operate very similarly to umbrellas but include a closed back to contain the light and add to the efficiency of the flash unit.

They mount to the stand in the same way an umbrella does, and they generate a wraparound, nondirectional type of lighting. They're available in

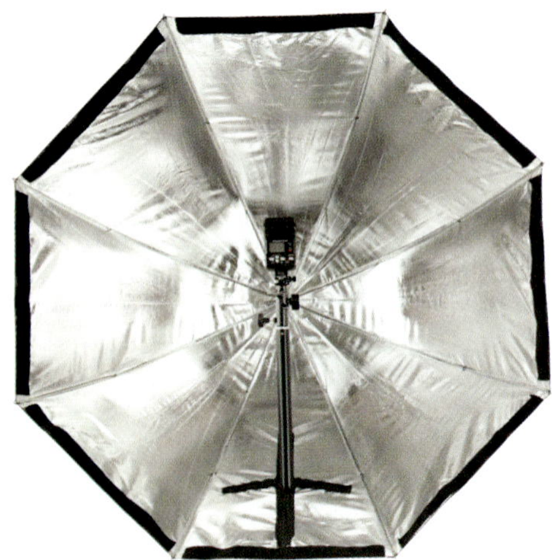

Courtesy of F.J. Westcott

5.18 Stand-mounted Apollo Orb octabank from F.J. Westcott

sizes ranging from medium all the way up to sizes larger than softboxes, and they can create soft light over very large areas.

Octabanks are considered by some photographers to be the most evenly lit (across their entire surface) large light modifiers available today. They have become more popular in large part because, compared to square and rectangular modifiers, they produce more natural, round catch-lights in subjects' eyes (see Chapter 6).

Stripbanks

Stripbanks are a key component of my lighting toolkit. Try to think about each of your light modifiers like the different brushes on a painter's palette. Each one is different and creates a different stroke and effect when applied to the canvas. As a photographer, you're painting, only with light instead of oils. Your brushes are light and the modifiers that you choose to create different effects and qualities of light in your images. Stripbanks, which are narrow rectangles, taller than they are wide, cast a dramatic narrow shaft of light on your subject. They are extremely useful tools for creating edge light, rim light, dramatic split lighting effects, and other cool effects that I cover in Chapter 6.

One of my favorites is F.J. Westcott's asymmetrical stripbank paired with a Magic Slipper bracket. It's sold as a kit (Style 2221) and allows mounting a Speedlite, radio receiver, and external battery pack onto one compact unit that can be directly mounted to any light stand. I favor this stripbank because of the gradual falloff and feathered light it creates due to its asymmetrical (tapered at one end) design (see Figure 5.19).

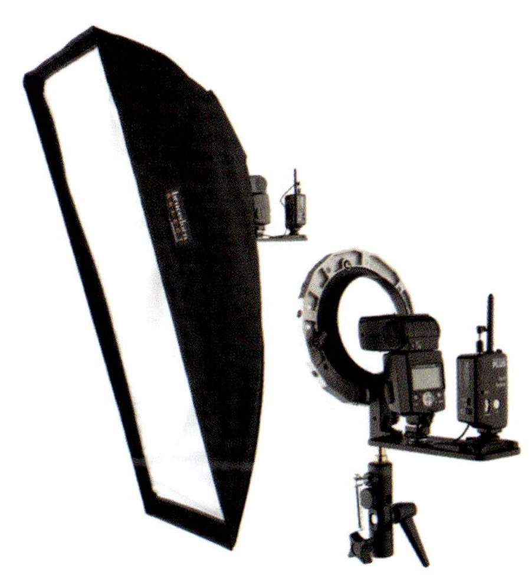

Courtesy of F.J. Westcott

5.19 F.J. Westcott Magic Slipper asymmetrical stripbank kit. Note the tapered design.

Softbox alternatives

A few other easily assembled and cost-effective alternatives to commercially available light modifiers deserve mention. A homemade diffusion panel is basically a frame made out of PVC pipe with a reflective or translucent material stretched over it. I've seen bed sheets and shower curtains used in a pinch. You can run a ¼-inch bungee cord through the pipe to keep all the pieces together, just like the professional ones. Because the PVC frame can be disassembled easily and packed away into a small bag for storage or for transportation to and from the location, it is a handy addition to the portable studio. This is good option until you're able to get your hands on a more full-featured commercial version.

Commercial diffusion panels are usually 4, 6, or 8 feet tall and some have a base that allows them to stand up without a light stand or grip heads. The diffusion panel is placed in front of your Speedlite, which is then mounted on a light stand. You can move the Speedlite closer to the diffusion panel for more directional light or farther away for softer and more even light. By using one of these panels for a full-length portrait, you could group two or three Speedlites behind the panel, evenly spaced near the top and bottom of the panel to achieve even lighting (see Chapter 6).

A diffusion panel can also be used as a reflector when used in conjunction with another light source. Diffusion panels can be purchased at most major camera stores at a fraction of the price you'd pay for a good softbox. Make your own until you're ready to invest in the real deal.

My favorite light modifier for product photography is the Lastolite Cubelite, available in sizes starting at 18 inches up to more than 6 feet. For those needing to photograph products both large and small regularly, these are worth a look.

Speedring conversion brackets

Many manufacturers offer hardware solutions that enable you to convert speedrings typically used in conjunction with studio strobes for use with Speedlites. This means that you can get double the use out of the studio light modifiers you may need or already own, such as softboxes, stripbanks, and octabanks. Speedring conversion brackets come in many configurations, providing options for from one to several Speedlites. One such adapter is the Magic Slipper from F.J. Westcott (shown earlier in this chapter).

Beauty dishes

Beauty dishes owe their name to their large parabolic shape and use in beauty photography. When used correctly, these modifiers produce a virtually shadowless light, similar to butterfly lighting, popular in today's beauty, glamour, and portrait photography. A more dramatic, contrasty, and shadowed effect can also be easily achieved with this important tool. Both are very popular looks.

Available in varying degrees of specularity depending on the interior surface finish (silver or white), beauty dishes produce a circle of light that rapidly falls off, creating a natural in-camera vignette. Optional diffusion socks and discs are available to further modify the light. When beauty dishes are used in combination with a honeycomb grid (www.honeycombgrids.com), a tighter circle of focused light with an even more rapid falloff light results. This is a very dramatic effect and one that I love. (See Chapter 6 for beauty dish lighting examples.)

Ontario-based Mola Softlights has been producing beauty dishes for the professional market for over 28 years. Mola's wide range of beauty dishes are used by many of the top pros in the industry. Recently, Mola released the Lumi Bracket which allows its 22-inch Demi beauty dish to be used in conjunction with Speedlites, a boon for Speedliters.

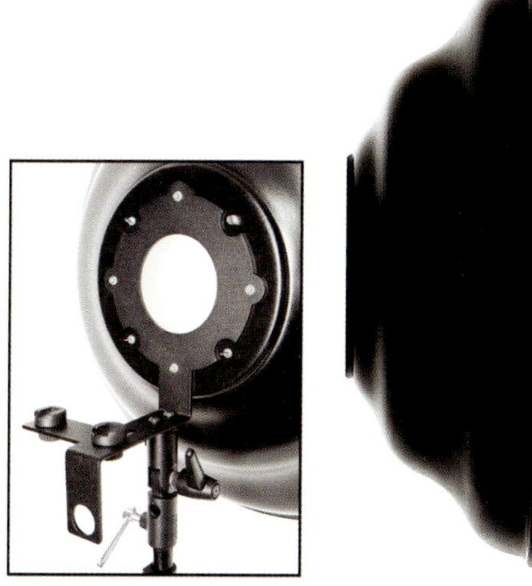

Courtesy of Mola Soft Lights, Inc.

5.20 Mola Softlights Demi deauty dish and Lumi bracket for Speedlites

Ring flash

Talk to most photographers about ring flash, and you'll get a decidedly passionate response. People either love the look or they don't. I definitely fall into the first category and have been a long-time ring flash user. If you're unfamiliar with the ring flash look, most of the celebrity portraits featured on *Saturday Night Live* are lit this way. The ring flash, a round flash tube that wraps around the lens in front of the camera, produces a flat, specular light with a telltale ring flash edge shadow around your subject and falling onto the background.

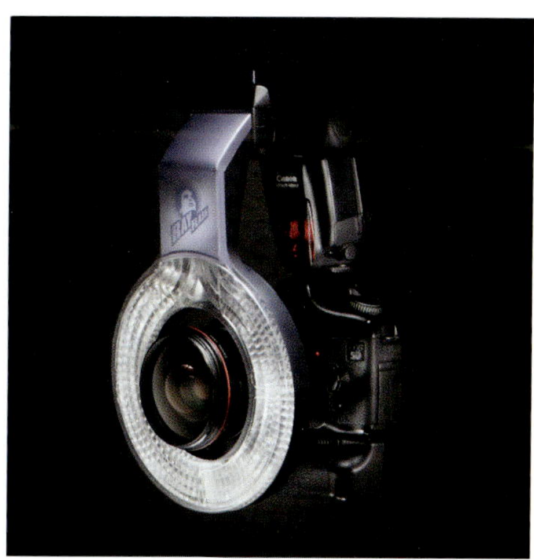

Courtesy of ExpoImaging

5.21 ExpoImaging's Ray Flash ring flash adapter for Speedlites

Long an expensive piece of studio equipment reserved primarily for fashion photographers, the ring flash is now available for Speedlite users, too! Czech photographer Dalibor Zyka has invented and manufactured a Speedlite ring flash adapter called the Ray Flash, distributed in the United States by ExpoImaging (www.expoimaging.com). I've fallen in love with this thing; it's really impressive, and it rivals my pro ring flash that costs about 10 times as much. (See Chapter 6 for a Ray Flash lighting example.)

Specialty brackets

There are many innovative specialty brackets now available for mounting individual Speedlites or groups of Speedlites on stands and in conjunction with various modifiers. These are available from major suppliers or in some cases designed, manufactured, and distributed by photographers and machinists. Here are three of my absolute favorites:

- ▶ **Lovegrove Consulting's Flash Bracket MkVII.** A custom-made and durable dual-locking ball-head design, this bracket allows a Speedlite to be mounted either vertically or horizontally on a light stand and positioned in virtually any direction.

- ▶ **Lovegrove Consulting's Gemini Twin Speedlite Bracket.** This high-quality bracket allows two Speedlites and a set of radio triggers (RadioPoppers or PocketWizard Flex) to be mounted on a light stand and easily locked into multiple positions with its lever arm. Speedlites can be used alone or with an umbrella by using the bracket's umbrella shaft. More information on both Lovegrove brackets is available at www.lovegroveconsulting.com.

- ▶ **The FourSquare Block.** Part of The FourSquare portable lighting system from Lightware Direct (www.lightwaredirect.com), the FourSquare Block is another innovative entry in this category. Used individually, it supports four Speedlites alone or inside a specially designed and easily portable softbox. If you would rather use umbrellas, the FourSquare block can also handle up to two umbrellas. In addition, there are numerous accessories available. When two FourSquare Blocks are used together, the second mounted behind the first, they are capable of holding an impressive eight Speedlites all in one convenient and rock-solid assembly.

Backgrounds and Background Stands

Whether you're shooting portraits, products, events, or macro work, the background is an extremely important element in your photograph. The right background can help set the mood, aid in the story telling of the image, and elevate the mundane to the fabulous. The wrong background can have exactly the opposite effect and end up distracting the viewer from your intended focus. Even in sports photography and photojournalism, the background can often make or break the shot.

Portrait and studio photographers have several different options at their disposal regarding backgrounds for their subjects. Obviously, you could use a room setting and just throw it way out of focus by selecting a large f-stop, but having a simple background to support your portrait is one of the keys to keeping the viewer's attention on your subject and making it stand out. Backgrounds come in a wide array of sizes, colors, and materials.

In environmental portraiture, a background can be as simple as a distressed brick wall in an urban alley or a beautiful mountain vista behind your subject. You are limited only by your imagination. The following sections discuss different types of commercially available backgrounds and their applications.

Seamless paper backdrops

Seamless backgrounds (also known as *sweeps*) got their name as a way to distinguish them from older canvas or muslin backgrounds that usually included a visible seam in their construction. The most common types of seamless backgrounds today are made of paper. Seamless paper backdrops are inexpensive and come in a broad range of colors. Standard rolls of background paper range from 3 feet to 12 feet wide rolls that are 36 feet long. The great thing about using paper as a background is that if it develops footprints, or gets dirty or ripped, you can cut off that piece and throw it away.

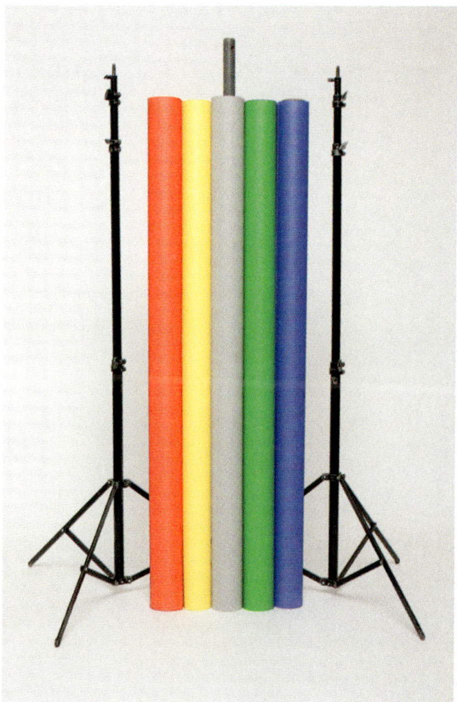

5.22 Seamless paper backgrounds, stands, and the crossbar that supports the paper are easily transported to and from portrait locations outside the studio.

> **TIP** It's best to store your seamless paper backgrounds vertically instead of horizontally if you can, to avoid them developing a washboard effect over time.

One trick you can employ to do away with footprints on your seamless is to pick up a sheet of thin Plexiglas from your local home improvement store. Lay this Plexiglas down on top of the portion of seamless paper on the floor, and your footprint issues and tears are a thing of the past. When you're shooting full-length or product shots, Plexiglas also produces a fashionable-looking reflection of whatever you put on top of it.

Starting out, obtaining a roll of the neutral gray paper is a good idea. You can use this background for just about any subject without worrying about the color of your subject clashing with the background. White paper is ideal for photographing subjects where you want a very clean or high-key look, just like many of the product shots used in this book. A black low-key background is good for making your subject pop where it appears to be the only thing in the shot, which is often desirable with dramatic portraits, lifestyle products, and jewelry.

> **CROSS REF** For more information on high-key and low-key images, see Chapter 6.

To keep your background kit to a manageable size when traveling, it's often more economical to buy larger-sized backgrounds and cut them down to the size you need with a hacksaw — your photo store can probably do it for you. This way, you can cut down the background to fit a case or bag you're already using for your stands, as long as it provides adequate coverage for your portraits. Lately, I've noticed several photographers using snowboard bags to transport their backgrounds and stands with great success.

> **TIP** When using white, gray, or black seamless backgrounds, I often use gels on a Speedlite behind the subject, aimed at the backdrop to create a background color. As previously mentioned, gels are pieces of colored polyester that you place over the light source to change the color of the light. Gels are readily available from professional camera shops and supply houses in a wide assortment of gel colors.

Collapsible backdrops

Collapsible backdrops are based on the same wire frame design as the collapsible reflectors and softboxes already discussed. They come in many sizes and colors, many being reservable, with a different color on each side. These backdrops twist down into compact carrying bags, require only one stand to support them from a center loop, and are a great option when traveling for everything but full-length work. F.J. Westcott has a full line of top-quality collapsible backgrounds that I use in my studio.

Muslin backdrops

Muslin is a durable, inexpensive, lightweight cotton material that can be folded, rolled up, or crammed into a stuff sack and still perform well as a background. When used for backdrops, it is usually dyed a few different colors with a mottled pattern to give the background the appearance of an out-of-focus texture. You can purchase muslin at most well-stocked photography supply houses or online. If you have very specific needs, there are companies that dye muslin fabric to a custom color of your choice.

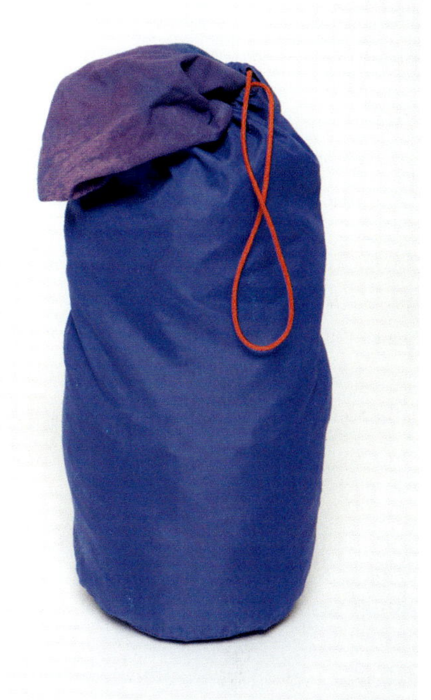

5.23 Muslin backgrounds compress to a very small size, making them ideal for location portraiture. This 10 × 20-foot muslin background easily fits into this 8 × 14-inch stuff sack.

TIP The Internet is great place to find sources and ideas for backgrounds. A few top background suppliers are Denny Manufacturing (www.dennymfg.com), Barbour Backdrops (http://barbourbackdrops.com), Backdrop Outlet (www.backdropoutlet.com), and Owen's Originals (www.owens-originals.com).

You can drape muslin over your background cross-member or easily tack it to a wall. Muslin is very versatile, and although it's much more suited to portraits, it can sometimes be used successfully for product shots as well.

Canvas backdrops

Canvas backdrops are very heavy duty. They are usually painted with a scene or a mottled color that is lighter in the center and darkens around the edges, which helps the subject stand out from the background by creating a vignette look. These types of backdrops are almost exclusively used for portraits.

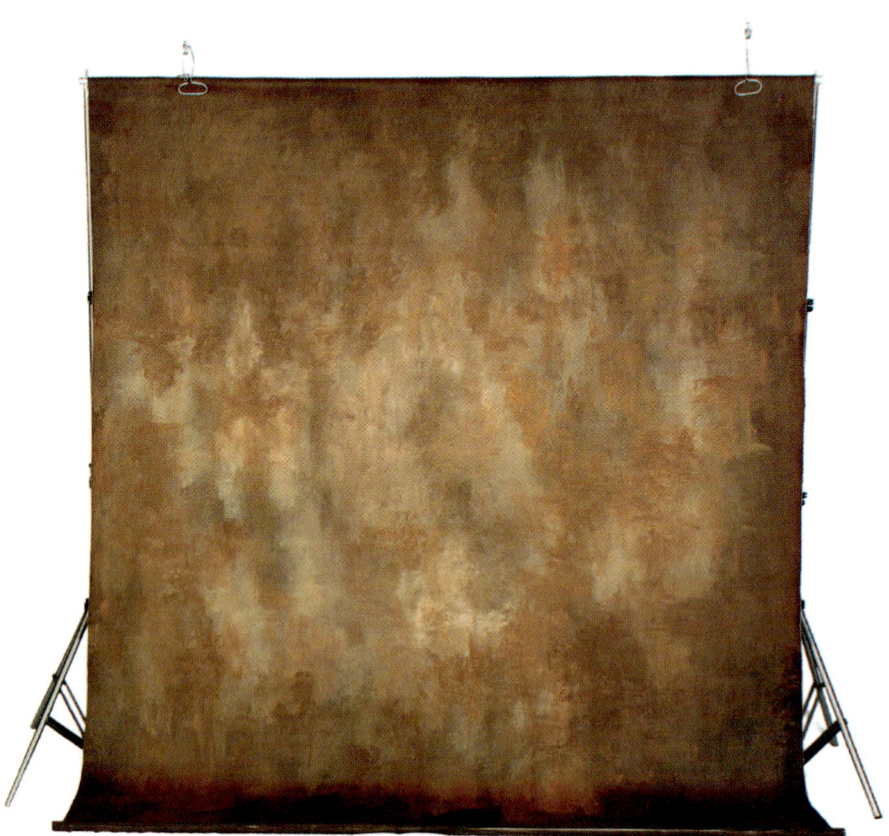

Courtesy of Maheu Backgrounds

5.24 Hand-painted backgrounds like this one from Backgrounds by Maheu (www.backgroundsbymaheu.com) and those from Barbour Backdrops (www.barbour backdrops.com) help create one-of-a-kind portraits and distinguish the pro from the amateur.

When considering a canvas backdrop, in addition to the weight, you should also consider the cost. They are fairly expensive but, if properly cared for, can last a lifetime. Although you can get them in lighter-weight, smaller sizes, they cannot be folded and must be rolled up, and you must take care when transporting them. These are best suited for studio use.

> **TIP** David and Julie Maheu of Backgrounds by Maheu (www.backgroundsby maheu.com) produce beautiful, custom hand-painted canvas and muslin backgrounds for some of today's top professional photographers.

Contemporary backdrops

A new wave of contemporary backdrops with more modern designs and styling has recently come to market from backdrop company Drop it Modern (www.dropitmodern. com). Manufactured from top-quality micro-chenille fabrics with velvet flocking, Drop it Modern backdrops have quickly become very popular, opening up the world of backdrops to many who felt existing styles where dated, unappealing, and lacking in style.

Backdrop stands

Most background stand kits have three pieces: two identical stands and a collapsible crossbar. The crossbar slides into a roll of paper or other backdrop material and two mounting holes, one at either end, which slide over a support pin on the top of the stands. The crossbar is usually adjustable from 3 to 12½ feet, to accommodate the various widths of backdrops. The stands are adjustable in height, up to about 10½ feet. Most kits also come with either a carrying case or a bag for maximum portability. In certain circumstances, A-frame clamps are needed to secure backdrop fabric to a crossbar or keep seamless paper from unrolling. Having a couple sets of A-frame clamps on hand is always a good idea; they're useful for all kinds of things.

There are varying degrees of quality in background stands, and the sturdier the stand, the more expensive it is. For a portable studio, a decent medium-weight background-stand kit suffices. Be careful when setting up stands and backgrounds, because they can become top-heavy and are easily prone to tipping over. Having a couple of properly placed sandbags helps to keep everything rock-solid.

Motorized backdrop support systems

If you're anything like me, after you start using backdrops you'll be hooked! More than likely, you'll soon have a ballooning collection of backdrops with different styles and colors, each one with a different purpose. Multiple rolls of backdrop material or stacks of fabric can quickly become a storage challenge. Manually swapping 9- and 10-foot backdrops regularly is also time-consuming and no fun. Plus, I like to save my workouts for the gym!

This is when motorized backdrop support systems can be a big help. These wonderful modern conveniences will help get you organized in a hurry and make your life in the studio a lot easier. Mounted either on the wall or ceiling, they provide a space-saving solution that makes changing backdrops fast and effortless. I use a six-roller system from online retailer Pro Photo Connect (www.prophotoconnect.com).

Space Considerations

If you are fortunate enough to be able to dedicate a place in your home for your studio, you are that much more ahead of the game. Being able to test and retest lighting setups allows you to work more smoothly and quickly when you have someone in front of your camera posing for you or have a lot of objects to shoot in a short time.

Depending on the type of photography you plan to do, space considerations often come up fairly quickly in the plan. If you intend to do full-body portraiture, including a hair light, you'll need at minimum a good 10 feet from the image's background to the photographer's back. Speedlites make it easy to do tabletop, macro, and still-life photography with a minimal amount of space, and they can also perform well with larger subjects. But remember that the larger your subject is, the larger the background needs to be. Everything expands from the camera's eye proportionally; a four-person rock band can easily require a 12-foot background.

However, there are workarounds if you have limited space. Shooting outside is one option. Most cities and towns have dedicated studio spaces that can be rented by the day or half day. Many photographers are willing to rent out their studios when not in use for a nominal fee. Don't be discouraged if you're working with limited space but rather use it as a challenge to find new and creative ways to make the images you want.

Setting up for indoor shoots

One thing to consider when setting up indoors is finding a space wide enough to accommodate the background and stands. Remember that although your backdrop may only be 6 feet wide, the stands extend 2 or 3 feet beyond that. Next, you want to be sure that you have enough room in front of the background to be able to move back and forth, even with zoom lenses, to enable you to frame your picture the way you want it. Again, don't be discouraged by space limitations; there are alternatives as discussed earlier.

Portraits

When photographing portraits, many prefer lenses with a medium-to-longer focal length. A lens in the 85-150mm focal length range is ideal because it compresses the scene slightly and keeps you a comfortable working distance away from the subject but not so far away that you're unable to communicate. Unfortunately, with longer lenses comes the dreaded *minimum focusing distance,* which becomes greater as the lens focal length increases.

My personal favorite for portraits is the Canon 70-200mm 2.8 IS L series lens. It's fast, meaning at its 2.8 aperture setting it lets a lot of light in, and provides beautiful background compression and blurred backgrounds at its wider apertures. One thing to be aware of when working with longer focal lengths is the possibility of increased camera shake issues at lower shutter speeds. Using a tripod or higher minimum shutter speed in these situations helps solve this problem. For example,

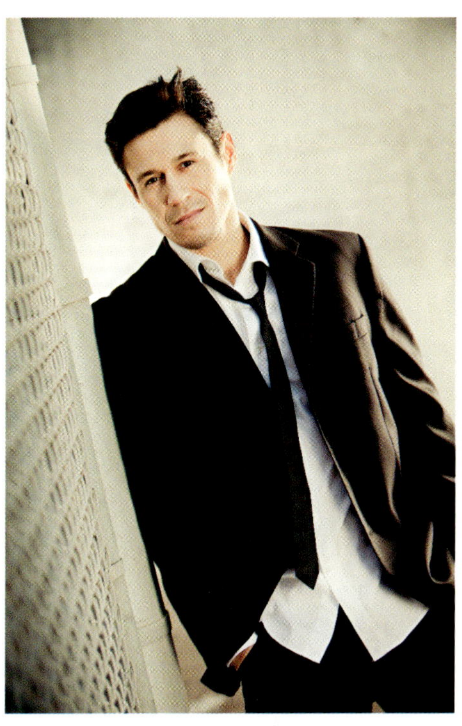

5.25 Using wider apertures helps soften backgrounds, blur distracting elements, and focus attention on your subject. Exposure: ISO 100, f/3.5, 1/60 second with an EF 70-200mm f/2.8L USM lens.

with my 70-200mm, I know that to be safe when shooting handheld I need to use a shutter speed 1/80 second or higher to avoid images blurred by camera shake.

Depending on the kind of the image I'm creating, I like to select an aperture somewhere between the widest aperture and f/8 on the lens I'm using. The wider the aperture used, the more any distracting background elements can be thrown out of focus and the attention is brought back to the subject in your foreground.

If you use a long focal-length lens to photograph a standard head-and-shoulders portrait, ideally there should be at least 10 feet between the camera and the subject, 2 or 3 feet behind the camera for you, and anywhere from 3 to 6 feet between the subject and the background to be sure the model isn't casting shadows on the backdrop because of your lighting placement. These sound like large spaces and they are; however, I've seen amazing things created in very tight spaces.

Be sure the area is wide enough to accommodate both the model and the lights comfortably. You want to have enough width to be able to move the lights closer or farther away from the model to fine-tune your light if need be.

Keep in mind the dimensions outlined here are ideal but definitely shouldn't prevent you from using any space you have available to hone your craft. You may simply need to alter the way you shoot to accommodate your space. For example, if your studio space provides less than 10 feet of separation between you and your model, or your ceiling is lower than what's desired, don't worry, just shoot tighter and lower. Consider shooting medium-length seated portraits instead of full-length images until you graduate to a bigger space. If your space isn't wide enough to accommodate six people, consider specializing in smaller groups. Everything doesn't have to be perfect; the main thing is to shoot as much as possible in whatever space you have available.

Small products

Photographing small products requires a lot less room than photographing people. When shooting small objects, you only need a few feet between the camera and the subject. That's almost half the amount of space you need for portraits. Use the 12mm and 25mm Canon extension tubes if you need to get in closer to fill the frame.

The ideal way to start lighting a simple product shot is to place the main light above and a little behind the product, or on the sides. This simulates a natural light and creates a slight rim light, which helps separate objects from the background. The next step is to note where the shadows fall and to fill them in if desired. You can either use an additional Speedlite as a fill light, or a bounce card or reflector to reflect light from the main light back into the shadow areas. Small, inexpensive, round, regular, and magnifying make-up mirrors can also work well for this.

Remember, pay attention to details when you are working with small subjects. Check and recheck your set before shooting. Dust can appear huge, and scratches and imperfections on the surface of an object can be very noticeable. Canned, nonaerosol air is great for removing dust from your setup right before you shoot. Some of this can be corrected later with retouching, but you should do anything you can to minimize your post-production time spent in Adobe Photoshop or Adobe Photoshop Lightroom at this point. This is what photographers call *getting it right in camera*!

Setting up for outdoor shoots

Putting a portable studio together ensures that you have beautiful light wherever you go. Remember, available light doesn't just refer to the sun; it's any light that's available, including a Canon Speedlite. With the Canon Speedlite System, you can bring your lighting gear just about anywhere and not have to worry about plugging in for power. Shooting outdoors offers its share of advantages — for example, as mentioned previously, you have none of the space restrictions that you have inside — but it also includes obstacles that you must overcome.

Using your 600EX/600EX-RT, 580EX II, or 430EX II on-camera (and you know how I feel about that!), you'd likely use

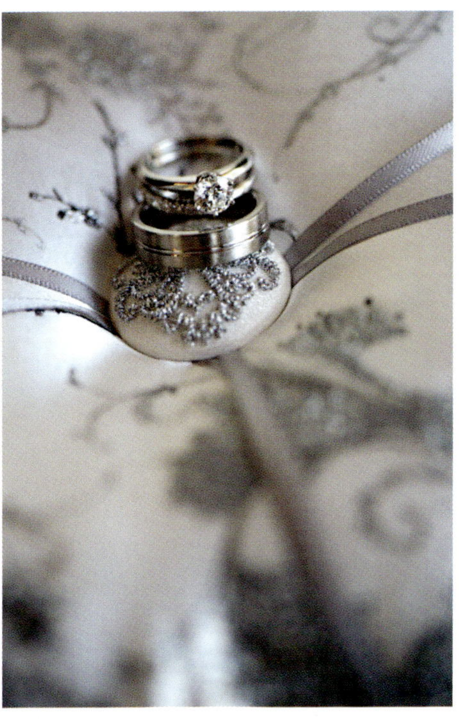

5.26 Ring shots taken during weddings present some of the same considerations as small product photography. Here I'm using a 100mm macro lens so I can work extremely close, show maximum detail, and blur everything else using the widest aperture available. Exposure: ISO 200, f/2.8, 1/160 second with an EF 100mm f/2.8 Macro USM lens.

the sun as your main light, set the flash to E-TTL, and shoot. This is known as *fill flash*. If you take my advice and use your flash off-camera with stands and modifiers such as umbrellas, softboxes, and octabanks, you need to set them up as level as you can and use sandbags or bungee cords and stakes to hold them down. E-TTL shooting can also be accomplished using a cord or E-TTL radio trigger. Cords can be a real danger on set, so pay special attention to their placement and consider carrying a roll of gaffers tape to secure them to the ground. To keep light stands in place, some photographers purchase used fitness weights at yard sales, wrap them in bubble wrap, run a loop of rope through them, and hook them on the light stands' adjustment knobs, a solution that works well.

Also, when you're using a softbox or umbrella, be very conscious of the wind. Wind can take your light and softbox or umbrella and send it flying into the next county or worse — right into your subject! Protect the people around you and protect your gear by taking the necessary precautions to create a safe working environment. I speak from experience!

When shooting outdoors, the same lighting styles and looks previously covered can be used, but you need to pay extra attention to the sun's position — note where it is now, where it's going, and where it's going to set — and plan accordingly. Different types of sunlight have different qualities and different color temperatures to consider:

- ▶ **Bright sunlight.** Bright sunlight can cause serious problems with exposure when using flash. When in bright sunlight, your camera may not be able to select a shutter speed that's higher than its rated flash sync speed if it detects a Speedlite is attached. You may need a higher shutter speed to achieve a proper fill flash exposure even at your smallest aperture.

  The way to solve this problem is to move your subject into a more shaded area or to use Canon's high-speed sync on your Speedlite; or one of the RadioPopper E-TTL transmitters discussed earlier. This enables you to shoot at speeds higher than the actual sync speed of the camera when using the 600EX/600EX-RT, 580EX II, 430EX II, or macro Speedlites. This is very convenient if you're shooting an outdoor portrait and need to use a wider aperture for less depth of field, which then requires a fast shutter speed. The High-speed sync mode causes the Speedlite to emit a series of lower-power flashes that coincide with the movement of the shutter across the digital sensor. The drawback to high-speed sync is that it diminishes the distance range and power output of the Speedlite. To compensate, you could gang up multiple Speedlites, increase the ISO or aperture settings, or switch the Speedlite to manual output settings. High-speed sync mode can be used all the way up to the maximum shutter speed of the camera.

  NOTE High-speed sync is also available on older Speedlite models such as the 580EX and 430EX.

- ▶ **Cloudy sunlight.** This lighting occurs when it is overcast, but when you still have slight shadows. This is wonderful light to photograph in and is comparable to the light from a good softbox. All you may need to do in this light is use your Speedlite to add a little fill flash and some warmth.

- ▶ **Open shade.** Open shade is another ideal lighting condition to shoot in and happens when your subject is in the shade with a clear light blue sky overhead. In harsh sunlight, seek out any shade you can to work in; this gets rid of the nasty harsh shadows you see. If the light is so soft in the shade that it has no character, you can use your Speedlites to design the light you want.

When using light stands outdoors, having sandbags or weights on hand to prevent the wind from blowing them over is highly recommended. Sandbags are commercially available through photography stores. Again, better safe than sorry!

Traveling with Your Wireless Studio

A range of lightweight and innovative products are available to help you get your get your gear from point A to point B. Whether that happens to be across town, across the globe, or on a mountaintop, there's a product for every need in this category.

Camera cases and bags

These are resources for the quality transportation and protection for your gear:

- **Think Tank Photo.** A company started by photographers for photographers, Think Tank Photo offers a huge array of smartly designed gear packs, airline cases, bags, and photo accessories for the traveling photographer. The company continues to innovate and come up with new products regularly. I've traveled all over the world with Think Tank bags, from its Airport Security rolling camera bag to its Retrospective shoulder bags, and I'm happy to report these products are top flight in build and quality. Think Tank Photo's "Be Ready Before the Moment" philosophy has inspired airport cases and bags that have been especially well-received by photographers who need to know their gear is safe, even on extended trips. Think Tank equipment can be found at major photography supply houses and online at www.thinktankphoto.com.

- **Lightware.** This company has been making professional photo gear cases for decades. Lightware cases use a variety of lightweight, shock-absorbing materials to produce extremely protective gear bags that protect equipment many times their weight. They look clean and professional and can be found at major photography supply houses and online at www.lightwareinc.com.

- **Pelican.** You've seen some version of these cases in nearly every James Bond movie. Pelican cases are watertight, airtight, dustproof, chemical-resistant, corrosion-proof, and nearly bullet proof! They are built to military specifications and are unconditionally guaranteed forever. That's right, forever. Pelican cases even float in salt water with a 55-pound load inside. A standard Pelican case holds two camera bodies, a wide-angle to medium zoom, a telephoto zoom, and two Speedlites and all the attachments. These cases are great for transporting lighting equipment; I've owned two large Pelican cases for years that I use for just this purpose. They can be found at major photography supply houses and online at http://pelican.com.

Cases are great for long-term storage, car transport, or airport shipping, but sometimes you have to carry all the gear to the location. Here are a couple of solutions for getting that gear where you need it:

▶ **Shoulder bags.** These are the standard, time-tested camera bags that you can find at any camera shop. However, choosing the right one makes all the difference. Materials and designs have changed significantly, and the new bags are sturdier than ever and come with user-configurable Velcro dividers and pads, sound dampeners, rain covers, and other perks. Bags come in a multitude of sizes to fit almost any amount of equipment you can carry. I use the Think Tank Photo Retrospective 30 and Urban Disguise 50 V2.0, both of which I love. These are easily found at major photography supply houses and online at www.think tankphoto.com.

▶ **Backpacks.** Backpack camera bags have grown in popularity as a new wave of participatory photography has attracted today's image-makers, and backpack bags make it that much easier. Many offer laptop-carrying capabilities that make it effortless to have everything in one case. The Think Tank Photo StreetWalker HardDrive backpack I use holds two camera bodies, a wide-angle and medium zoom, a 70-200mm telephoto, two Speedlites, a battery pack, and a 15-inch laptop. It also has an attachment for a tripod and fits all the plugs, batteries, gels, sync cords, slaves, and other small accessories that go along with my gear.

Portable light stands

There is no way around it. You want the most stable stands you can find, so they won't blow away in the wind, but you also need to be able to move them around quickly. Additionally, they need to fit inside your cases, along with the umbrellas and related gear, and be lightweight. This is no small order.

This is where the previously mentioned Manfrotto 5001B Nano Retractable Compact light stand comes in. This is the perfect stand for supporting Speedlites on location. Surprisingly strong for such a small size, it extends to 6.2 feet and folds down to 19 inches, making it very easy to fit into a location case like the one I use.

I wouldn't attach a studio strobe to one of these stands in the studio, but their light weight makes them perfect for small flash support on location. Manfrotto's Avenger and C Stand lines are substantially heavier and perfect for supporting larger softboxes and octabanks. Whichever one you decide to use, just remember to sandbag or weigh them down even in the studio.

Practice Makes Perfect

Here are a few key techniques to practice. Repeated practice is an indispensable way to learn what's possible with each technique and get to know your gear.

▶ **Source-to-subject distance.** Using a Speedlite with a Sto-Fen diffuser, umbrella, or softbox, make one exposure with the light source as close as possible to your subject. Then move the light back 6 feet and make a second exposure of the same subject. Note the different quality of light this creates. Look at how much harder the transitions from the highlights to the shadows are. For beautiful soft light, keep your lights as close as you can.

▶ **Reflectors.** Pick up a piece of white foam core from your local art shop. With your Speedlite on one side, foam core on the other, and your subject in the middle, experiment with bouncing light back into the shadow areas on your subject created by the flash.

▶ **Grids and snoots.** Convert an empty round Quaker Oats container into a snoot by cutting off the closed end and cutting a shape in the plastic cap to fit your Speedlite (pointing directly into it). You may need a bit of gaffers tape. Notice how this funnels the light into a narrow beam. Pump up the effect by lining the inside with aluminum foil.

▶ **Diffusers.** Experiment with softer light by using a diffusion panel, handheld diffuser, or even an inexpensive semitransparent shower curtain! Trigger your Speedlite through the diffusion material. Start with your flash close to the diffusion fabric and then farther away.

▶ **Convertible umbrellas.** Experiment with the different qualities of light produced by bouncing light using the standard configuration, creating specular light using the silver interior, and shooting through the umbrella to create a softer light.

▶ **Softboxes.** Using the foundation lighting patterns in Chapter 6 as your guide, reposition your Speedlite and softbox and create six exposures, one for each lighting pattern.

5

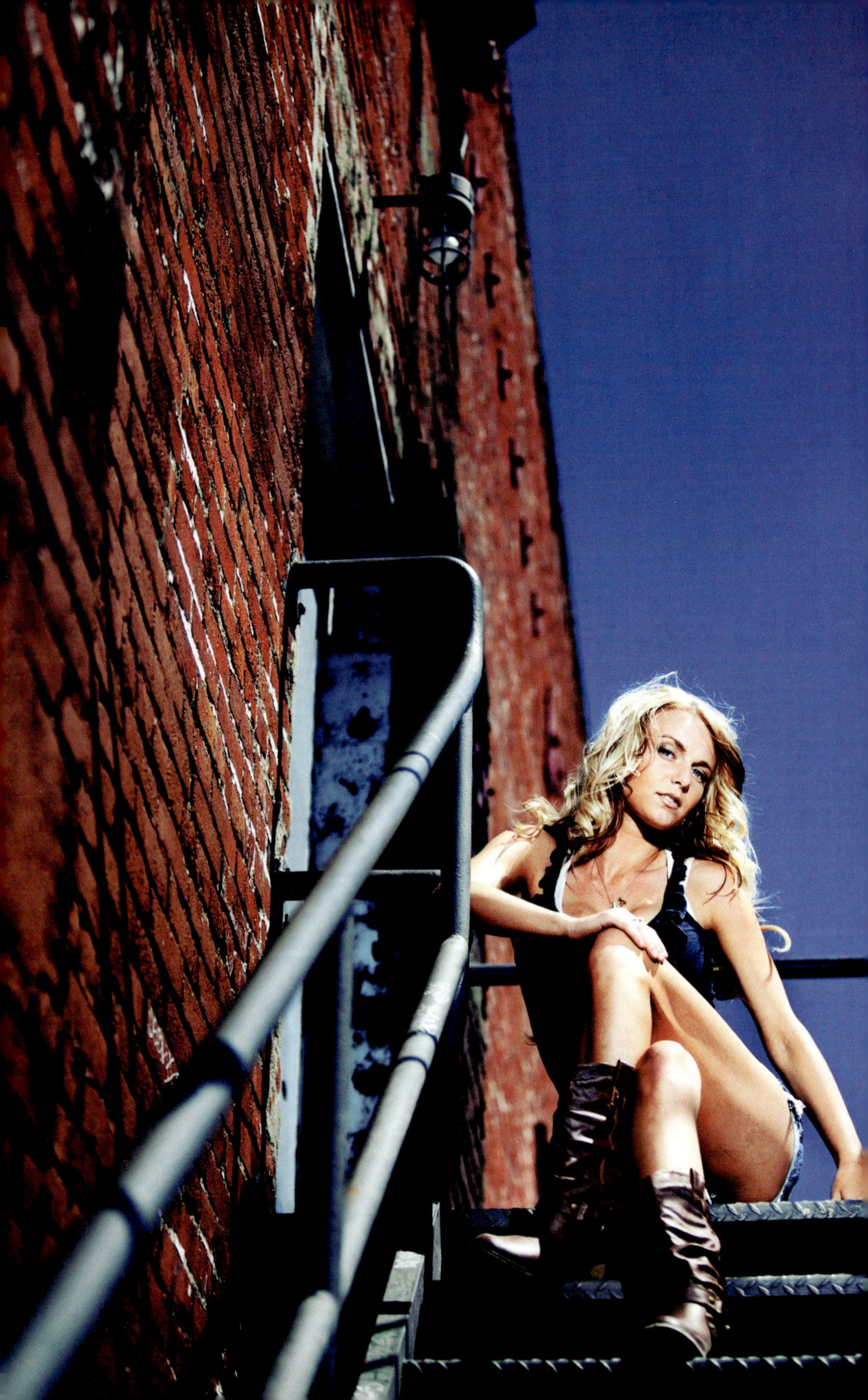

Lighting Concepts and Patterns

Congratulations — you've made it to the fun stuff! Now that you have a solid understanding of the technical aspects governing your Speedlite, it's time to put all that knowledge into practice and start creating great images. You've learned how to control your flashes off the camera wirelessly, how to set up and work with masters, slaves, ratios, and groups, and how to dig deep into your Speedlite's menus. So what's missing? One word — practice! This is the entire point of the book: to get you out there creating the kind of light you've always wanted. In this chapter, I pull it all together by showing you practical applications for your new Speedlite know-how. Combined with details about my recommended gear, example images, and tons of lighting diagrams and behind-the-scenes shots, this chapter is your recipe guide for great lighting. Let's get cookin'!

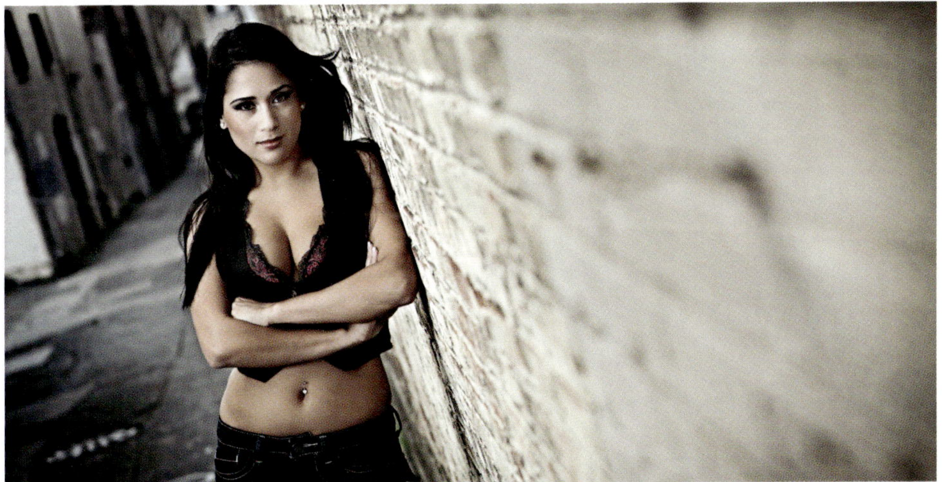

In this edgy portrait, two 580EX II Speedlites were placed camera left and fired at a low power setting through a diffusion panel to create a soft quality of light. Exposure: ISO 100, f/4, 1/200 second with an EF 70-200mm f/2.8L USM lens.

Concepts of Lighting

Speedlites enable you to produce professional lighting in the studio and on location in a variety of situations, such as environmental portraits, business portraits, weddings, and events. When working on location, you will often use your Speedlites in conjunction with natural light (possibly from a window, skylight, or the sun), incandescent light, fluorescent light, or some combination of the three. Location lighting can be tricky outdoors, sometimes fooling the camera's metering system. Seeking open shade for your subject, using an overhead diffusion panel, and having multiple Speedlites to light the subject, create fill, and illuminate the background are a few of the ways to manage the challenges of exterior shooting.

Using multiple Speedlites wirelessly is the way I like to work because it offers maximum creative flexibility, portability, and convenience. The wireless E-TTL system does a great job on its own in most cases, but it also allows you creative control over the lighting output through ratio controls and Exposure Compensation. These options are essential in shooting situations where you want to able to control and fine-tune the lighting that's been created by the E-TTL system.

Studio lighting

If you are fortunate enough to be able to set up a dedicated space for indoor photography or want to establish a studio of your own, Speedlites can help you create professional looks and styles. If you're just starting out and experimenting with studio lighting, a living room, basement, or garage will do just fine. Creating lighting diagrams and making notes about exposure settings, flash ratios, and power levels in a small book or on a diagram creation website, such as www.sylights.com offers the advantage of quick reference and repeatable results. The more you work with your equipment, the more intuitive the process will become, and the easier it will become for you to create the light you want.

When you set up for shoots, it's a good idea to have a plan of action, otherwise known as *the concept.* I like to sketch out a detailed plan of how the subject will be lit, the lighting pattern I'll be using, and the necessary equipment, makeup, wardrobe, and props. Most importantly, I jot down a few thoughts about the intent of the image. Addressing these issues well before the shoot helps clarify the way you want the final image to look and helps the shoot day run smoothly. Developing a concept for the finished image is known as *previsualizing* and is a tactic used by top portrait photographers, including Annie Leibovitz and Mark Seliger. Careful planning helps create more thought-out images and gets you one step closer to achieving your goals.

When you're planning out your photographs, keep these ideas in mind:

▶ **Visual impact.** The first thing to consider is how to create a photograph of your subject that has strong visual impact. You have several tools at your disposal to achieve this, such as composition, color, background, your f-stop and shutter speed selection, and lighting intensity and placement. Breaking down the shot in terms of the individual problems that need to be solved will reveal several creative solutions.

▶ **Direction of light.** Especially when you shoot with a mix of ambient and flash lighting, the direction of the lighting is very important. You must take into account where the ambient light is coming from and where the shadows are falling, and try to mimic that in your lighting placement. You can use reflectors and fill flash to brighten dark areas, but avoid crossed, overlapping shadows. We live in a world with only one sun, and your lighting pattern should appear natural. Overlapping shadows is a dead giveaway of poor flash use. The indoor studio relieves you of that burden and gives you complete control over the lighting, so this consideration becomes less significant.

▶ **Amount of light.** The terms *high-key* and *low-key* are designations photographers use to describe bright and dark lighting setups. High-key lighting is bright and evenly lit, usually with a bright background, as illustrated by Figure 6.1. Conversely, low-key lighting is dramatic, often featuring dark, shadowy areas, as demonstrated in Figure AA.1 in Appendix A.

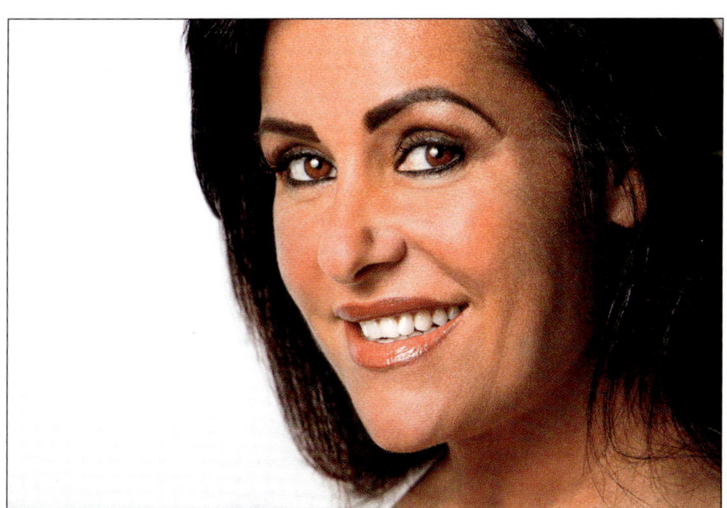

6.1 This headshot of entrepreneur Frauka Kozar is an example of high-key lighting. Exposure: ISO 100, f/10, 1/100 second with an EF 70-200mm f/2.8L USM lens.

By comparing Figures 6.1 and AA.1 in Appendix A, you can see how using high- or low-key lighting can completely change the feeling of an image.

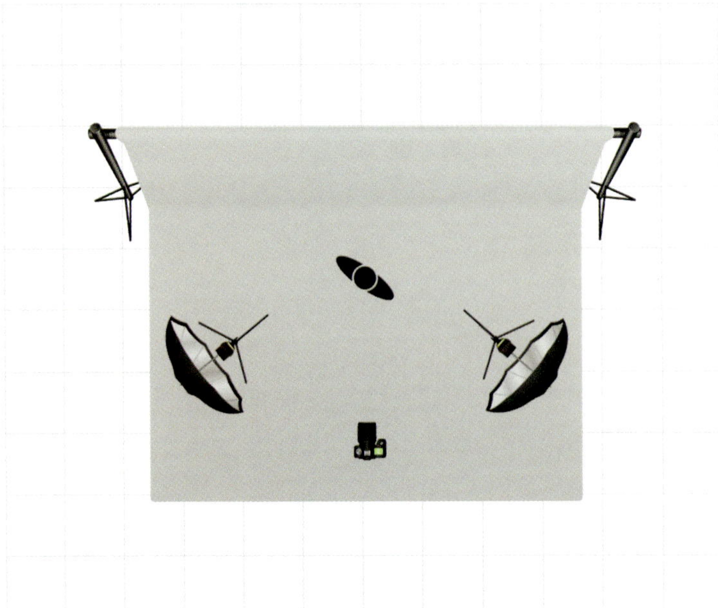

6.2 For the lighting setup in the high-key headshot shown in Figure 6.1, I used two Canon 580EX II Speedlites, one left and one right, each fired into a Photek Softlighter II umbrella light modifier using the RadioPopper PX System for full E-TTL control. Placing the subject close to the background allowed maximum use of the two lights in the setup, lighting not only the subject but also creating a high-key background.

Portrait lighting types

Lighting patterns are described using terms like *key, fill,* and *backlight,* which address lighting placement, intensity, and the size of the light source. Familiarizing yourself with these terms will help you better understand and be more conversant in the language of light.

▶ **Key.** The key or main light is the dominant light source that illuminates the subject and tells the story. It can be a shaft of sunlight, a reflected light source, cloudy sunlight, or a flash.

▶ **Fill.** This is an additional light source directed toward or reflected back onto the subject to open up the shadow areas in an image.

▶ **Backlight.** This is a light source placed behind the subject (or coming from behind the subject in the case of the sun). Backlight is used to help separate subjects from backgrounds and to add edge or rim light to the subject.

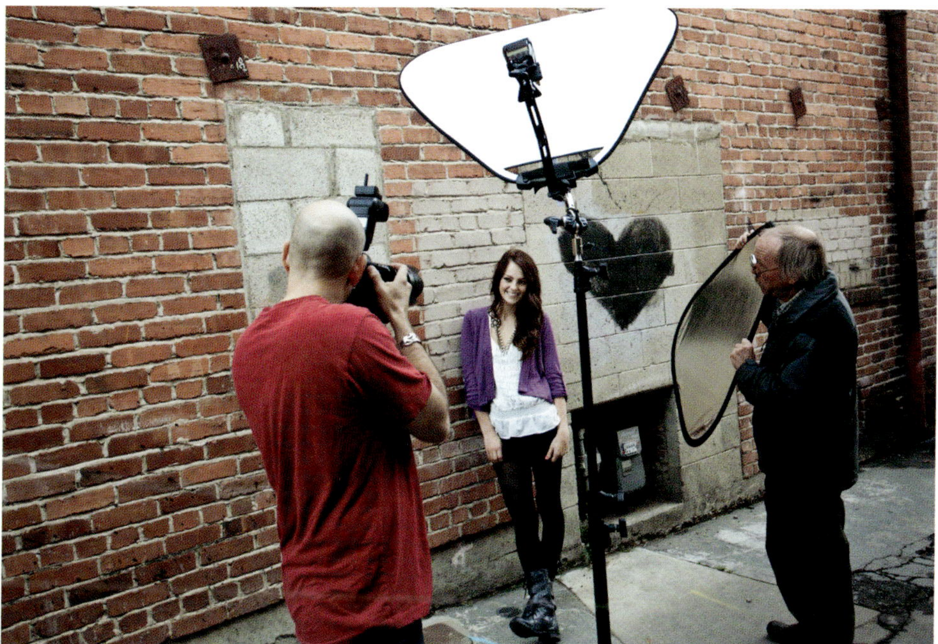

6.3 In this setup, I'm using one Canon 580EX II Speedlite to light my subject, a Lastolite TripGrip diffusion panel to soften the light, and a Lastolite TripGrip gold reflector to add fill light and warmth. I've got a second Speedlite on the camera acting as a master in conjunction with the RadioPopper PX System; however, you could just as easily use a long E-TTL cable.

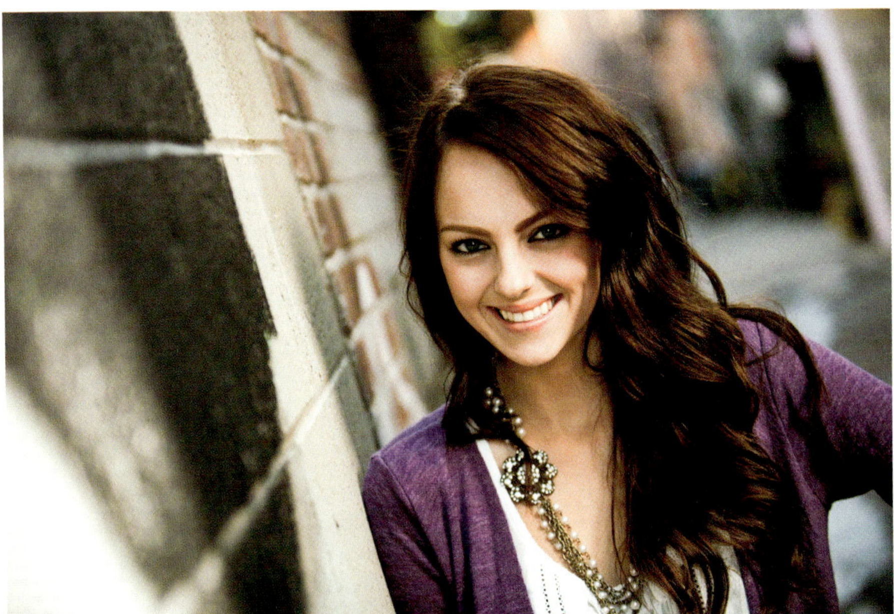

6.4 The resulting image proves that with a little know-how and the right equipment you can achieve professional-looking results. Exposure: ISO 200, f/2.8, 1/160 second with an EF 70-200mm f/2.8L USM lens.

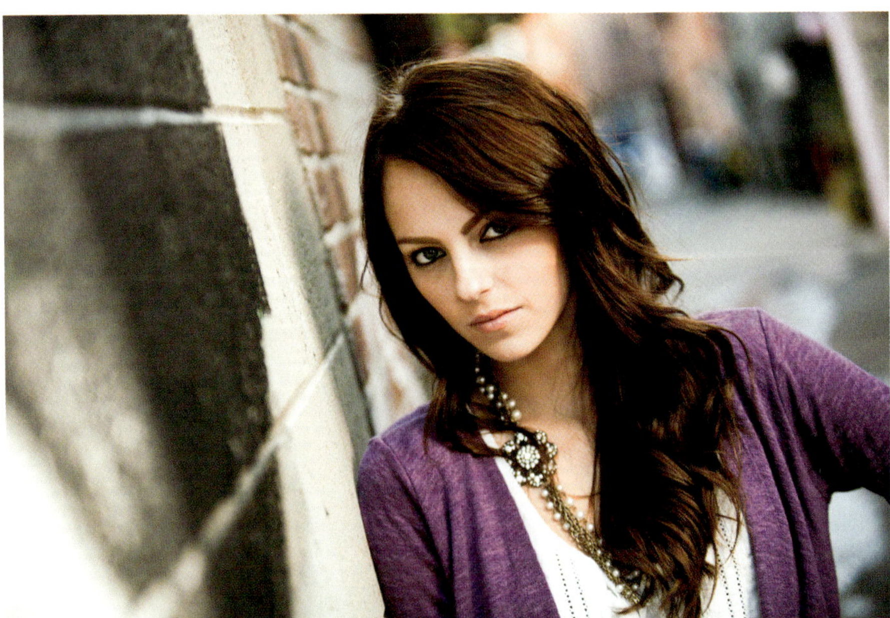

6.5 Here the gold reflector has been removed; notice the reduced warmth in the highlights of the subject's hair. Exposure: ISO 200, f/2.8, 1/125 second with an EF 70-200mm f/2.8L USM lens.

The two basic types of studio lighting techniques for making portraits are called *broad* and *short* lighting. You have probably already shot some portraits using these styles and not even thought about it. I like to try different types of portrait lighting patterns during shoots to produce a variety of images with disparate looks and feelings.

Broad lighting refers to lighting patterns where the largest portion of the subject's face, angled toward the camera, is illuminated by the key (main) light (see Figure 6.6). Short lighting, on the other hand, is created when the key light is positioned to illuminate the side of the subject's face that is turned away from the camera, emphasizing facial contours and slimming the face (see Figure 6.8).

Both the broad and short light example images are lit using a 43-inch Westcott Apollo Orb and one Speedlite. Notice the round catch-lights in the eyes and soft quality of the light. The catch-lights produced by octabanks are considered by some to be more natural looking and, therefore, favored over softboxes.

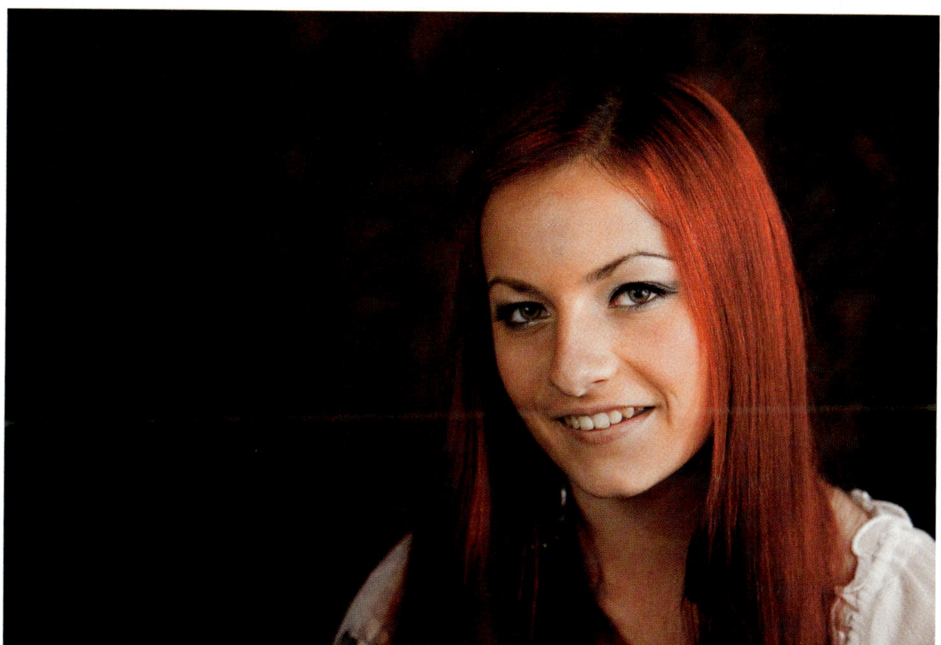

6.6 Model Samantha Hagle lit with broad lighting. Simply said, when most of the face is lit and facing the camera, it is called as broad lighting. This lighting pattern is not ideal for women in most cases, as it adds weight to the face. Compare this image with the short light example that follows (Figure 6.8) and you see why short light is preferred for its slimming effects on the face. Exposure: ISO 100, f/3.5, 1/60 second with an EF 70-200mm f/2.8L USM lens.

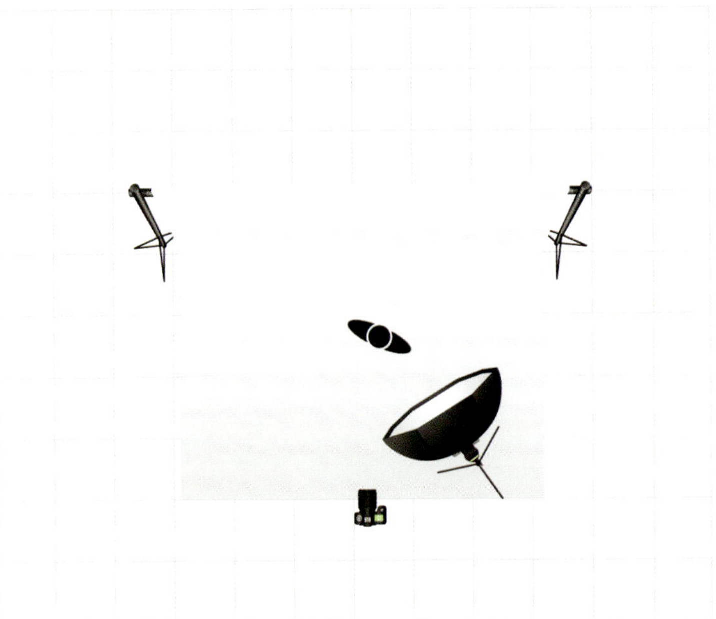

6.7 Broad light diagram. With broad light, the side of face toward the camera is lit.

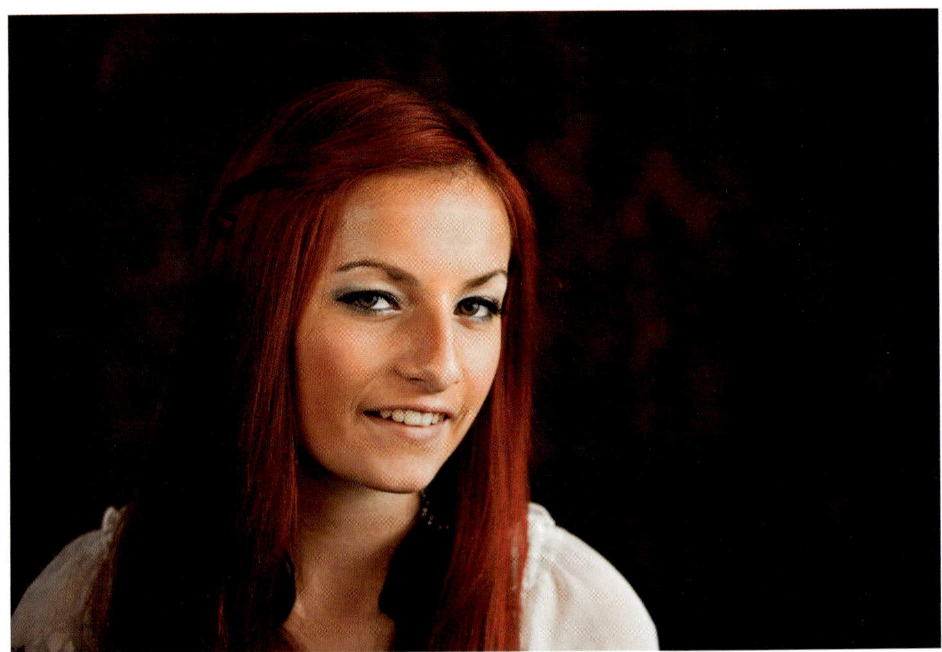

6.8 Short lighting illuminates the side of the subject that is turned away from the camera. Exposure: ISO 100, f/3.5, 1/60 second with an EF 70-200mm f/2.8L USM lens.

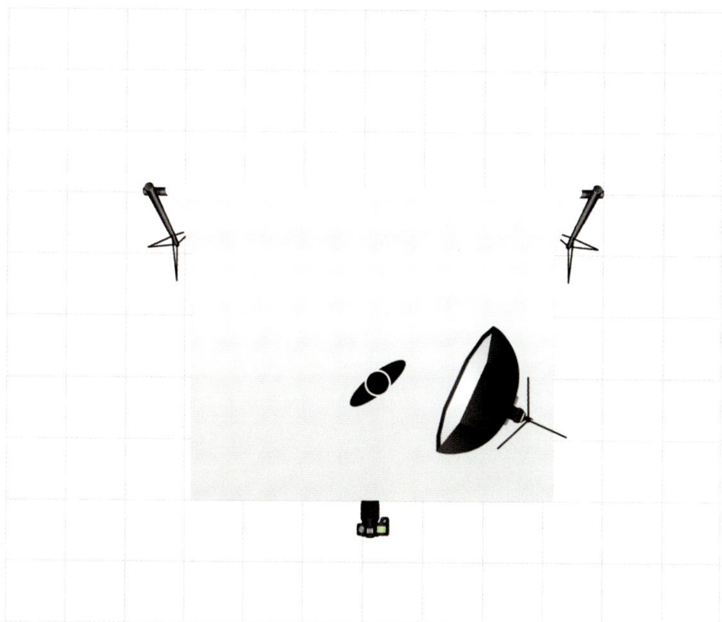

6.9 Notice how the light is positioned to illuminate to side of face turned away from the camera in this short light diagram.

Broad and short lighting techniques apply outdoors as well. When you're shooting portraits outdoors and using the sun as your main light and the Speedlite as a fill, the same techniques can be applied. Using sunlight as your main light source, positioning your subject to take advantage of these principles can produce flattering results for your outdoor portraits.

> **NOTE** Lighting ratios represent the difference in light intensity between the shadow and highlight areas of your subject and how much detail they contain. Lighting ratios are expressed numerically, for example, 2:1, which means one side of the subject is twice as bright as the other. You use ratios when you are planning how much contrast you want in a lighting pattern. You can get very accurate measurements for lighting ratios using Speedlites in E-TTL mode. You can adjust ratios by making adjustments on the master unit for each flash or the Canon ST-E2 or ST-E3-RT transmitter.

Other lighting styles to consider include the following:

▶ **Hard lighting.** Hard light, also known as specular light, can be used in photographs to create contrast, drama, texture, and highlights. Typically light from an undiffused source or a source placed a good distance from the subject, it's considered harsh, especially for portraits, because the light is strong, contains a lot of contrast, brings out skin texture, and highlights flaws.

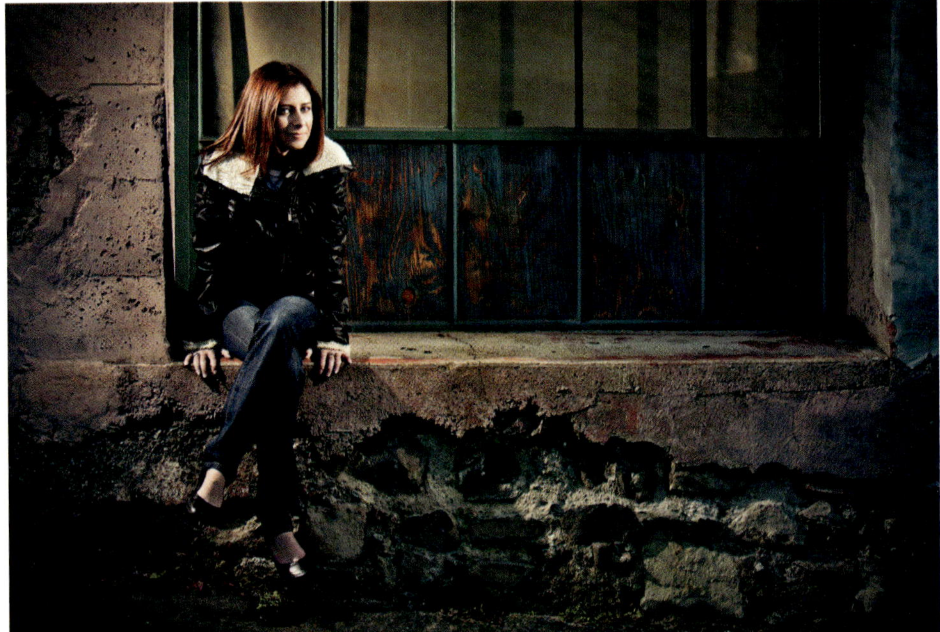

6.10 Bare flash aimed directly at the subject produces hard and moody light. This look is great with fashion and gritty urban portraits. Exposure: ISO 100, f/2.8, 1/250 second with an EF 70-200mm f/2.8L USM lens.

> **NOTE** The farther the light source is from the subject, and the smaller it is, the harder the light will appear.

▶ **Diffused/soft lighting.** Soft light is more desirable when producing portraits that are meant to be flattering. Soft lighting is created by firing your Speedlite through a translucent umbrella, softbox, fabric panel, or diffusion dome over your flash head. These techniques produce a more natural-looking lighting effect with more realistic-looking skin, as shown in Figure 6.12.

▶ **Bounced/angled lighting.** Creating bounced or angled lighting involves aiming your Speedlite toward a white or lightly colored ceiling. Alternatively, the flash can be moved off the camera and trigged remotely, into a reflective umbrella or reflector, using the previously mentioned OCF extra-long E-TTL cord or OC-3 Off-Camera Shoe Cord. Bouncing the light off these reflective surfaces scatters it and causes the light rays to strike the subject from many different angles, producing a softer, more diffused quality of light.

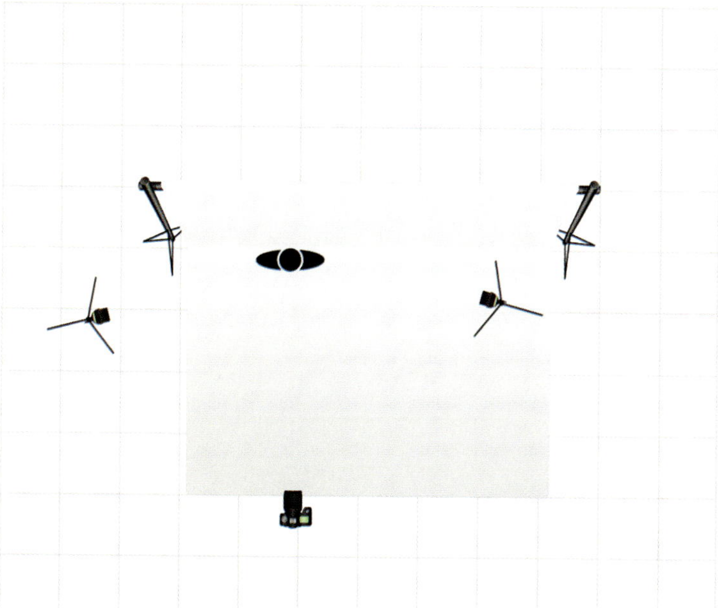

6.11 Two bare Speedlites placed at opposite sides of the subject in Figure 6.10 provide key and fill light. Using the RadioPopper PX system allows me to operate wirelessly in full E-TTL mode using High-speed sync. Doing so enables me to shoot with a wide aperture. For urban location shoots like this, the Manfrotto 5001B compact light stands are fantastic.

▶ **Front lighting.** This is the kind of light created from a camera-mounted Speedlite or an onboard pop-up flash and is often the least flattering type of lighting. This is because front lighting from Speedlites creates flat lighting with no modeling, compresses the subject, and exacerbates any shiny areas on a subject's skin. However, when used in the studio with large diffused light sources like a beauty dish, an octabank, or a softbox at slight to steep angles, this type of lighting can be very forgiving and provide a beautiful, glamorous look.

▶ **Mixing ambient light with flash.** Requiring slightly more skill to manage, photographers are often faced with situations that necessitate mixing ambient light sources in a scene with light produced by flashes. Available light can be the existing indoor ambient lighting or the naturally occurring light streaming in from a window. You may even want to preserve the warm tone of the existing ambient room light and only use flash to add fill light to the scene. Or you may want to omit the ambient light altogether and rely solely on your Speedlites.

6.12 For this family portrait, two Canon Speedlites were fired into a large 7-foot octabank positioned camera left and very close to the subjects. The proximity of the source to the subject and size of the source contribute to the soft quality of light. Exposure: ISO 160, f/5, 1/80 second with an EF 50mm f/1.2L USM lens.

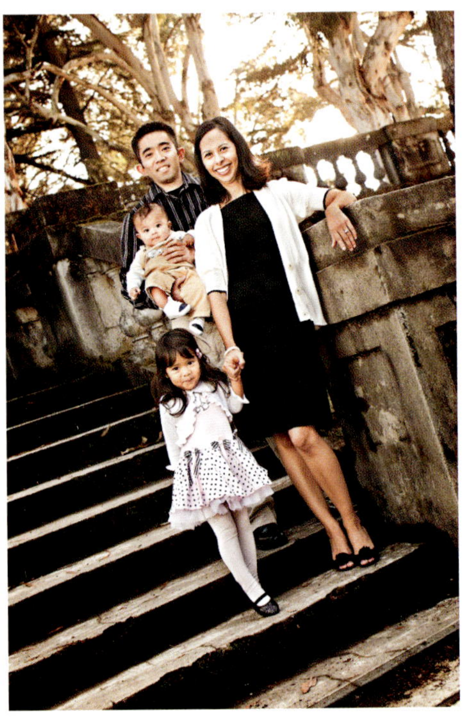

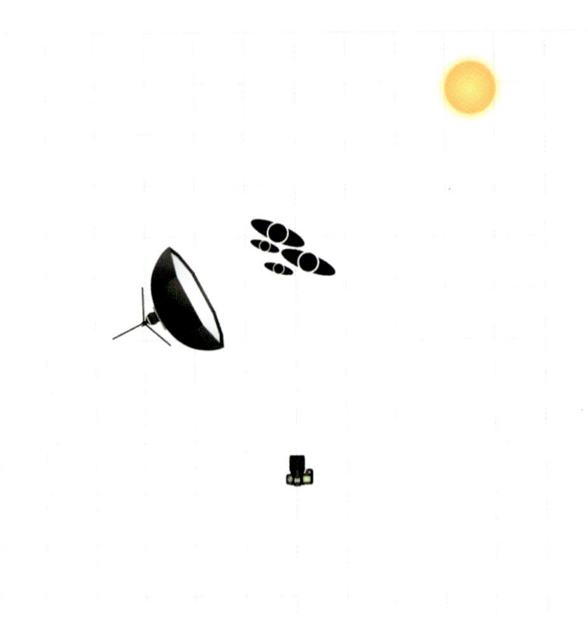

6.13 The soft lighting in Figure 6.12 is achieved by using a very large light modifier (source) and placing it very close to the subjects.

Mood and drama

The subject can be strong and visually interesting, but you create the most mood and drama in your images with creative use of lighting where it's all about the feel of the photograph. Hard lighting can be useful in this instance, where you may want a harder look, stronger shadows, and chiseled features. It can mimic the lighting of an urban street scene at night or full-on direct sun.

Mood and drama work in concert with your subject to establish a sense of time, place, or location in your given scene. The lighting you choose to use, whether natural or stylized, should serve a storytelling purpose for your subjects and the image. It should be a supporting element that helps create a unique image about who they are, what they do, and what their lives are about. Mood and drama are the cornerstones of successful portraiture and are driven by creative use of lighting as well as composition. Being sensitive to the role lighting plays in creating mood and drama will help take your photography to the next level and differentiate you from less skilled photographers.

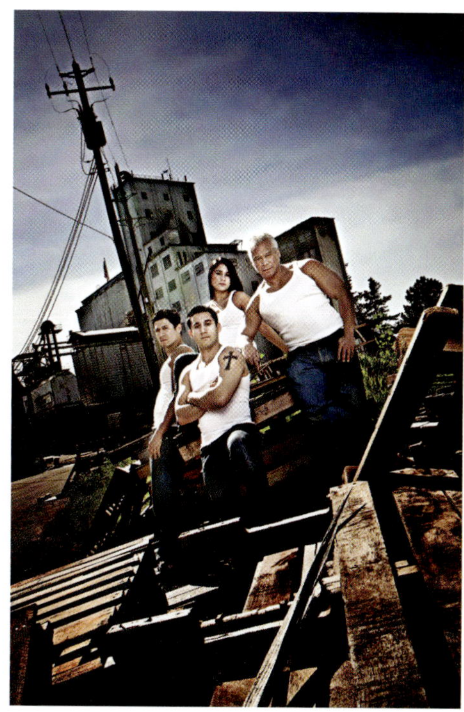

6.14 In this family portrait with a very different look than Figure 6.12, one light was placed camera right. However, the light was much smaller and considerably father away. Along with the harsh midday sun in the background providing rim light, the size and position of the light source helped create a harder, edgier image. Exposure: ISO 100, f/20, 1/60 second with an EF 17-40mm f/4 USM lens.

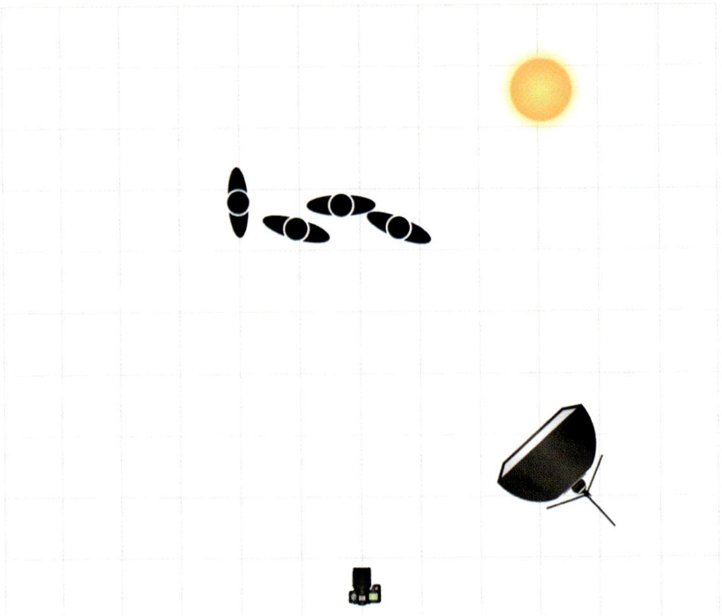

6.15 The harder quality of light in Figure 6.14 was created by using a smaller source, a Westcott 3 × 4-foot softbox placed approximately 10 feet away.

Lighting patterns

Most portrait photography utilizes some variation of five foundation lighting patterns: butterfly/Paramount, loop, Rembrandt/45, split lighting, and modified split/rim lighting. You have probably used these patterns before (and definitely seen them) and just didn't know what they were called. When planning your portraits, consider these five lighting patterns, each with their own strengths and weaknesses. I also include shadowless lighting information for situations when a modeled lighting pattern is not desired.

Butterfly/Paramount

Also referred to as Hollywood glamour style, this type of lighting is often used in model and celebrity photography. It gets its butterfly designation from the shape of the shadow that the nose casts on the upper lip. You achieve this type of lighting by positioning the main light directly above and in front of your model. Studio photographers usually use a softbox, octabank, umbrella, or beauty dish to create this look.

6.16 Dennis Urbiztondo poses for an example of butterfly-style portrait lighting. Exposure: ISO 100, f/11, 1/200 second with an EF 50mm f/1.2L USM lens.

This lighting style is also referred to as Paramount in some circles. It was used so extensively by Paramount Studios in Hollywood's golden age that this lighting pattern became synonymous with the studio's name.

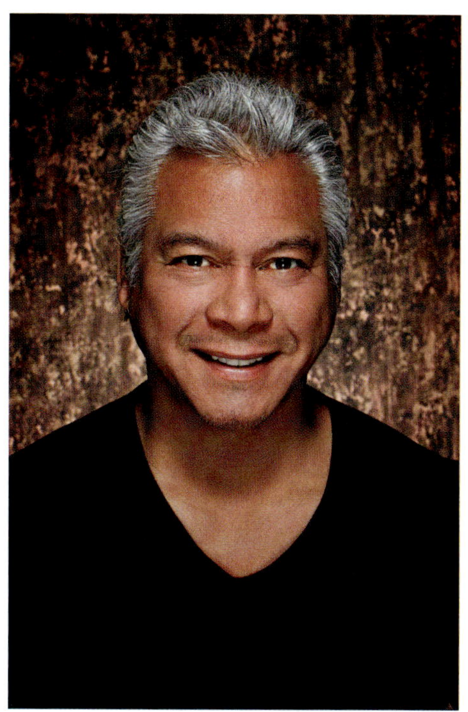

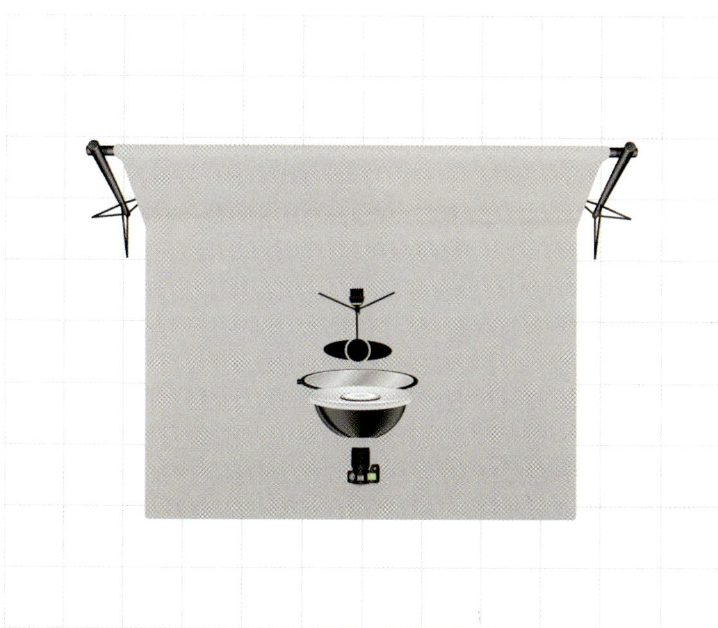

6.17 The lighting pattern for butterfly-style portrait lighting. In this image, I used one Canon Speedlite mounted on Mola Lumi bracket and fired into a Mola Demi beauty dish, one Speedlite for background light, and a Westcott 6-in-1 reflector (silver fabric) placed on the subject's lap.

Loop

Probably the most commonly used lighting technique for portraits today, a minor variation of Paramount lighting, loop lighting is achieved by lowering the key light and moving
it more to one side of the subject. Make sure to keep the light high enough so that the
shadow cast by the nose — the loop — is at a downward angle on the shadowed side
of the face yet low enough to create catch-lights in the eyes.

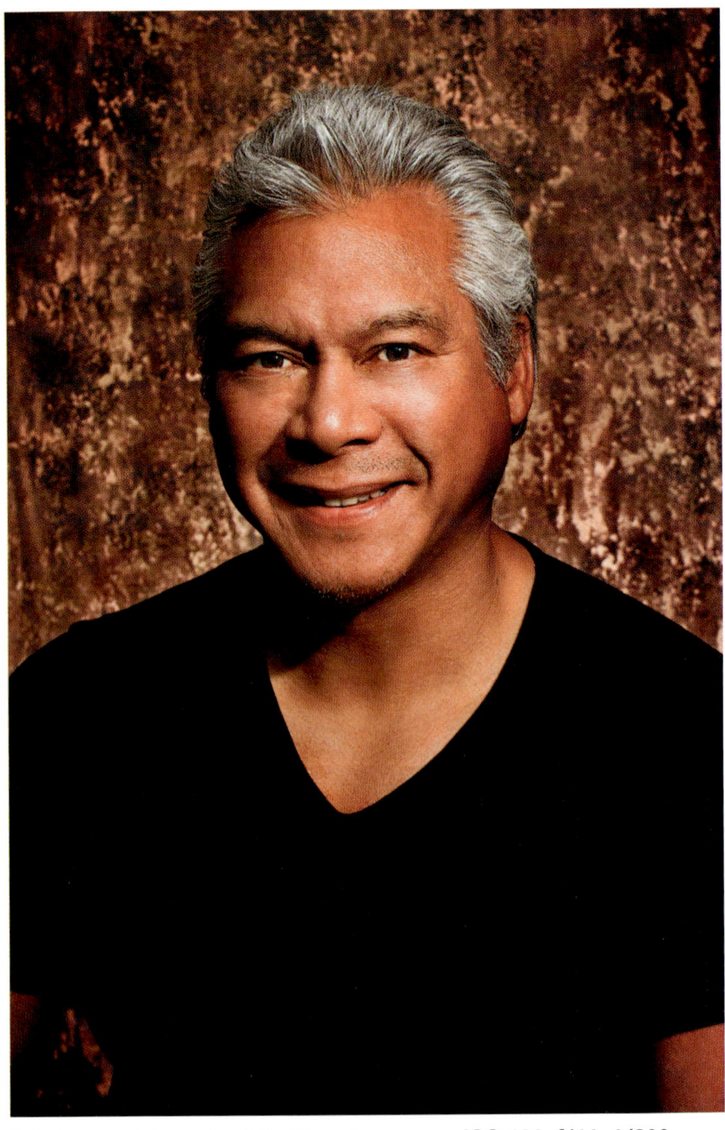

6.18 Loop-style portrait lighting. Exposure: ISO 100, f/11, 1/200
second with an EF 50mm f/1.2L USM lens.

In loop lighting, the fill light is positioned on the camera-subject axis. The fill light's intensity is lower than the main so that it does not cast a shadow of its own to maintain the one-light look of the portrait. To be considered true loop lighting, the loop shadow from the nose area should not touch the shadow area on the side of the face. This is a very flattering lighting pattern used often by most photographers.

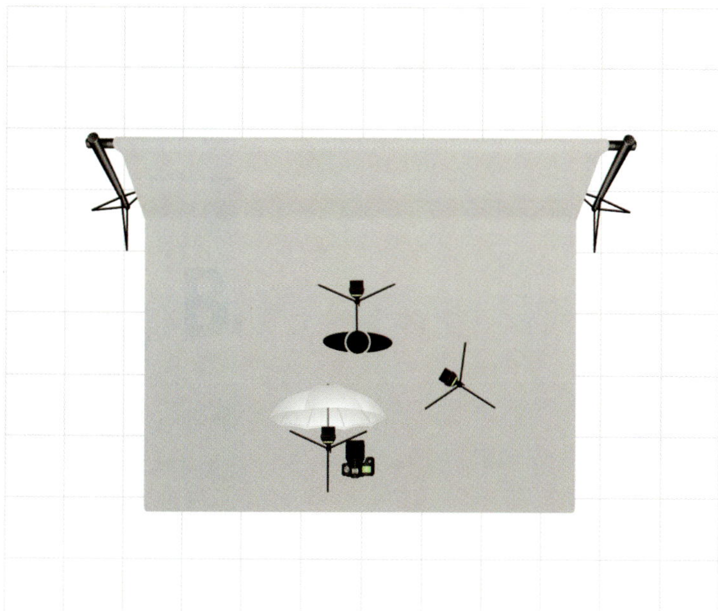

6.19 Loop-style lighting pattern. Three Speedlites were used to produce this image. The key Speedlite was placed camera right with a Sto-Fen diffuser, the fill Speedlite right next to the camera fired through a Westcott collapsible shoot-through umbrella, and the third Speedlite was behind the subject pointed toward the background to add separation.

Rembrandt/45

Rembrandt lighting is the name given to the lighting pattern used by the master painter in his studio. This was the naturally occurring lighting pattern caused by a skylight above his subjects. It's basically broad lighting where the shadow from the nose connects with the shadow on the short side of the face, thus creating a triangle of light on that side of the face. If the nose shadow doesn't connect with the cheek shadow, it's not considered Rembrandt lighting, just broad lighting. The Rembrandt style is created with the key light positioned at a 45-degree angle, higher than the subject but still low enough to produce a catch-light in the eyes.

6.20 Rembrandt-style portrait lighting with a background by Barbour Backdrops. Exposure: ISO 100, f/11, 1/200 second with an EF 50mm f/1.2L USM lens.

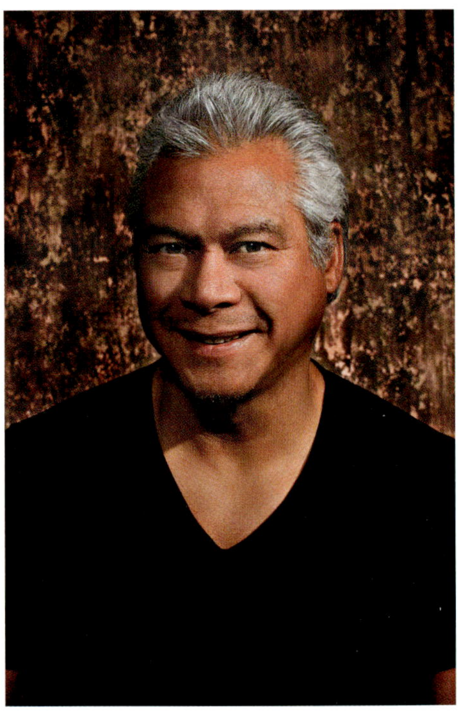

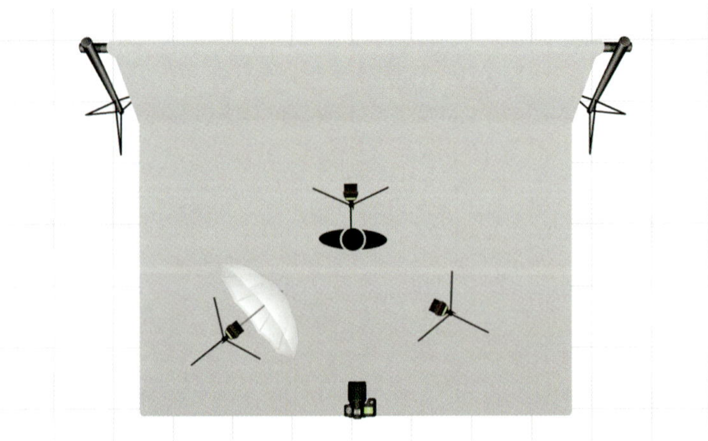

6.21 Rembrandt-style lighting pattern. Three Speedlites were used to produce Figure 6.20. The key Speedlite was placed camera right with a Sto-Fen diffuser, a fill Speedlite camera left fired through a Westcott collapsible shoot-through umbrella, and a third Speedlite behind the subject pointed toward the background to add separation.

Split lighting

Placing the main light at a 90-degree angle to the subject throws the other side of the face into deep shadow and creates mood, drama, and a bit of mystery in your portrait. This technique gives the photographer less of a canvas to work with, because half the face is in shadow, but it can add great power to a portrait. Having a little concealer make-up or powder on hand to help your subjects look their best can help lessen the amount of apparent skin texture. This type of lighting from the side shows off any texture in the light's path and highlights any skin imperfections. Generally, this pattern is a better choice for portraits of men.

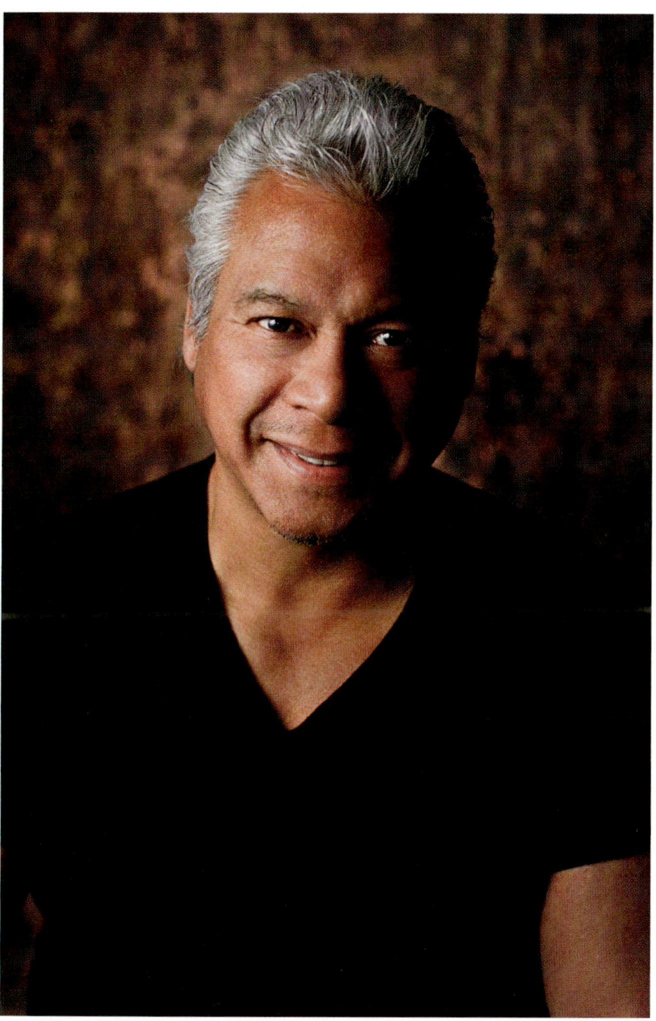

6.22 A portrait using the split lighting style. Exposure: ISO 100, f/3.5, 1/200 second with an EF 50mm f/1.2L USM lens.

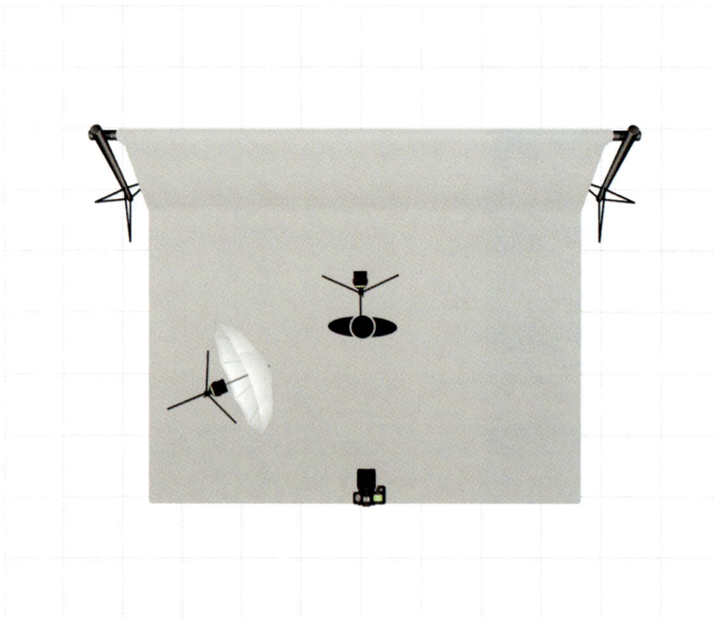

6.23 Split lighting pattern. Two Speedlites were used to produce this image. The key Speedlite was placed left fired through a Westcott collapsible shoot-through umbrella and a Speedlite behind the subject with a 25-degree ExpoImaging Rogue Grid pointed toward the background to add separation and a natural vignette.

Modified split/rim lighting

This style of lighting involves adding a secondary light source, often undiffused, to the split-lighting mix to create a rim of light around the subject that separates that person from the background. In Figure 6.24, a rim light is used to create separation of Dennis's silver hair from the background. This establishes boundaries for his head shape and provides a more three-dimensional look to the portrait. This rim light can also be fitted with a colored gel to add some contrasting or complementary color to the image, while retaining all the separating qualities created by the lights' positions. In this case, I added a 25-degree grid to both the rim and background light. The grid on the Speedlite illuminating the background helps create separation and a natural vignette.

CROSS REF For more information on grids and gels, see Chapter 5.

6.24 A portrait using the modified split/rim lighting style. Three Speedlites were used for this image: A Speedlite fired through a shoot-through umbrella is the key. The second Speedlite, undiffused, is used for the rim light on the subject. A third Speedlite was placed behind the subject to create separation from the background. Notice how moving the subject away from the background and using wider apertures helps create additional separation from the background. Exposure: ISO 100, f/3.5, 1/200 second with an EF 50mm f/1.2L USM lens.

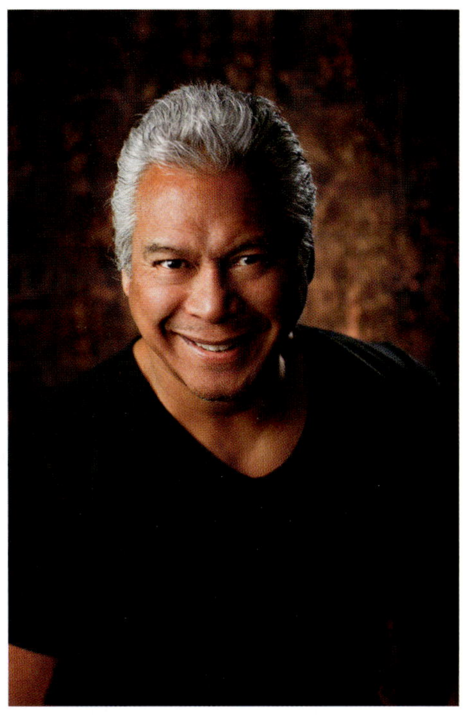

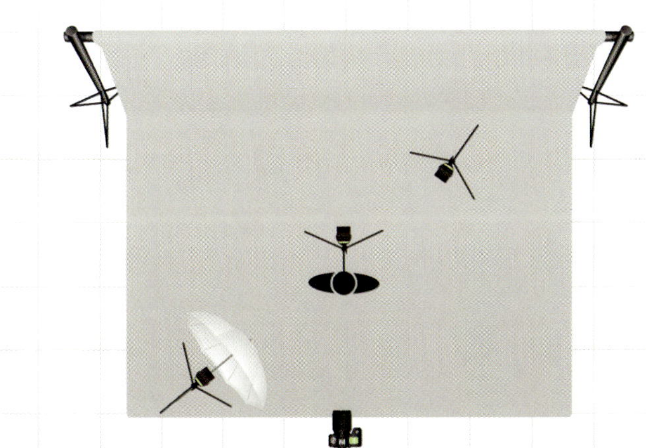

6.25 Modified split/rim lighting pattern. Three Speedlites were used to produce this image. One was placed camera left and fired through a Westcott collapsible shoot-through umbrella; two were fitted with 25-degree ExpoImaging Rogue Grids and placed behind the subject. I pointed one toward the background to add separation, and I angled the other and placed it off to the right, aimed at the back of the subject's head and shoulders to create rim light.

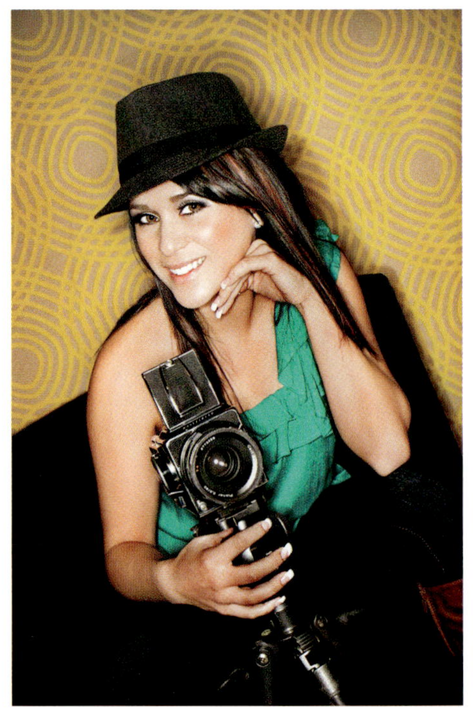

6.26 A portrait of model Lauren Urbiztondo using the shadowless lighting style. Exposure: ISO 400, f/10, 1/60 second with an EF 50mm f/1.2L USM lens.

Shadowless

Several configurations of equipment will get you into the realm of shadowless lighting. Ring lights that encircle the lens are often used, as well as positioning light sources above and below or to the left and right of the subject's face. Combined with setting the light output to equal ratios, shadowless lighting is very forgiving to skin tones and delivers a very clean, stylized look.

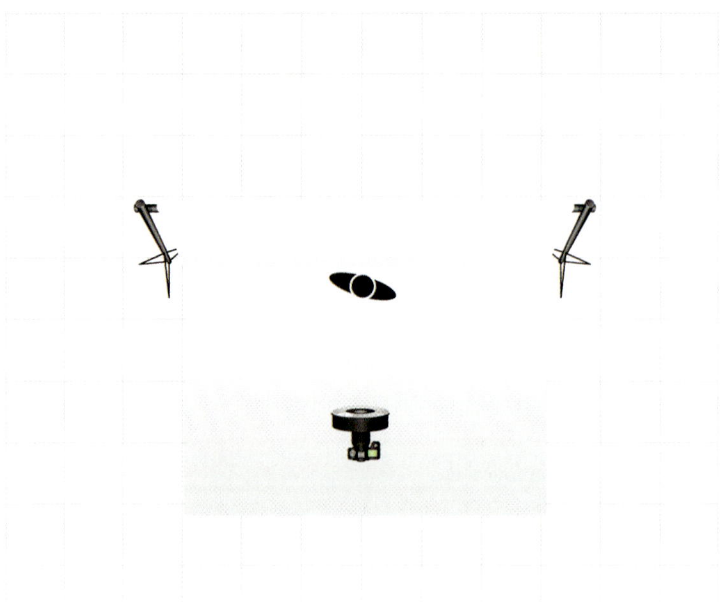

6.27 Shadowless lighting pattern. A Ray Flash Ring Flash Adapter from ExpoImaging was used to produce this image.

Using Speedlites for Outdoor Locations

Having several Speedlites to work with is great and something to work toward, but remember, just because you only have one Speedlite in your bag doesn't mean you can't create stunning photographs. Photographers do all the time. Although I love having as much gear with me as possible to keep my creative options open, sometimes when you're on the road you need to travel light. Using reflective surfaces at the locations you're shooting at to open up shadow areas or using collapsible reflectors is effectively like having that second light source you wish you had but without the expense. Position the subject to take advantage of the reflective surfaces you have at your disposal. Keep in mind that any colors that are part of the surface will also be reflected and can contribute unwanted colorcasts. Surfaces like the exterior walls of light-colored or white buildings work really well. Another approach I like when working with only one Speedlite is to use OCF Gear's extra-long E-TTL cord. Moving the Speedlite off-camera results in greater control over the lighting angle, and connecting the Speedlite with this accessory still gives you all the advantages of flash-to-camera E-TTL communication. Using the sun as an edge or rim light and a flash as the main light is another useful technique.

Despite their small size, Speedlites deliver a solid punch of light that's well suited for outdoor lighting. Their small size is also an asset because unlike studio strobes, you can stick them in tight spaces where larger lights wouldn't fit and create dramatic lighting effects. In outdoor environments, ambient light becomes a major player in your lighting considerations, so you have to decide how you want to handle it.

The first approach is to use E-TTL with fully automatic camera settings and hope for the best. In some fast-breaking shooting situations, this is all you can do, but in my opinion, it should be your last resort. The next method involves using E-TTL but changing the white balance settings to accurately match the natural lighting conditions and adding a colored gel to the flash to match those dominant conditions. The third approach that is a little more creative, and the one I favor from time to time, is to shoot with manual settings, forget accurate white balance for a moment, pick a totally opposite color temperature than what's needed for the ambient light, and add a gel to the flash to push the Speedlite back to neutral or even warmer. For example, by choosing a tungsten white balance setting when shooting outside (daylight balanced) and putting a tungsten colored gel (full CTO) on your Speedlite, you can create cool-looking images where the background goes blue but the foreground remains tungsten balanced. I discuss color temperature, white balance, and balancing for ambient light in the next section.

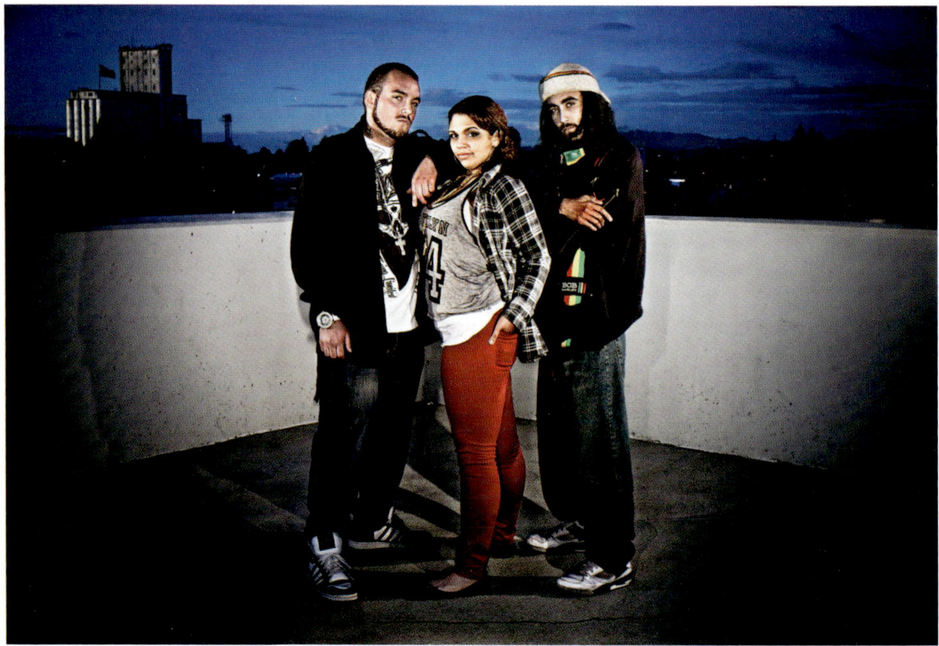

6.28 This image of musicians Brittanie England, Nino Angelo Joseph Bosco, and Auston S. Cowan-Bent was made using six Speedlites. Exposure: ISO 100, f/10, 1/125 second with an EF 50mm f/1.2L USM lens.

Whatever you decide, taking a Speedlite along on location shooting is smart insurance that you will get the shot, even under the worst of conditions. Because of their small size, you can quickly make many of the light-shaping tools you may need on the fly from some paper and cardboard. A wide variety of professional third-party accessories is now available for hot shoe–mounted flashes.

The advantages of using flash when making images outside include the following:

▶ **Creating fill and edge light.** Using a Speedlite as a fill light complements the ambient light and opens up shadowed areas, providing more information and less contrast to the viewer. It also adds nice catch-lights to the eyes that add a little sparkle and pizzazz to the images. Using your Speedlite as an edge/rim light while the dominant light (key light) in the scene is the ambient light is a great way to add separation and dimension. By reducing the flash output, with Flash Exposure Compensation (FEC) or power output adjustments in Manual mode, to levels just under the ambient light, the flash's contribution to the scene will look natural and less apparent.

▶ **Reducing contrast.** Speedlites can also improve the tonal range of an outdoor portrait in high-contrast situations. Mostly, I try to avoid direct sun for shooting portraits, but when I can't, such as during a wedding ceremony, using a Speedlite can help reduce the difference between the brightest and darkest values of the image by raising the values of the darker areas to be more in line with the darker middle tones.

▶ **Creating light in the dark.** You can create extremely dramatic portrait images by using the changing colors of an evening sky as your background. With your Speedlite as the main light, simply keep shooting as night falls. Watch as the city lights appear, and a whole new background palette is revealed. The shadows grow long, colors intensify, and daylight fades away. As long as there's enough light to make focusing possible, having a Speedlite along can extend your shooting time and provide a lot of enjoyment in the process.

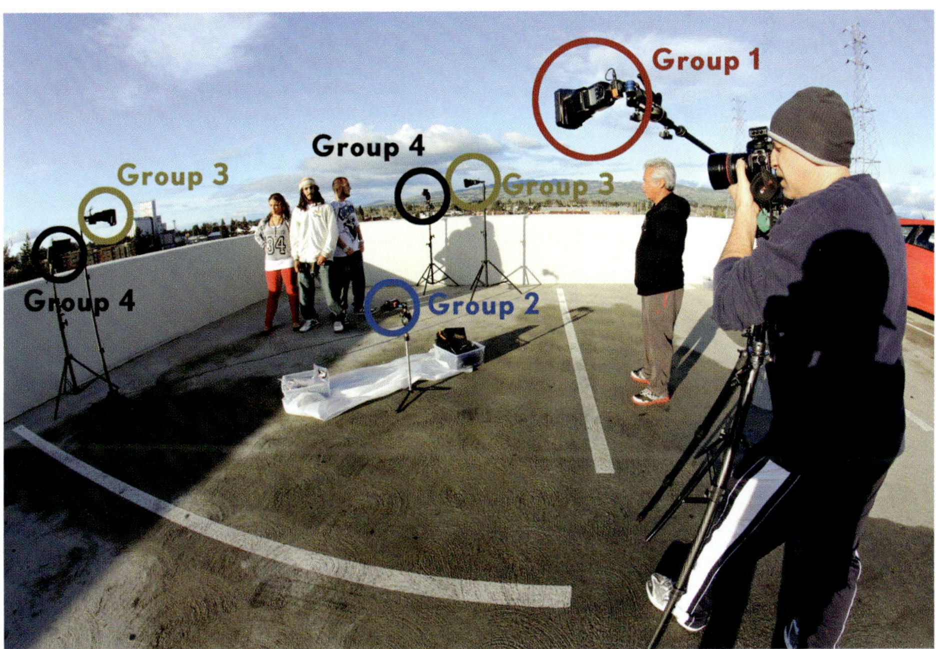

6.29 Here you see where the six Speedlites were placed and grouped for easy power adjustment at the camera using the RadioPopper JrX System. To get the otherworldly blue sky while keeping the subjects looking like they were from Earth, I shot the image using tungsten white balance and added a full cut of CTO (color temperature orange) gel to each Speedlite. I added 25-degree Honl Photo grids to the flashes in groups 1 and 3, aimed those at the subjects' faces, and added Honl Photo flags to group 4 to prevent flare from these rim and edge lights.

The preflight

The day before an outdoor shoot, I test all the equipment and systems I'll be using. I call this *the preflight*. Referring to my plan for the shoot, I gather all the listed gear, including Speedlites, light modifiers, brackets, light stands, radio triggers, cords and cables, gels, gaffers tape, and so on, and I set up everything as it will be used during the shoot to make sure all systems are go. I make sure the Speedlites are each set up for their respective roles as master and slave, set up channels and groups, dial in any special Custom Functions I may need, test all triggers, make sure I have all necessary brackets, and so on. Taking this extra step has saved me on more than one occasion. There are just so many little odds and ends to remember. Without setting up set and working with your gear, it can be really easy to forget that one small but essential piece. Having everything nailed down the day before and creating a solid plan for the shoot allows you to arrive confident, relaxed, and ready to go.

Remembering light theory

Without getting into a dissertation on photons and Sir Isaac Newton, the light theory I'm suggesting you remember here is simply that light goes in one direction unless diffused or broken up. Of course, you can bend light and shape it with modifiers, but the light should look consistent within the scene. Opposing lights can be used as rim lights or fill, but it should remain low enough in value so as not to confuse the viewer and create crossed shadows. You can get away with more rule-breaking in advertising and product photography than you can in documentary or photojournalist work. Keep the light as simple or dramatic as you want, but remember to pay attention to the shadows to see where they fall.

When you're using flash, keep in mind that aperture selection controls the amount of light from the flash on the subject and shutter speed controls the light value of the ambient light in the photograph. It is critical to understand this distinction. This is how photographers control flash output and ambient light levels and select settings that make the combination look natural.

> **TIP** Aperture controls the amount of light from the flash on the subject and shutter speed controls the amount of ambient light in the photograph.

Setting power output

With location photography, the ambient light must be carefully evaluated to determine if it is adequate to use as the main light source. The ambient light can provide a sense of the subject's environment that helps set the prevailing scene, particularly in indoor locations. I try to make the most of ambient light and use it as the main or fill light source when possible. As a result, I use Speedlites to boost ambient light and to help define areas in the scene that are poorly lit or to create edgier light.

To this end, I use the Speedlite's E-TTL ratio settings or manual power output controls to choose and fine-tune my light for the look I want. Adding light modifiers may absorb some of the power output, but this is no problem for E-TTL to automatically compensate for and is noted and figured into the exposure calculation. Manual flash mode may require you to boost the flash power, which is diminished slightly by modifiers. Make sure that any light modifier or gel does not cover the flash sensors.

Modifiers and Their Qualities of Light

One of the questions I'm often asked is in what situations to use various light modifiers. This is a very personal, artistic, and sometimes business-related decision; therefore, it is pretty subjective. There are some general guidelines, such as using softboxes for softer looks, octabanks for round catch-lights, beauty dishes for fashion, and so on. Lighting is all about modifiers, and as discussed earlier, the right modifier can turn an average image into something truly special. I collect them like baseball cards! Seriously, along with all the other gear you have in your arsenal, your lighting modifiers are just like the tools carried by a skilled carpenter or craftsmen. Each tool has a different purpose and produces a different result. Modifiers with white interiors produce softer results while those with silver interiors produce more specular results; larger modifiers provide a more diffuse light while those that are small yield a

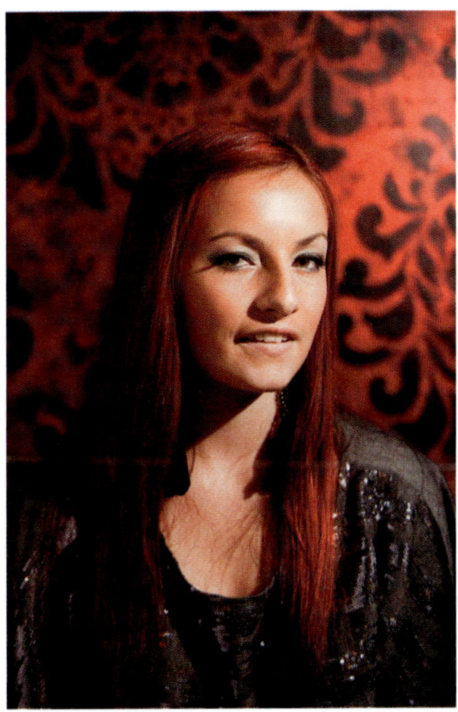

6.30 **Bare flash. This is hard light, and it produces hard transitions between the highlights and shadows. Background by Barbour Backgrounds. Exposure: ISO 100, f/3.5, 1/60 second with an EF 70-200mm f/2.8L USM lens.**

harder light. I thought it would be helpful to show examples of images produced with different light modifiers. The following images start with bare flash and build from the there to the very soft light of a medium softbox. Each example was produced using only one Speedlite and one modifier.

Build your collection of light modifiers slowly and take time getting to know what's possible with each of them. Sometimes I pick out one light modifier and use it for an entire day, exploring the different kinds of light I can coax from it. Again, experiment often and have fun!

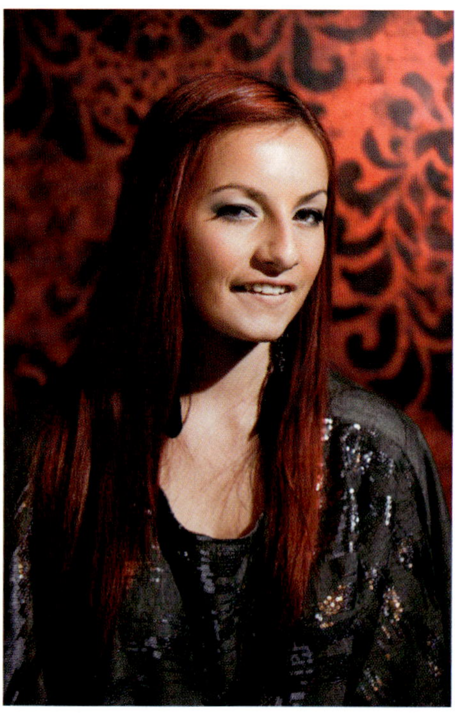

6.31 Flash with Sto-Fen. The Sto-Fen plastic cap is placed over the flash head and scatters light, helping diffuse and soften it slightly. This will likely be your first light modifier. Exposure: ISO 100, f/3.5, 1/60 second with an EF 70-200mm f/2.8L USM lens.

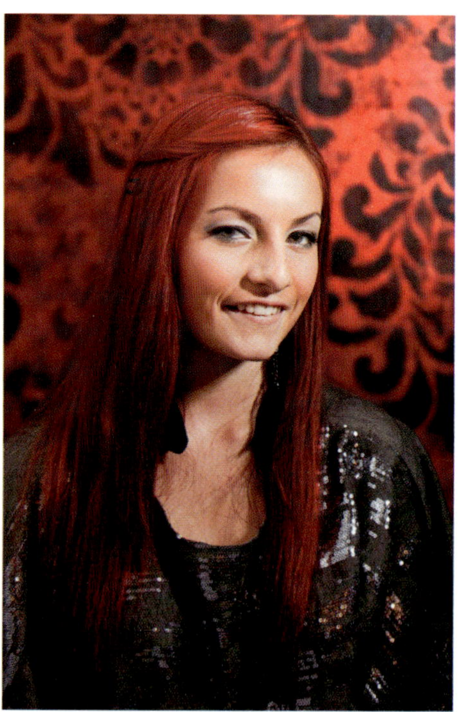

6.32 Flash with bounce card. This image was produced using the Hanson Fong bounce card, a large piece of plastic that mounts to the back of the flash head with Velcro. Large bounce cards like this broaden and soften the light by bouncing it back toward the subject. Notice how the background and shadows start to open up and even out. Exposure: ISO 100, f/3.5, 1/60 second with an EF 70-200mm f/2.8L USM lens.

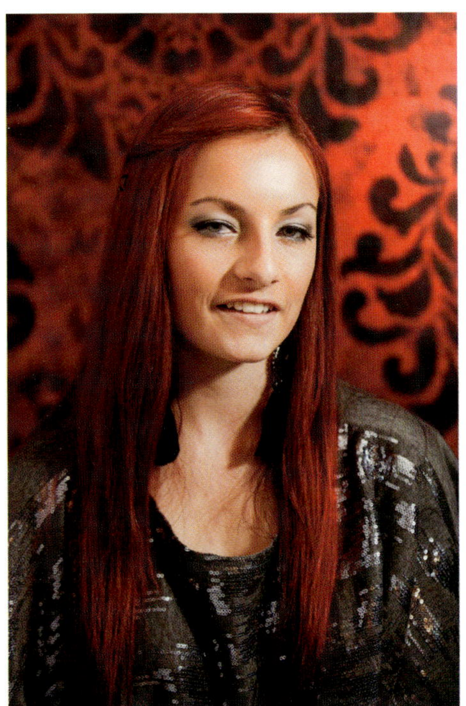

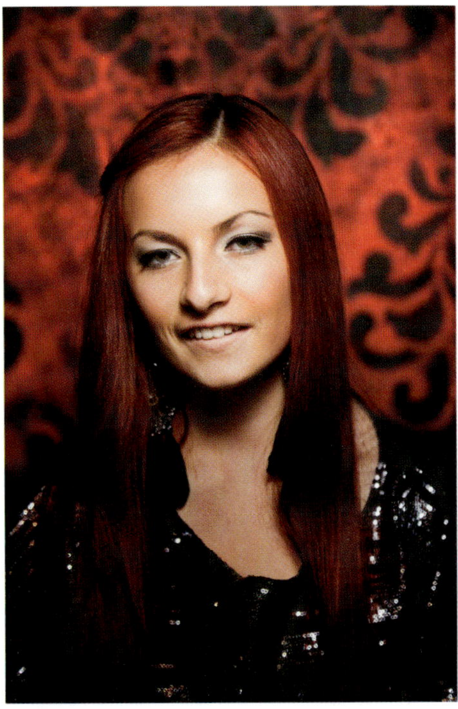

6.33 Flash with Lightsphere. This image was produced using the Gary Fong Lightsphere, a large, clear plastic housing that mounts on top of the flash head. A favorite with event photographers, this modifier does a good job of creating relatively shadow less light. Exposure: ISO 100, f/3.5, 1/60 second with an EF 70-200mm f/2.8L USM lens.

6.34 Flash with beauty dish and grid. This image was produced using a Mola Softlights Demi beauty dish with a 25-degree honeycomb grid from HoneyGrids attached to its front. Grids confine the light to a narrow beam, confining its spread. These large dish-shaped modifiers are one of my absolute favorite tools because of their versatility and the fact that they make great hats! Beauty dishes with both white and silver interiors are used in fashion, beauty, portraits, studio, and location — you name it. Exposure: ISO 100, f/3.5, 1/60 second with an EF 70-200mm f/2.8L USM lens.

CROSS REF See Chapter 5 for more information on light modifiers.

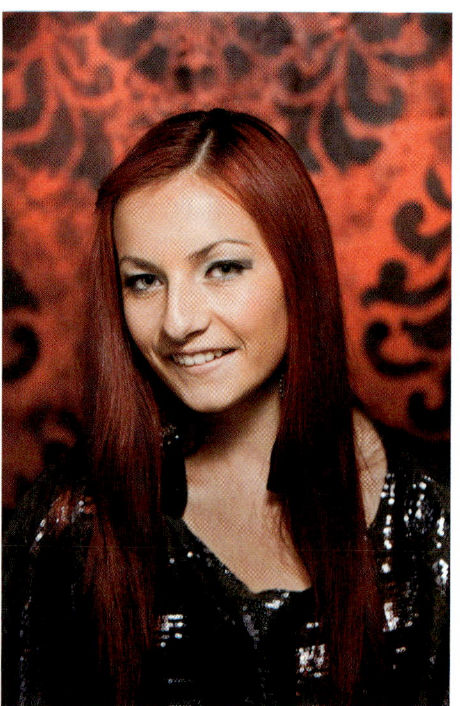

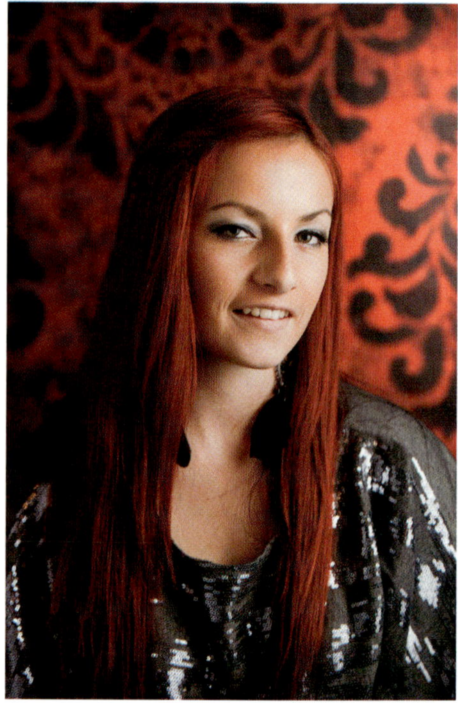

6.35 Flash with beauty dish. This image was produced using a Mola Softlights Demi beauty dish without a grid. Exposure: ISO 100, f/3.5, 1/60 second with an EF 70-200mm f/2.8L USM lens.

6.36 Flash with stripbank. This image was produced using a Westcott Bruce Dorn asymmetrical stripbank and Magic Slipper Speedlite adapter. Stripbanks allow you to channel light in a narrow and long shaft that can produce images that vary from soft to edgy. I've included a few examples of what's possible with this versatile tool in the next section. Exposure: ISO 100, f/3.5, 1/60 second with an EF 70-200mm f/2.8L USM lens.

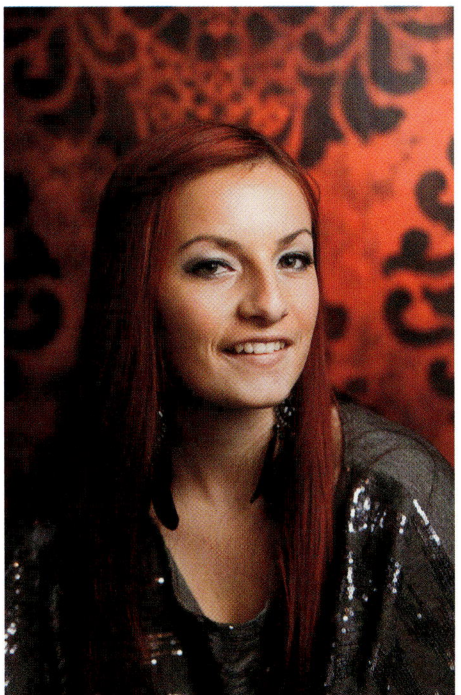

6.37 **Flash with softbox. This image was produced using the Westcott 28-inch Apollo softbox, a portable, umbrella-style modifier that produces beautiful, soft light. Both the stripbank used in Figure 6.36 and this modifier have interior baffles and exterior diffusion panels that can be removed alone or in combination to increase specularity. Exposure: ISO 100, f/3.5, 1/60 second with an EF 70-200mm f/2.8L USM lens.**

One Light, Two Lights, Three Lights!

Whether you've got one light or ten, your only limit is your imagination. One light, along with a reflector or diffuser, opens up a whole world of possibilities. Add to that an extra-long E-TTL cord for off-camera flash, and the world is your oyster! In this section, I walk you through a series of one-, two-, and three-light sample images and diagrams that explain how the images were created, what gear was used, and why. I've included a healthy collection of one-light images because I know many people have just one light! Two-light images follow with plenty of behind-the-scenes images giving you a peek at the process. Last but not least are the three-light images; this is where things get really interesting!

One light

Don't be discouraged if all you have is one light. One light is power; one light is magic! That lonely little light you're holding in your hands is capable of greatness. If you have any doubts, refer back to Figures 6.3 through 6.5 right now. The following images can all be produced with one Speedlite and various modifiers. In some cases, I've shown examples where I've used two Speedlites together as one light source to get more power, quicker recycle times, and longer battery life, but they're all possible with just one light.

Images 6.38, 6.40, and 6.42 are each examples of a technique I learned from my friend and top commercial shooter Joel Grimes. If you ever have an opportunity to take one of Joel's workshops, do it.

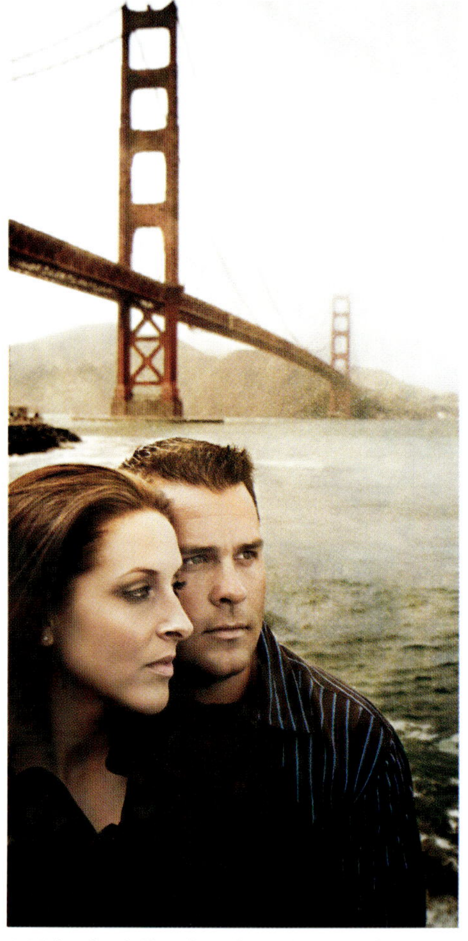

6.38 In the following three images, I used two Speedlites in E-TTL II mode triggered by the RadioPopper PX system, fired into one 3-foot Photoflex OctoDome (using only one Speedlite would have produced similar results). The OctoDome and flashes were attached to a paint pole operated by an assistant (voice-activated light stand). Many cities require permits to put down light stands, so this is a great option. Exposure: ISO 100, f/10, 1/50 second with an EF 17-40mm f/4L USM lens.

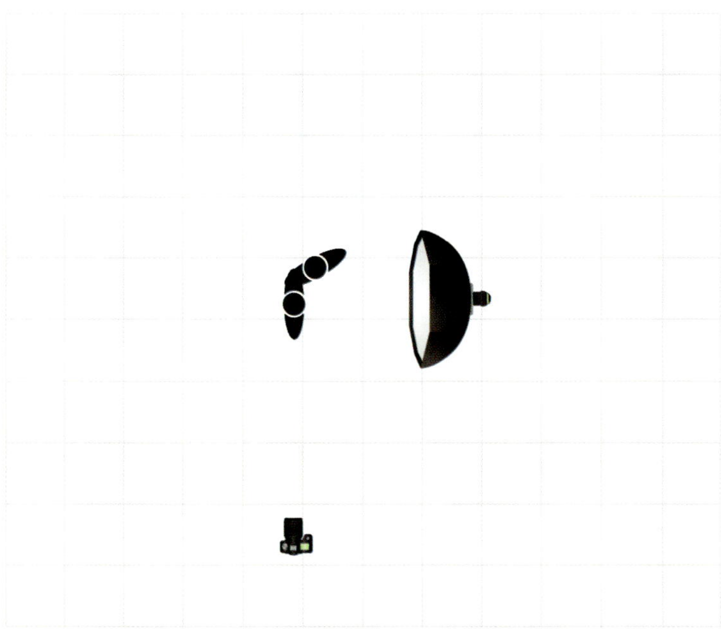

6.39 Lighting diagram for Figure 6.38.

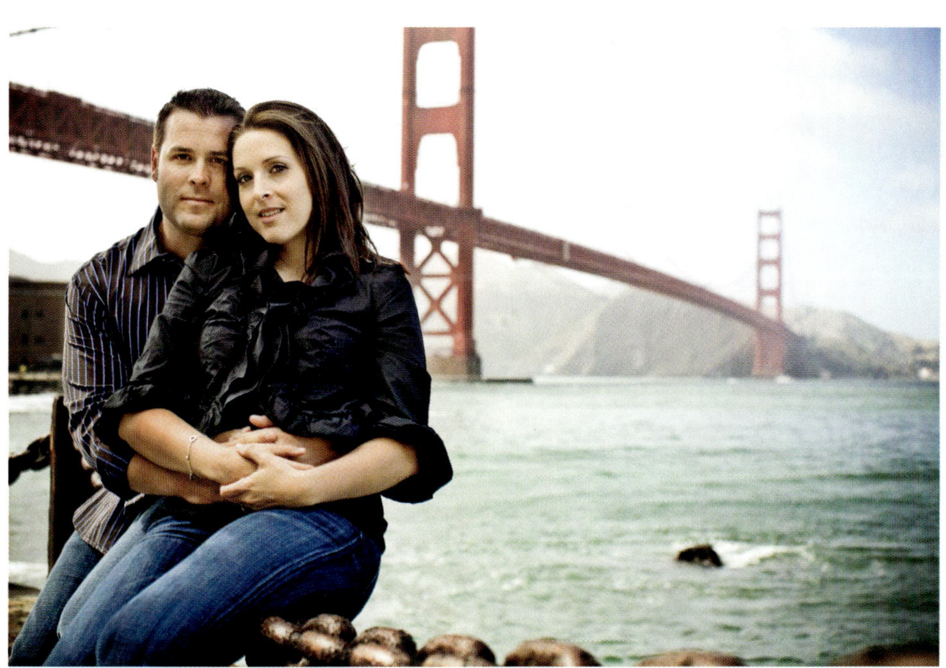

6.40 Changing the position of this one light source creates an entirely different look.
Exposure: ISO 100, f/4.5, 1/250 second with an EF 50mm f/1.2L USM lens.

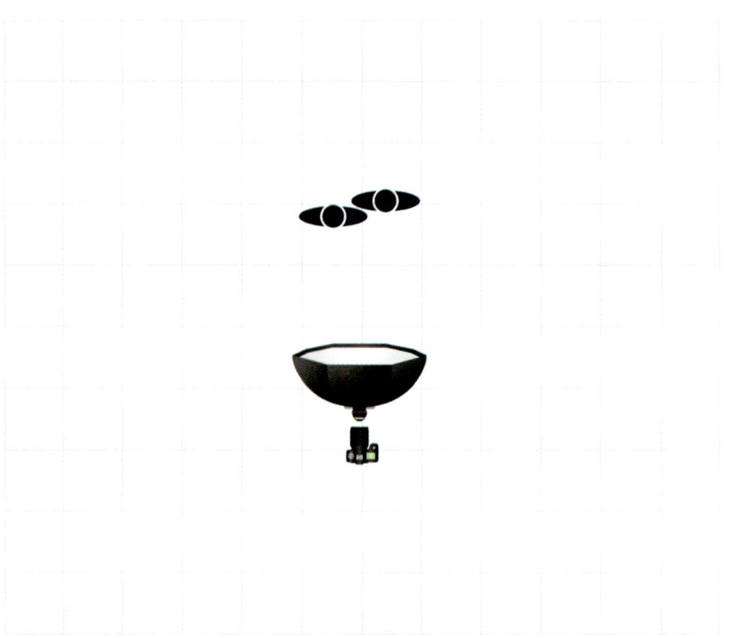

6.41 Lighting diagram for Figure 6.40.

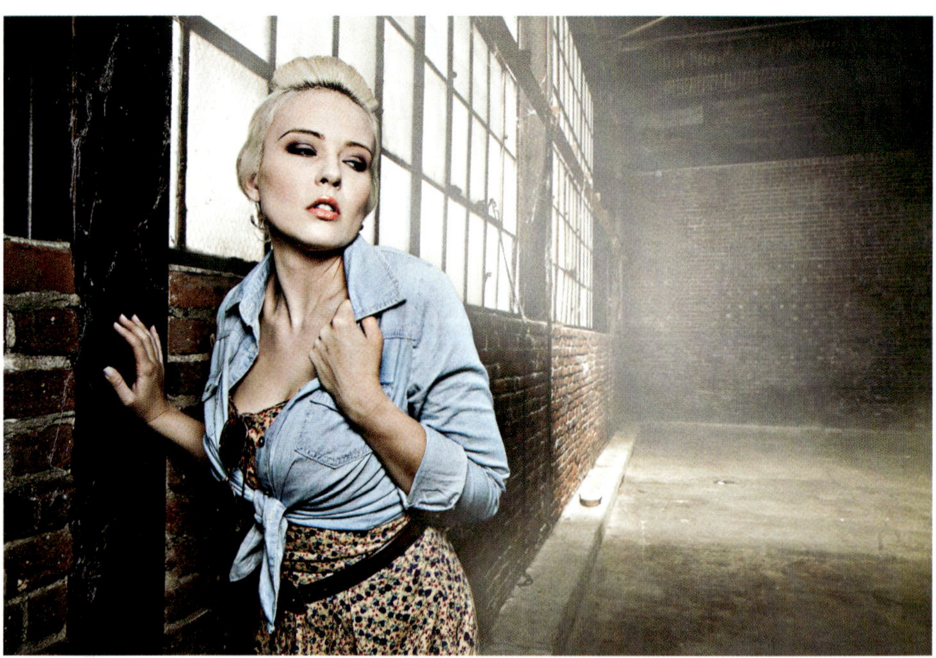

6.42 Moving the light source closer and directly over the lens on camera produces this soft, fashion-oriented quality of light. Exposure: ISO 100, f/11, 1/50 second with an EF 16-35mm f/2.8L USM lens.

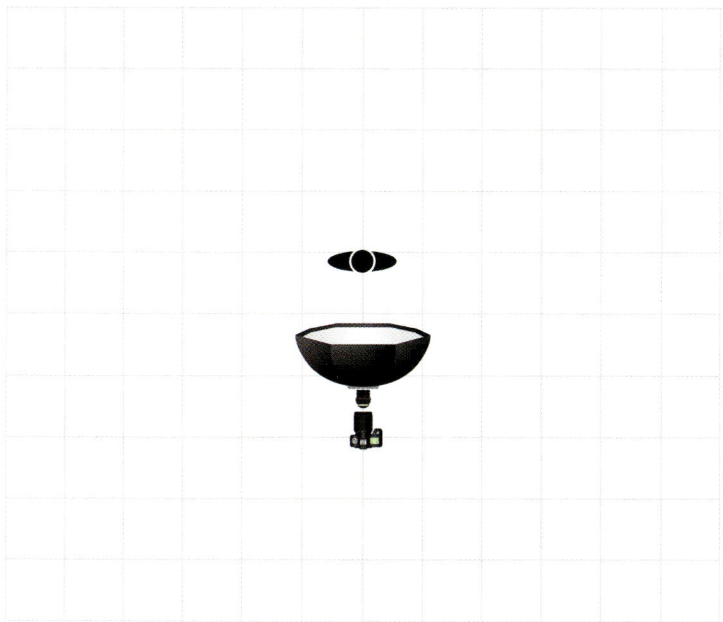

6.43 Lighting diagram for Figure 6.42.

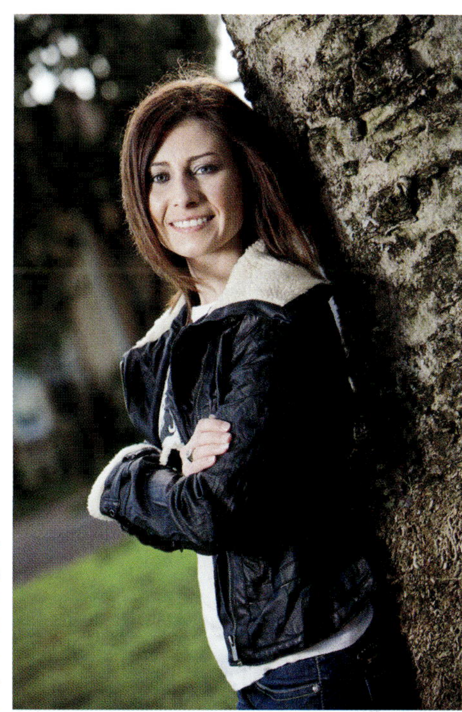

6.44 The sun is a powerful ally in your one-light arsenal. Here I've placed my subject with the sun behind her and used it as a second free light source to provide rim light on her hair. Exposure: ISO 100, f/4.5, 1/200 second with an EF 70-200mm f/2.8L USM lens.

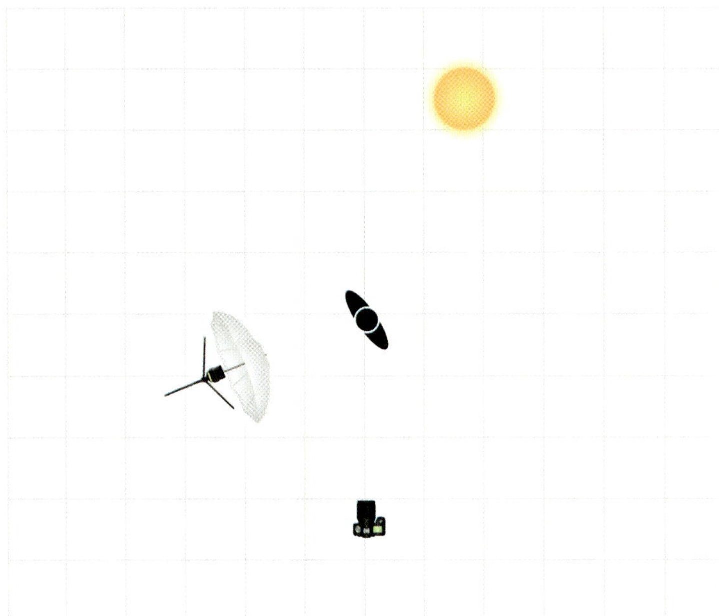

6.45 Lighting diagram for Figure 6.44. Here I'm using two Speedlites fired into a Westcott collapsible shoot-through umbrella. Both Speedlites and the RadioPopper PX receivers are attached to the umbrella with a Lovegrove Consulting Gemini Bracket.

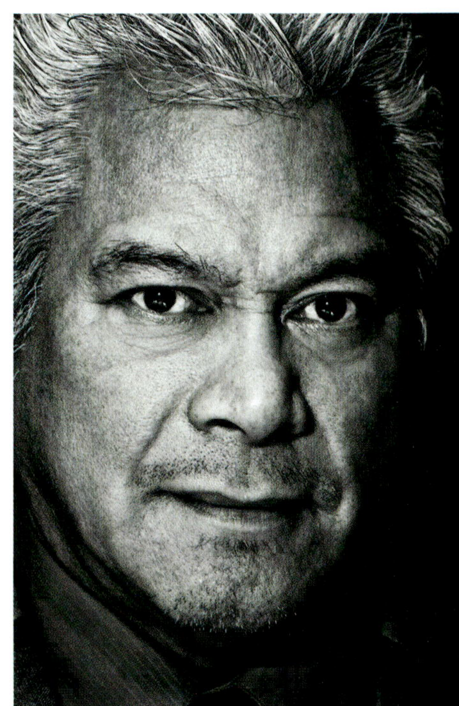

6.46 This image was inspired by the work of amazing photographer Kelly Castro. Here a car's sun reflector is used in conjunction with Gary Fong Lightsphere to produce a really gritty and specular look. The accordion catch-lights in the subject's eyes are very unusual. Don't try this on your women friends! Exposure: ISO 100, f/11, 1/100 second with an EF 70-200mm f/2.8L USM lens.

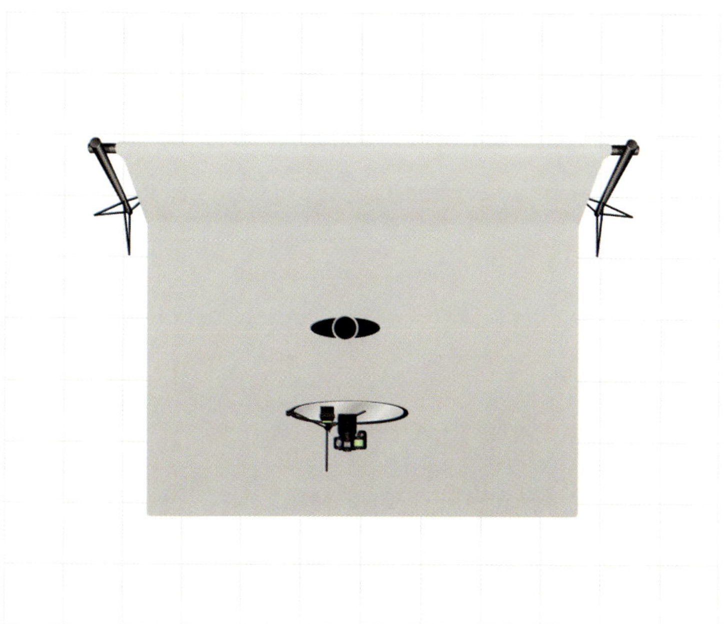

6.47 Lighting diagram for Figure 6.46.

Next I've included two variations of split lighting using one Speedlite and various modifiers. See the split lighting section earlier in this chapter for additional examples.

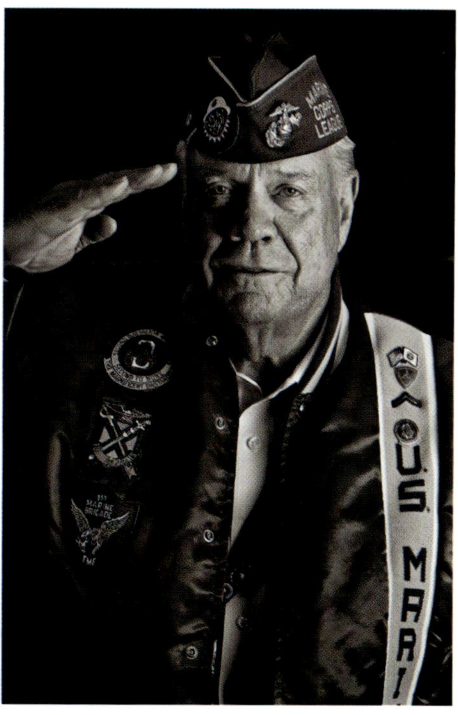

6.48 This image, part of a series of veterans portraits I made, shows what's possible when split light is feathered. Note the position of the softbox (a Westcott 28-inch Apollo) in relation to the subject's shoulder; setting it up this way helps feather the light across the subject and reduces hot spots. A large portable Westcott 6-in-1 silver reflector is used camera left to open up the shadows. Exposure: ISO 200, f/5, 1/100 second with an EF 85mm f/1.2L USM lens.

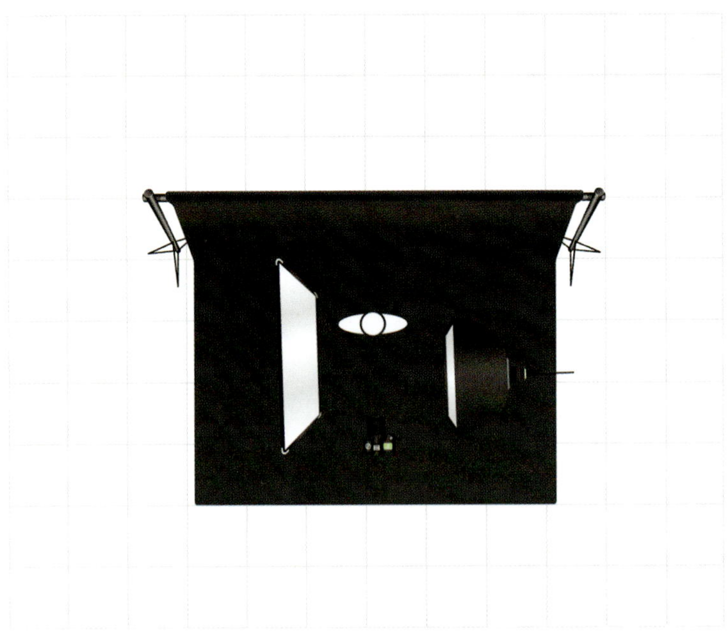

6.49 Lighting diagram for Figure 6.48.

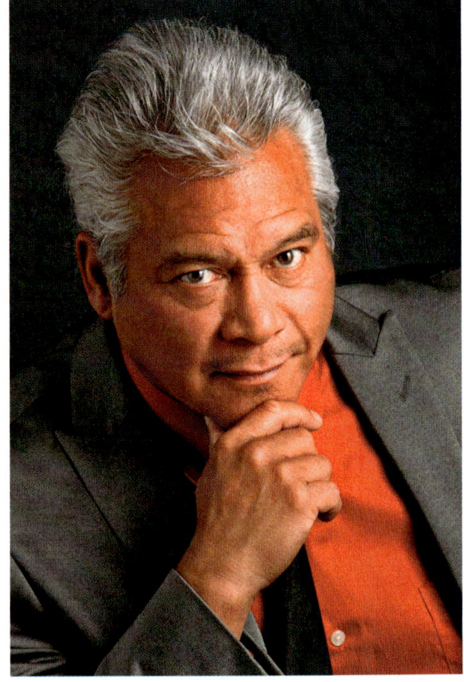

6.50 This next image shows the softer side of what's possible with split-style lighting. To produce this image, I used a Westcott asymmetrical stripbank camera right and a large California Sunbounce silver reflector on the left, just outside the frame. This gives the image a very soft and open feeling. Exposure: ISO 100, f/14, 1/100 second with an EF 700-200mm f/2.8L USM lens.

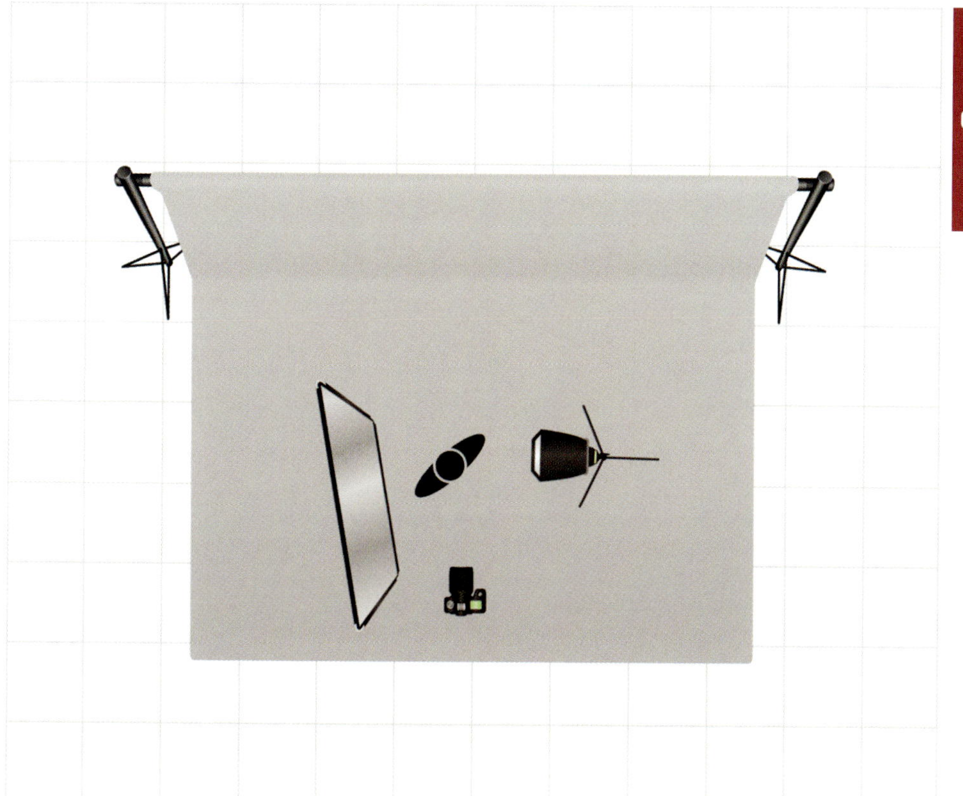

6.51 Lighting diagram for Figure 6.50.

Two lights

With two lights come two times the fun, two times the possibilities, and two times as much stuff to carry! Two-point lighting allows modeling and sculpting, the use of rim and fill light, lighting in ratios, groups, and many other options. Here are a few examples of how I've used two lights.

Two-point lighting is a classic way to light and one that affords many creative possibilities. In the following two light images, I explore how you can achieve multiple looks using the same lighting setup by simply changing your position, the subject's position, or both.

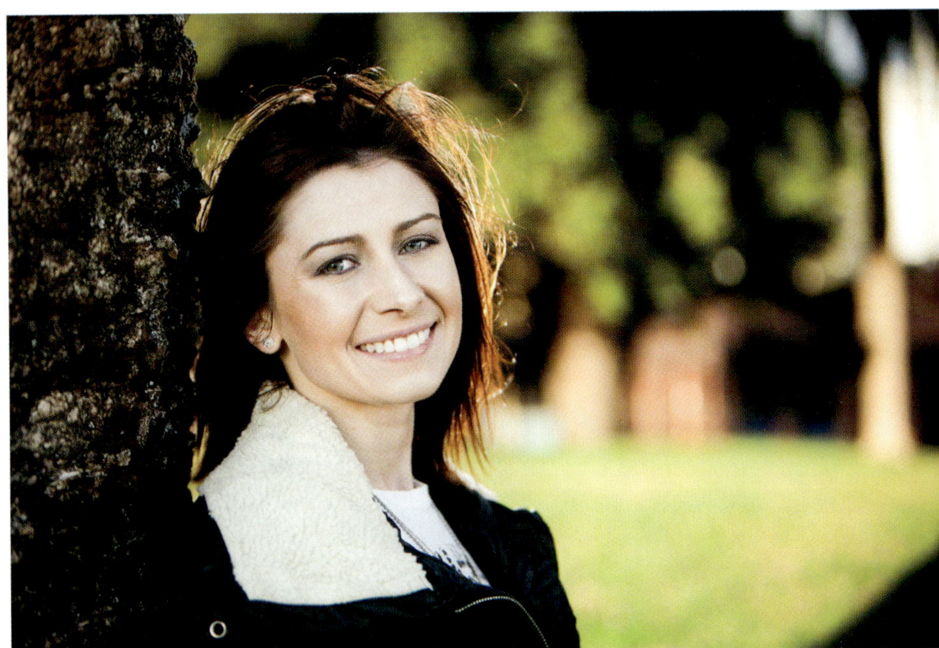

6.52 Figure 6.44 shows how the sun can be used as a kicker or rim light. In this image, I'm achieving that same look by using a second Speedlite behind the subject's head. Exposure: ISO 100, f/2.8, 1/320 second with an EF 70-200mm f/2.8L USM lens.

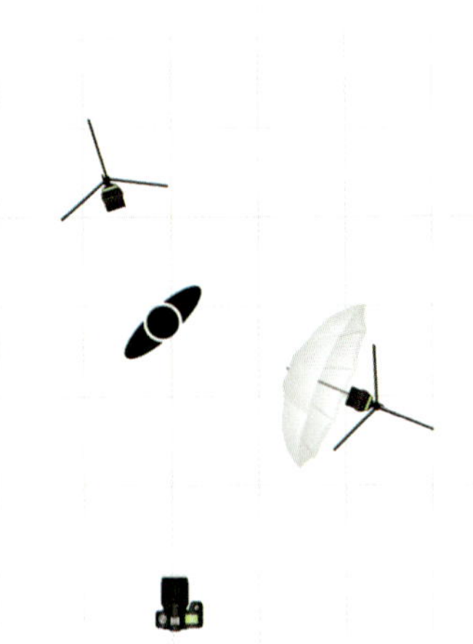

6.53 Lighting diagram for Figure 6.52.

6.54 This image of model Taylor Anderson in an urban doorway uses a simple two-point lighting setup. Lights are placed opposite one another in a wedge shape, allowing key, fill, and edge light. These images were produced using Lastolite EzyBox hot-shoe softboxes, Manfrotto light stands, and the RadioPopper PX System. Exposure: ISO 200, f/2.8, 1/160 second with an EF 70-200mm f/2.8L USM lens.

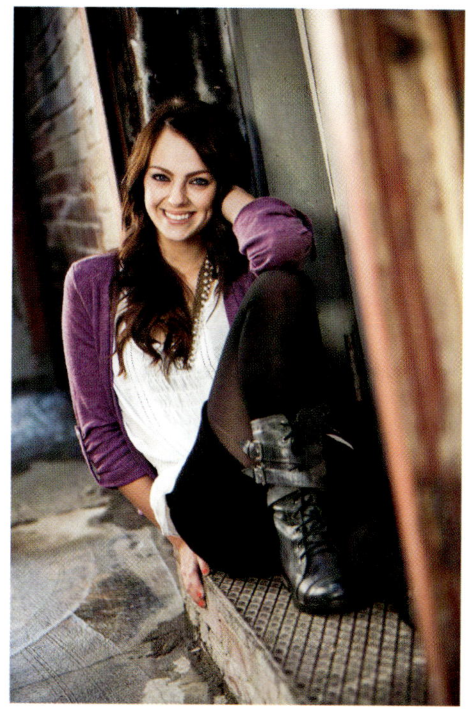

6.55 Behind the scenes! Notice how close I have the two lights placed in relation to my subject. These softboxes are relatively small light sources, so if I want the soft light I'm getting in Figure 6.54, I need them close. One light out in front and camera left is acting as my key light and another behind the model is providing accent light on her hair.

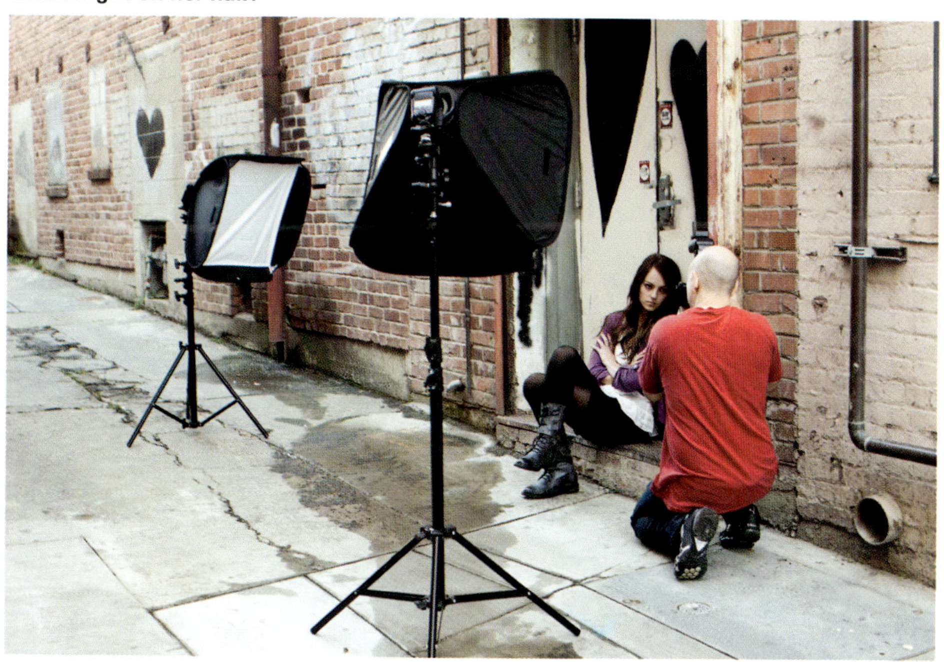

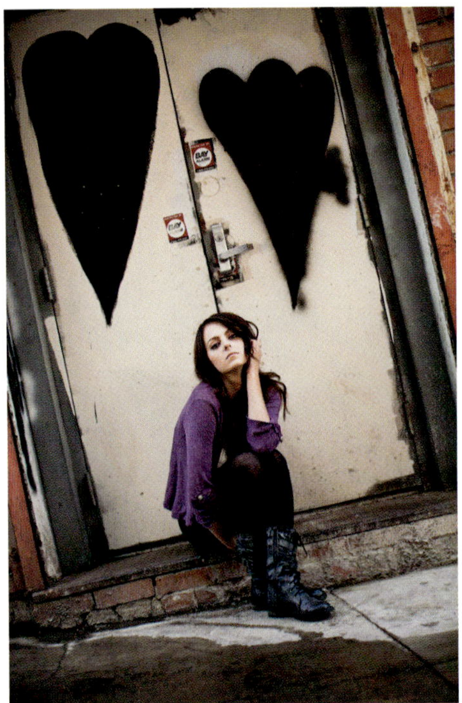

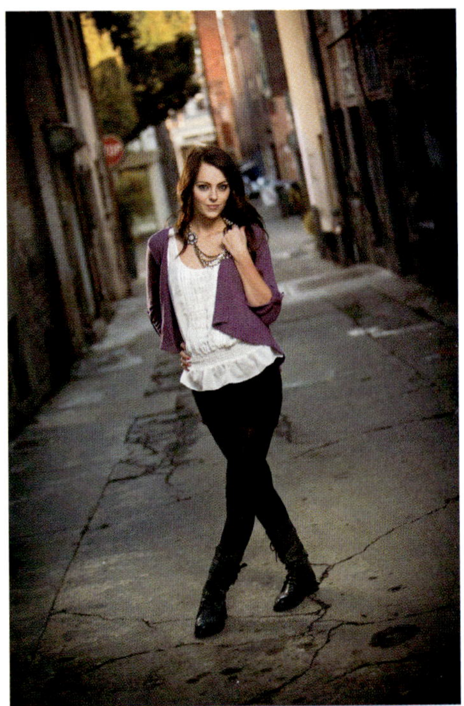

6.56 By leaving the lights exactly where they were in Figure 6.55, turning the model, and simply changing my position, I'm able to achieve a completely different quality of light that's flat and even. Exposure: ISO 200, f/2.8, 1/160 second with an EF 70-200mm f/2.8L USM lens.

6.57 Moving down the alley where we were shooting, I arranged the lights front to back again. However, this time I positioned the lights farther apart and farther away from the model. I did this to produce yet another quality of light, harder and with more contrast. Exposure: ISO 100, f/2.8, 1/125 second with an EF 70-200mm f/2.8L USM lens.

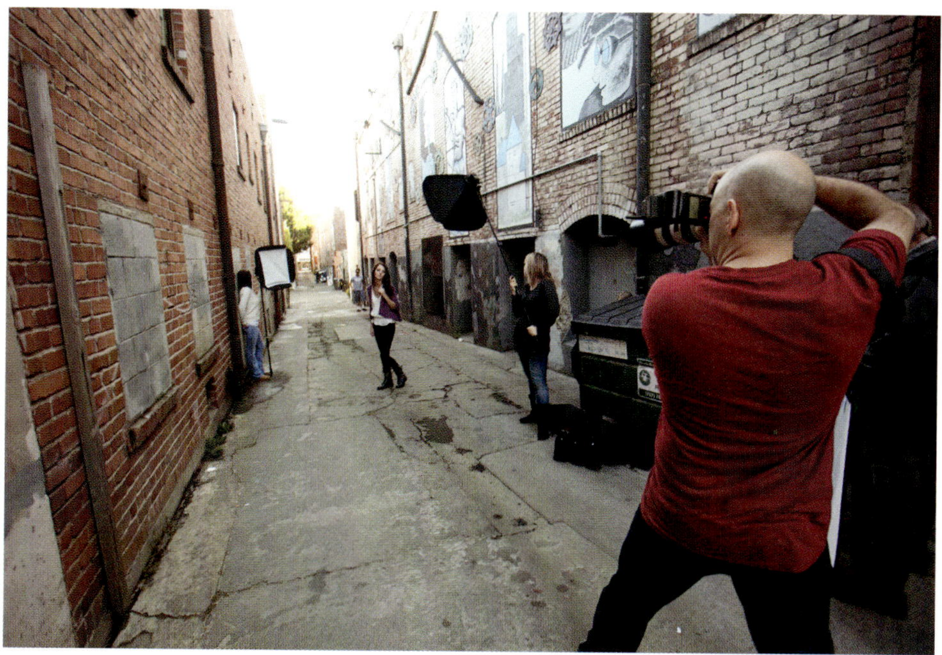

6.58 Behind the scenes!

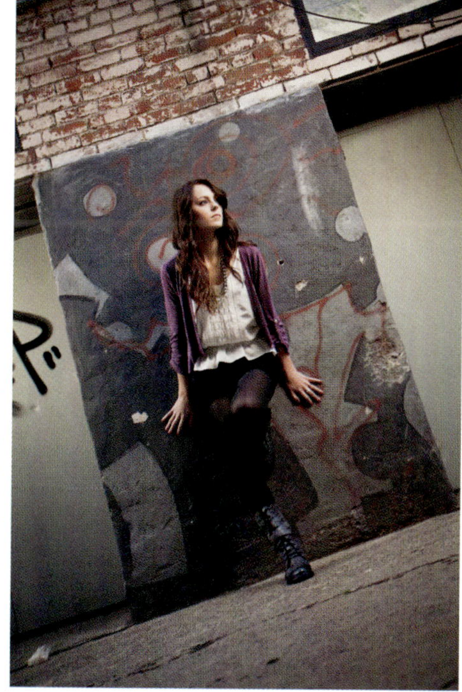

6.59 Architectural elements make great props, and this doorway is no exception. By placing the model between the two doors, I'm able to create an interesting frame for her. Even though my lights are placed on her left and right, having the model turn and look toward one side creates a more interesting light. Instead of the light being flat, as it was when she was facing the camera, it's now modeled. Exposure: ISO 200, f/4.0, 1/100 second with an EF 17-40mm f/4L USM lens.

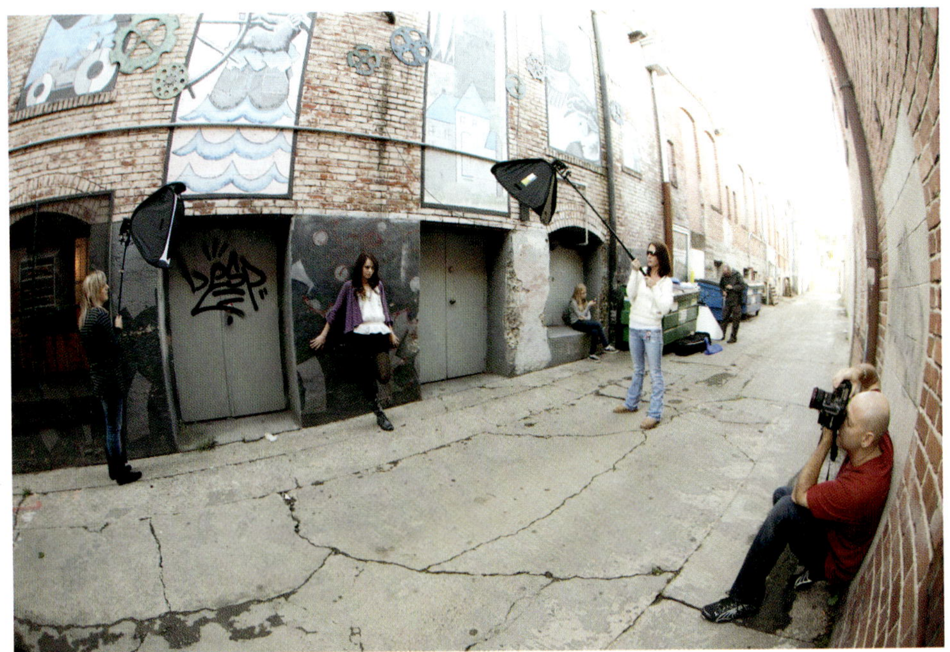

6.60 Behind the scenes!

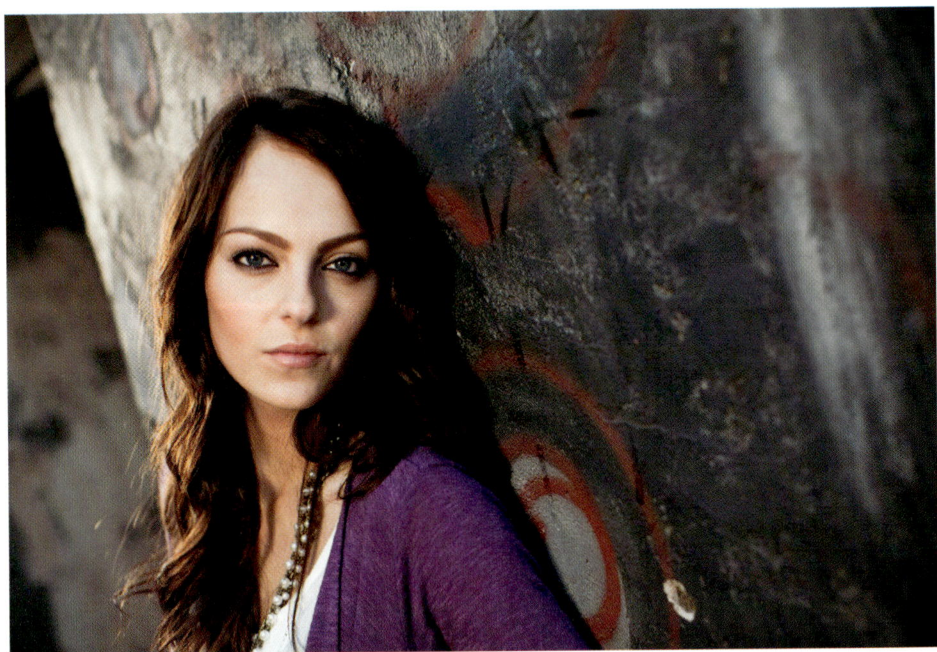

6.61 Keeping the lights exactly as they were positioned in Figure 6.60, but changing my position, I'm able to achieve another interesting quality of light. Exposure: ISO 200, f/2.8, 1/400 second with an EF 50mm f/1.2L USM lens.

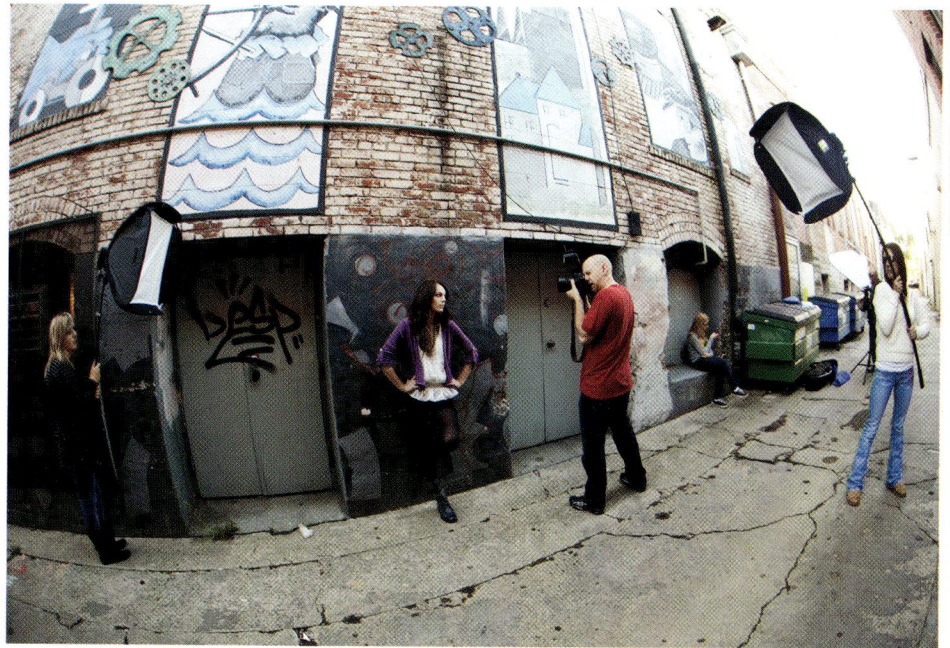

6.62 Behind the scenes!

Three lights

Three times a charm? You bet! Using three lights opens up even more options to mold, sculpt, wrap, and chisel with your lights. You've seen some of the classic three-light setups earlier in this chapter, but now it's time to break out and get a little crazy! The great thing is that after you've learned the foundation lighting patterns, you'll be able to bust out and experiment when the mood strikes you. Lighting patterns are like recipes used in cooking: The real fun is in experimenting! You may have a kitchen disaster every now and then, but that's half the fun.

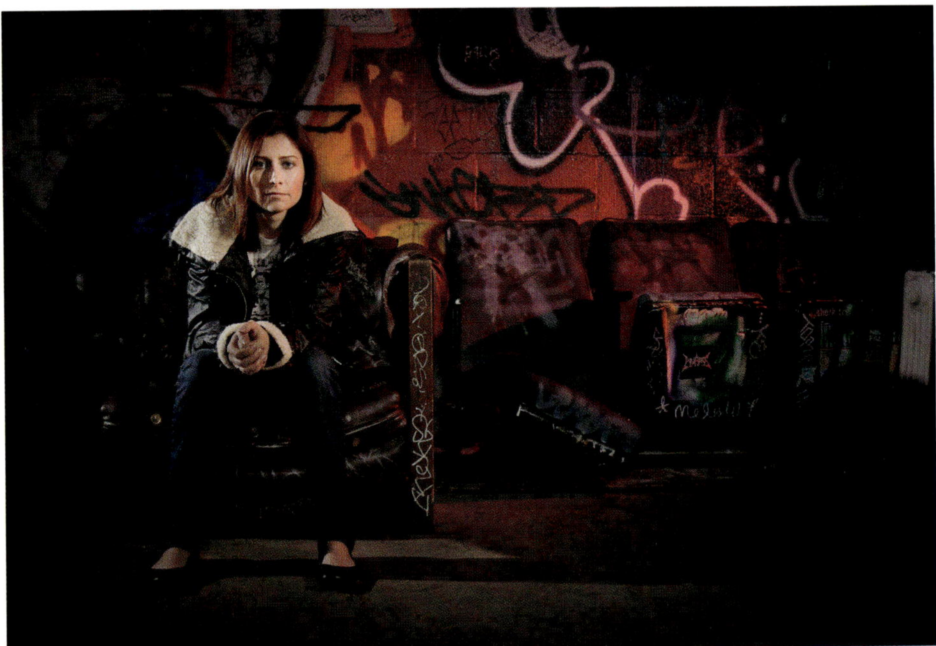

6.63 This portrait of engineer Carrie Janello was made in the loading area of the Phoenix Theater in Petaluma, CA. I used three 580EX II Speedlites, Lastolite Strobo 25-degree grids and gels, Lovegrove Consulting MkVII brackets, Manfrotto 5001B light stands, and the RadioPopper PX system. Exposure: ISO 400, f/4.0, 1/60 second with an EF 28-70mm f/2.8L USM lens.

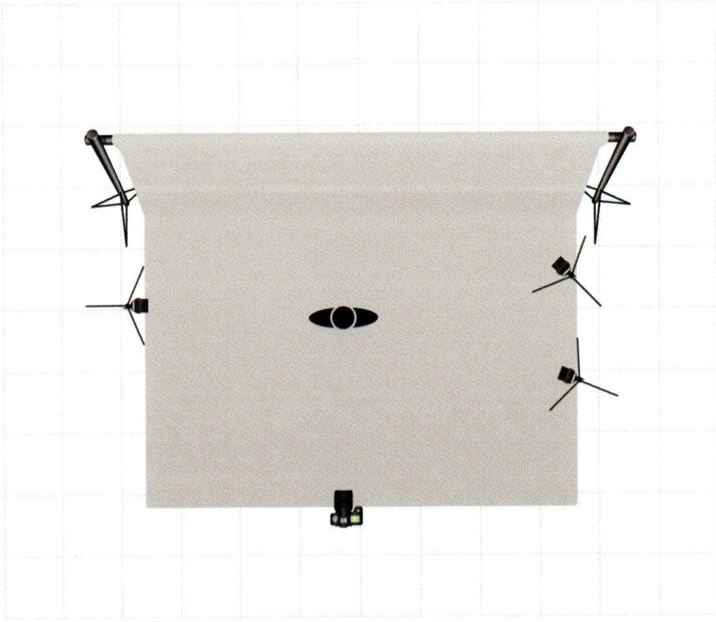

6.64 Lighting pattern for Figure 6.63

6.65 For this portrait of musician Nino Angelo Joseph Bosco, I placed one Westcott asymmetrical stripbank on the left and right sides of Nino and used a Mola Demi beauty dish overhead and angled in front of him. The three 580EX II Speedlites were triggered using the RadioPopper PX system. Exposure: ISO 100, f/4.0, 1/125 second with an EF 28-70mm f/2.8L USM lens.

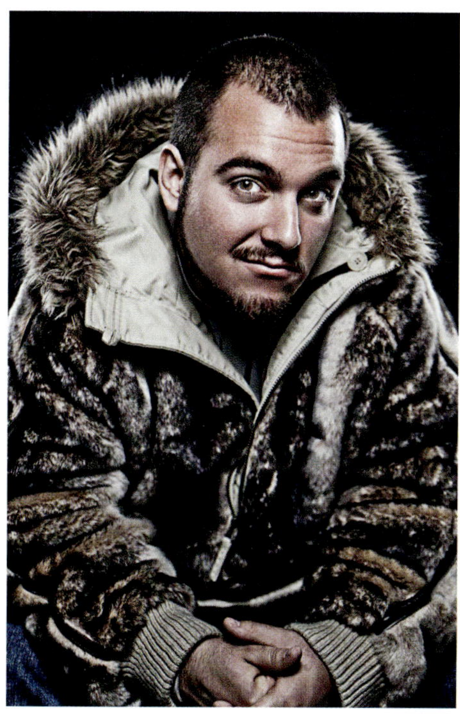

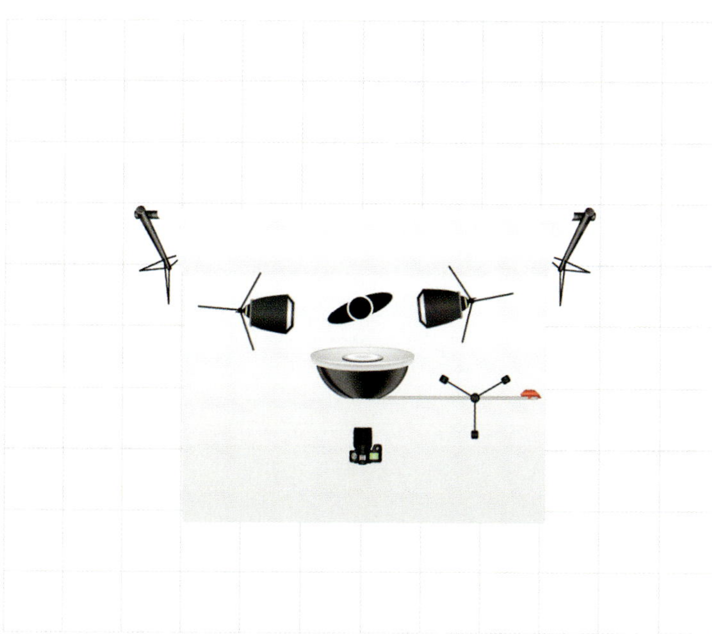

6.66 Lighting pattern for Figure 6.65

Practice Makes Perfect

I've covered a lot of exciting information about lighting in this chapter. When you're ready, set aside time to try the following exercises to practice what you've learned. Reading is one thing, but doing is another. The best way I know to learn is to get out there and start lighting! You'll be glad you did.

▶ **Use your flash off camera.** Pick up an extra-long E-TTL cord (see Appendix C) and start experimenting with off-camera flash. Have a model or friend sit in one place, and make photographs of them while moving your Speedlite to different positions around them. Create sidelight, backlight, and so on. Try to replicate some of what you've seen in this chapter.

▶ **Decode it.** Next time you're looking at a magazine or movie poster or advertisement, try decoding the lighting patterns used in the images you're looking at. The catch-lights in the eyes provide great clues!

▶ **Experiment with gels and grids.** Along with the Sto-Fen filter, gels and grids are very affordable light modifiers. When you can, pick up a few and start experimenting. Try aiming your Speedlite at a white wall and taking a picture without a grid and then with a grid. You'll see how the spread of the light has narrowed considerably.

▶ **Create diagrams.** Sign up for a free account at www.sylights.com and start creating your own lighting diagrams and seeing those created by others. Diagrams are a terrific way to start brainstorming your ideas and keep track of what you'd like to try later.

▶ **Pick one.** Choose one light modifier and dedicate yourself to only working with that modifier for a day, a week, or a month. Restricting yourself like this will help you think outside the box, get to know your equipment, and help you discover new ways to use it.

Posing Basics

Why include a section on posing in a book about Canon Speedlites? The answer is simple: Posing and lighting are the two biggest factors differentiating the pro from the amateur. The responsibility of posing subjects can strike fear into the hearts of even the most intrepid photographers; many feel unsure about directing people they're photographing. Think of it this way: It's your job! The people who seek you out are counting on you to help them look their best. Most people who you'll be photographing won't be professional models, and they'll expect you to be a confident leader. They'll want guidance about what to do in front of your camera. Absent this direction, you'll have nervous clients and uncomfortable sessions. Countless books and DVDs by some of the best in business are available on the topic of posing, and I encourage you to seek them out. Look for educational materials and examples from Hanson Fong, Bambi Cantrell, David Williams, Doug Gordon, and Robert Lino (see Appendix C for more resources). Here I cover some important basics to help get you started.

Your personality and your ability to connect with your subjects and put them at ease is an essential component in the posing equation. No one approach works for everyone or every situation. This is where your intuition and ability to read people and judge their temperaments comes into play. Should you be gregarious, soft and contemplative, or something completely different? Ask yourself these kinds of questions on a case-by-case basis. Figuring out the best way to reveal something truly unique in each person is essential to really good portraiture. Photographer Peter Hurley's DVD with Fstoppers. com, *The Art Behind the Headshot,* covers this subject well and demonstrates how to use your personality during sessions to get what you want from clients.

Posing, much of which is based on paintings of the old masters, is sometimes perceived as stiff, old, and stale. I agreed with this view before I took the time to really investigate the concepts behind posing and the work of its master practitioners. These stereotypes are misrepresentations based on poor examples of something really worthwhile. Posing at its best can be traditional, contemporary, or many variations in between. For inspiration, look at fashion magazines, movie posters, and advertising campaigns — you'll see that posing is everywhere! Whether traditional or modern, a pose should be the result of careful thought about body placement. With posing and lighting, your aim is to create a mood, tell a story, or evoke a feeling. Body language is a huge part of this! Developing a good foundation in the basics of posing and knowing how to apply these techniques will add depth to your portraits.

Start by letting your subjects know what space to occupy in the scene. To use a theater term, you're essentially *blocking* out the subject's space, showing them the acceptable range of movement. You want your subject to know how to stay within the bounds of the light you've created, allowing you to consistently achieve great results. I also call my subjects' attention to the key light in the scene by asking them to look toward it during the shoot. Letting subjects know the kind of framing you'll be working with also helps in guiding expectations. Are you shooting full-frame, three-quarter-length, or head-and-shoulders images? If your subjects know you're using head-and-shoulders framing, they don't have to worry about the position of their feet.

Clearly communicating that you want clients to shift positions, change their angle, and turn or tilt their head can be a linguistic challenge. I find that by first explaining a series of hand gestures you can make with one hand can help tremendously in conveying your message. Clench your fist and explain to your subjects that it represents their head, then tilt it backward and forward and twist it left and right. Ask your subjects to mimic these movements with their head. Try the same thing with your hand flat and turned with its thin side facing the subject, also twisting it to the left and then right. Again, explain that it represents their body and asking them to follow along when you signal. This little technique has been a big help!

Here are some basic poses for individuals:

- ▶ **Feet placed naturally.** If you're shooting full-length portraits, foot positioning is important. You want the feet positioned close enough together but not so close that it looks like they cannot support the shape of the body. Additionally, if your subjects face you at an angle, have them place most of their weight on the back leg. To help create the desired and classic S-curve when posing females, ask them to push their front hip toward the camera. This is what photographers mean when ask a model to *pop the hip*. These are slimming techniques that naturally bend the front leg toward the camera.

- ▶ **Shoulders at an angle.** This is the most common pose in portraiture. When the subject's shoulders are turned at an angle to your camera, you create a slimmer profile. Having the shoulders squared and directly facing the photographer makes the subject look boxy, unflattering, and wide. In other words, not good!

- ▶ **Head tilted.** After subjects turn their shoulders so that they're at an angle to the camera, have them tilt and turn their head slightly so it isn't in the same position as their shoulders. When you have your subjects tilt and turn their head slightly while still making eye contact with the camera, you're also changing the position of the eyes and making the eyes appear larger.

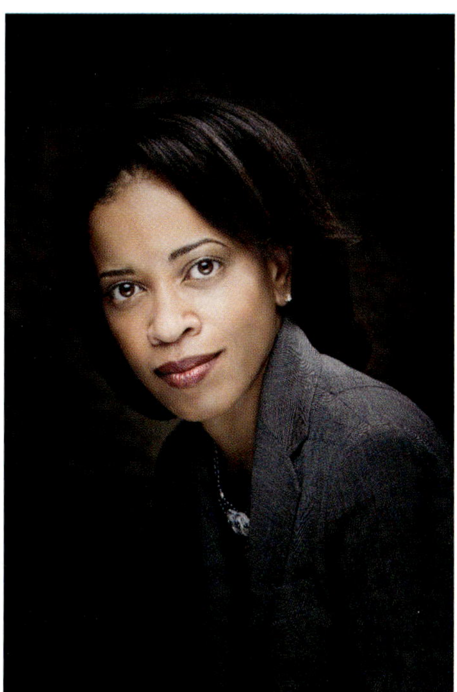

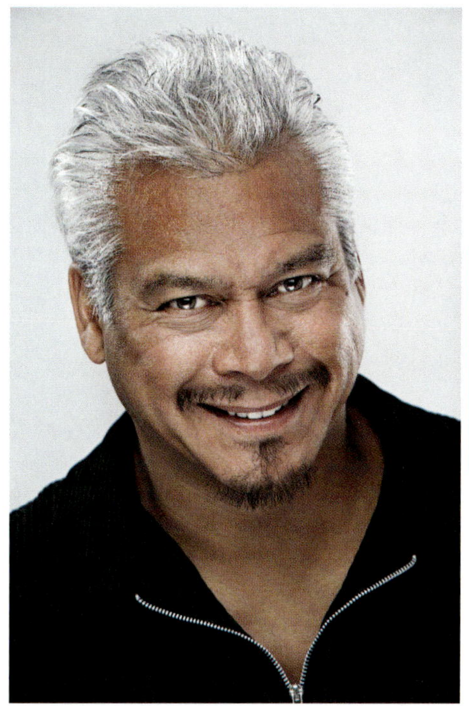

AA.1 Posing your subjects with their shoulders at an angle to the camera creates a slimmer, less boxy profile. Placing the front shoulder higher than the back created a more formal pose appropriate for this law school professor. Taken with two Canon 580EX II Speedlites. Exposure: ISO 200, f/14, 1/100 second with an EF 70-200mm f/2.8L USM lens.

AA.2 A slight tilt of the head makes the eyes break a visual line from the shoulders, as in this portrait of photographer Dennis Urbiztondo. Taken with three Canon 580EX II Speedlites. Exposure: ISO 100, f/9, 1/125 second with an EF 70-200mm f/2.8L USM lens.

After you get these basic posing techniques down, you're ready to move on to more creative portrait-posing techniques.

TIP When you're directing changes to your subject's posture, make slight adjustments. Small movements go a long way when shooting portraits. You want poses to feel natural, not overworked or contrived. Keep it relaxed and fun, and you'll be sure to have repeat clients. Remember, it's as much about the photography as it is about the experience clients have working with you!

Developing Your Style

You can learn a lot by working with professional models or even just watching them work. Notice how professional models place their bodies and angle their movements in a scene. Look at where they're placed in the composition and think about why these choices were made. They are extremely aware of where the camera is and how to play to that angle. If you don't have that opportunity, don't worry — there are many semiprofessional and aspiring models you can work with. You can connect in online communities like Model Mayhem (www.modelmayhem.com) and One Model Place (www.onemodelplace.com). These are also fantastic places to network with other photographers and learn about lighting and equipment.

This is the kind of keen awareness you need to develop. As I mentioned earlier, magazines (fashion and editorial), movie posters, ad campaigns, and Google image searches are also great educational resources and inspirations for posing ideas. Not to mention the scores of posing DVDs available (see Appendix C). Create a scrapbook of your favorite poses and try to replicate them. Eventually you will develop your own signature style. Practice makes perfect!

Positioning the body

Slimming the body is almost always an important goal in posing. As a photographer you're only working with two dimensions (height and width), so how you handle them is very important. By angling the body away from your camera instead of positioning it squared and straight, you create a noticeably slimmer appearance. Try it — photograph someone straight on, and then angle the body away from the camera and photograph that person again. You'll be amazed at how much slimmer this technique makes them look.

Slimming poses include the following:

▶ **Torso twisted, with legs slightly separated.** In addition to having your subject turn his or her hips slightly to the left or right, you should also suggest a stance with the legs slightly separated, or one in front of the other. This reduces the silhouette of the body and makes the hips and legs appear slimmer. Black or dark-colored clothing also achieves this effect. Northern California–based wedding and portrait photographer Bambi Cantrell's DVD *The Language of Lighting and Posing* is a great resource and addresses the positioning of legs.

▶ **Leaning on a chair or table.** Have your subject turn at an angle, either left or right (preferably toward the main light), and slightly arch the back. With correct lighting, this places much of the body in shadow, and more emphasis is on the face and upper body. Turning a chair around and positioning its back toward the camera at a slight angle while having the subject sit with his or her arms folded on top is another look worth exploring. Using chairs, tables, couches, stairs, walls, and other props helps create more interesting posing situations.

When subjects sit, I request that they shift forward a little and not use the back of the seat. I ask them to sit upright, pull their shoulders back and down, and extend their chin forward. This avoids slumping shoulders and helps slim the face and neck. Turning the head slightly also helps tighten loose skin around the neck and jawline.

People often get nervous when posing, tensing their bodies, raising their shoulders, and looking somewhat hunched over. I like to help clients by using my own body to show what I want them to do with theirs. I often demonstrate by pulling my shoulders back and down and giving an example of a more open appearance with my body language.

Clothing can also help or hinder your efforts to capture a thinner and pleasing appearance for your clients. Having a conversation with your clients about clothing prior to their portrait session is a good practice that can help avoid extra work during the session and in post-production. Ask clients to bring several wardrobe options, so you'll be able to choose different colors and styles and create a variety of looks, enabling you to sell more pictures.

In situations where my client is wearing loose clothing, I use clothespins to tighten clothing closer to the side of the body that's away from the camera; reducing wrinkles.

NOTE Ask before touching clients! When you're in the middle of a portrait session and caught up in the moment, you may be tempted to jump right in and reposition your client's clothing, body, hair, hands, arms, and legs. However, exercise caution and realize this may make some people very uncomfortable, or worse, expose you to legal liability! This is why you should always ask first. This is especially true when working with minors. I find having a female assistant on hand for these adjustments is best.

Positioning the hands and arms

The position of the hands and arms in relation to the subject's body can make or break a portrait. Handled correctly, hands can look beautiful, adding curves and attitude. Handled incorrectly, they can look like wide claws. The same is true for arms, which can add line, dimension, and once again, attitude. If arm positioning is ignored, arms can look like meat hooks.

Follow these guidelines when working with hands and arms:

▶ **Triangular pose using the arms and hands.** Try using this pose as an alternative to standard vertical portrait positioning. Back away slightly with the camera in the vertical position or switch to horizontal framing. Then fill the bottom of the frame with your subject's arms folded, filling in the bottom of the triangle, where the arms and shoulders lead up to the peak of the triangle, which is the face of your subject. Don't be afraid to try cropping in below the top of your subject's head. This is a very contemporary look.

▶ **Shoulders diagonal.** Shoulders are great for adding an imaginary diagonal line to your portraits to help break up the symmetrical qualities of the face and body. Lowering the front shoulder creates an inviting line up toward the face, while raising the front shoulder creates more attitude and a perception of detachment. Titling the camera left or right off its horizontal access, known as a *dutch angle* or *dutch tilt,* is also a great technique for creating visual interest and tension.

▶ **One arm away from the body.** Because bodies are so linear and faces symmetrical, adding more visual interest to the image often involves breaking these perceived lines. Having the subject

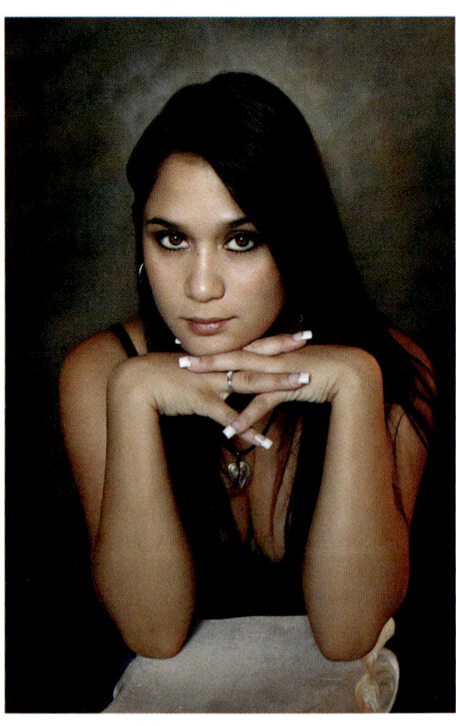

Courtesy of Dennis Urbiztondo

AA.3 Pose subjects with the arms crossed and resting on the back of a chair or other surface to create a triangle shape that leads from the bottom of the frame to subject's face. Taken with two Canon 580EX II Speedlites. Exposure: ISO 400, f/3.5, 1/160 second with an EF 28-70mm f/2.8L USM lens.

put a hand on a hip or the waist can break these lines and help define the midsection.

▶ **Hands relaxed.** Hands and fingers in a portrait can include key storytelling elements — the kind of jewelry worn on them, the character and quantity of their wrinkles, and the way they're used to cover portions of the face, to point, or to touch another person are all elements that can add to an image. Hands are one of the main ways people express themselves, so use them carefully when building your images. Be aware that anything closer to the camera appears larger, and anything farther away appears smaller. This means that hands, more often than not, should be turned to present their slimmest profile when positioned near the face. Hands placed one over top of the other (ring hand up) look more relaxed than with the fingers interlaced. With two people in a portrait, resting one's fingers on the other's shoulder instead of the entire hand conveys caring without possessiveness.

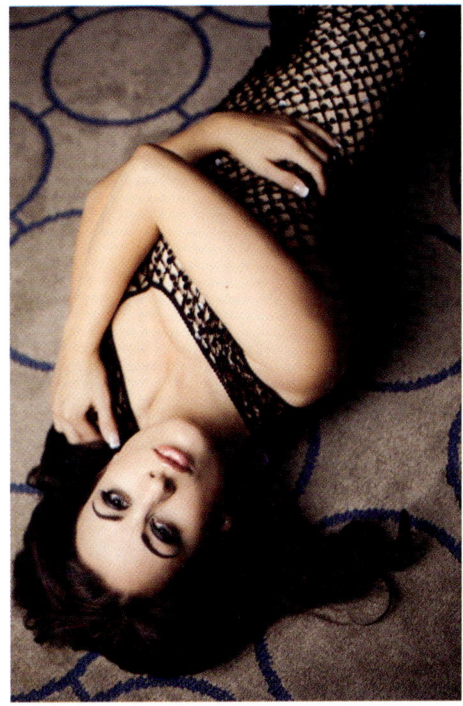

Courtesy of Stacie Frazier

AA.4 Positioning the arms crossing the body helps break the linear quality of the figure to add visual interest. Notice how the body is angled away from the camera position and the hands are shown almost in profile. Both techniques contribute to a slimming effect. Exposure: ISO 100, f/3.5, 1/100 second with an EF 50mm f/1.2L USM lens.

CAUTION Be sensitive to your subject's feelings about their bodies when photographing them. Many people find posing for pictures uncomfortable, and these feelings translate to their body language. The trick is to show clients you're on their side and truly invested in how they look in the final images. If they trust you and relax, you can more easily produce images that make you both shine. Try posing for another photographer to deepen your understanding of what it feels like to be on the other side of the camera.

Paying attention to the details

Your final posing considerations before pressing the shutter button are positioning the head and neck and directing the angle of the eyes to help your subjects look their best. Subtle adjustments can add a lot to the visual interest of the shot, so spend time on these details to fine-tune your images.

The eyes are often said to be "the windows to the soul" and can be the most important part of a portrait. You make eye contact with the person in the portrait, and by doing so, you make a connection with that person. For most business portraits, this is quite true. In these situations, my portrait subjects want to make a personal connection with their potential clients, employers, or customers. Direct eye contact communicates that they've got nothing to hide, creates an open and friendly feeling, and portrays subjects as people you'd be comfortable meeting.

When shooting portraits, producing a broad range of looks from the session should be your goal. Concentrate on getting the expected, tried-and-true (otherwise known as *safe*) images nailed, and then flex your creative muscles. Have the subject look away from the camera lens to achieve a more contemplative, less camera-aware expression. Try several different angles, directing clients to look left, right, slightly up, or slightly down. Moving the head around and changing pupil orientation opens up more white around the eyes, making them appear larger. When creating these variations, I like to change the composition of my subjects framing as well so that I've got images of the subject looking into and out of the frame.

> **TIP** When shooting portraits, either indoors or outdoors, consider using fill flash to create catch-lights in your subject's eyes. Catch-lights are tiny reflections in the eyes from the main light source, whether it's a flash, bright sky, or the sun. The eyes are one of the most important elements of your overall portrait, and this attention to detail adds a natural feeling and polished quality to your portraits.

Here are a few more details you need to consider when posing your subjects:

- ▶ **Beware the hair.** To save yourself a lot of unnecessary retouching headaches during post-production, pay special attention to your subject's hair. I don't know how many times I've had to learn this lesson! Be sure hair looks neat and orderly, without strays going across the face, eyes, nose, or mouth. Also watch for unwanted gaps in the hair that allow skin to show through. Check and recheck the hair, strays, and gaps every time you change a pose. Having a professional hairstylist (or even an assistant, friend, or spouse) on hand to help watch for and correct hair as needed is an even better plan, allowing you to focus on your client. Having hair and makeup professionals on hand also puts clients at ease and reassures them that they're in good hands.

▶ **Jewelry and accessories.** It's easy to get so caught up creating the best lighting and posing for a subject that you can miss other important elements, like what's happening with jewelry and accessories. Again, this is a good argument for having an assistant on hand tasked with keeping an eye on things. Remember to make sure that necklace clasps are hidden and necklaces centered, rings turned the right way, and earrings positioned correctly. These simple steps produce the best results possible and require the least amount of retouching.

NOTE Be careful with the way you photograph a subject's neckline. The position of camera, clothes worn, and age and weight of the subject all play important roles. Many older women are particularly sensitive about their necks. To minimize these factors and achieve the most pleasing portrait, hide portions of the neck with clothing, position the camera to reduce the amount of the neck shown, or shoot down from a position slightly higher than your subject. This technique is also a great way to reduce double chins and the overall perceived weight of your subject.

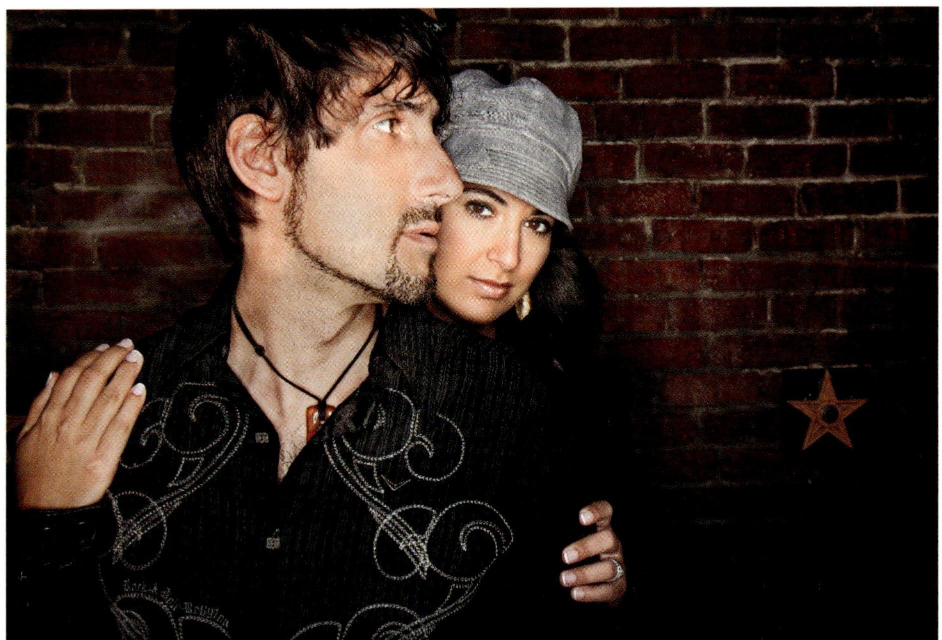

AA.5 Having subjects positioned on the left or right of the frame and looking into or out of the image adds direction and drama. Exposure: ISO 100, f/13, 1/200 second with an EF 16-35mm f/2.8L USM lens.

Positions to Avoid

I've briefly discussed some helpful concepts to keep in mind when designing your portraits. Practice them, find what works for you, and incorporate them when and where you see fit. Keep in mind there are no set rules, so develop an informed posing vocabulary and then let taste and creativity be your guide. Here are a few posing pitfalls that you should avoid:

- **Straight on to the camera pose.** This pose might work well for portraits in which you want to make the body appear larger and the subject seem heroic. This kind of image is usually captured from a low angle to further accentuate this larger-than-life quality. At almost all other times, this arrangement looks rather stiff, artificial, two-dimensional, and unflattering. Avoiding rigid poses that call attention to the symmetrical and linear quality of the body helps make your subjects look more natural, casual, relaxed, and three-dimensional. Break up the body shape by bending legs and arms whenever possible.

- **Repetitive poses.** Using the same pose repeatedly and lighting it the same way is lazy and will quickly bore you and potentially cast a pallor on your images. Part of the fun of creating portraits and being an artist is keeping things fresh and exciting. This is also important for your business. Try regularly introducing new skills and equipment into your repertoire. Challenge yourself to develop new photographic, business, and interpersonal skills. A great habit is to set yearly goals for yourself, such as, "This year I'll work on mastering Speedlites." I look at every subject and shoot as unique and an opportunity to choose different tools, backgrounds, or lenses, depending on the look I'm going for. Be creative and push yourself to new heights.

- **Chins too low or too high.** Head positioning is all-important. Make sure that your portrait subject's chin isn't directed too low to a point where the eyes are shadowed, and watch out for having the chin so high that your model looks too snooty, aristocratic, or thug-like.

- **Negative body language.** Be upbeat, relaxed, patient, and confident. Remember that you're the leader, so clients look to you to set the tone and tempo of the session. Body language is subjective and depends entirely on the type of image. Folded arms, a back toward the camera, or a subject looking down might work great for a senior portrait or commercial image but be perceived as off-putting in a family portrait. Being aware of the impact body language has on the message of the image is your best preparation. And if the vibe in the studio is negative, you can bet the images will reflect it. You want your subjects to have a good time during their sessions. Winning images, happy clients, and repeat business are dependent on the experience clients have when working with you.

Have fun with your subjects. A successful portrait session depends on your subjects feeling comfortable, as well as your skill and creativity. Practice your craft often so you can be confident with clients. Being well prepared and knowing your techniques and equipment inside and out is essential for you to be relaxed. When you're calm, clients are able to relax knowing they're in the trusted hands of a trained professional. Encourage your subject to relax and just be natural; keep an eye out to capture any special looks they create on their own, even when not posing. Often those fleeting, non-camera-aware moments are where the true magic lies. Things such as wrinkling the nose, winking, or rolling the eyes can reveal much about a subject's personality. All these little things that people instinctively do every day can be special moments that end up making a great portrait image. Engage your clients and see what kind of expressions you can coax out of them. Get the safe stuff first and then have fun!

Planning Poses

Part of the excitement and creativity involved in shooting portraits is the decision-making process determining the eventual look and feel of the portrait. This planning (or *previsualization*) is an important step in the way I like to work. Typically, this is a collaborative effort between you and your client. Obviously, if you've been hired, you should make sure you and you're client are in agreement about the look, style, and purpose of the final images. The important thing to remember is to always speak with your subject beforehand and make sure you're on the same page. If you keep the client's expectations in mind, you'll both be pleased with the final results.

The flexibility of digital capture allows you to shoot as many different poses as time permits and immediately review them to see which poses work and which lack impact. When at all possible, shoot tethered and take

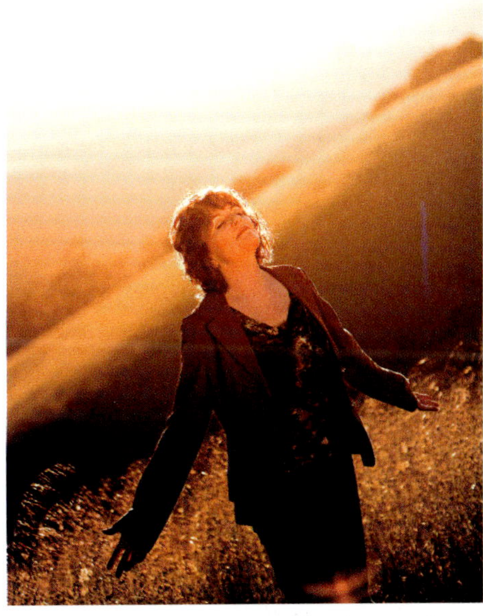

AA.6 Choosing a pose and background that fits the client's needs is your goal. In this portrait for spiritual singer Melissa Phillippe's CD cover, I suggested a background of awe-inspiring natural beauty and a pose looking toward the heavens. Exposure: ISO 100, f/2.8, 1/1600 second with an EF 85mm f/1.2L USM lens.

advantage of the large and accurate previews possible on a computer screen. The ability to compare images side by side on a large computer screen is also worthwhile.

Traditional posing

Traditional or more conservative posing is popular with business leaders and professionals. There are many uses for a headshot, such as website bios, speaking engagement announcements, marketing materials, annual reports, and newsletters. Having a good foundation and skill set for creating these kinds of portraits is money in the bank. There's a time and a place for the creative projects photographers all strive for and love, but as a well-rounded professional, you must address the needs of a broad range of clientele.

Many traditional poses share these characteristics:

- ▶ **Conservative expressions.** A slight smile, but not laughing, is key with traditional posing. For business media and publications, subjects often have more serious facial expressions and strong, direct eye contact.

- ▶ **Subtle backgrounds.** For traditional portraits, plain, subtle backgrounds are used. The most common looks are solid or mottled colors on dyed or printed fabric and painted muslin.

- ▶ **Seated positions for portraits and headshots.** The most common position for traditional posing is the sitting. It allows the subject to relax and stay in a designated area to be photographed. An adjustable posing stool is ideal for making small adjustments to the height and angle of your subjects as they face the camera.

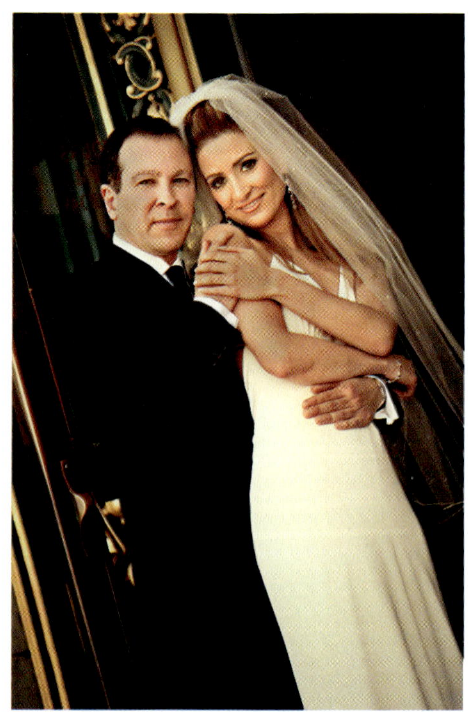

AA.7 Standing poses, popular in business, editorial, and wedding photography, portray strength and directness. Directing standing couples to embrace and positioning their heads close together along the same focal plane of the image allows crisp focus at wider apertures. Taken with one Canon 580EX II Speedlite. Exposure: ISO 100, f/3.2, 1/250 second with an EF 700-200mm f/2.8L USM lens.

▶ **Standing positions for environmental portraits.** Having subjects stand is sometimes a good way to convey a commanding presence and can work well for business leaders and executives photographed in environmental settings. Standing poses are also very common in the wedding industry, as the participants are often dressed stylishly, in a suits or more formal attire, and standing can make them look and feel more comfortable and also shows off the wardrobe.

Editorial posing

Editorial posing, common in environmental portraiture, differs from its traditional cousin in that it captures subjects in a context relative to their surroundings, possessions, life events, and careers. These kinds of portraits, most often shot on location, are more relaxed and, at their best, tell a more complete story about people being photographed and how they live.

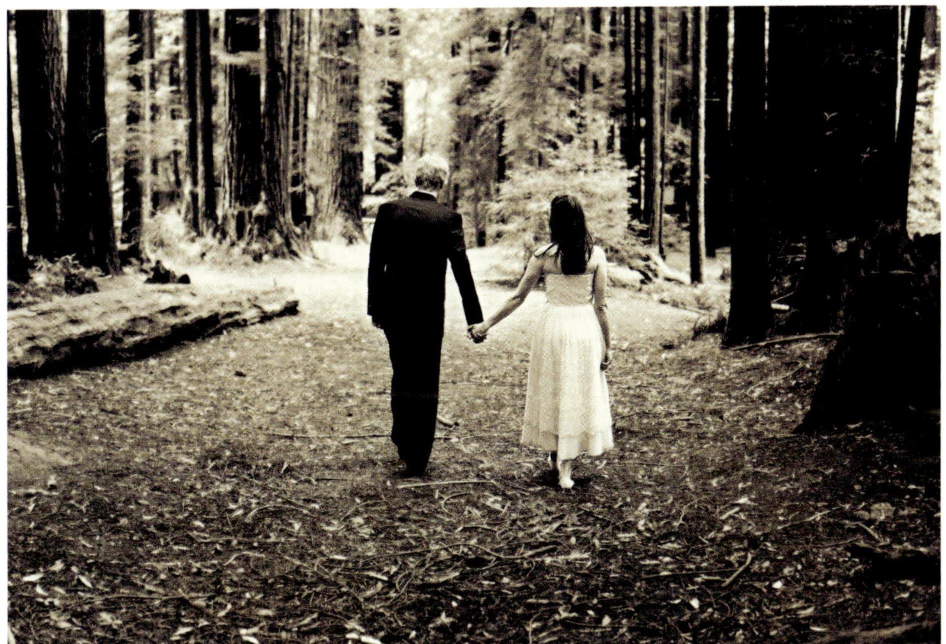

AA.8 Creating images that appear natural and unposed but that are still in perfect light and at a perfect location most often requires some planning and slight direction. Here the couple was asked to turn and walk away hand in hand down a nearby forest path that seemed perfect for this kind of image. Exposure: ISO 1250, f/3.5, 1/60 second with an EF 50mm f/1.2L USM lens.

Environmental portraiture is also increasingly popular in wedding photography where more relaxed and less camera-aware styles are preferable with many clients and photographers. Most of my wedding clients come to me for what they refer to as my *unposed* style. Although this is a compliment that I appreciate and means that I've done my job correctly, it is also a misconception. The trick is to make it look that way! Here's the way I work: My first step is finding a great spot for my clients to interact, in an ivy-covered archway, nestled between the rows of a vineyard, lying on the grass, or walking along the beach, to name a just a few examples. Next I give the couple some subtle direction — stand here, face each other, lean in and kiss, touch foreheads, walk toward me, pretend I'm not here, and so on. Then I hang back, give the couple space to interact, and shoot with a mid to long focal-length lens. This kind of shooting is where the magic often happens, and these kinds of photographs from the wedding day are what many photographers refer to as *the Romantics.*

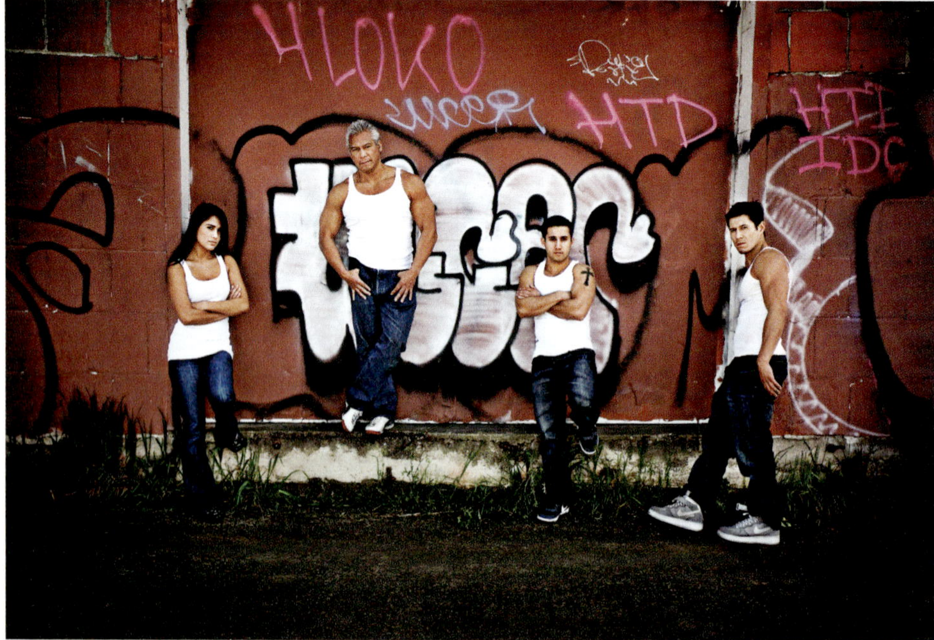

AA.9 For this portrait of an urban family with a love of fitness, rap, and pop culture, the right setting was key. Finding locations that fit your subjects' personalities is an essential part of environmental portraiture. Creating an image catalogue of locations you like is a great way to keep track of spots you find. This can easily be accomplished with GPS on a smartphone. Taken with two Canon 580EX II Speedlites. Exposure: ISO 100, f/4.5, 1/320 second with an EF 17-40mm f/4L USM lens.

These techniques allow you to capture images that are relaxed and natural-looking to the viewer, appearing unplanned and unposed. However, the secret is that without the couple first being placed in an ideal location, chosen by an experienced photographer with an eye for such details, and some subtle directions given to clients to spark their interaction, these images would not exist.

Environmental portraiture tells a visual story and gives insight into the subject's background and motivations. Styles can vary from gritty to beautiful to humorous, but all environmental portraits share the goal of going beyond the traditional. The best examples convey something more than just the face to reveal deeper contextual elements about the subjects, the way the world sees them, and how they see themselves in the world. This style of photography is something you're exposed to daily in magazines and advertising and is very popular.

Glamour style

Glamour-style photography involves creating images that are sexy and sultry. The poses are usually slimming and provocative, with eye contact directed toward the camera. For the most part, these photos are created using very flattering lighting.

The pin-up girls of the 1940s were the first subjects of glamour shots, and today that style can be found in advertising, boudoir, and even wedding and maternity photography. True glamour shots produce an air of romance and sexiness without ever crossing the boundaries of good taste.

For today's digital portrait photographer, thinking of glamour photography as an art form is key to understanding the possibilities of the medium. When shooting glamour-style photographs in your studio or on location, remember to be professional at all times. This is extremely important to build trust and future referrals. Make sure your models are comfortable with the types of poses they are expected to assume, and invite them to suggest poses themselves. Being verbally supportive behind the camera can go a long way to making your subjects feel confident and truly beautiful in front of the camera.

One of two situations usually exists when shooting glamour. The first is where the subject (usually a model) is familiar with his or her body and already knows what poses work best. In this case, the photographer is more concerned about lighting, placement, and location, as the model already has the posing routine down. If the photographer does need to request something, it's usually quickly understood and executed by an experienced model. The second situation occurs when working with subjects with little or no formal training in modeling and involves the photographer taking a more proactive role in directing the entire look of the shoot through posing direction, lighting, placement, and location.

You can frame poses for head-and-shoulders portraits, three-quarter-length body shots, and full-length images. The flash or flashes should be positioned to take advantage of and define the contours of the body, face, and hair, typically without harsh shadows. It usually helps to give your subject a broad area in which to pose, allowing the model to feel comfortable moving freely and not confined to a certain rigid lighting pattern. Posing for glamour-type photography should follow all the previously discussed posing suggestions with special emphasis paid to the eyes and, to a lesser extent, the mouth. Even slight changes of expression in these areas, along with the tilt of the head, can create a wide range of looks for successful glamour-style photography.

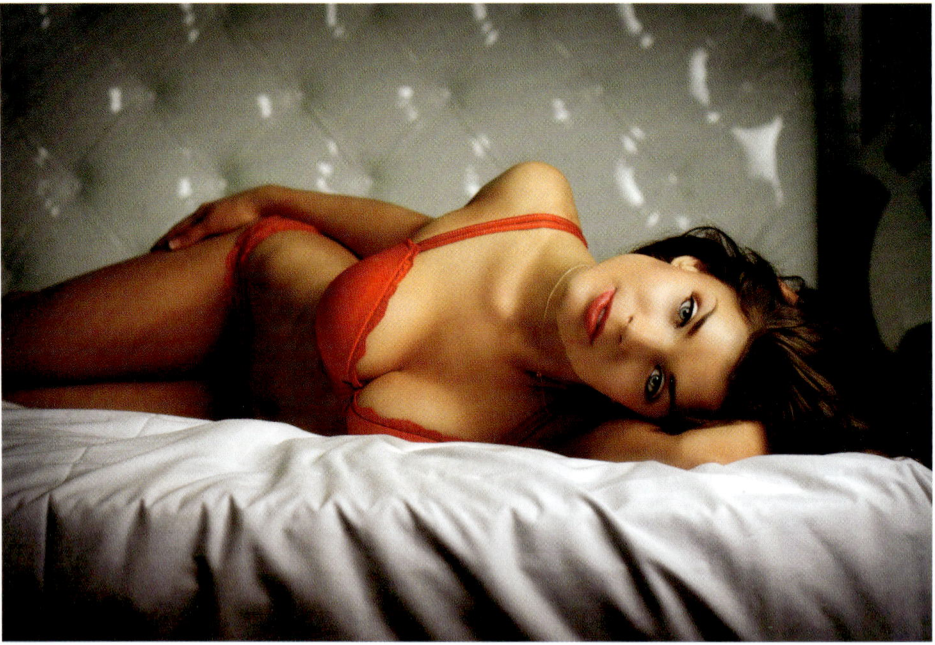

Courtesy of Stacy Frazier

AA.10 Glamour portraits are images meant to convey a lifestyle brimming with a certain vitality and sexuality. Images such as these can be used to market any number of products to a specific demographic. Exposure: ISO 100, f/3.2, 1/200 second with an EF 50mm f/1.2L USM lens.

Props and clothing accessories can also add visual interest and appeal to the image and can hide less-than-flattering features of your subjects, allowing them to look their best. Resist the urge to clutter your image with too many of these items, as the intent should always be to show your subject in the best possible light.

Rules of Composition

By this time, I hope you've gained a better understanding about the creative possibilities of lighting in general and Canon Speedlites in particular. Ideally, you've been inspired and learned how to begin lighting your subjects and scenes in new and more visually interesting ways. Keep in mind that great lighting is only part of the picture; you also need an understanding of the conventions and rules governing composition. Granted, when it comes to matters of creativity, "rules" can be hard to quantify. Just call them visual guidelines to keep in mind as you create images and edit your work.

At first, applying these concepts might seem strange and uncomfortable, like holding your camera in a different way or composing scenes through a new lens, and you may struggle a bit. Understand that these are the foundations on which your best shots will be built, and that a conscious working knowledge of them is essential to creating more dynamic and compelling images. Ultimately, these practices will become more innate sensibilities than rote memorization, occurring naturally and almost subconsciously while you work.

Consider these concepts as tools and techniques you can call on when a situation or location is not working or has been exhausted photographically. Mentally going through the list of ideas presented in this appendix can often yield new ways of looking at camera angles, lens choices, and perspective. After all, you should always be on the lookout for new and exciting ways to expand your photographic skills and style.

Keep It Simple

Keeping your compositions simple is probably the easiest yet most important rule in creating powerful and memorable images. Studies have shown that the human eye/brain combination begins to repeat itself, that is, to focus again on areas of an image it has already registered, after less than four seconds of viewing the total work. In today's image-saturated world, that means you have a very limited time in which to capture the viewer's attention. Keeping it simple means getting rid of visual clutter in the picture, limiting the elements, and then arranging them in compelling ways.

Each day, you are increasingly bombarded by images for myriad reasons — to sell you products, relate current events, share family milestones, and so on. Eventually, image overload can set in. You want your images to be clear and to the point. Keeping your compositions simple can go a long way toward this goal.

Ideally, your subject should be immediately recognizable to your audience. When considering a subject to photograph, I rarely come upon a scene that needs no adjusting or finessing. This is what distinguishes the professional from the amateur. The amateur simply *takes* a photograph, while the professional *makes* a photograph. Although this may seem like semantics, it's actually an all-important distinction. It takes expertise and careful consideration of all the elements to make a truly remarkable image.

After you've determined the goal of your image and what you're trying to convey about the person you'll be photographing (the portrait's viewpoint), the next task is to locate a background

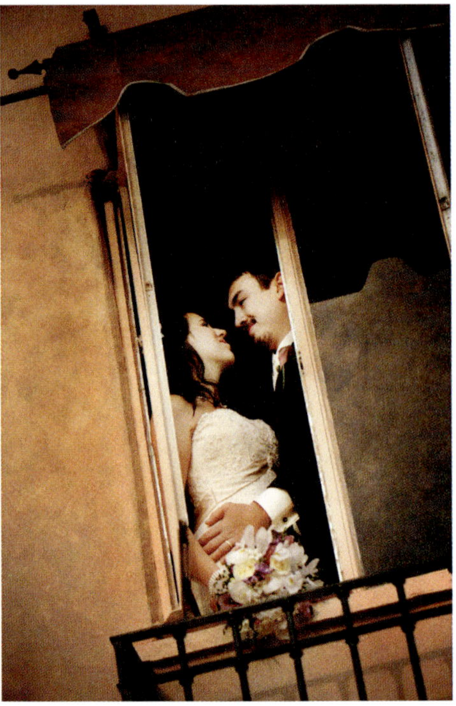

AB.1 I placed this just-married couple in the window of a room in the villa above where we were shooting family pictures. It set the perfect scene for this romantic Tuscan-styled wedding. The room wasn't theirs and they weren't staying in the villa; I just made it happen. This is what I mean by "making" an image. Exposure: ISO 800, f/3.5, 1/5000 second with an EF 700-200mm f/2.8L USM lens.

that supports and complements that goal. Once you're at a location or in the studio, keep your options open and don't get locked in to one idea. Circle your subject 360 degrees and see what other visual possibilities and nearby locations jump out at you. New ideas will flow into your head, and you may end up creating additional images that are entirely different, and often better, than what you first imagined. Edward Weston once remarked, "My own eyes are no more than scouts on a preliminary mission, for the camera's eye may entirely change my idea."

Try to come up with backgrounds that have different colors, tones, and textures than your subject does; this way you won't accidentally camouflage the subject. Having a brighter-toned subject against a darker background, or vice versa, is another way to command more of your viewer's attention by adding contrast and making your subject stand out. A simple background allows the viewer's eye to remain largely on the subject and provides the time to make an emotional connection.

To create better photographs, it's helpful to learn to see the world like your camera does. Think of your camera like a digital sketchpad. Use the flexibility and freedom of digital capture to your advantage by shooting as much and as often possible. Visually experimenting and playing will help you quickly develop your eye and style. By understanding how the camera sees, you'll begin to craft your own visual language.

This disconnect between what you see when capturing an image and your expectations of what the final photograph should look like is where many photographers stumble. Your eye/brain combination is capable of differentiating between thousands more tones than today's camera sensors or film can. Your eyes also perceive depth of field very differently. The result of these disparities can lead to unrealistic expectations about how an image should look based on how you remember it when it was captured. Learning to see the way your camera and lenses do goes a long way to improving your photography. Spend the time getting to know your camera and lenses and how they see the world. After you do, you'll be rewarded with spectacular and compelling imagery.

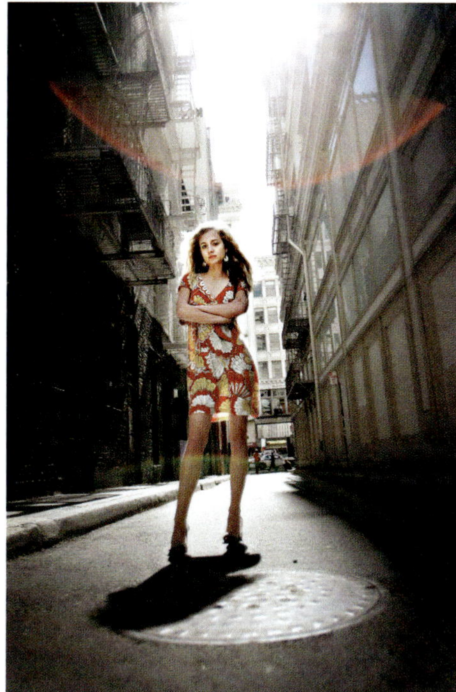

AB.2 For this cool and fashion-forward senior, I had something completely different in mind when the back alleys of San Francisco inspired me to create this image for her. Taken with a Canon 580EX II. Exposure: ISO 500, f/2.8, 1/4000 second with an EF 16-35mm f/2.8L USM lens.

Silhouettes

Using silhouettes as main or supporting elements is a great way of keeping compositions simple and directing viewer focus in your images. With silhouettes, the shape delivers only minimal information and adds mystery as well as a contrast to the background. Whether used as standalone images or as part of a series, silhouettes add impact and an emotional quality that resonates with viewers. They can be a powerful way to add punch to your images. If you've never attempted silhouettes before, consider giving them a try.

The basic approach is to find a dynamic background and underexpose the image by 1 to 2 f-stops or shutter speeds. Another technique I like is something I call *the reverse silhouette.* This is achieved by *overexposing* the background by 1 to 2 f-stops, the reverse of a traditional silhouette, creating a glowing and ethereal feeling while still maintaining detail in the foreground. This works particularly well with backlit subjects standing in an alley, in front of a window, or in front of an open set of doors.

The following two photos show how silhouettes can add visual power to your images.

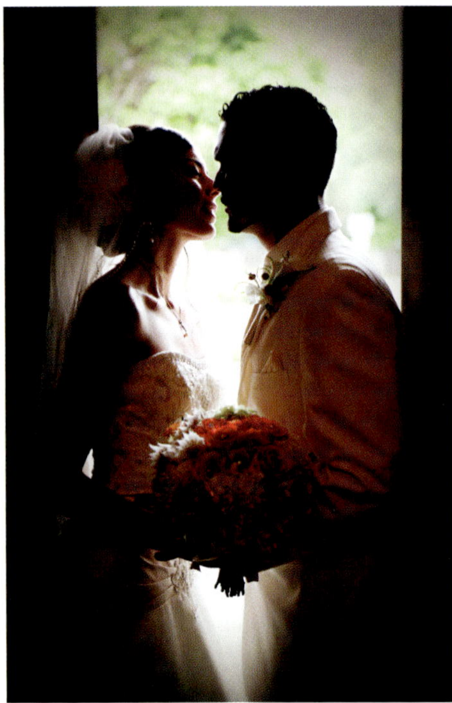

AB.3 **Silhouettes add drama to your image. Exposure: ISO 1600, f/2.8, 1/640 second with an EF 70-200mm f/2.8L USM lens.**

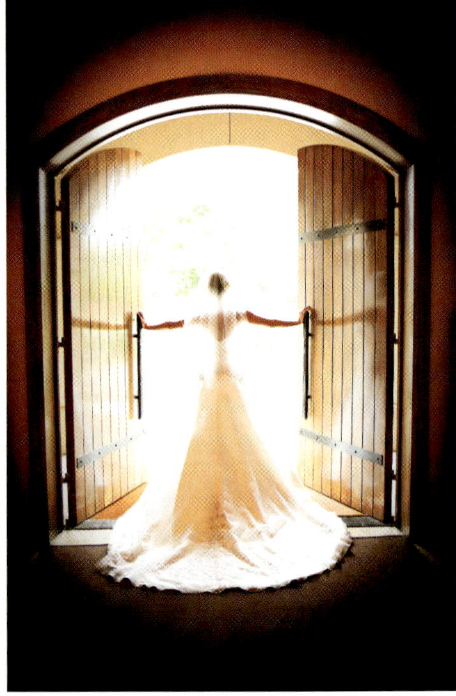

AB.4 **Here is a reverse silhouette — the background is purposely blown out to create an ethereal and dreamlike quality. Exposure: ISO 1600, f/2.8, 1/200 second with an EF 16-35mm f/2.8L USM lens.**

Limiting focus

Another way to simplify your images is to limit the focus range to cover only the subject, rendering elements in front of or behind the subject partially out of focus. You can achieve this by using larger-number apertures (f-stops), all the way down to your smallest (widest), to reduce the amount of depth of field in that image. This is one of the main reasons, besides image clarity, that professionals opt for big, expensive lenses. These lenses come equipped with large apertures that are used to throw backgrounds completely out of focus. Because these lenses let in more light, they're often referred to as *fast*.

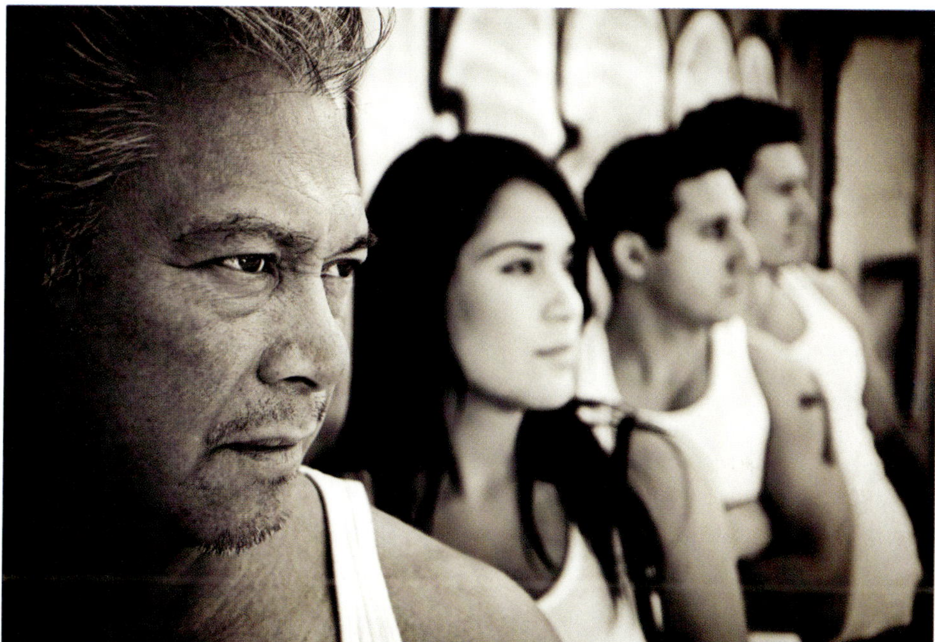

AB.5 Selective focus creates drama, builds tension, and shifts the viewer's focus to the desired area of the image. Exposure: ISO 100, f/4.0, 1/320 second with an EF 17-40mm f/4L USM lens.

By shifting the plane of focus this way, photographers blur the background or foreground and guide the viewer's attention to the important areas in the image. This is a great technique to employ when you're stuck with an unattractive or distracting background. A good example would be urban portraits where architecture, trash cans, and signage can all steal attention away from your subject.

With lenses, bokeh is an important consideration. The term refers to the way an out-of-focus point of light is rendered in an image. The word *bokeh* is actually derived from the Japanese word *boke,* meaning fuzzy.

Obviously, bokeh can make the out-of-focus areas aesthetically pleasing or visually obtrusive, and the interpretation is almost entirely subjective. In general, you want the out-of-focus points of light to be circular and to blend or transition nicely with other areas in the background. The illumination is best if the center is bright and the edges are darker and blurry.

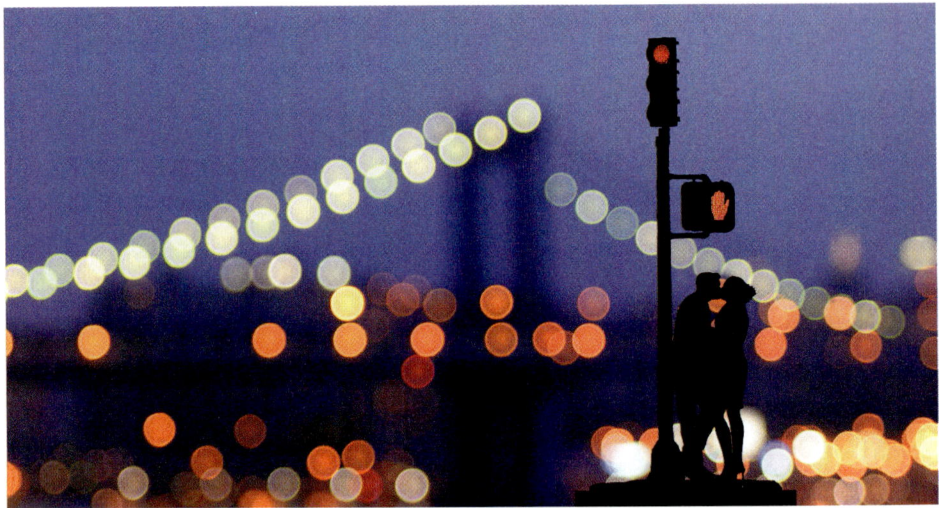

Courtesy of Dennis Urbiztondo

AB.6 This night shot is a beautiful example of the bokeh created around lights when shooting at very wide apertures. Exposure: ISO 1600, f/2.8, 1/60 second with an EF 17-40mm f/4L USM lens.

The Rule of Thirds

One of the easiest ways to take your compositions to the next level is by breaking the unfortunately common habit of centering subjects within the image. You've probably seen this many times, especially in the case of horizontal images where one person's face is dead center in the picture. The downside of this type of composing, in addition to being potentially visually boring, is underutilizing all the other real estate at your disposal: the top and sides of the image. The face appears to float in the middle of the picture. Recomposing and shifting the subject to the left or right side of the image easily remedies this situation. Including more of the background increases the visual interest, adds context, and can imply movement within the scene.

Perhaps the best-known principle of photographic composition is the Rule of Thirds. Also common in painting and film, the Rule of Thirds involves breaking down your image into an imaginary grid of thirds (both horizontally and vertically). Doing so gives you nine sections or boxes with two vertical and two horizontal lines, each a third of the way across its dimension.

The resulting lines and intersections are your "sweet spots." The objective is to keep the subjects and areas of interest (such as the horizon) out of the center of the image, by placing them on or near one of the lines or intersections that would divide the image into three equal columns and rows.

Two techniques that I've found helpful when utilizing the Rule of Thirds are worth noting. The first technique is to have my subjects (either on the right or left side of image) look across and into the image toward its center. This helps adds balance and direction for the viewer's eye to follow. The opposite approach, centering the subject, may weigh the image down, giving it an unbalanced feeling. However, as with any "rule" in the creative realm, there are exceptions, and centered images can be quite effective from time to time. Being armed with a thorough knowledge of these compositional conventions or rules and understanding the visual effect they have on an image will help you make informed decisions about where and when to use them.

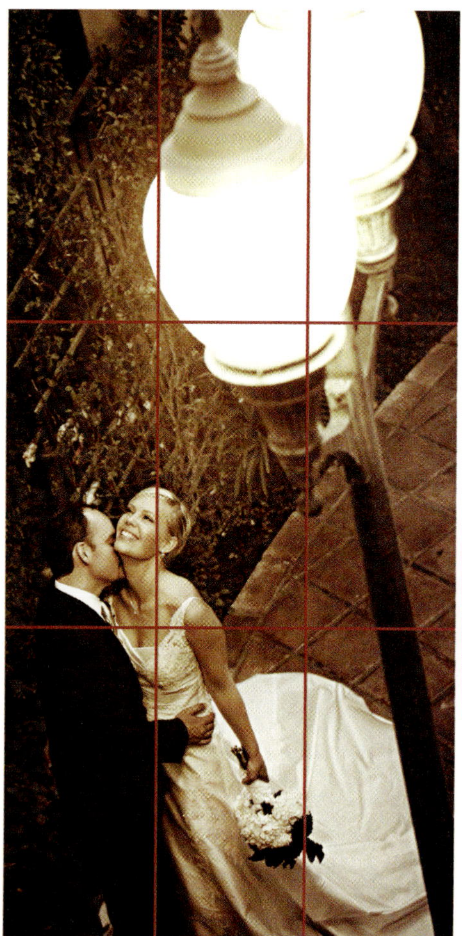

AB.7 Notice how the subjects in this image have been composed near the bottom-left portion of the image and see where they fall relative to the Rule of Thirds grid. This arrangement creates a more pleasing image when compared to a centered composition of the same subjects. Exposure: ISO 1600, f/2.8, 1/30 second with an EF 70-200mm f/2.8L USM lens.

The second technique applies when shooting landscapes with the sky as an element of the scene. If you see an incredible sky, try placing the horizon on or near the lower horizontal line. For skies without any interesting cloud formations but very good light, move the horizon up to the higher horizontal line and find some interesting element in the good light of the foreground.

At this point for me, after so many years of shooting, these decisions have become unconscious, based simply on what feels right visually at the moment of capture. You, too, will gain this intuition as you develop your visual vocabulary and hone your skills.

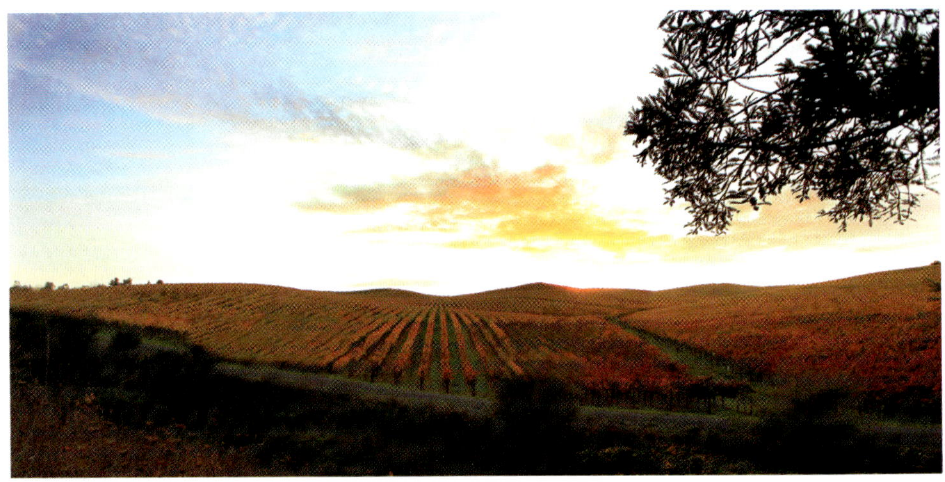

Courtesy of Dennis Urbiztondo

AB.8 Careful attention to the placement of the horizon line when making landscape photographs will add balance and tranquility to your images. Exposure: ISO 400, f/7.1, 1/100 second with an EF 17-40mm f/4L USM lens.

Field of View

Many times, better compositions can be achieved by merely moving the camera slightly up, down, left, or right. Distracting elements can be eliminated by taking a few steps to the right or left of the subject. By making subtle or not-so-subtle alterations to the subject's position, your position, and the camera's position, you can modify the background of the composition to include fewer distractions. Moving laterally, or vertically adjusting the camera's position and angle, can also help achieve this.

Controlling the field of view can also mean getting closer to your subject by zooming in, changing lenses, or physically moving closer. Personally, I favor a mix of up-close-and-personal shooting with shorter focal-length lenses and working at more of a distance with longer focal lengths. They both have their charms. Working with shorter focal lengths in closer proximately to your subject helps create a bond and build rapport between the photographer and the subject, resulting in more compelling and authentic images than those shot strictly at a distance. On the other hand, shooting with longer focal lengths allows clients more breathing room, freedom of movement, and has the added benefit of beautifully compressing and blurring the background at wider apertures. One of my favorite lenses for this kind of shooting is the Canon EF 70-200mm f/2.8 L IS USM.

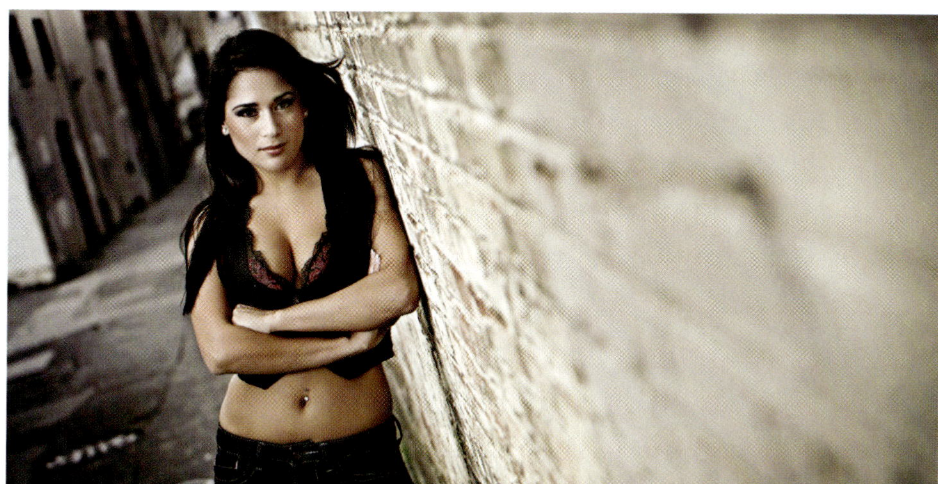

AB.9 Working with a long lens (Canon 70-200mm f/2.8) allows distance from the subject and blurs the background. It helps minimize unwanted distractions. Exposure: ISO 100, f/4.0, 1/200 second with an EF 70-200mm f/2.8L USM lens.

Creating a unique and interesting visual perspective with your images should always be your goal. Try not to fall into the habit of shooting all of your images standing at eye level. This is the way everyone is used to seeing the world, and it results in images that are common looking and not very compelling. Changing the perspective to something unexpected can quickly elevate the mundane image to something superior and worthy of attention. You're also creating more personal images when you tell the story of how things look from a vantage point other than your own. Images of children and pets, for example, are more interesting photographed from their eye level rather than yours. Also, remember that anything closer to the camera appears larger and any elements farther away appear smaller. That's the reason many family portraits are most often composed with the children in front and the adults in the back.

To create more heroic-looking images of people, I frame them with the camera at about waist high or lower, making them seem larger than life, towering, and statuesque. By contrast, in tight situations where space is limited, such as a wedding cocktail hour or a party with guests whooping it up on the dance floor, I hoist a camera with a wide-angle lens attached to a monopod and shoot down on the crowd, triggering the shutter with a Vello ShutterBoss wireless cable release. onOne Software makes an iPhone and iPad app called DSLR Camera Remote that allows live previews and control of many of the camera's most important functions such as the shutter release, aperture, and shutter speed. This setup is ideal when shooting overhead images for event photography.

After getting the "safe" shots, investigate more interesting options, like offbeat camera angles. Don't be afraid to stand on a chair (don't ask permission, beg for forgiveness!) or get down and dirty on your belly to create a more interesting camera angle of your subject. Any personal embarrassment will be long forgotten when you see the killer images you've captured.

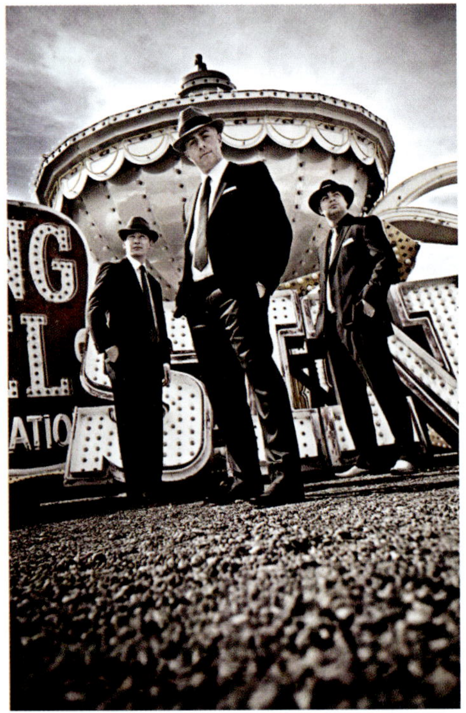

AB.10 Shooting from a low angle with a wide lens creates images that make subjects look heroic and larger than life. Exposure: ISO 400, f/3.5, 1/3200 second with an EF 16-35mm f/2.8L USM lens.

Leading Lines and S-Curves

Leading lines create an illusion of perspective and a feeling of depth by merging at what is called the vanishing point. Oblique and angular lines convey a sense of dynamic balance and a sense of action. Lines can also direct attention toward the main subject of the photograph or contribute to the photograph's organization by dividing it into sections.

A straight, horizontal line, commonly found in landscape photography, gives the impression of calm, tranquility, and open space. Be on the lookout for horizontal lines that cross a subject's eye line, ear height, neck, or head because these can subconsciously create an uncomfortable feeling for the viewer. An image filled with strong vertical lines tends to give an impression of height, power, and grandeur. Tightly angled diagonal lines give a dynamic, lively, and active feeling to the image — a stylistic approach very common in contemporary wedding and portrait photography.

Curved lines or S-curves are generally used to create a sense of flow within an image. The eye scans these flowing lines with ease and enjoyment as it follows them through the image. Compared to straight lines, S-curves provide a greater dynamic influence in a photograph. When paired with soft-directional lighting, curved lines can give gradated shadows, which usually results in a very harmonious line structure within the image. Perspective is also important with S-curved lines; generally speaking, higher viewpoints produce more open lines.

Symmetry

Although I do suggest steering clear of centering your subjects in the frame too often and employing the Rule of Thirds when possible, there are definitely times when a centered composition works best. Centered compositions can work well occasionally for business portraits, editorial images, wedding images, and images with a square crop. I look for balancing colors in the background or some architectural items that I can use to frame my subject. Balance is what you're striving for, and sometimes putting the subject directly in the middle creates the most powerful impact.

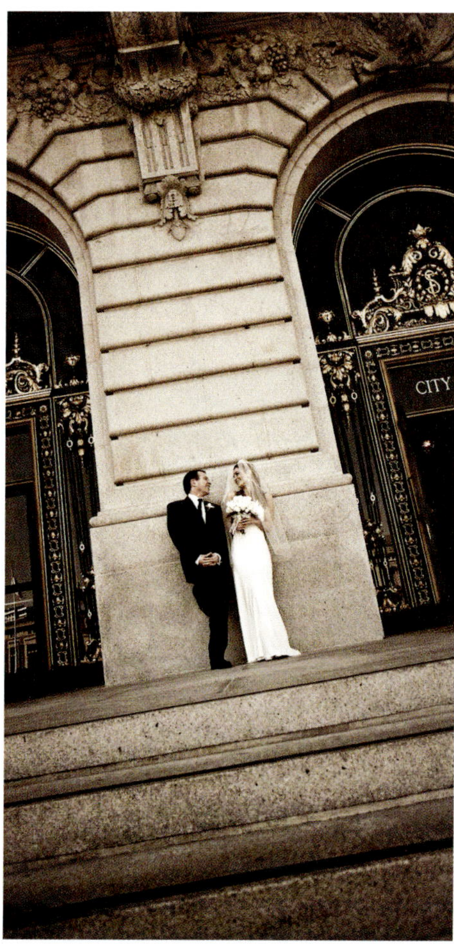

AB.11 Strong architectural lines and a tall vertical crop help accentuate the grandeur of San Francisco's City Hall, an important element in this wedding. Exposure: ISO 100, f/4.0, 1/500 second with an EF 17-40mm f/4L USM lens.

When shooting engagement sessions or couples, I often compose the shot in a way that creates visual diagonals, balancing the shot by having one person slightly higher than the other or farther away.

Also, pay close attention to the edges of your frame, and try to make use of all of them. Avoid having bright spots or colors or sharp focus directly on the edges of your picture. Areas such as these give the viewer's eye an easy way out of the image and are the main reason many digital photographers today add slightly darker vignettes to their images to contain the edges of the frame.

Remember to always ask yourself what it is that you're not seeing, what you are missing, and how you can improve upon what you're seeing in the viewfinder to make your image more interesting. Think about new ways of seeing, step back to take another look, and circle your subject to look for different opportunities. Be open to suggestions from those you're working with. You've got one opportunity to capture lightning in a bottle, so use it wisely!

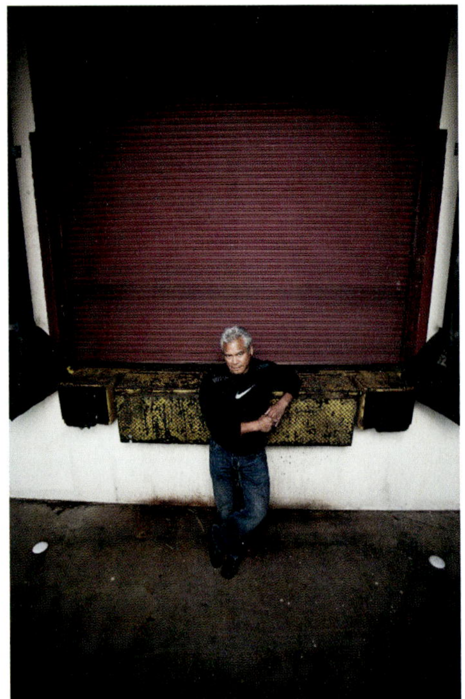

AB.12 Choose centered compositions carefully and capitalize on their ability to convey balance, strength, and directness. Exposure: ISO 200, f/4.0, 1/30 second with an EF 17-40mm f/4L USM lens.

Resources

When it comes to learning photography, there's never been more information and resources available. The immediate feedback of digital capture and elimination of consumable expenses, like film and processing, make it easy to keep practicing and developing new skills. Online learning sites, how-to DVDs by top pros, iPad apps, books, workshops, magazines, and trade shows all help put high-quality, reasonably priced photographic education within the reach of just about everyone.

For this appendix, I pulled together the best of the best here for you. These are the resources that have helped me grow as photographer, craftsman, and businessperson. I continue to turn to these resources daily to keep learning, improving, and striving to be the best I can be. In this appendix, you find my favorite resources to help you learn more about using the Canon Speedlite System, lighting, posing, working with handheld flashes, starting and maintaining a business, and improving your photography in general. I include my favorite websites, workshops, iPad apps, trade shows, trade associations, DVDs, books, and equipment.

NOTE Download a PDF file of this section for clickable links to the resources at www.wiley.com/go/canonslsdfg3e.

Websites and Online Learning

Creative Edge. www.creativeedge.com

creativeLIVE. www.creativelive.com

Kelby Training. www.kelbytraining.com

Lighting Essentials. www.lighting-essentials.com

Lynda.com. www.lynda.com

Model Mayhem. www.modelmayhem.com

One Model Place. www.onemodelplace.com

Photo Resource Hub. http://photoresourcehub.com

PhotoshopCAFE. www.photoshopcafe.com

PhotoTraining4U. www.phototraining4u.com

Salvatore Cincotta, Training for Professional Photographers. www.behindthe shutter.com

Steele Training: Photography Tutorials and Courses by Phil Steele. www.steele training.com

Strobist. www.strobist.com

Studio Styles. www.studiostyles.net

DVDs and Video Downloads

Bambi Cantrell's Weddings Volume 3 DVD: The Language of Lighting and Posing DVD. http://cantrellportrait.com/extra/online_store.php

Bob Davis's A Master's Approach DVD. http://davisimpact.wordpress.com/2008/ 01/28/a-masters-approach-with-bob-davis-dvd-finally-here

Boudoir Photography with Master Craftsman Photographer James Schmelzer DVD. www.amazon.com/Boudoir-Photography-Craftsmen-Photographer-Schmelzer/dp/ B006M4D0NC

Damien Lovegrove's Speedlight Mastery DVD. www.lovegroveconsulting.com/ dvds.aspx

Damien Lovegrove's Studio Portraits DVD. www.lovegroveconsulting.com/dvds. aspx

Dean Collins DVDs. www.software-cinema.com/trainers/6/dean-collins

Don Chick Confident Photographer DVD Series. www.donchick.com/store

Don Giannatti's Lighting Essentials Advanced: Creating Dimension with Light.
www.dongiannatti.com

Don Giannatti's Lighting Essentials Basics: Understanding Subject Centric Light. www.dongiannatti.com

Doug Gordon's Posing DVDs. http://douggordonworkshops.myshopify.com/collections/videos

Evans Creative Training Downloads. www.evanscreativetraining.com/products.html

Frank Doorhof's Lighting DVDs. www.frankdoorhof.com/shop2

Hanson Fong's Posing DVDs. www.hansonfong.com

Inspiring Beauty: Photographic Techniques of Matthew Jordan Smith DVD. www.software-cinema.com/training/photography/matthew-jordan-smith/131/inspiring-beauty-photographic-techniques-of-matthew-jordan-smith

Jack Reznicki's Lighting Essentials DVD. www.software-cinema.com/training/photography/jack-reznicki/18/lighting-essentials

Joe McNally's The Language of Light DVD Set. www.joemcnally.com/blog/the-language-of-light

Joel Grimes Video Tutorials. www.joelgrimesworkshops.com/Joel_Grimes_Photography/Video_Tutorials.html

Joey Lawrence's Session with Joey L DVD or Download. www.joeyl.com/shop/package/session-with-joey-l

Karl Taylor's Photography Masterclass DVD. www.karltaylorphotography.com/learn-photography-dvd-series.htm

Ken Cook's Facial Analysis and Corrective Lighting Double Volume DVD. www.cooksphotography.com/Seminars.aspx

Ken Sklute's Location Lighting for the Wedding Photographer DVD. www.software-cinema.com/training/photography/ken-sklute/20/location-lighting-for-the-wedding-photographer

Mark Wallace's Studio Lighting Essentials DVD. www.studiolightingessentials.com

Mike Larson's Photographic Business and Lighting DVD Set. www.sunbounce.com/en/workshops/mike-larsons-photographic-business-and-lighting-lecture-dvd/mike-larson-dvd-3.html

Monte Zucker's Portrait Photography for Everyone. www.software-cinema.com/trainers/14/monte-zucker

Peter Hurley's The Art Behind the Headshot. www.peterhurley.com/dvd

PhotoVison DVDs and Online Training. www.photovisionvideo.com

Scott Kelby's Lighting DVDs. http://kelbytraining.com/dvds

Shannon Michelle's boo.dwa Workshop DVD. www.shannon-michelle.com

Strobist Lighting Seminar DVD Set. http://mpex.com/strobist-lighting-seminar-dvd-box-set.html

Tim Kelly Portrait Lighting and Marketing DVDs. http://timkellyportraits.com/proshop

Tony Corbell's Portrait Lighting on Location DVD. www.software-cinema.com/training/photography/tony-corbell/21/portrait-lighting-on-location

TriCoast Wireless Flash TTL 2 DVD Set. http://tricoastseniors.photobiz.com/cart/product_detail.cfm?productID=159309&categoryID=29200

Zack Arias's OneLight DVD. www.zackarias.com/workshop/onelight-dvd

iPad Apps

DSLR Camera Remote Professional Edition. http://itunes.apple.com/us/app/dslr-camera-remote-professional/id316771002?mt=8

Fashion & Beauty Photography Lighting Secrets by Karl Taylor. http://itunes.apple.com/us/app/fashion-beauty-lighting-secrets/id386806696?mt=8

iRelease. www.ireleaseapp.com

Kevin Kubota's Lighting Notebook. http://kubotaimagetools.com/lighting-notebook/app.html

Light It Digital Magazine. http://itunes.apple.com/us/app/light-it-digital-magazine/id455243692?mt=8

Lights, Camera, Capture! http://itunes.apple.com/us/app/lights-camera-capture/id399732384

RadioPopper JrX Guide. http://itunes.apple.com/tw/app/rp-jrx-guide/id459281316?mt=8

Sylights (lighting diagrams creator and community). www.sylights.com

Books

Kevin Kubota's Lighting Notebook: 101 Lighting Styles and Setups for Digital Photographers, Kevin Kubota, 2011

Lights, Camera, Capture: Creative Lighting Techniques for Digital Photographers, Bob Davis, 2010

Workshops

After Dark Education. www.afterdarkedu.com

Bob and Dawn Davis Workshops. www.davisworkshops.com

Damien Lovegrove. www.lovegroveconsulting.com

Doug Gordon Workshops. www.douggordonworkshops.myshopify.com

FisheyeConnect. www.fisheyeconnect.com

Joel Grimes. www.joelgrimesworkshops.com

Kubota Digital Bootcamp. www.kubotaimagetools.com

Lighting Essentials Workshops. www.learntolight.com

C

Salvatore Cincotta Workshops. www.behindtheshutter.com

Santa Fe Workshops. www.santafeworkshops.com

Skips Summer School. www.mei500.com

TriCoast Photography Workshops. http://tricoastphoto.com/blog/about

Zack Arias OneLight Workshops. www.zackarias.com/workshop

Trade Shows

Imaging USA. www.imagingusa.org

PDN PhotoPlus International Conference + Expo. www.photoplusexpo.com

Society of Wedding & Portrait Photographers. www.swppusa.com

Wedding Photographers Association (WPPI). www.wppionline.com

Magazines

Photo District News. www.pdnonline.com

Professional Photographer Magazine. www.ppmag.com

Rangefinder. www.rangefinderonline.com

Associations

Your local Professional Photographers of America affiliate group

Find your local Strobist group on Google.

American Society of Media Photographers (ASMP). www.asmp.org

Professional Photographers of America (PPA). www.ppa.com

Light Modifiers

Enlight. www.orbisflash.com

ExpoImaging. www.expoimaging.com

F.J. Westcott. www.fjwestcott.com

Fotodiox. www.fotodiox.com

Foursquare. www.lightwaredirect.com/mm5/merchant.mvc?Screen=CTGY&Store_Code=LightwareDirect&Category_Code=GSR

Gary Fong Lightsphere. www.garyfongestore.com

Honey Grids. www.honeycombgrids.com

Honl Photo. www.honlphoto.com

Lastolite. www.lastolite.us

Mola Softlights. www.mola-light.com

Photek. www.photekusa.com

Light Stands

Manfrotto 5001B. www.manfrotto.com/nano-black-stand

Photogenic. www.photogenic.com

Reflectors

California Sunbounce. www.sunbounce.com

Eyelighter. www.theeyelighter.com

F.J. Westcott. www.fjwestcott.com

Foam Core Stands. www.foamcorestands.com

Lastolite. www.lastolite.us

Brackets

F.J. Westcott. www.fjwestcott.com

Foursquare. www.lightwaredirect.com/mm5/merchant.mvc?Screen=CTGY&Store_Code=LightwareDirect&Category_Code=GSR

Frio Cold Shoe Adapter. www.friocoldshoe.com

IDC Photo. www.idcphotovideo.com/store/lighting

Lovegrove Consulting. www.lovegroveconsulting.com/lovegrove_collection.aspx

MF-X II. www.ep-designs.com

Lenses

Canon. www.usa.canon.com

Lensbaby. www.lensbaby.com

Radio Triggers and Remotes

PocketWizard. www.pocketwizard.com

PocketWizard Accessories. www.hildozine.com

RadioPopper. www.radiopopper.com

Vello. www.vellogear.com

Backdrops and Support Systems

Backgrounds by Maheu. www.backgroundsbymaheu.com

Barbour Backdrops. www.barbourbackdrops.com

Drop it Modern. www.dropitmodern.com

Pro Photo Connect. www.prophotoconnect.com

Cords and Cables

Michael Bass Designs. www.michaelbass.blogspot.com

Off-Camera Gear E-TTL Cord. www.ocfgear.com

Equipment for Tethered Shooting

Tether Tools. www.tethertools.com

Filters

ExpoImaging. www.expoimaging.com

Honl Photo. www.honlphoto.com

Lastolite. www.lastolite.us

LEE Filters. www.leefilters.com

Rosco International. www.rosco.com

Bags and Cases

Lightware Direct. www.lightwaredirect.com

Think Tank Photo. www.thinktankphoto.com

StandBagger. www.standbagger.com

How to Use the Gray Card and Color Checker

Have you ever wondered how some photographers are able to consistently produce photos with such accurate color and exposure? It's often because they use gray cards and color checkers. Knowing how to use these tools helps you take some of the guesswork out of capturing photos with great color and correct exposures every time.

The Gray Card

Because the color of light changes depending on the light source, what you might decide is neutral in your photograph, isn't neutral at all. This is where a gray card comes in very handy. A gray card is designed to reflect the color spectrum neutrally in all sorts of lighting conditions, providing a standard from which to measure for later color corrections or to set a custom white balance.

By taking a test shot that includes the gray card, you guarantee that you have a neutral item to adjust colors against later if you need to. Make sure that the card is placed in the same light that the subject is for the first photo, and then remove the gray card and continue shooting.

> **TIP** When taking a photo of a gray card, de-focus your lens a little; this ensures that you capture a more even color.

Because many software programs enable you to address color correction issues by choosing something that should be white or neutral in an image, having the gray card in the first of a series of photos allows you to select the gray card as the neutral point. Your software resets red, green, and blue to be the same value, creating a neutral midtone. Depending on the capabilities of your software, you might be able to save the adjustment you've made and apply it to all other photos shot in the same series.

If you'd prefer to made adjustments on the spot, for example, and if the lighting conditions will remain mostly consistent while you shoot a large number of images, it is advisable to use the gray card to set a custom white balance in your camera. You can do this by taking a photo of the gray card filling as much of the frame as possible. Then, use that photo to set the custom white balance.

The Color Checker

A color checker contains 24 swatches that represent colors found in everyday scenes, including skin tones, sky, foliage, etc. It also contains red, green, blue, cyan, magenta, and yellow, which are used in all printing devices. Finally, and perhaps most importantly, it has six shades of gray.

Using a color checker is a very similar process to using a gray card. You place it in the scene so that it is illuminated in the same way as the subject. Photograph the scene once with the reference in place, then remove it and continue shooting. You should create a reference photo each time you shoot in a new lighting environment.

Later on in software, open the image containing the color checker. Measure the values of the gray, black, and white swatches. The red, green, and blue values in the gray swatch should each measure around 128, in the black swatch around 10, and in the white swatch around 245. If your camera's white balance was set correctly for the scene, your measurements should fall into the range (and deviate by no more than 7 either way) and you can rest easy knowing your colors are true.

If your readings are more than 7 points out of range either way, use software to correct it. But now you also have black and white reference points to help. Use the levels adjustment tool to bring the known values back to where they should be measuring (gray around 128, black around 10, and white around 245).

If your camera offers any kind of custom styles, you can also use the color checker to set or adjust any of the custom styles by taking a sample photo and evaluating it using the on-screen histogram, preferably the RGB histogram if your camera offers one. You can then choose that custom style for your shoot, perhaps even adjusting that custom style to better match your expectations for color.

D

Glossary

AE (Automatic Exposure) A general-purpose shooting mode where the camera automatically sets the aperture and shutter speed using its metered reading. On some cameras, the ISO settings are also automatically set.

AE/AF Lock A camera setting that allows you to lock the current exposure and/or autofocus setting prior to taking a photo. This button lets you recompose the scene without holding the shutter button halfway down.

AF-assist illuminator Useful in low-light and low-contrast shooting situations, a feature that automatically projects a red grid onto your subject to aid the camera's autofocusing system. The AF (autofocus) assist illuminator is located on the bottom front of the flash. The AF-assist beam is compatible with most recent Canon cameras, helping the camera to focus properly in poor light.

ambient light The natural or artificial light within a scene. This is also called available light.

aperture Also referred to as the diaphragm or f-stop setting of the lens. The aperture controls the amount of light that is allowed to pass through the lens. The higher the f-stop number setting, the smaller the aperture opening on the lens. Larger f-stop settings are selected by lower numbers, such as f/2 or f/1.2. The larger the aperture, the less depth of field the image will possess. A smaller aperture means that the image will have more depth of field, and that more of the background will be in focus.

Aperture Priority (Av) A camera exposure setting where you choose the aperture, and the camera automatically adjusts the shutter speed according to the camera's metered readings. Aperture Priority is often used by photographers to control depth of field.

background light Light that is generally placed behind the subject and pointed toward the backdrop to create separation between the subject and background. Also known as a separation light.

backlighting Light that is positioned behind and pointing to the back of the subject, creating a soft rim of ligwht that visually separates the subject from the background.

bokeh The shape and illumination characteristics of the out-of-focus areas in an image, depending on the focal length, optical design, and aperture blade pattern of the lens.

bounce flash A technique of pointing the flash head in an upward position or toward a wall, thus softening the light falling on the subject. Bouncing the light often eliminates shadows and provides a much smoother light for portraits.

bracketing To make multiple exposures, some above and some below the average exposure calculated by the light meter for the scene, either by flash output or exposure settings. Some digital cameras can also bracket white balance to produce variations from the average white balance calculated by the camera.

bulb A shutter speed setting that keeps the shutter open as long as the shutter button or cable release is fully depressed.

cable release An accessory that connects to a port on the camera and allows you to trigger the shutter by using the cable release instead of pressing the shutter button, to reduce camera/shutter vibrations over slow or timed exposures.

Canon EOS Speedlite System Also referred to as simply "Speedlite System," a lighting system that allows for multiple flash capabilities in a wireless environment, taking advantage of communication of exposure information between the camera, master flash unit, and remote Speedlites. Presently, the Canon lighting system includes the 600EX/600EX-RT, 580EX II, 430EX II, 320EX, 270EX II, 270EX, ST-E3-RT and ST-E2 wireless transmitters, MT-24EX Macro Twin Lite, and MR-14EX Macro Ring Lite.

catch-light panel A pullout panel located on the top front of the 320EX, 270EX II, 580EX II, and 600EX/600EX-RT Speedlites. Using the catch-light panel while pointing the flash head straight up provides the light needed to create sparkle in a portrait subject's eyes, called a catch-light, and a small amount of fill flash.

channel Also referred to as communication channel. To avoid interfering with other wireless flash users in the same location, the master and slave units can communicate on one of four channels. Communications in the Speedlite System are partially based on setting the master and all additional Speedlites to the same channel. If by chance another photographer is using the same channel as you are, your Speedlite System units may fire from the other photographer's controls. To avoid this, you can set the master and your other Speedlites to a different channel.

chimping Reviewing images on the LCD right after you've taken them. This is derived from photographers making the "ooooh-ooooh" chimp sound when reviewing impressive images.

color balance The color reproduction fidelity of a digital camera's image sensor and of the lens. In a digital camera, color balance is achieved by setting the white balance to match the scene's primary light source. You can adjust color balance in image-editing programs using the color Temperature and Tint controls.

colored gel A color gel or color filter, or a lighting gel (or simply gel), is a transparent, colored material that is used in theater, photography, videography, and cinematography to color light and for color correction. Modern gels are thin sheets of polycarbonate or polyester, placed in front of a light source. Gels are often used to change the color of a black background when shooting portraits or still-life photos. The name *gel* stems from the early form of filters used in theaters, which were typically made from gelatin.

color temperature A numerical description of the color of light measured on a Kelvin scale. Warm, early, and late-day light have a lower color temperature. Cool, shady light has a higher temperature. Midday light is often considered to be neutral light (5500 K) and flash units are often calibrated to 5500–6000 K.

daylight balance A general term used to describe the color of light at approximately 5500 K, such as midday sunlight or an electronic flash.

dedicated flash A flash unit designed to work with one particular camera system, and which can operate in conjunction with the camera's internal metering. Dedicated flash units exchange information with the camera via a proprietary digital data line. These lines require small data pins on the flash hot shoe to communicate.

depth of field The distance in front of and behind the subject that appears in acceptably sharp focus.

E-TTL and E-TTL II mode Evaluative Through-the-Lens metering is a Canon EOS flash exposure system that uses a brief preflash before the main flash to obtain a more correct exposure. Like TTL, the sensor is internal to the camera and takes its exposure reading via the lens so any filters added to the lens will also affect the E-TTL readings, giving more accurate exposure information to the camera.

Exposure Compensation A setting that allows you to adjust the exposure, in 1/2 or 1/3 stops from the metered reading of the camera, to achieve correct exposure under mixed or difficult lighting conditions.

fill light Subordinate in power to the key light, fill light lightens shadow areas and is generally placed opposite the key light. Fill light can be either a dedicated Speedlite or a reflector.

first-curtain sync The default setting that causes the flash to fire at the beginning of the exposure when the shutter is completely open. See also *second-curtain sync*.

flash color information communication Color temperature information is automatically transmitted to the camera, providing the camera with the correct white balance setting, and giving you accurate color in your image when you shoot photos with a Speedlite.

Flash Exposure Bracketing (FEB) This concept is similar to Auto-Exposure Bracketing (AEB), only instead of changing ambient exposure settings, you shoot a series of three photographs with normal, positive flash compensation and negative flash compensation. You can apply the bracketing value in half, third, or full stop values. FEB auto-cancels after you've taken the three-photograph sequence and uses whatever drive mode your camera is set to. FEB can be used in conjunction with both Flash Exposure Lock (FEL) and Flash Exposure Compensation (FEC).

Flash Exposure Compensation (FEC) Adjusting the flash output by +/–3 stops in 1/3-stop increments. If images are too dark (underexposed), you can use FEC to increase the flash output. If images are too bright (overexposed), you can use FEC to reduce the flash output.

Flash Exposure (FE) Lock A feature that allows you to obtain the correct flash exposure and then lock that setting in by pressing the FE Lock button. You can then recompose the shot, with the main subject either on the right or the left, and take the picture with the camera retaining the proper flash exposure for the subject.

flash head The part of the Speedlite that houses the flash tube that fires when taking a flash photo. Flash heads can be adjusted for position. See also *flash head tilting.*

flash head tilting Adjusting the flash head horizontally or vertically by pressing the Bounce Lock Release button and repositioning the flash head. This is often used to point the flash in an upward position, such as when using bounce flash. You tilt the flash head up toward the ceiling when using the catch-light panel on the 580EX II or 600EX/600EX-RT.

flash mode The method the flash uses to determine flash exposure. On most EX-series Speedlites, flash modes include E-TTL, Multi-stroboscopic mode, and Manual mode.

flash shooting distance and range The actual range in which the Speedlite has the ability to properly illuminate a subject. The range, determined by the guide number, is typically between 2 and 60 feet, and dependent on the ISO sensitivity, aperture setting, and zoom head position.

flash sync mode A mode which, set in conjunction with camera settings, allows you to take flash photos in either first-curtain or second-curtain sync. For most flash photos, the default is first-curtain sync. When using first-curtain sync, the flash fires right after the shutter opens completely. In second-curtain sync, the flash fires just before the shutter begins to close. Using second-curtain sync in low-light situations avoids unnatural-looking photos due to subject or camera movement. See also *first-curtain sync* and *second-curtain sync.*

front light Light that comes from behind or directly beside the camera to strike the very front of the subject.

f-stop A number that expresses the diameter of the entrance pupil in terms of the focal length of a lens; the f-stop number is the focal length divided by the "effective" aperture diameter. A larger f-number denotes a smaller aperture opening, while a smaller f-number means a larger aperture opening. See also *aperture.*

gobo Short for "Go Between," this is typically a piece of material with a pattern of holes or shapes that's placed in front of the light source to cast a pattern. Many common household objects, such as lattice and house plants, can be used as gobos to create interesting and inexpensive patterns.

gray card A card that reflects a known percentage of the light that falls on it. Typical grayscale cards reflect 18 percent of the light. Gray cards are standard for taking accurate exposure-meter readings and for providing a consistent target for color balancing during the color-correction process using an image-editing program.

grid Available in fabric for softboxes and plastic for Speedlites, this light modifier shapes the light into a narrow beam and is also useful in reducing glare.

grip A general term that includes but is not limited to clamps, light stands, extension arms, and any hardware used to attach and support lights and other equipment.

group A collection of Speedlites, where each flash shares the same output setting controlled by the master flash unit.

guide number (GN) A number that indicates the amount of light emitted from the flash (at full power). Each model Speedlite has its own guide number, indicating the Speedlite's maximum capability. The guide number is calculated based on an ISO setting, flash zoom head position, and the distance to the subject.

highlight A light or bright area in a scene, or the lightest area in a scene.

high-speed sync This feature allows you to shoot with flash up to the maximum shutter speed of the camera. With high-speed sync, the camera actually changes the way the flash fires. Rather than a single, strong burst, it tells the flash to send out an ultrafast series of low-power flash pulses. Because the flash pulses are so short, the light appears to be continuous. When the High-speed sync mode is not engaged, the camera with a hot shoe–mounted Speedlite does not allow you to set the shutter speed to faster than the camera's rated sync speed. High-end flashes, such as the 580EX II and the 430EX II, have this feature. See also *sync speed.*

hot shoe A camera mount that accommodates a separate external flash unit. It is called a hot shoe because it also provides an electronic connection between the flash and the camera. Inside the mount are contacts that transmit information between the camera and the flash unit, and that trigger the flash when the shutter button is pressed.

ISO sensitivity The ISO (International Organization for Standardization) setting on a camera indicates the camera's light sensitivity. Lower ISO settings provide better-quality images with less image noise; however, the lower the ISO setting, the more exposure is needed.

Kelvin Different than Fahrenheit and Celsius degree scales, the Kelvin scale for measuring color temperature. The lower the Kelvin number is the warmer the color of the light is and conversely, the higher the Kelvin number is, the cooler the color of the light is. The scale is used in photography to quantify the color temperature of light.

key light Also known as the main light, this is the dominant light source in a scene. Often, you direct subjects to look toward the key light.

kicker light Also known as rim or edge light, this is side light that can come from either the left side, the right side, or both. When working with kicker light in conjunction with natural light, pay careful attention to where the shadows are falling. Avoid creating unnatural opposing shadows that don't occur in nature. In the studio, you have much more latitude with kicker light placement.

leading line An element in a composition that leads the viewer's eye toward the subject or deeper into the scene.

lighting ratio A ratio used to describe the difference in brightness between two light sources. A 1:1 ratio means both light sources are equal. A 1:2 ratio denotes that the second light is half as bright as the first, a 1:4 ratio describes the second light as being one-fourth as bright as the first, and so on.

Manual exposure A mode in which the photographer adjusts the lens aperture and/or shutter speed to achieve the desired exposure. Many photographers need to control aperture and shutter speed independently because opening up the aperture increases exposure but also decreases the depth of field, and a slower shutter speed increases exposure but also increases the opportunity for motion blur.

master The flash unit that is mounted on the camera when using multiple Speedlites in a wireless flash configuration. The master flash unit controls the flash output of all remote units. The built-in Speedlites of some camera models can also act as a master flash. The master flash unit is also sometimes called a commander. See also *remote* and *slave*.

metering Measuring the amount of light utilizing the camera's internal light meter. For most flash uses, Speedlites emit a preflash for the camera's light meter in order to achieve a properly exposed photo.

midtone An area of medium brightness; a medium-gray tone in a digital image or photographic print. Midtones are usually found halfway between the darkest shadows and the brightest highlights.

mirror lock-up A camera function that allows the mirror, which reflects the image to the viewfinder, to flip up without the shutter being released. This is done in order to reduce vibration from the mirror moving on slow or timed exposures or to allow manual sensor cleaning.

modeling light A secondary light, usually tungsten or halogen, built into a studio strobe in order to visualize what the flash output will look like. The Canon EX series Speedlites have a modeling "flash" that fires a short burst of rapid flashes that allow you to see the effect of the flash on the subject.

multiple flash setup A configuration that uses multiple Speedlites, wired or wirelessly, to illuminate a subject and/or scene. This allows the photographer to create natural-looking photographs by creatively placing multiple flashes in different positions (and/or flash output) to achieve the desired lighting results.

noise Extraneous visible artifacts that degrade digital image quality or that are creatively added in post-production for effect. In digital images, noise appears as multicolored flecks, also referred to as grain. Noise is most visible in high-speed digital images captured at high ISO settings.

Program Auto Exposure A mode where the shutter speed is automatically set to the camera's sync shutter speed when using a Speedlite. On the camera, the shutter speed and aperture are automatically set when the subject is focused.

Quick flash A state the Speedlite enters into before recycling to full power as indicated on the flash by a green ready light. Quick flash fires the unit at 1/6 to 1/2 power but enables it to fire faster. For full flash, wait until the pilot lamp turns red. The Quick flash only will fire in Single drive mode, not in Burst mode.

Red-eye Reduction A function of certain EOS cameras that is used to prevent the subject's eyes from appearing red. The camera emits a bright light before the shutter is opened that shrinks the pupils. As a general rule, the farther the flash head is located from the axis of the camera lens, the less chance you have of experiencing the red-eye effect. You can combine Red-eye Reduction with slow-sync in low-light situations.

remote A radio device that triggers cameras or off-camera flashes to fire. See also *master* and *slave*.

scene modes Available on some cameras, automatic modes in which the settings are adjusted to predetermined parameters, such as a wide aperture for the Portrait scene mode and high shutter speed for the Sports scene mode.

second-curtain sync A camera/flash setting that allows the flash to fire at the end of the exposure, right before the second or rear curtain of the shutter closes. With slow shutter speeds and flash, this feature creates a blur behind a moving subject, visually implying forward movement. See also *first-curtain sync.*

Shutter Priority (Tv) A camera exposure setting where you choose the shutter speed and the camera automatically adjusts the aperture according to the camera's metered readings. Action photographers often use Shutter Priority to control motion blur.

shutter speed The length of time the shutter is open to allow light to fall onto the imaging sensor. The shutter speed is measured in seconds, or more commonly, fractions of seconds.

side lighting Light that strikes the subject from the side, often utilized to show the texture of the subject.

silhouette A view of an object or scene consisting of the outline and a featureless interior, with the silhouetted object usually being black. The term has been extended to describe an image of a person, object, or scene that is backlit, and appears dark against a lighter background.

slave A Speedlite used in a multiple flash configuration that is not attached to the camera; also a remote triggering device. The Speedlite attached to the camera is called the master, while all the other Speedlites are referred to as remotes, or slaves. See also *master* and *remote.*

stroboscopic flash A flash mode on the 580EX II that fires multiple flashes with which to capture multiple images of a moving subject in a single photographic frame. A dark background helps greatly for successful multi-stroboscopic images.

sync speed The fastest shutter speed that you can set the camera to and have the flash expose for the whole exposure duration. Canon cameras prevent you from setting a faster shutter speed when a Speedlite is powered on and attached to the camera or when the pop-up flash is in the open position. See also *high-speed sync.*

TTL (Through-the-Lens) A flash metering system that reads the light passing through the lens that will expose film or strike an image sensor.

tonal range The range from the lightest to the darkest tones in an image.

tungsten lighting Common household lighting that uses tungsten filaments. Without filtering or adjusting to the correct white balance settings, pictures taken under tungsten light display a yellow-orange color cast.

vignetting The darkening of edges on an image that can be caused by lens distortion, using a filter, or using the wrong lens hood. This is also used creatively in image editing to draw the viewer's eye toward the center of the image.

white balance A setting that you use to compensate for the differences in color temperature common in different light sources. For example, a typical tungsten light bulb is very yellow-orange, so when adjusted properly, the camera's white balance setting adds blue to the image to ensure that the light looks like standard white light.

wireless remote A controller that communicates with its respective devices via infrared (IR) signals (and in some cases, via radio signals) and that can be used to trigger cameras or flashes. See also *master* and *slave.*

zoom head Also referred to as the Speedlite's flash head, the mechanism that can automatically move the flash tube forward or backward during automatic flash operations to match the focal length of the lens being used.

Index

K

L

M